Inspiration

Contemporary Design Methods in Architecture

Mark Mückenheim | Juliane Demel

BIS Publishers
Het Sieraad
Postjesweg 1
1057 DT Amsterdam
The Netherlands
T (+) 31 (0)20 515 02 30
F (+) 31 (0)20 515 02 39
bis@bispublishers.nl
www.bispublishers.nl

ISBN 978 90 6369 267 4

Printed in China

Content

Inspiration: Contemporary Design Methods in Architecture is a comprehensive compilation of work samples and ideas on design and gestalt, illustrations and graphic configurations, textures and structures, as well as form and spatial development. This book features more than 800 examples of abstract compositions that relate to architectural design methods and principles. These methodologies find their ground in the work of contemporary architectural design practice, while still being highly applicable to other related creative fields.

Inspiration showcases hundreds of examples, models, sketches, and renderings of abstract architectural design applications. In addition to this substantial body of visual work, the book also documents and details the generative process and production of these design creations.

About the Book

The knowledge of contextual relationships and their requisite translation into a process of design or form requires a certain abstract comprehension of different cultural phenomena.

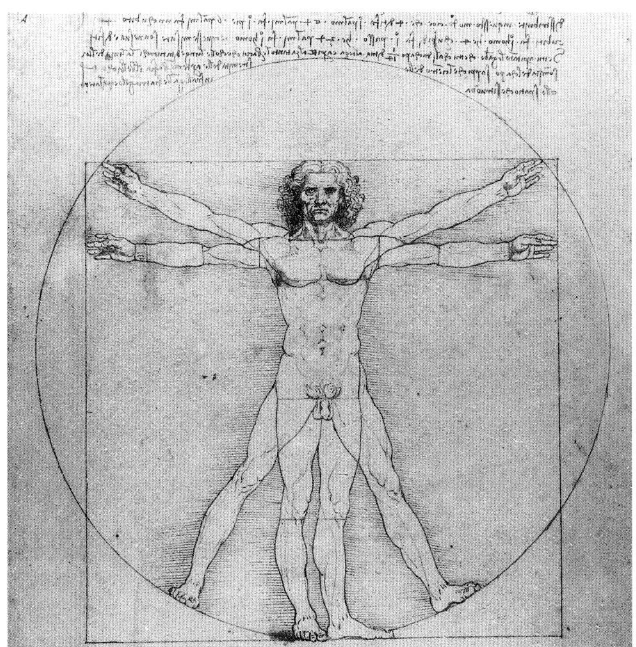

0.1 Leonardo da Vinci: Vitruvian Man

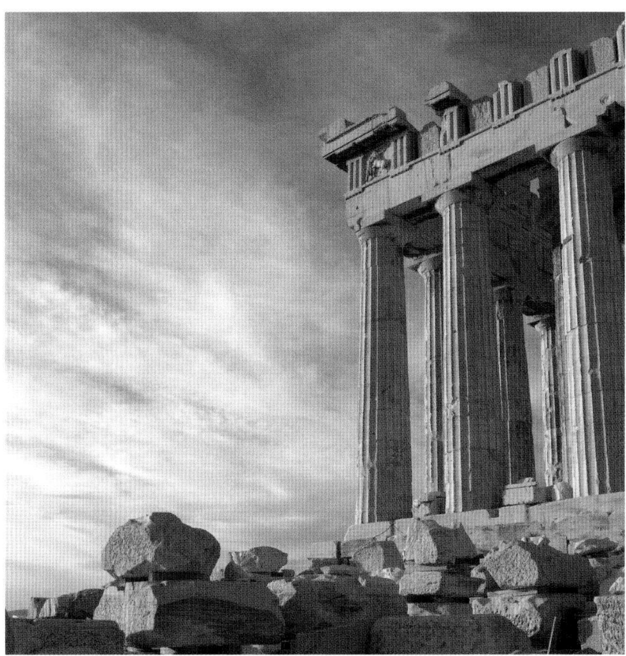

0.2 Parthenon Temple, Athens, Greece

Introduction

The book *Inspiration: Contemporary Design Methods in Architecture* focuses on the contemporary use of emblematic design strategies, laws, and procedures in the field of architecture. The book features process-oriented design approaches through the illustration of abstract exercises, intended to develop genuine solutions that place themselves within architectural design and theoretical discourse. The content and methodologies in this book are universal: although the focus of the book is on architectural design, generally accepted design parameters such as perceptional theory and proportion studies will also apply to other related creative fields. We believe that designers, landscape architects, artists, illustrators and students will find this book a source of inspiration.

The conformation of our environment is a reality whose basic prerequisite lies in the reflection of our cultural or natural context by constitutive and creative individuals. Besides fundamental design principles, this particular process has historically been driven by societal phenomena, theory and science (ref. 0.1). A strong affiliation with up-to-date knowledge of cultural and scientific facts respective of their context has therefore proved to be crucial in the development of our own consciousness and existence.

Our society has reached such a high degree of understanding that even simple design tasks often require a highly complex system of intellectual realizations and resulting design procedures in order to gauge solutions that effectively reflect our cultural development. The knowledge of contextual relationships and their requisite translation into a process of design or form therefore requires a certain abstract comprehension of these different phenomena. The mastery of these methods and the intellectual ability to transfer a multifaceted issue into a design statement is an obligation for future generations of architects and designers.

To work within these challenging parameters, process-oriented research in conjunction with a thorough knowledge base are necessary to consistently cultivate fluctuating and ever-evolving design approaches. Only innovative and conceptually sophisticated

0.1 for example mathematical science and musical harmony in ancient Greek architecture (fig. 0.2)

0.3 Cathedral of Cologne, Germany

0.4 St. Patrick's Cathedral, New York City

solutions can achieve a comprehensive and long-ranging design value. To strive for this kind of architectural quality is therefore the only way to render a design capable of generating cultural relevance and societal value.

Design Methodology + Cultural Significance

Design methods in architecture never lose their relevance. The now-globalized profession is increasingly searching for architectural individuality, giving the principles of architectural design an even greater significance in city marketing and corporate identity. For better or worse, many highly celebrated "signature buildings" have been executed since the completion of the influential and undoubtedly brilliant Guggenheim Museum by Frank Gehry in 1997, unleashing a stream of ever progressing fashion styles in architecture. Having taken these trends in consideration, the design methods in this book will not follow a style or fashion or postulate form for the sake of form. Instead, the book will strive to demonstrate how abstract design elements can playfully interact with building constituents to achieve a harmonious whole that is comprehensible and artistically significant. At their best, these relationships will lead to what we would like to introduce the aspect of "cultural relevance."

The search for architectural individuality or uniqueness can be considered one of the central themes in contemporary architectural design. But uniqueness and inimitability on their own will not create architectural quality. To achieve architectural quality, designers must consider the cultural relevance of their work by placing it within a cultural context.

This term can be used to gauge how well an idea or production of an idea speaks to society as a whole: a building or an architectural solution of any kind has cultural relevance if it has the capacity to demonstrate the following principles: deep roots in a greater cultural idea, concept or heritage; inherent qualities and design concepts of non-economic value; innovative and progressive ideologies; communication with its cultural and environmental context; and finally, capability to enrich cultural human life.

0.5 Façade of the Guggenheim Museum, Bilbao, Spain, Frank O. Gehry and Associates

The current trend towards architectural individuality and uniqueness seems to be highly tailored to the individual designer. A process like this is in danger of becoming arbitrary if one is not carefully considering all aspects of all design parameters at hand within any architectural assignment. One can argue that contemporary building activities of an ever globalizing society tend to negate the classic design elements of local origin and material-specific composition, which can for instance be found in vernacular architecture. (ref. 0.2)

The design quality and relevance that is inherent in a local building and craftsmanship culture results from a long evolution of traditions, available material, and lore of crafting abilities. Nowadays, these qualities often converted to luxury items, relegated to a niche existence, and only able to survive in confined geographical areas. As these examples are already deeply rooted within their cultural context, it is safe to say that by nature these are already cultural relevant designs. If this classical form of cultural relevance is replaced through a combination of random products from the building industry that are executed through standardized detailing by the lowest possible bidder, a cultural relevance is obviously lost. On a larger scale this means that the cultural and also natural harmony of any given geographical region is potentially disturbed, if not destroyed. This "cultural neutrality" can be found in almost every region of the earth. However, this book does not aim to continue the ideological discourse between modernism and traditionalism, nor does it propagate critical regionalism. Instead, this book seeks to establish and explore certain constant design parameters which are always inherent qualities in architecture, regardless of context, site, or scale of time. Finally, Inspiration strives to link these parameters to contemporary architectural practice.

Globalization – specific vs. generic

Historically, the propagation of certain architectural styles has always exceeded boundaries and continents (ref. 0.3). Current architectural development is characterized and trenchantly described by Hans Ibelings as "supermodernism" (ref. 0.4). Ibelings categorizes two types of supermodernist architectures:

0.2 Bernard Rudofsky: Architecture Without Architects: A Short Introduction to Non-Pedigreed Architecture

0.3 for example gothic architecture or art deco

0.4 Hans Ibelings: Supermodernism, Architecture in the Age of Globalization

0.6 Casa da Musica, Porto, OMA. Does Supermodernism really disregard its context?

0.7 Cuandixia Village, China

buildings of high architectural value that have the power to give meaning to their context, and buildings that are absolutely generic and could be found just about anywhere. If we consider every manmade structure, the majority of the built environment, which is falling into Ibelings second group, was never meant to last. We would therefore like to concentrate on the first group and establish the qualities and aspects that are necessary to gain such a power of presence. The thorough reflection of the cultural context through an individual designer or design team, and the linkage from the subject of the architectural design to the current endemic culture, prevents the neutrality of the latter group, and creates a potential for the genesis of cultural relevance within a globalized architecture.

Design Methodology + Architecture

A valuable example of cultural relevance in contemporary architecture can be found in the designs of Kazuyo Sejima and Ryue Nishizawa (SANAA). Although their work is rooted in the cultural understanding of space in Japan, it can also be interpreted as a reflection of the cultural context of the digital revolution and the resulting virtualization of our current society. Similarly, Sou Fujimoto's radical spatial concepts under the slogan "primitive future" (ref. 0.5) introduce ideas about the nature of architecture and architectural space in a global society. More than any other architect of his generation, Fujimoto takes a stance towards a nonspecific and flexible use of space, ultimately connecting basic human needs to the reality of our globalized society. So in its best way, this very sensitive form of "global architecture" begins to reflect the current societal context while still being highly influenced by its local culture or history.

It should be noted that while the design methodology of these architects follows a very personal approach, their work also relies on universally valid aesthetic principles. Due to the unique nature of their work, it is not advisable for young designers to merely follow these styles, but rather understand the underlying universal principles behind the architect's design decisions. It is therefore essential for designers to develop their own stance and handling of the relevant architectural composition elements. For this reason, it is more important to look beyond the emblematic

0.5 Sou Fujimoto: Primitive Future

0.8 Wooden model displaying the additive design elements of „Tokyo Apartments“ by Suo Fujimoto

quality of a given piece of architecture in order to find and understand the inherent design harmony that operates beyond the personal and sometimes subjective criteria of the author. If we stay with the example of SANAA or Fujimoto, we can easily look beyond the fascinating personal predilection of dematerialisation or spatial indetermination and always find general qualities such as additive design elements, emergent effects and self-similarities. It is precisely these attributes that this book will elucidate. There are many more works within the current architectural discourse which highlight this point. The examples featured are not intended to present a style or endorse a certain kind of architecture, but rather reveal principles that constitute good design. It should be noted that most examples are also chosen for their contextual and cultural relevance. Without this type of integration none of the featured works in this book would be possible.

Design Methodology + Digital Culture

The references of the examples shown in this book complement the design methods featured in each chapter. These methods are also examined by various creative analysis methods, including digital investigations. Computational technologies have given rise to many new design methods and to experimentation, making it possible for designers to seek solutions using emergent digital tools and techniques. This book features examples of digital explorations in conjunction with their design principles, in an effort to establish a foundation of contemporary and fundamental design methods in architecture.

The research and application of digital design and fabrication methods continuously impacts architectural practice. Innovative material and product applications will not only lead to new design possibilities in architecture and product design, but also allow a direct communication between designer and production facility. The resulting design and production possibilities for specific custom-tailored building parts allow for the realization of complex and highly specialized building components. Computational techniques have the potential to be valuable design tools.

0.9 Zollverein School of Management and Design, Essen, Germany, Kazuyo Sejima + Ryue Nishizawa / SANAA

Although the work presented in this book has been influenced by current digital developments, it was not only conceived through multiple iterations of various digital investigations but as well as through hand sketching, model building, and drawing. These techniques mirror contemporary professional practice where design work is still executed through a highly integrative process involving a diverse range of media and tools. It is therefore vital to understand that the human brain is still the best computer when it comes to analysis, design, and the development of a rigorous creative process. Aspects of traditional design methodology such as the theory of proportion or theory of perception for example, are oftentimes faster and more successfully applied through manual techniques.

Didactics and Intuitive Decisions in the Design Process

On a more abstract level, the essence of the examples in this book can be sorted into three categories (ref. 0.6). The first is applied methods; the second, theoretical methods which come into play when designing architecture or single architectural elements. The third is a category that underlies all creative work, the emotional or intuitive. We would like to focus on this third category and the idea of developing an emotional intelligence for design.

This intuitive ability consists of a knowledge that cannot be clearly explained. It is a highly trained "gut feeling" that becomes apparent when we instinctively apply the right choices in a given work of architecture or try to solve a complex set of design problems. This phenomena is described by Michael Polanyi as tacit knowledge (ref. 0.7). According to Polanyi, tacit knowledge differs from person to person and is a non-communicable form of knowledge, such as the ability to ride a bicycle or draw a picture. The corresponding didactic part is implicit learning, where the acquisition of a certain skill or knowledge is playful and unconscious, independent from the conscious attempt to learn (ref. 0.8). The key qualification for any design task is creativity, which can not really be learned consciously. Therefore, this book can only provide the information for understanding the necessary procedures to create a particular design. It

0.6 The first two categories link to Vitruvius 80-15 BC. According to Vitruvius, the knowledge of architecture is structured by two entities "fabrica" (craft) and "ratiocinatio" (cognitive abilities) in De Architectura – The Ten Books of Architecture 15 BC

0.7 Michael Polanyi: Tacit Dimension

0.8 Shanks, D.R. / St. John, M.F.: Characteristics of dissociable human learning systems

0.10 Serpentine Gallery Pavilion, London, UK, Kazuyo Sejima + Ryue Nishizawa / SANAA

0.11 Rolex Learning Center, Lausanne, Switzerland, Kazuyo Sejima + Ryue Nishizawa / SANAA

cannot supply the ability to develop original design ideas or even deliver the ultimate solution for a given design problem.

In a further propagation on the subject of tacit knowledge by Ikujiro Nonaka and Hirotaka Takeuchi, there is a differentiation in between physical and mental dimensions that can also be described as cognitive and technical (ref. 0.9). This delineation is congruent to the previously described terms. According to Nonaka and Takeuchi, the key for the creation of new knowledge lies in the conversion from tacit into explicit knowledge. This process is described as externalization. In simple terms, this can be seen as the emergence of ideas and innovations associated with creative work. The opposite is described as internalization, which can very roughly summarize the didactics of conveying creative abilities (ref. 0.10). The texts and examples in this book give a first introduction allowing the reader to broaden and expand his or her idea of design methods in architecture.

In this book, the underlying cognitive examination creates a foundation for the artistic and abstract character of some of the individual works. Therefore, despite their seeming field departure, they remain architectural in their structure and concept. The approach of the works is balanced with the manifested architectural and spatial accumulation of relevant design criteria, which often considers the functional, constructive, tectonic, and structural aspects of the discipline. At the same time the book partly focuses on design as a craft and evaluation of design and architectural conformation in its context, by deliberately setting an abstract frame that does not mean to show possible solutions but rather possibilities and processes.

The conscious and subconscious point of view that this book offers on the subject matter opens the possibility to inform and reflect at the same time and therefore open up one's own imagination. We hope you are inspired.

0.9 Nonaka, Ikujiro / Takeuchi, Hirotaka. The Knowledge-Creating Company

0.10 Even if Nonaka and Takeuchi are describing these models in the broader context of organizational theory the comparability to creative processes and creative learning is evident

Architectural design education usually starts with the point, the line, and the square. Here, these basic elements will be considered for their aesthetic design possibilities.

Architectural design education usually starts with the point, the line, and the square. Here, these basic elements will be considered for their aesthetic design possibilities.

Chapter 1 : Primary Elements of Design – Points

component assembly

point, line, surface

loss of gestalt quality

additive composition

visual effects

emergent effects

In architectural design, it is imperative to assemble elements, building components, and materials. In addition to the tectonic, constructive, and structural makeup of a given element, architects must also consider the potential of its inherent aesthetic and design qualities. The design can begin as a simple combination of a number of single entities and component parts starting with the point, the line and the surface. The compositional alignment of these elements is a vital attribute of a cohesive design.

Without this design consistence, there is a loss of gestalt quality. For example in extremely heterogenic or generic places such as landfills, many industrial areas, most suburban housing developments or other such spatially inconsistent places, one will find little compositional conformation or compositional harmonic qualities. These conditions illustrate a loss of constitutive organization. Conversely, by the limitation of one or only a few elements (in this chapter circles and pixels) or a comprehensible rule structure in their arrangement, an initial design quality can be established.

One way to assemble a design consisting of single elements is through additive composition (ref. 1.1). The effects of additive composition can be found almost everywhere: in nature, culture, art, design and architecture. Children

Page 14 15:
Danish Pavillon, World Expo Shanghai.
Bjarke Ingels Group

1.1 among many other sources additive composition is most actually described in Richard Weston: 100 Ideas that Changed Architecture

1.1 Rice Terraces in China: Radical transformation of a landscape through a repeated alteration

1.2 Imperial cathedral, Aachen, Germany. Different building periods are reflected in an additive compostion

1.3 Falling Water, Mill Run, Pensillvania. Frank Lloyd Wright. Additive composition of horizontal and vertical elements

configure LEGO bricks with joy and fascination into infinite constructions and formations. Terraced rice paddies in Asia reflect the same design principle (fig 1.1). The landscaping of rice fields and colorful combinations of plastic blocks are only two examples of additive compositions: they appeal to us and capture our attention because of their inherent order and fascinating repetition. Similar qualities can of course also be found in many artworks, for example Andreas Gursky's photographs or the manic drippings of Jackson Pollock's paintings; both draw their allure from this simple but very effective design method.

Repetitive or similar elements can sometimes begin to constitute a new and a unique whole that ultimately possesses exclusive characteristics in its constituting substructure. This phenomenon is called emergence: the occurrence of new properties on a macroscopic level as a direct result from the interaction of its single parts on a microscopic level – or as simply put by Aristotle, "the whole is greater than the sum of its parts." (ref. 1.2)

An example of a historic and relatively simple additive composition can be found in Germany's Aachen Cathedral (fig 1.2), whose structure comprises the arrangement of building sections, each of which reflect the architectural style of the era they were erected. The differentiating building parts reveal the captivating spatial continuum of the interior, while their resultant cluster-like urban qualities create an emergent effect. Another example that shows the material and spatial qualities of additive design can be found in the cantilevered balconies that are horizontally read against the vertical quarry-stone walls at Frank Lloyd Wright's Fallingwater in Mill Run, Pennsylvania (fig 1.3).

1.2 Aristotle, Metaphysica. Vol. VII 10, 1041 b. ca. 330 B.C

1.4 Atomium, Brüssel

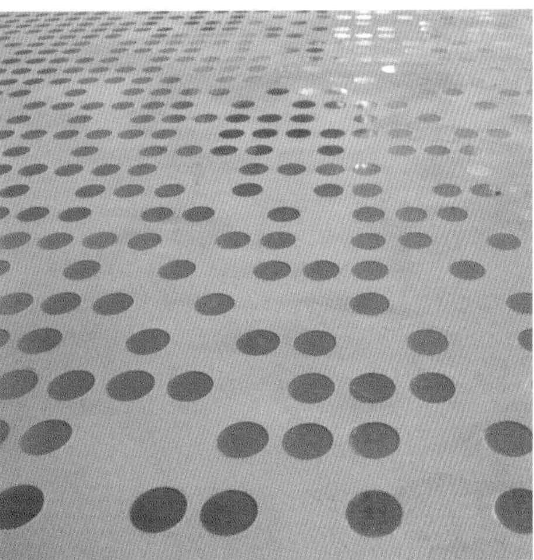
1.5 Façade texture incorporating glass mosaic. „Five Courtyards", Munich. Herzog & de Meuron

1.6 Danish Pavillon interior, World Expo Shanghai. Bjarke Ingels Group

Many examples of modernist architecture display these principles, and their application is even more obvious in recent architectural developments. Contemporary examples of additive compositions and emergent effects in architecture can be found for example in the Guggenheim Museum Bilbao by Frank Gehry (page 9, fig. 0.5), where building parts clearly share similarities in texture and shape, as well as the dotted embossed, and perforated façade of the de Young Museum by Herzog and de Meuron in San Francisco (page 54, fig 3.1). The architectural designs of an even younger generation of architects such as Sou Fujimoto and Bjarke Ingels often utilize these strategies to achieve spectacular spatial and material effects. The examples in the first three chapters of this book delve deep into this design method.

In the first section, additive compositions will begin with designs achieved by the manipulation of points and dots. In our examination, the points will not yet be regarded as a means to derive architectural space, but as a method to achieve a graphic quality and derive a two-dimensional composition.

The works in the following chapter will illustrate the potential of additive configuration of points. The intention is to achieve and develop a design that is not generated by using digital filters or programming, but through a habitual approach. The final products are derived through physical design techniques like hand-sketching, followed by manual manipulation and simple transformation steps in a two-dimensional CAD program.

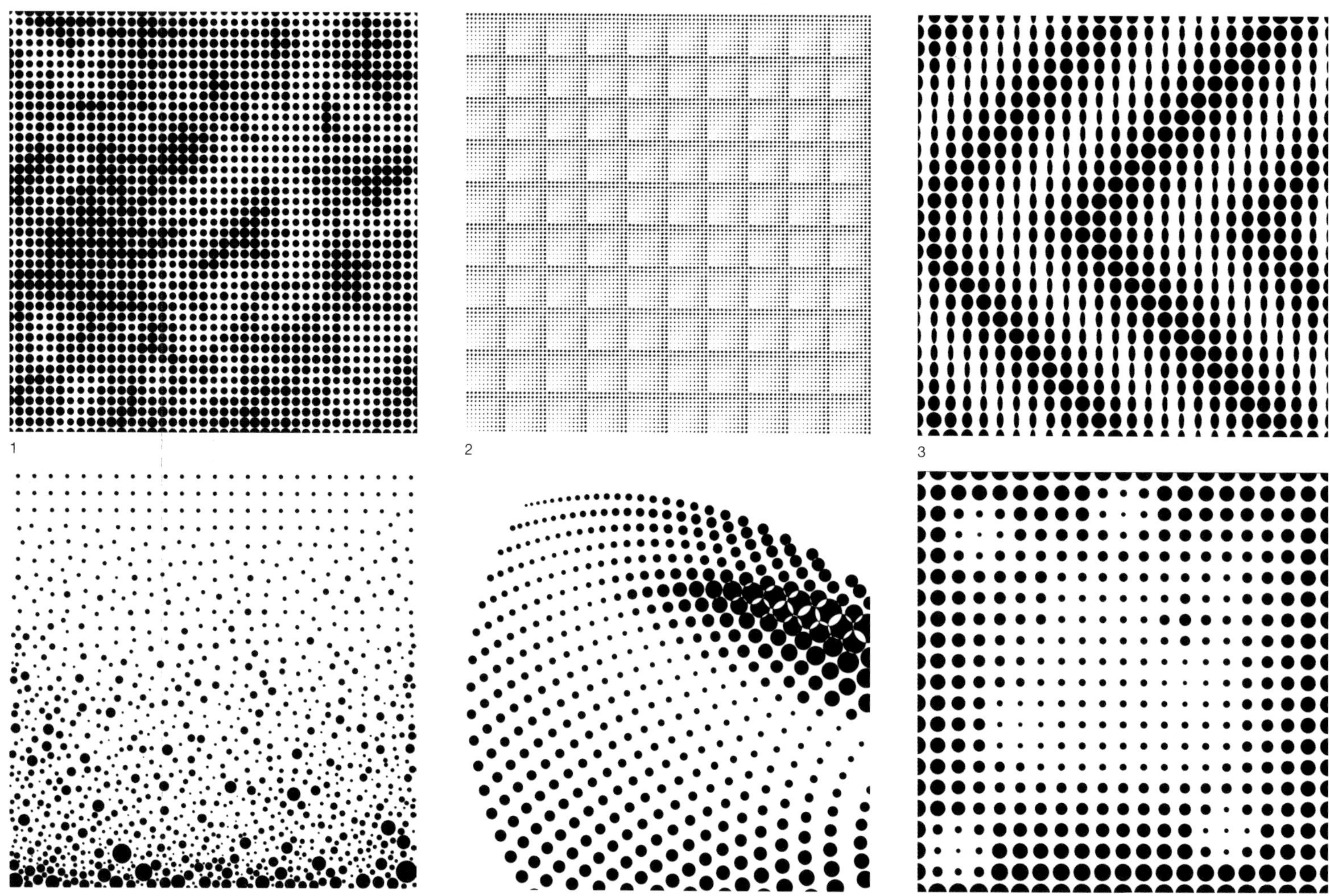

1 Dots with slight differentiations in scale generate a diffuse abstract pattern
2 Regular grid with spatial effect created by dots with dynamically increasing size
3 Optical illusion of rotating spherical disks achieved through ellipses with varying diameter
4 Transition from order to chaos
5 Fan-like arragement of dots with superimposition
6 Illusion of embossing through the configuration of small dots

7

7 Various sized dots create a diffuse spatial definition

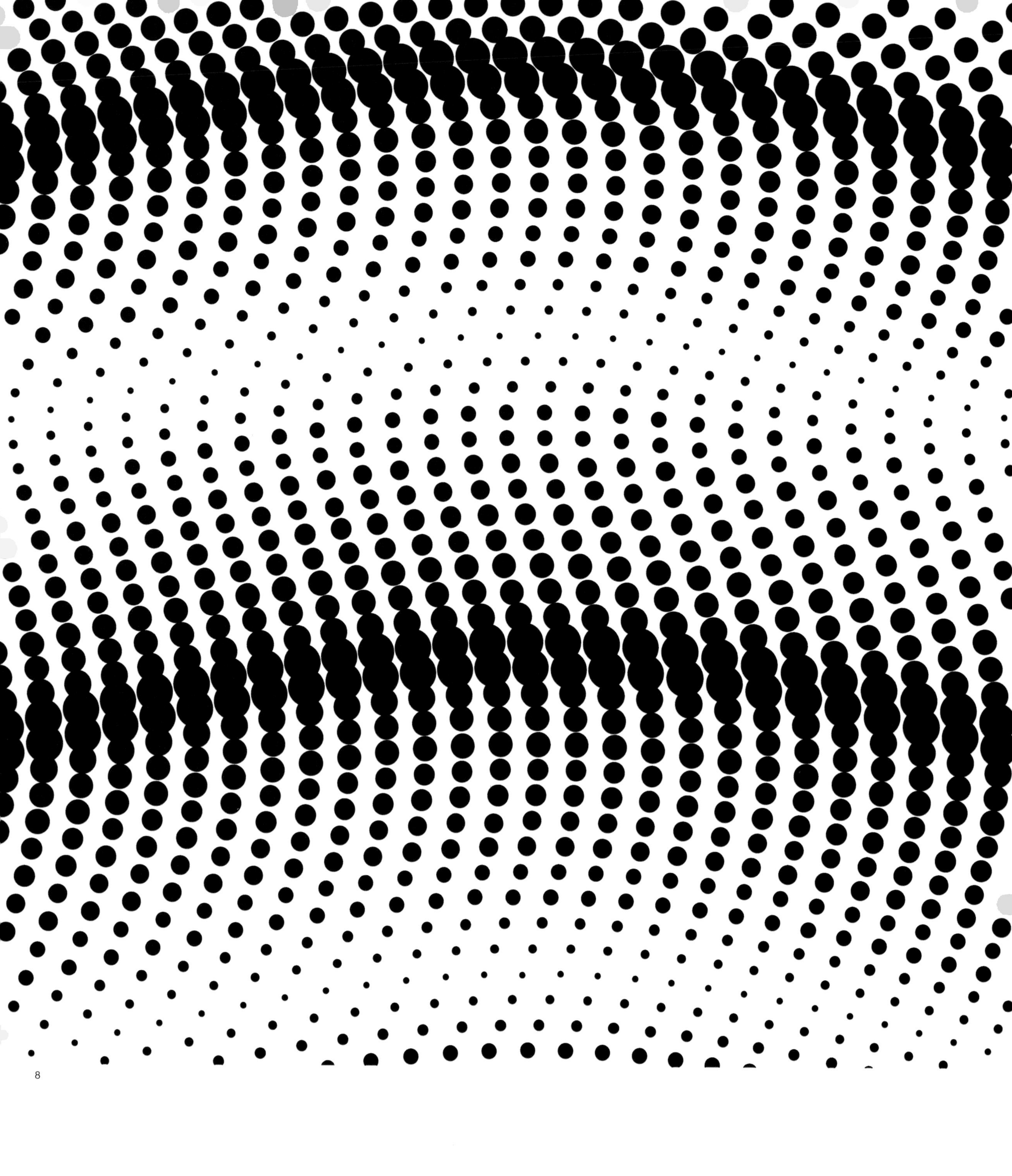

8

8 The impression of a wavy surface is generated by dots with varying sizes along curved invisible lines

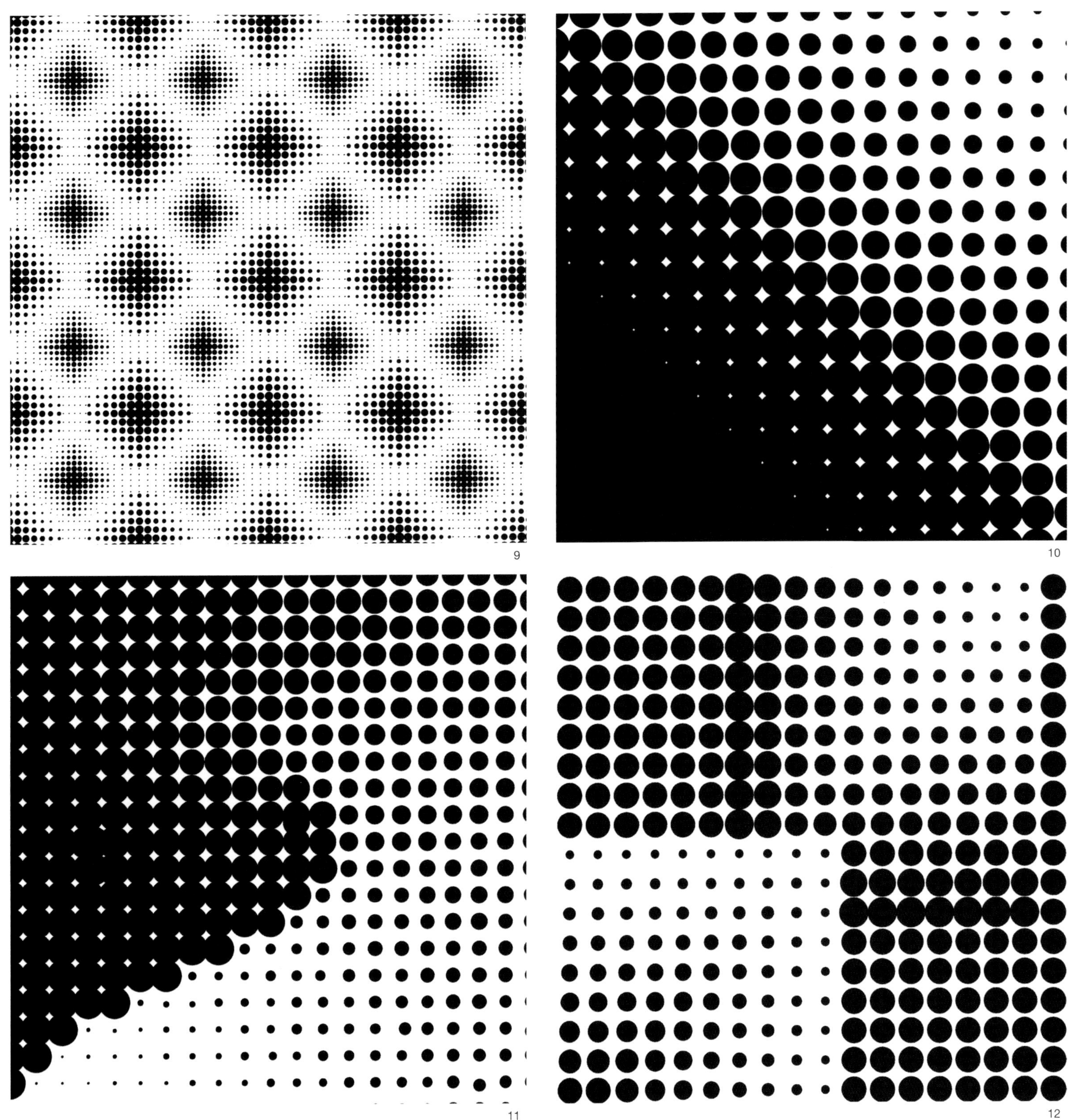

9 Impression of three-dimensional checkered grid caused by dots with different size

10 11 12 Spatial and gradient effects generated by dots of varying size that are aligned to a regular grid

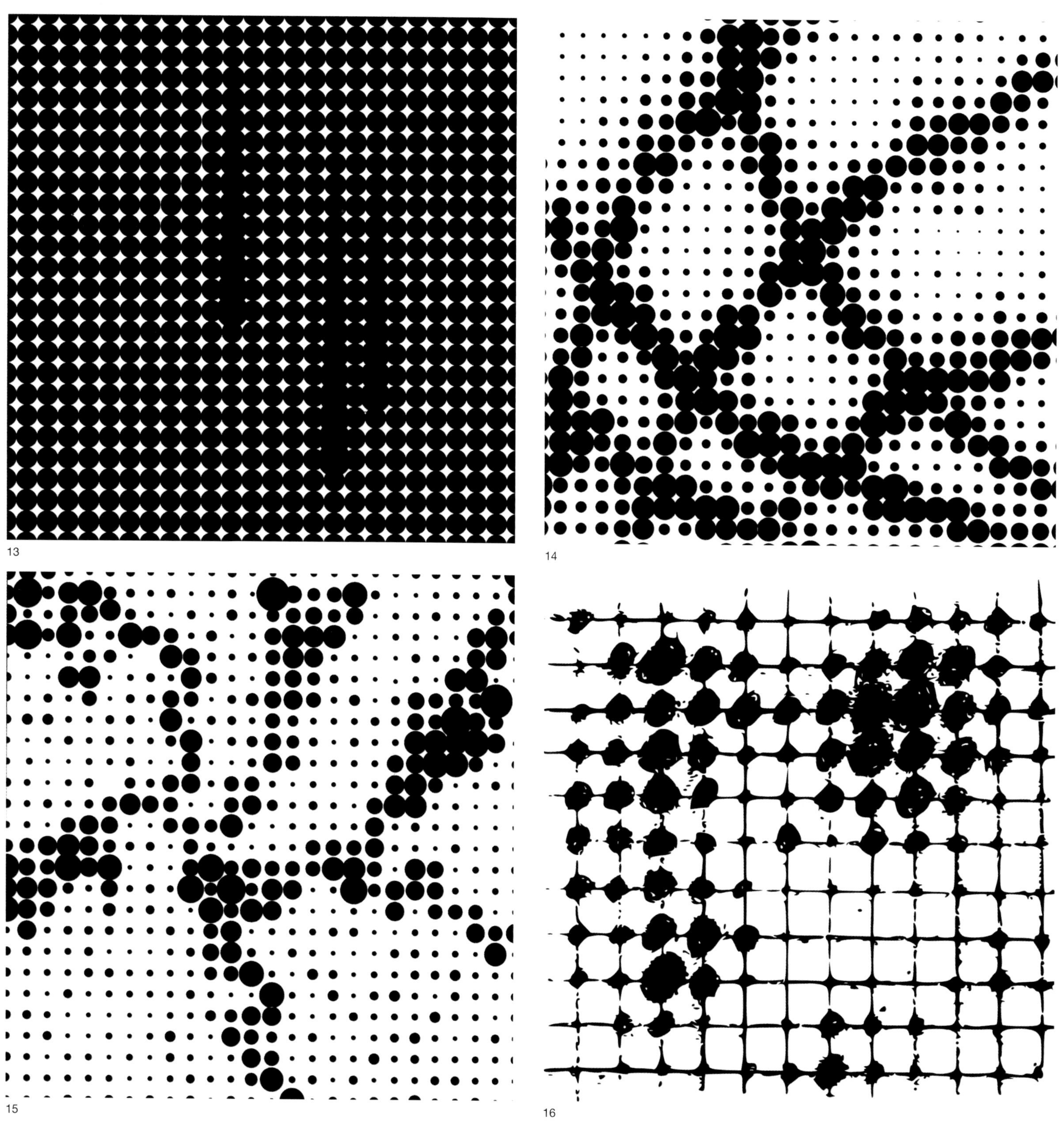

13 Gradually expanding dots within a tightly spaced grid evoke the impression of water droplets runnig down a glass surface

14 Superposition of an orthogonal grid and a dynamic net pattern achieved through selective scaling of dots

15 Organic cluster

16 Study on grid and dots

17

18

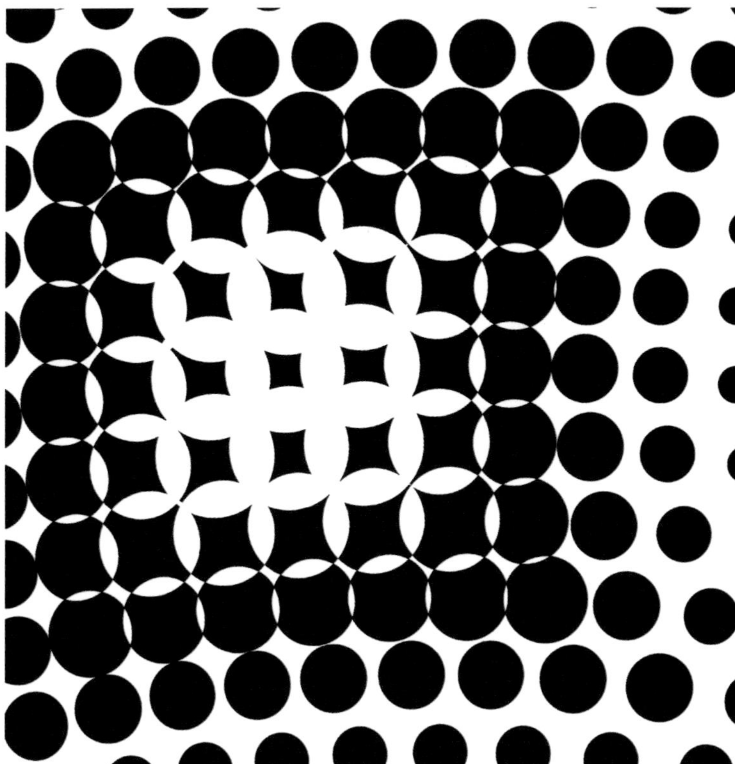

19

17 Small dots with varying distances along a curved line generate a spatial effect

18 Dots aligned within a spiral create a fractal-like geometry

19 Pattern created by subtractive overlapping of black circles

20 21 22
23 24 25

20 Gradually scaled dots aligned to a transformed grid create the impression of a spatial force field
21 Pattern created by subtractive overlapping of black circels
22 Spatial impression of a corrugated surface
23 Freely configured and scaled dots along a regular grid
24 Curved grid lines and gradually expanding circels create the illusion of a sphere
25 Different sized dots on a regular grid create a spatial illusion

26

26 Linear arranged dots with equal spacing and different sizes: the subtractive over-lappings create a shimmering effect

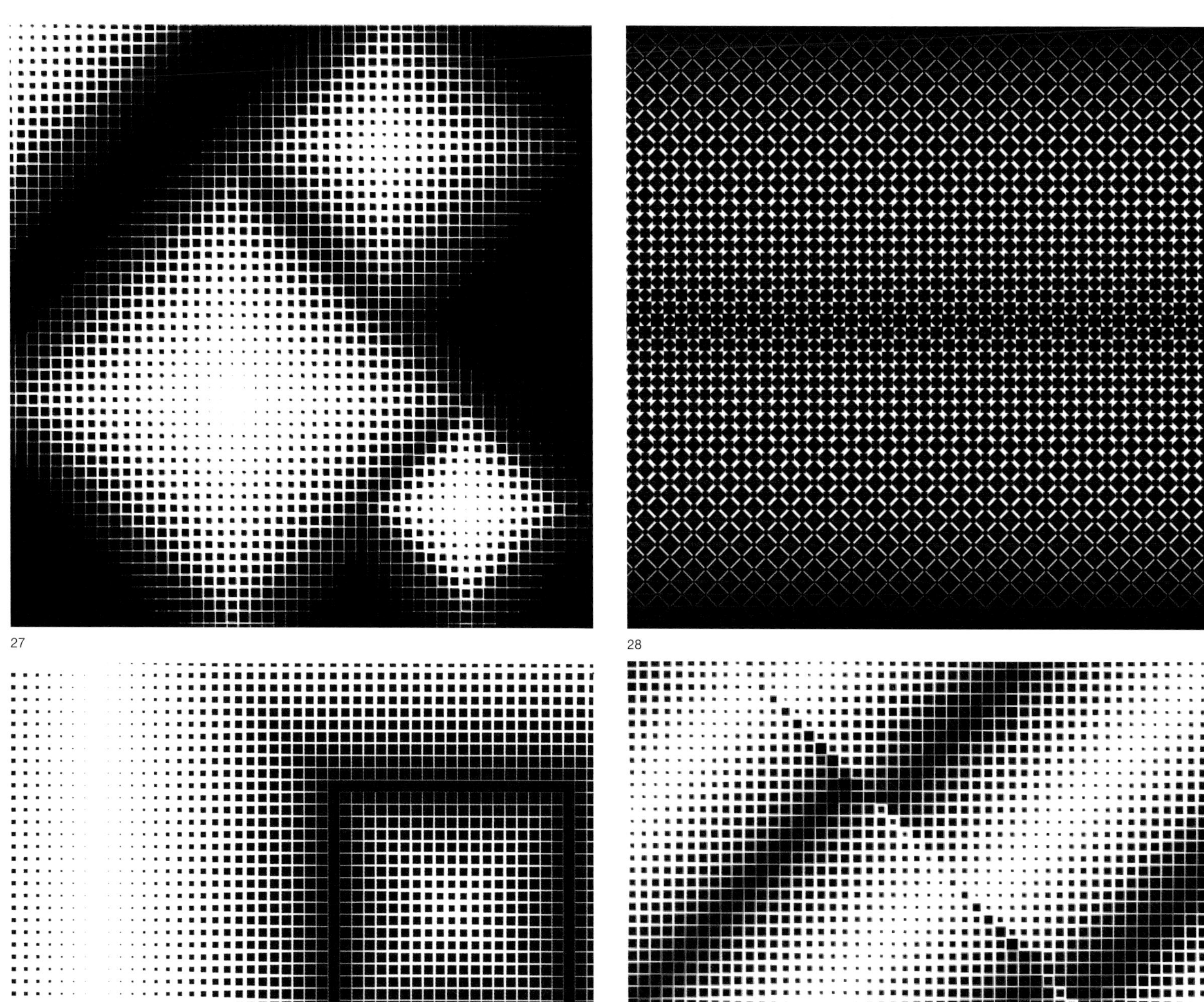

27

28

29

30

27 - 30 Studies of different sized
squares aligned to various grids

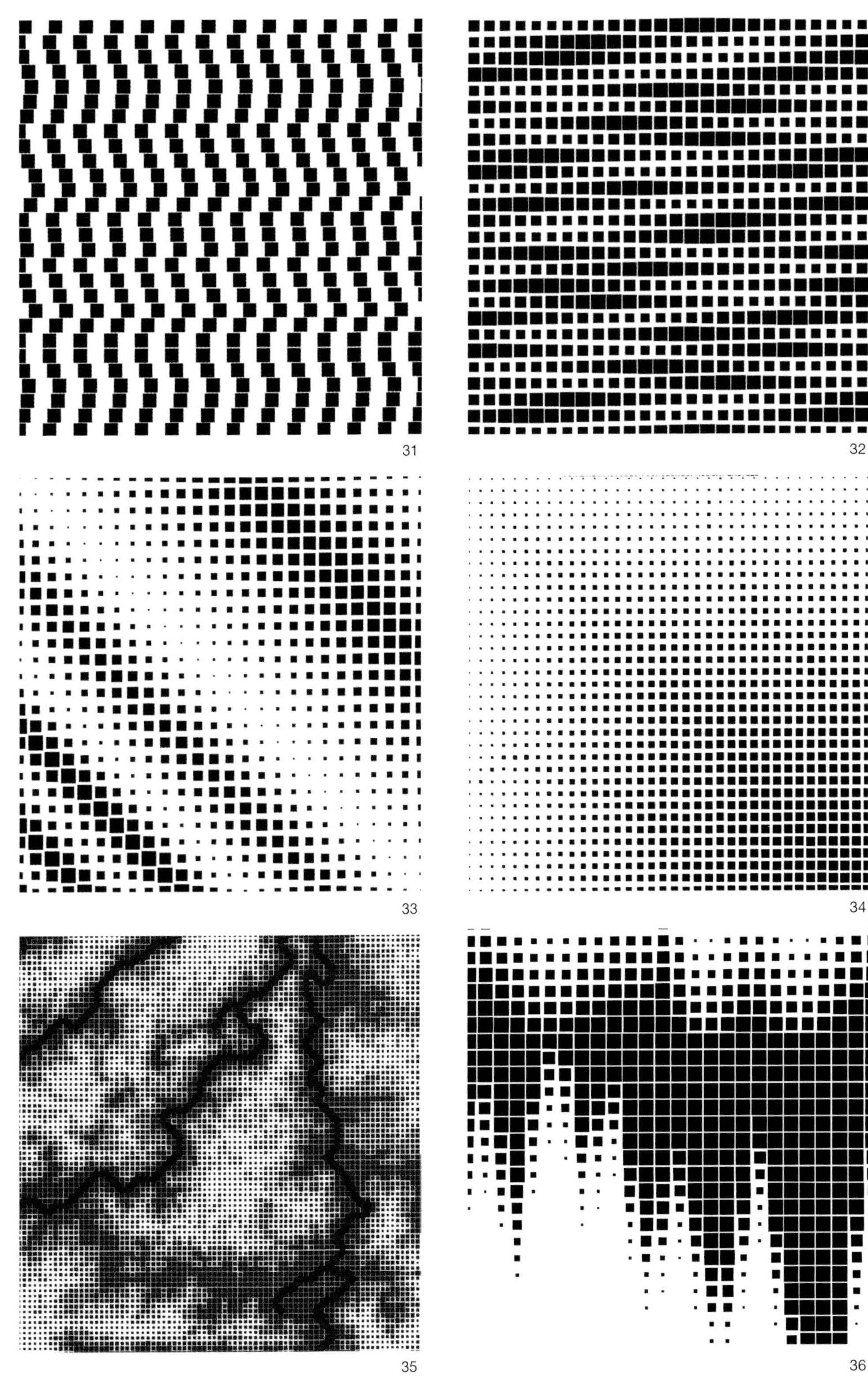

31 Squares slightly displaced evoce the optical illusion of tilted horizontal axes

32 - 36 Squares slightly different in size create gradient and spatial effects

An important primary element in architectural design is the line. Numerous building components are arranged in a linear order. It is therefore essential for any architectural designer to cultivate a good command of designing with linear elements.

An important primary element in architectural design is the line. Numerous building components are arranged in a linear order. It is therefore essential for any architectural designer to cultivate a good command of designing with linear elements.

Chapter 2: Primary Elements of Design – Line to Surface

lines

emergent effects

optical illusions

surface composition

three-dimensionality

two-dimensional subtraction

additive design

visual effects

optical illusion

The line manifests itself in many ways in the communication, representation, and physical form of architecture. It can become a wall within a floor plan, a beam within a constructive spatial framework, or an abstraction, connecting an urban axis to a city grid. Many building components in architecture are of linear nature: lines of mortar between bricks, joints, battens, louver blades, columns and joists. It is imperative for an architect to master the language of the line, as this basic entity establishes a sensible and poetic design composition. One of the first architectural design strategies deals with using the line in combinatory fashion to generate effect and intention.

The student works shown in this chapter illustrate how lines have the ability to activate the perception and recognition of space in a given design. The emergent effects, optical illusions and visual ramifications of these examples play with the cognition of surface and space. The ambiguous, pulsating, shimmering, flickering, irritating and oscillating effects of these additive compositions are used consciously to implement a spatial dimension into otherwise two-dimensional graphics.

These emergent effects are a good example for pre-digital non-cognitive design processes that can be easily explored manually and later be enhanced

---

Page 30 31:
Dee and Charles Wyly Theatre, Dallas, Texas. REX | OMA

2.1 Structural application of lines. Structural cables of the Erasmus Bridge Rotterdam, UN Studio. Ben van Berkel and Caroline Bos

2.2 Linear elements within the membrane structure of the Alianz Arena, Munich. Herzog & de Meuron

2.3 The grooved in-situ concrete texture of the wall is intended to give the surface the appearence of stacked paper. Public record office, Basel Liesthal. EM2N

through the use of digital technology. Throughout the manual two-dimensional design process, the designer derives a possible three-dimensional effect through deliberate manipulation. In this case, a spatial illusion is created through a willful act. From this method of designing, the vital principle of subtractive composition emerges. Subtractive design techniques will be discussed in a later chapter; as this chapter's examples are still in a two dimensional realm, layering might be a better term to describe this method of two-dimensional design.

The interaction and composition of linear elements has a strong connection to the schools of Bauhaus, op art or visual art, as well as the pedagogy of the Ulm School of Design (HfG Ulm) (ref. 2.1).
These references illustrate the timeless principles of an aggregative and linear approach. They can be considered very good tools for instilling simple design principles and basic computer-aided design tools.

When it comes to real world applications in architectural surfaces and façades, some of the works of Herzog and de Meuron illustrate these design principles and demonstrate how a design may stimulate the borders of perception. The railway control center in Basel (fig. 2.4) and the inner surface of the Five Courtyards building in Munich (page 19, fig. 1.5) are only two of many examples that illustrate the application of the earlier described optical effects within architectural projects.

In addition to optical works, the student examples in this chapter illustrate the effects of an aggregative linear approach. There is a certain sophistication and challenge within the simplicity of this method. The following steps were taken in the production of these examples.

As part of their assignment, the students were asked to completely fill a sheet of paper with a series of parallel lines. Following this initial step, the students manipulated the composition

2.1 Cyril Barrett: An Introduction to Optical Art

2.4 Oscillating emergent effect on the facade of the Rail Switchtower at Basel railyard, Herzog & de Meuron

2.5 Temppeliaukion church, Helsinki. Timo and Tuomo Suomalainen

through differentiating the distances and thicknesses between lines. After a number of such experiments, various degrees of complexity were introduced and the rules of the initial assignment were broken. Over time, the applied operations and outcomes became increasingly compelling and sophisticated. As in the previous chapter, the students were asked to manually develop their ideas through sketching before bringing them into a CAD program.

In the second step of the assignment, the one and two-dimensional productions that resulted from the use of the point and the line were transformed into two- and three-dimensional compositions through the multiplication and layering of numerous lines onto a surface.
The results of this exercise offer a diverse array of effects and atmospheres: nuances of compositional calmness or optical dithering, complex visual illusions like fuzziness or flickering, in addition to emergent effects like spatiality or movement. These results can quickly show beginners the challenging and demanding opportunities of such a simple assignment.

If a spatial effect emerges from the interference or the coexistence of a number of lines, this effect is the result of an initially conscious decision within a design process. This design decision manifests itself through a more or less deliberate process and string of experiments.

The examples in the following pages show different assemblies of emergent and cognitively derived three-dimensionalities and interferences, as part of the results generated by the exercises described above. The addition of similar or disparate elements, directed visual effects and impressions, emergent effects and visual illusions can be achieved through those combinations. These examples may relate to a more graphic design, but can also be related to the design of building components in a physical third dimension.

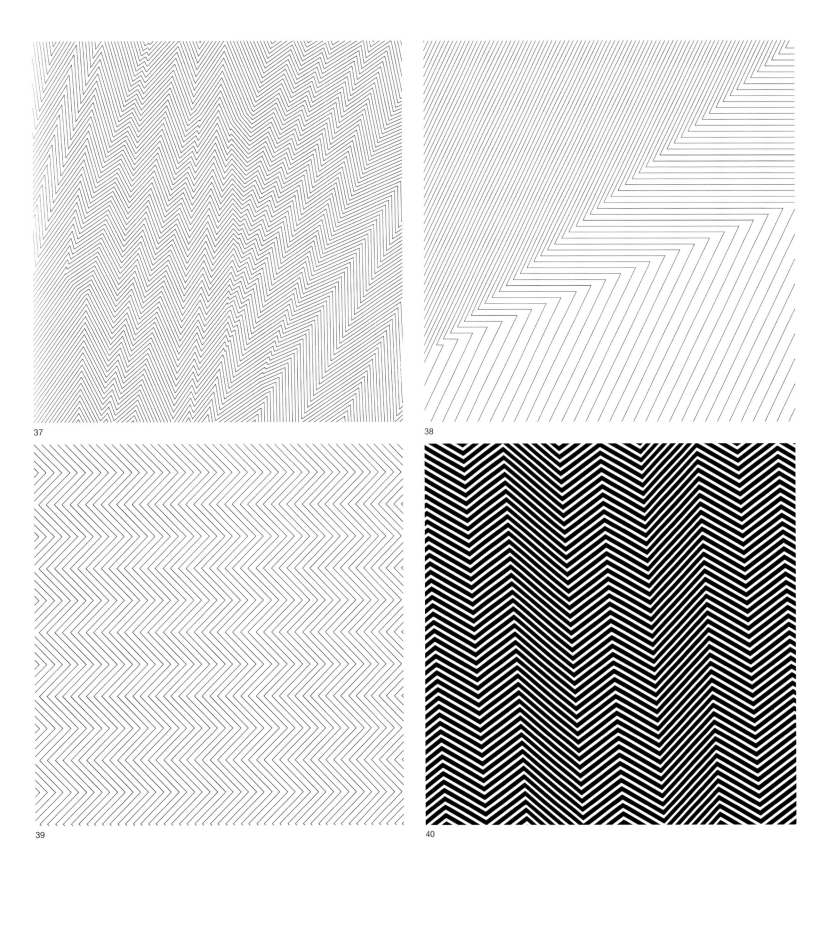

37 38 39 40

37 - 40 Parallel lines with changing directions create the impression of a folded surface. A change within the angle of a line also changes the spacing between lines - thereby visual effects of different grey shade levels and various flickering effects are created

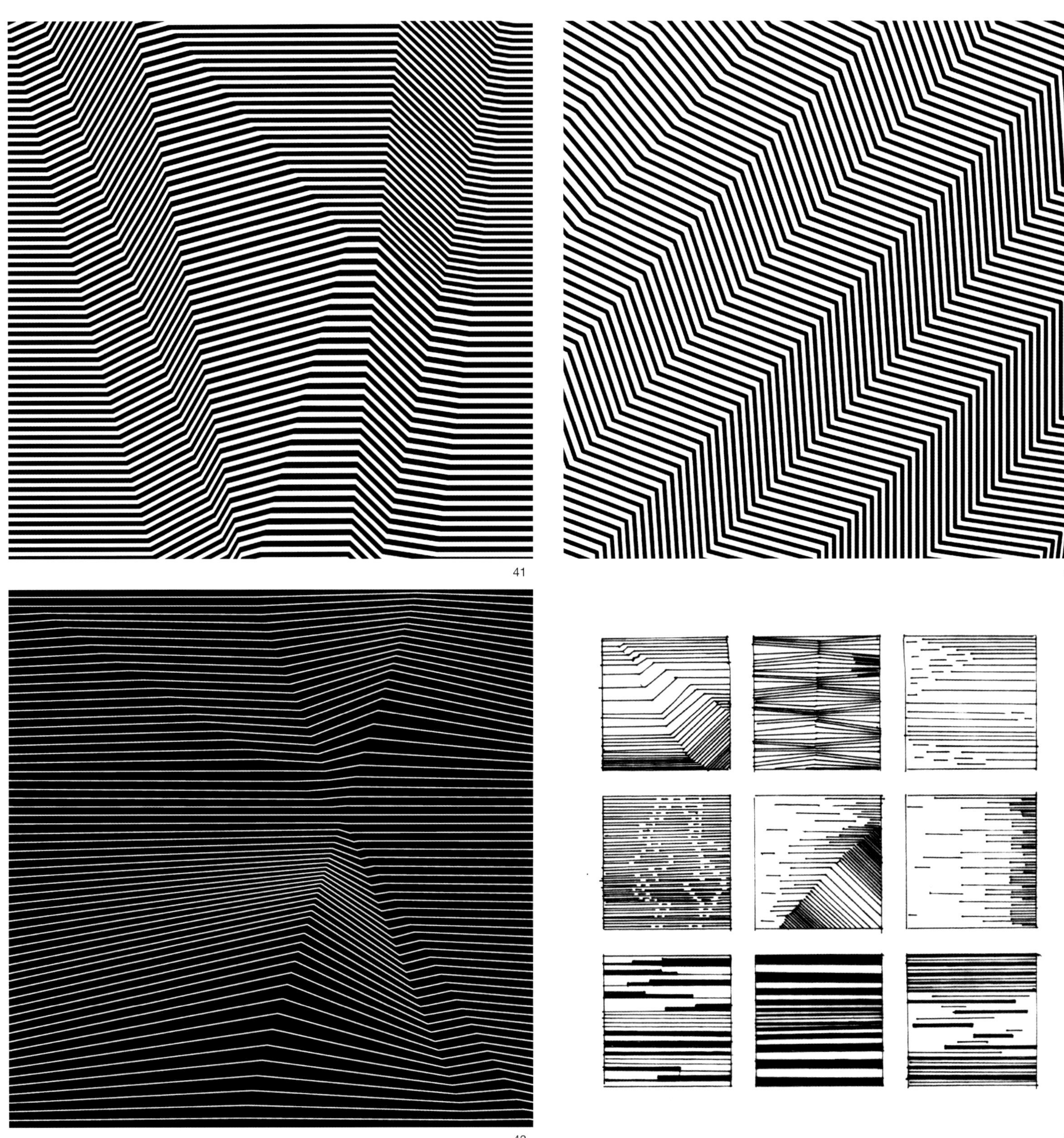
41 42 43 44

41 42 Ambiguous relationship between line and background: the dichotomy of white lines on black or black lines on black ground create strong flickering effects

43 Same design procedure as in fig. 41 - 42 but with inverse colors: white lines on black ground

44 Hand sketches: studies on the behavior of a sum of lines - rhythm, spatial effects, and velocity

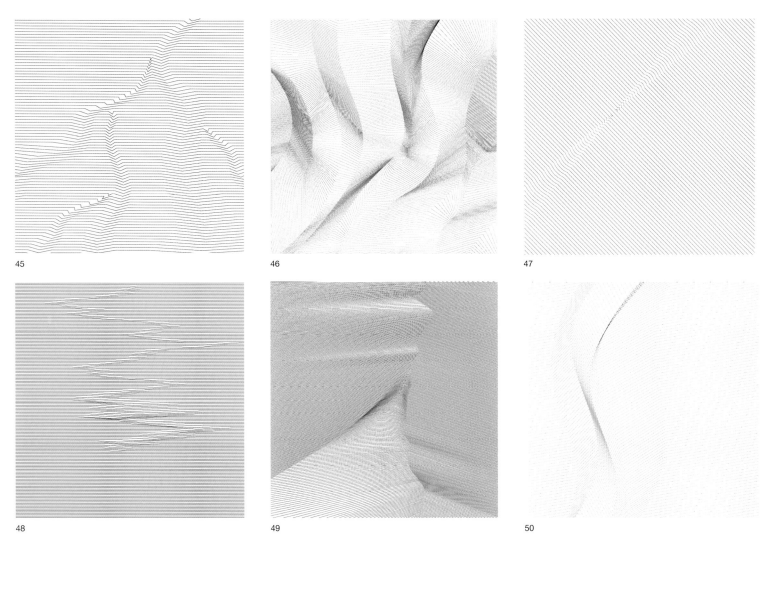

45

46

47

48

49

50

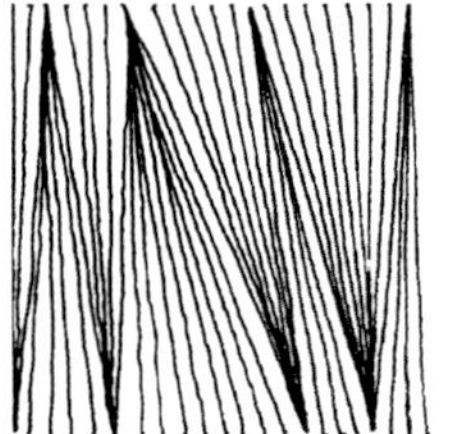

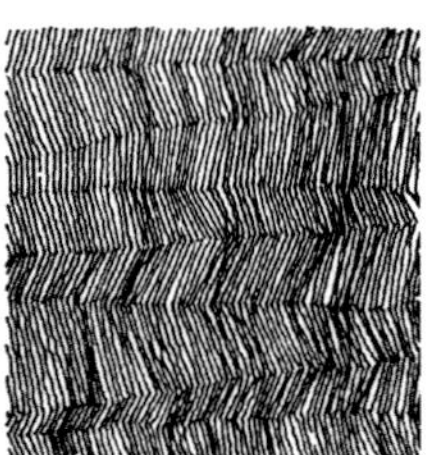

51

45 - 50 The arrangement of unbroken linear lines evoke the impression of organic structures through simple changes in direction

51 Study sketches are not as precise as computer drawings, but already give a good insight in testing numerous design options

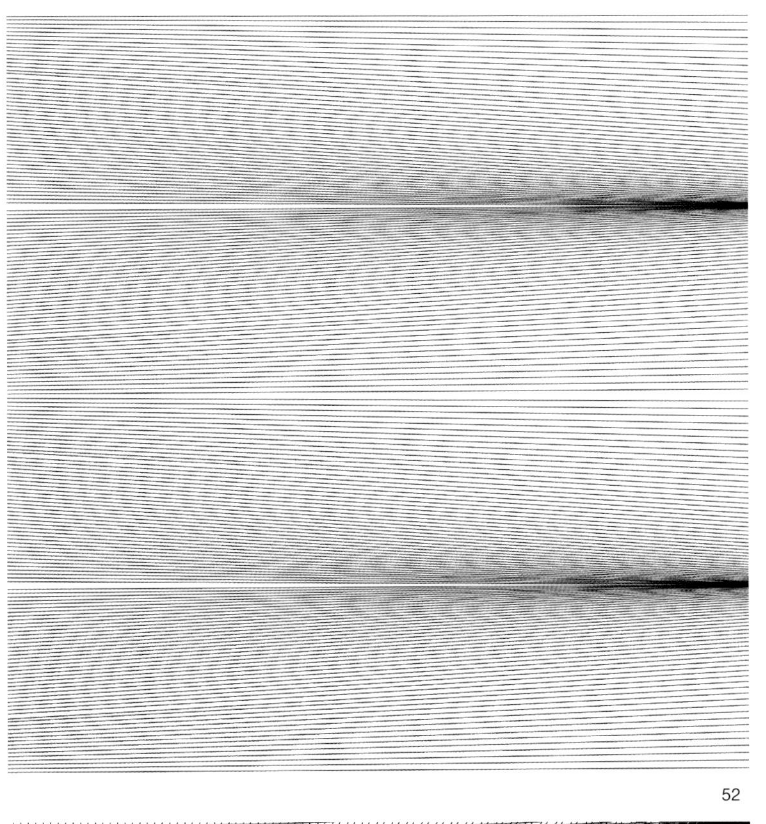

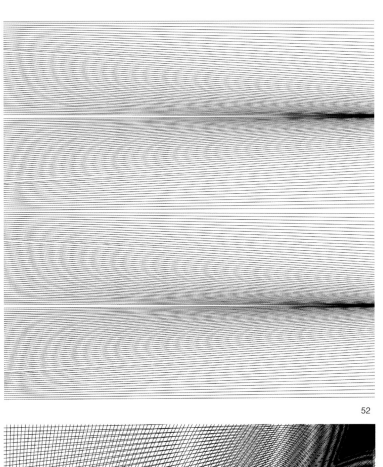

52

53

54

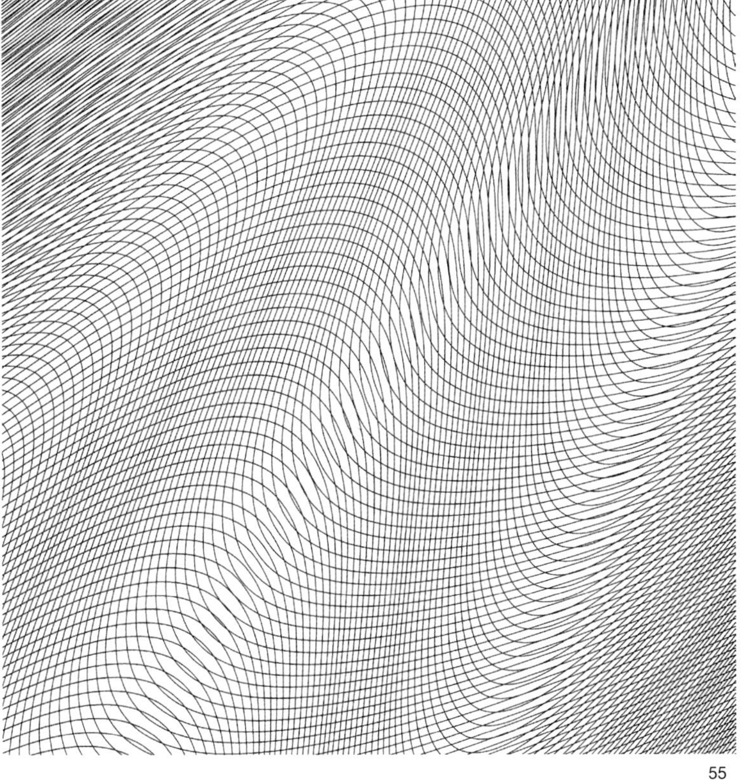

55

52 - 54 Moiré pattern created by the superposition of linear structures

55 Moiré pattern created by the superposition of a curved structure

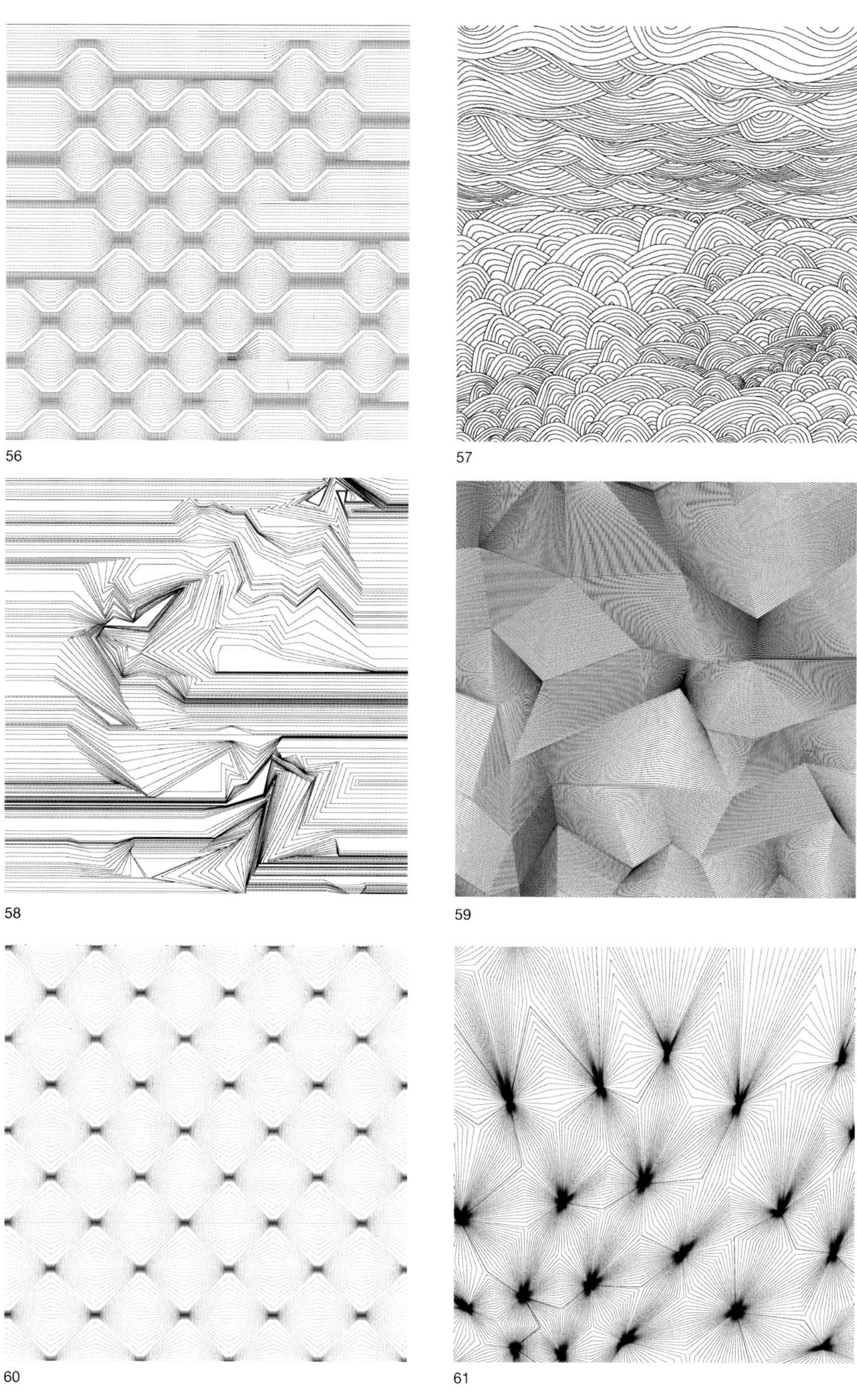
56 57 58 59 60 61

56 - 61 Studies on different line compositions dealing with the interplay of distance and proximity, density and vastness creating spatial and other visual effects

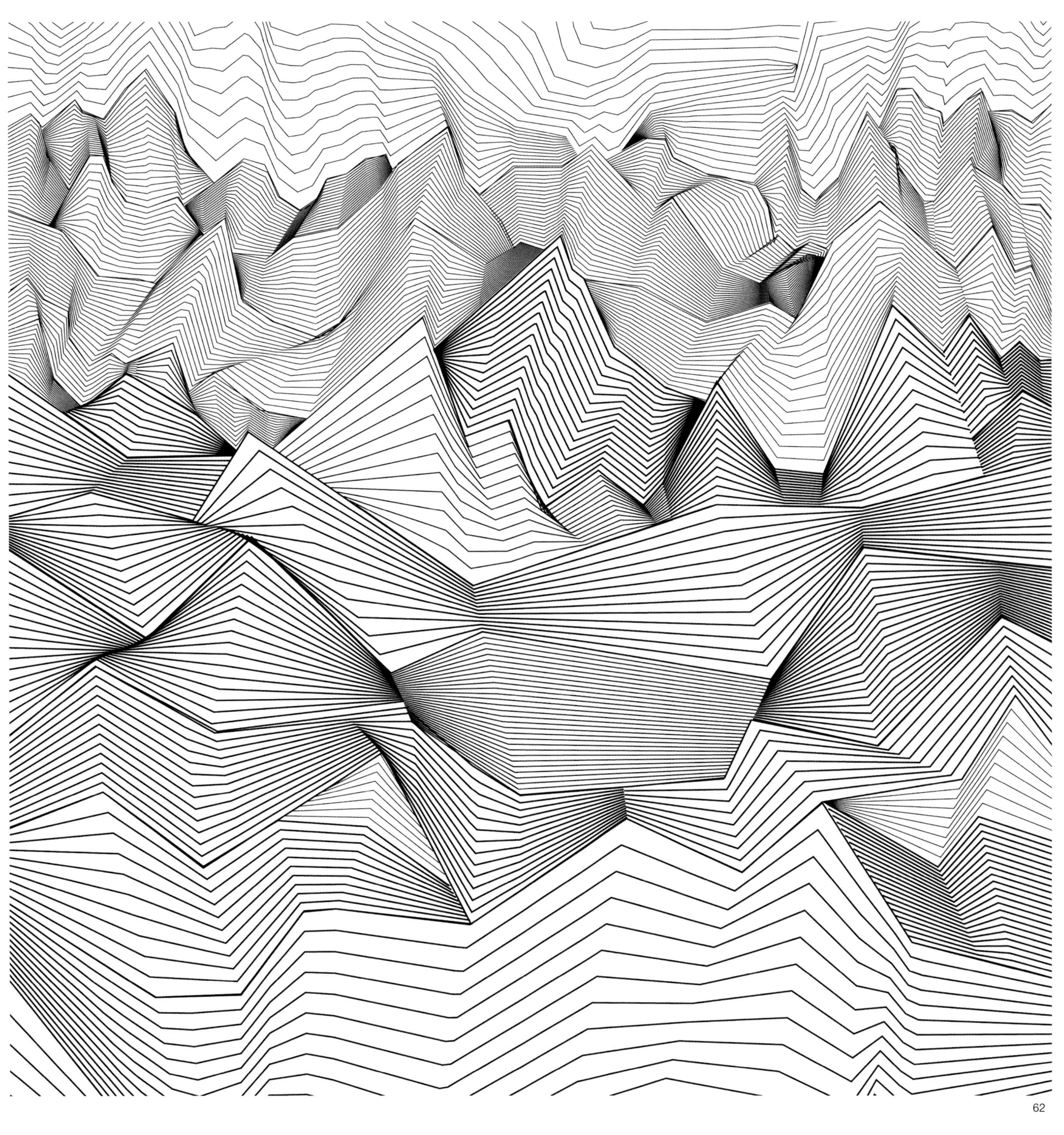

62

62 Continuous lines with varying distances evoke the image of a deeply staggered landscape

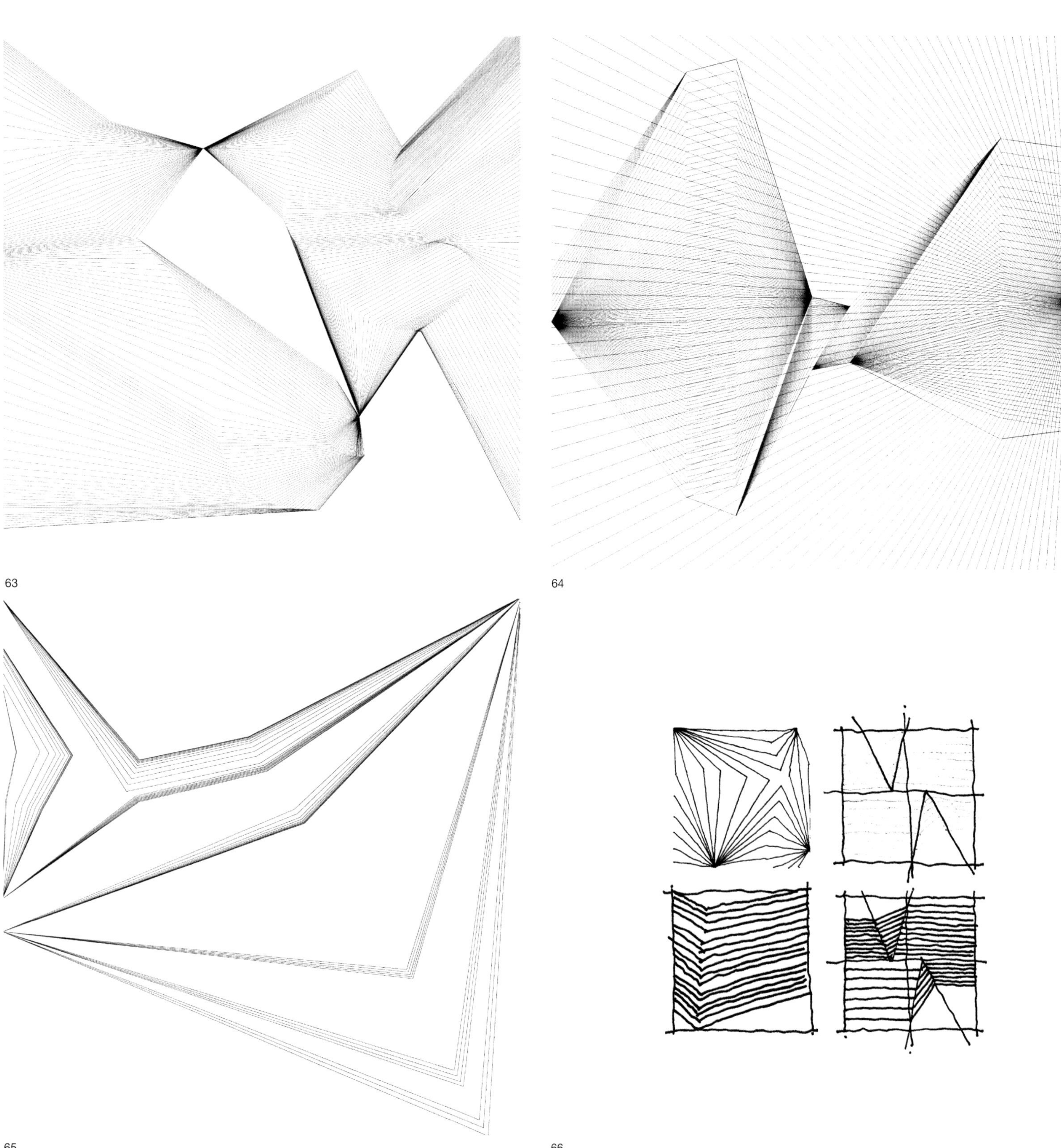
63 64 65 66

63 64 65 Cluster of lines alternating between dense and open configurations

66 Design development sketches

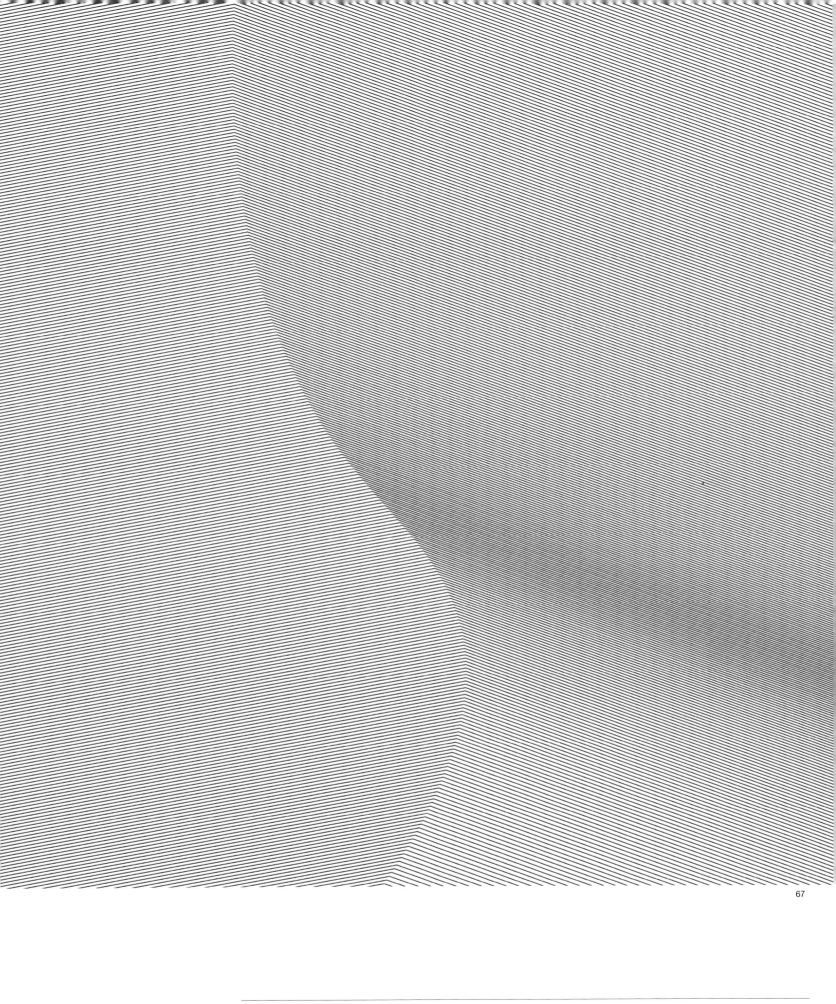
67

67 The sum of the lines that are deviated along an invisible curve, create a very calm composition that in this case, evokes an image of fictive dune landscape

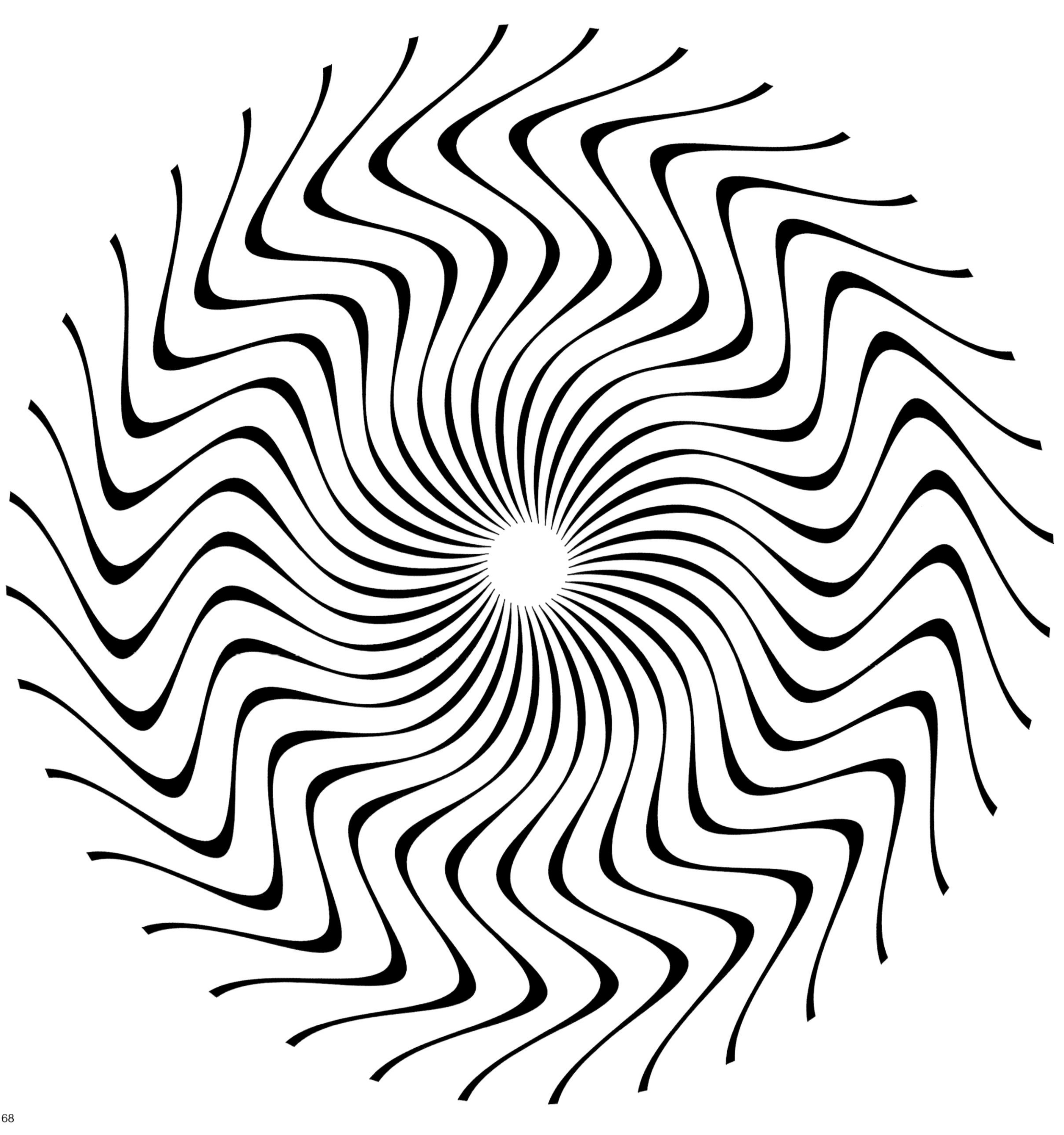

68

68 Spatial effect generated by radially configured and curved lines with deliberate changes in thickness

69 70 Curved lines with varying spacing generate the impression of natural surfaces whereas the strict spacing of fig. 71 seems to simulate an artificial surface

72 Multilayered line segments create the impression of an ostensive oscillation

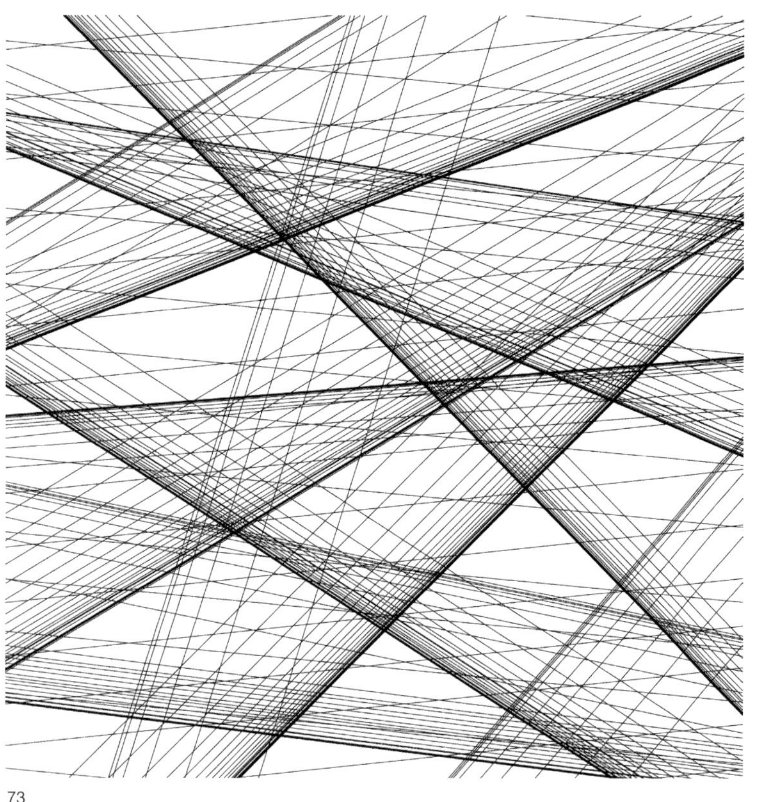

73

74

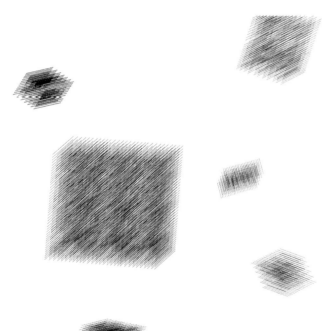

75

73 Spatial depth effect evoked by intersecting diagonal bundles of lines

74 Addition and superposition of curved and orthogonal line segments

75 Only through the multiple overlaying of line segments the illusion of blurring and apparently moving cubes is created

76

77

78

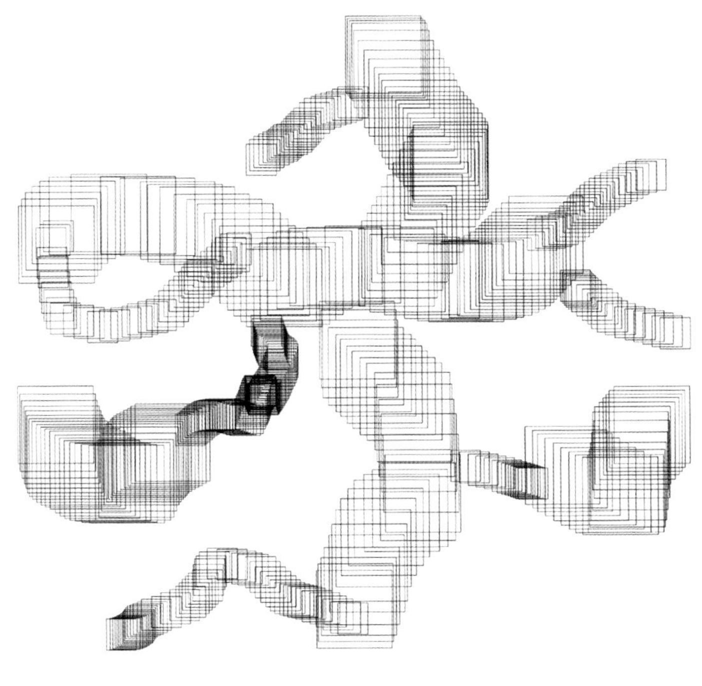

79

76 77 Successively displaced squares simulate a dynamic movement

78 Centralized arrangement in groups: shades of grey, foreground and background relationships create an interesting repetition of the initial square shape

79 Figurative configuration of staggered square contours

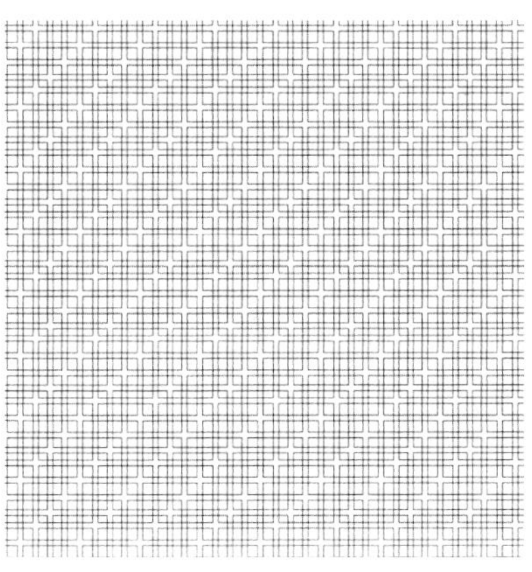

80

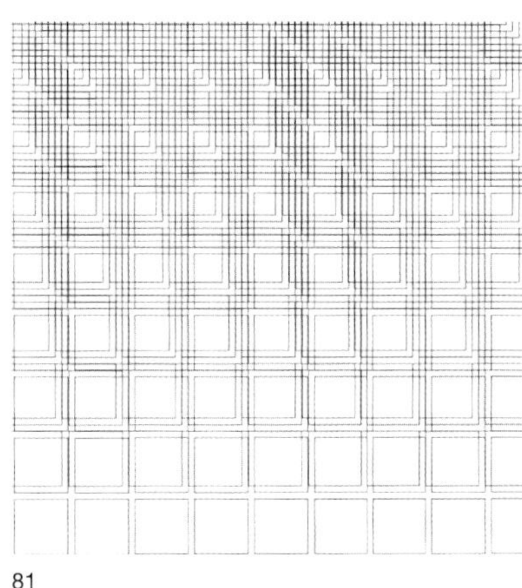

81

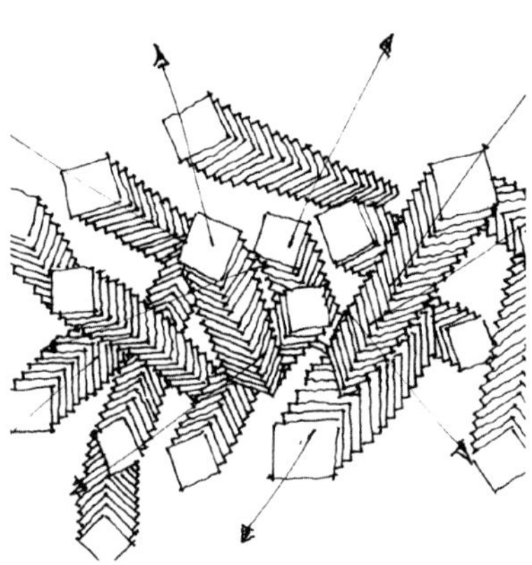

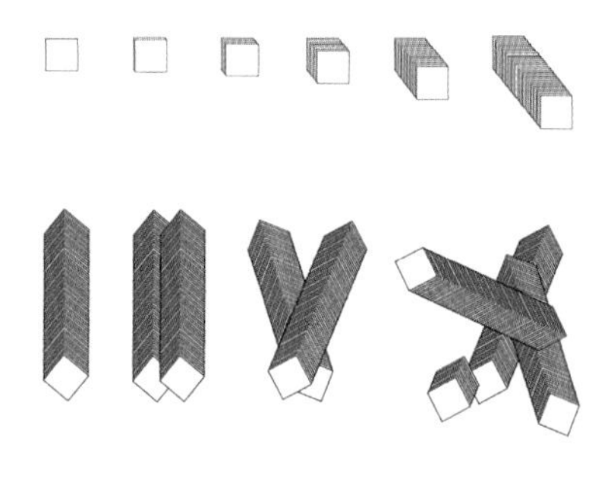

82

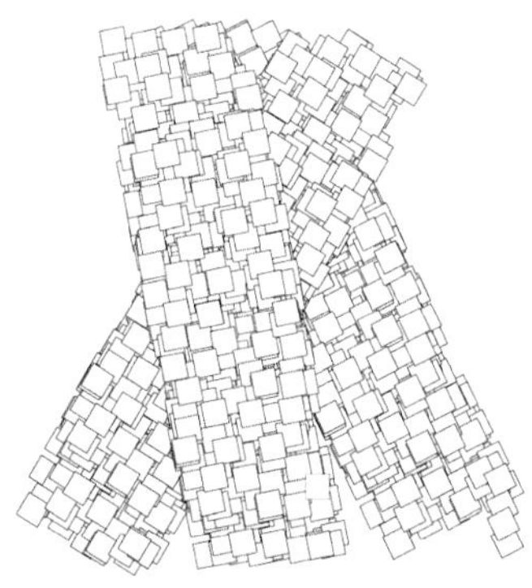

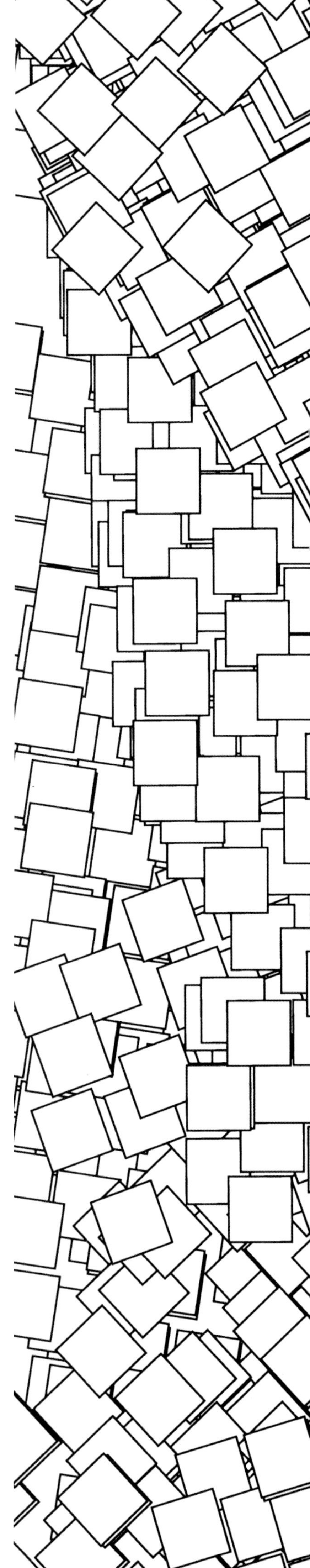

83

80 Pattern effect created through overlapping outlines
81 Spatial, gradient pattern effect created through overlapping outlines

82 Different preliminary studies for the arrangement of squares

83 Superimposition and intensive overlapping of grouped and rotated squares create a fascinating spatial depth effect that triggers an imaginative process for the viewer

Textures highlight the haptic character of any given object, this can also be regarded on a much larger scale. For example, the texture of a building or city can be the consequence of a design process, dealing with immanent spatial qualities of the given texture.

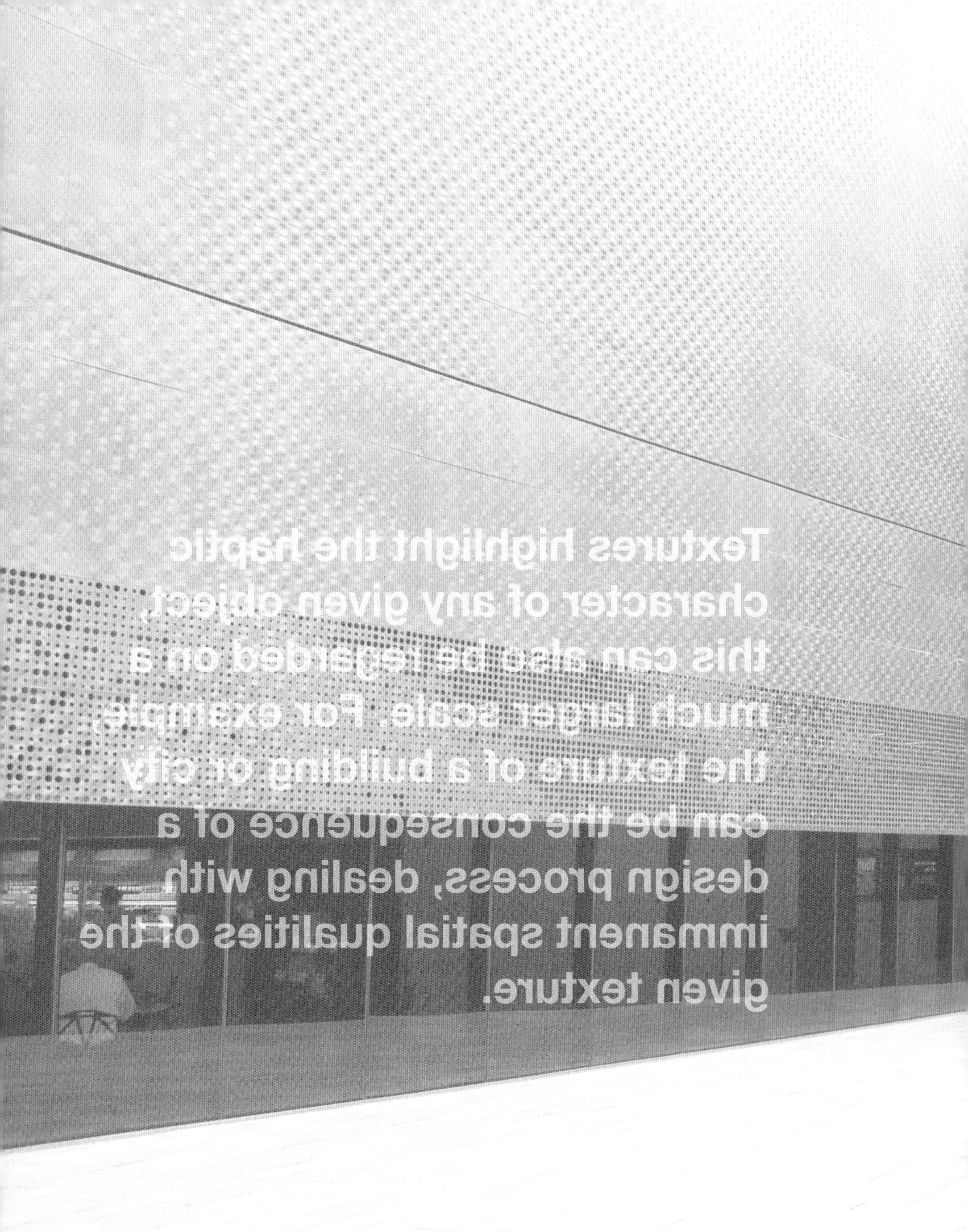

Textures highlight the haptic character of any given object, this can also be regarded on a much larger scale. For example, the texture of a building or city can be the consequence of a design process, dealing with immanent spatial qualities of the given texture.

Chapter 3 : Pattern Development – Texture

axes

grids

patterns

ornamental patterns

textures

performative properties

spatial reliefs

pattern tectonics

Axes and grids are the basis of efficient construction techniques. Although the use of modular grids can be traced throughout building history, perhaps their most common implementation emerged in modern architecture, the Bauhaus, and later within structuralism. Unlike the line, which is defined by the connection of two points, an axis is an imaginary grade that is potentially endless and possibly repeated as an organizing principle for building components. In geometry or three-dimensional modeling, this can be a rotational axis of a volume, a symmetry axis, or the visual axis within an urban fabric. Grids that are constituted by the repetition and crossing of imaginary axes function as an important structural principle for the construction and design of many buildings. The following examples take the intersections of grids as a basis for pattern design into focus. This examination will emphasize the design possibilities of pattern generation that are derived through working with grid points and the resulting tectonic possibilities of those patterns. In this first step, the grid will serve as a base for two-dimensional graphics and textures, with the potential to be further transformed into ornamental patterns.

Not even a hundred years have passed since Adolf Loos' manifesto "Ornament and Crime," and recent architectural developments are already gathered towards design ornamentation in contemporary buildings. (ref. 3.1)

Through up-to-date research, these ornamental patterns may soon transform into structural and typological principles. (ref. 3.2)

Page 50 51: De Young Museum, San Francisco, Herzog & de Meuron

3.1 „The evolution of culture marches with the elimination of ornament from useful objects" Adolf Loos: Ornament und Verbrechen / Adolf Loos: Ornament and Crime: Selected Essays

3.2 For example see: Michael Hensel, Achim Menges, Michael Weinstock: Emergent Technologies and Design

3.1 Structured and textured façade, De Young Museum, San Francisco. Herzog & de Meuron

3.2 Concrete façade panels with embossed texture, University Library Utrecht, the Netherlands. Wiel Arets

3.3 Translucent façade panels, University Library Utrecht, the Netherlands. Wiel Arets

The digital revolution and the use of digital tools in architecture in the last 25 years, resulted in the development of performative patterns that greatly contributed to this design shift. (ref. 3.3)

The graphic design possibilities of image processing and illustration tools, which are widely available and easy to use, and the graphic interface of the internet have resulted in a rapid expansion of graphic elements in everyday life, increasingly permeating into the field of architecture.

The recent renaissance of the pattern façades of the space age has been proliferated by actual research in parametric architecture. The basis for this fascination for pattern design is closely related to the necessity for deploying grids in order to efficiently construct buildings. The repetition of similar building components into a structural or constructive pattern is a natural design procedure for any architect. The principle of additive design also explains the attraction many people have towards patterns. The recent advancement of pattern façades do not just follow a formal design fashion: they are also capable of delivering concrete building applications and functions like structure, shading or ventilation, among others.

Often, certain capabilities like adaptive or supersurface structures are incorporated into pattern designs with the ability to intelligently adjust their functionality according to their environmental conditions and resulting exigencies. In these cases, the limitations of the two-dimensional pattern as a simple surface texture are exceeded, and the pattern becomes spatial, and possibly structural. The following chapters will highlight more of this aspect in architectural pattern design.
Textures and patterns not only activate architectural surfaces but add to or question the sense of scale in a given architectural design. When designing with a computer, the reference to scale within the natural environment can easily be lost. While visualizing an architectural project digitally, the process of

3.3 also see chapters 8 and 11 in this book

3.4 Arts Centre De Kunstlinie, Almere City, the Netherlands. Kazuyo Sejima + Ryue Nishizawa / SANAA

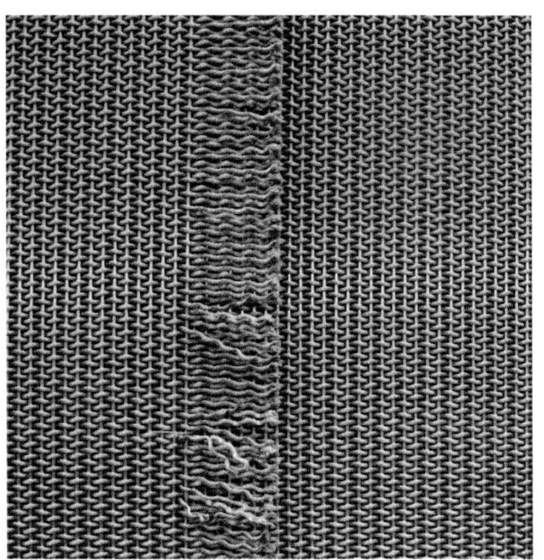

3.5 Wall covering. French National Library, Paris. Dominique Perrault

3.6 Wooden wall paneling, Kolumba Museum, Cologne, Germany. Peter Zumthor

texturizing relates to the role that natural textures on surfaces and designed textures in façades play within a real building. The sensible use of materials with their respective patterns and textures evokes a heightened perception of closeness and distance. This allows for a better perception of the size and dimension of an architectural design. The materiality in the metal fabric of the staircases in Dominique Perrault's National Library in Paris, France (fig. 3.5), and the grain of the wood veneer in the interior of Peter Zumthor's Kolumba Museum in Cologne, Germany, (fig. 3.6) are excellent examples of this effect.

The following examples illustrate the design and construction of different patterns that are based on simple grid organizations. As part of an exercise, students were asked to follow assigned principles of a grid pattern with a number of variables that consisted of a minimum of three axes, the first two of which had to cross each other repeatedly, while the third independently positioned axis had to intersect some of the cross-points of the other two, depending on its angle and alignment. This grid or network served as the base for developing a pattern that was loosely oriented within the axes and cross-points.

Through the development of the pattern, students were free to either highlight or omit any number segments or surfaces, and to add multiple connections between points in the grid. Some patterns were also derived through the repetition of a freely developed abstracted element. After the initial graphic composition, every pattern was than projected into a spatial relief incorporating the development of a textural design within a three-dimensional pattern. This served as a first step towards the next assignment that dealt with structure.
The examples illustrate the possibility of deriving a variety of diverging pattern designs from a grid network. These two dimensional graphic patterns can further be translated into spatial formations that can eventually be assigned to functional and tectonic attributes in later stages of the design.

84

85

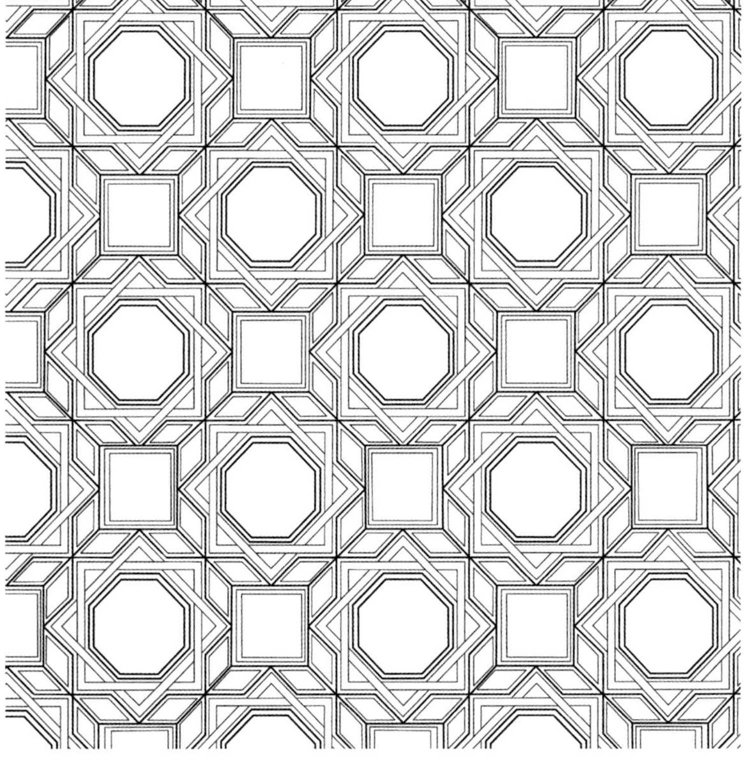
86

84 Default grid for the development of the pattern

85 Evolution of a complex pattern structure by selectively erasing segments of the given grid

86 Final pattern

87

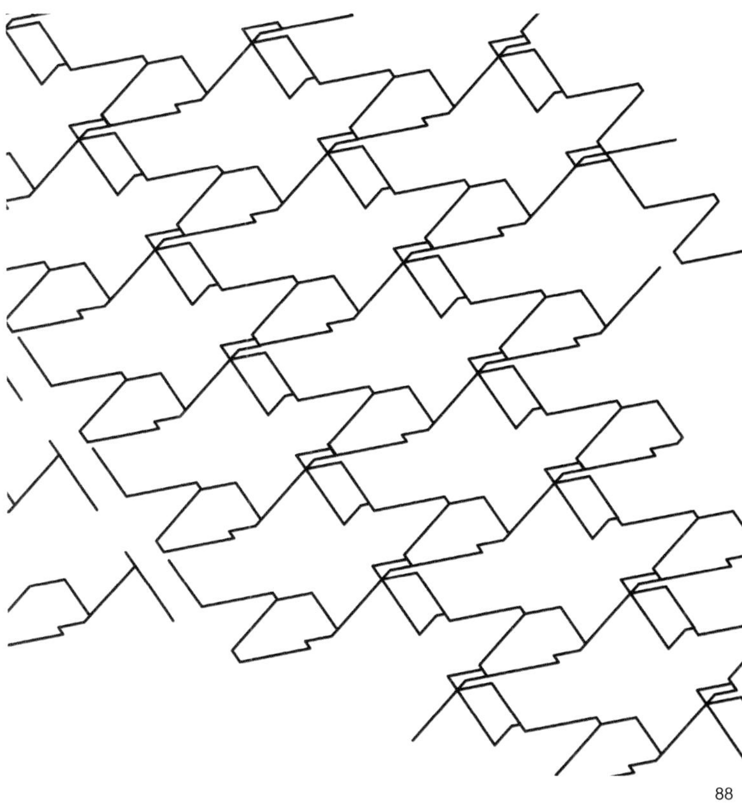
88

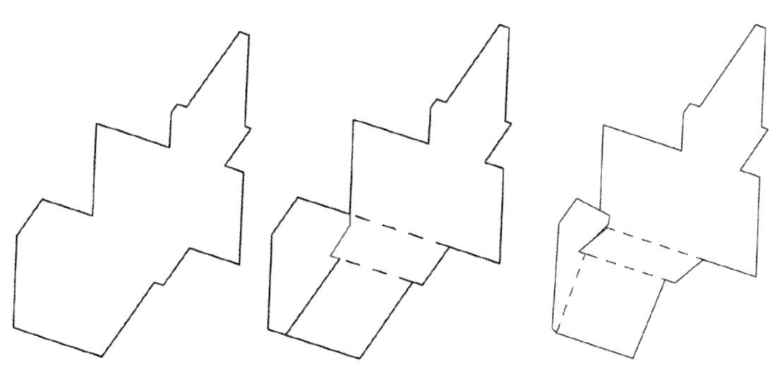
89

90

87 Pattern lines with grid overlay
88 Pattern structure without grid

89 Transformation study for a modular element folded in three dimensions

90 Model as the result of a three-dimensional transformation process

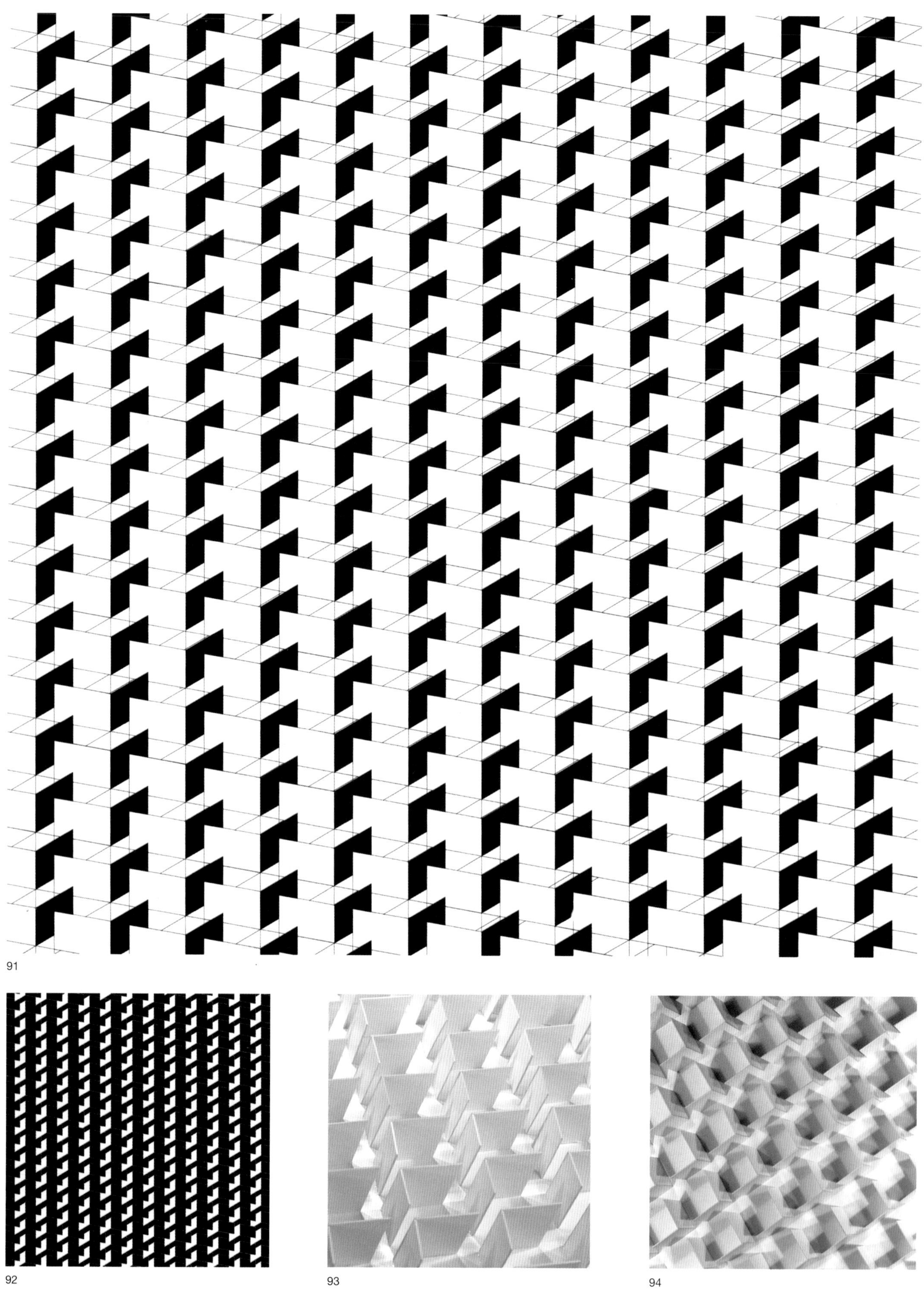

91

92

93

94

91 92 Similar patterns in positive-negative variations

93 94 Model derived from patterns in fig. 91 and 92. Light and shadow increases the complexity enhancing the texture as a non physical layer of complexity

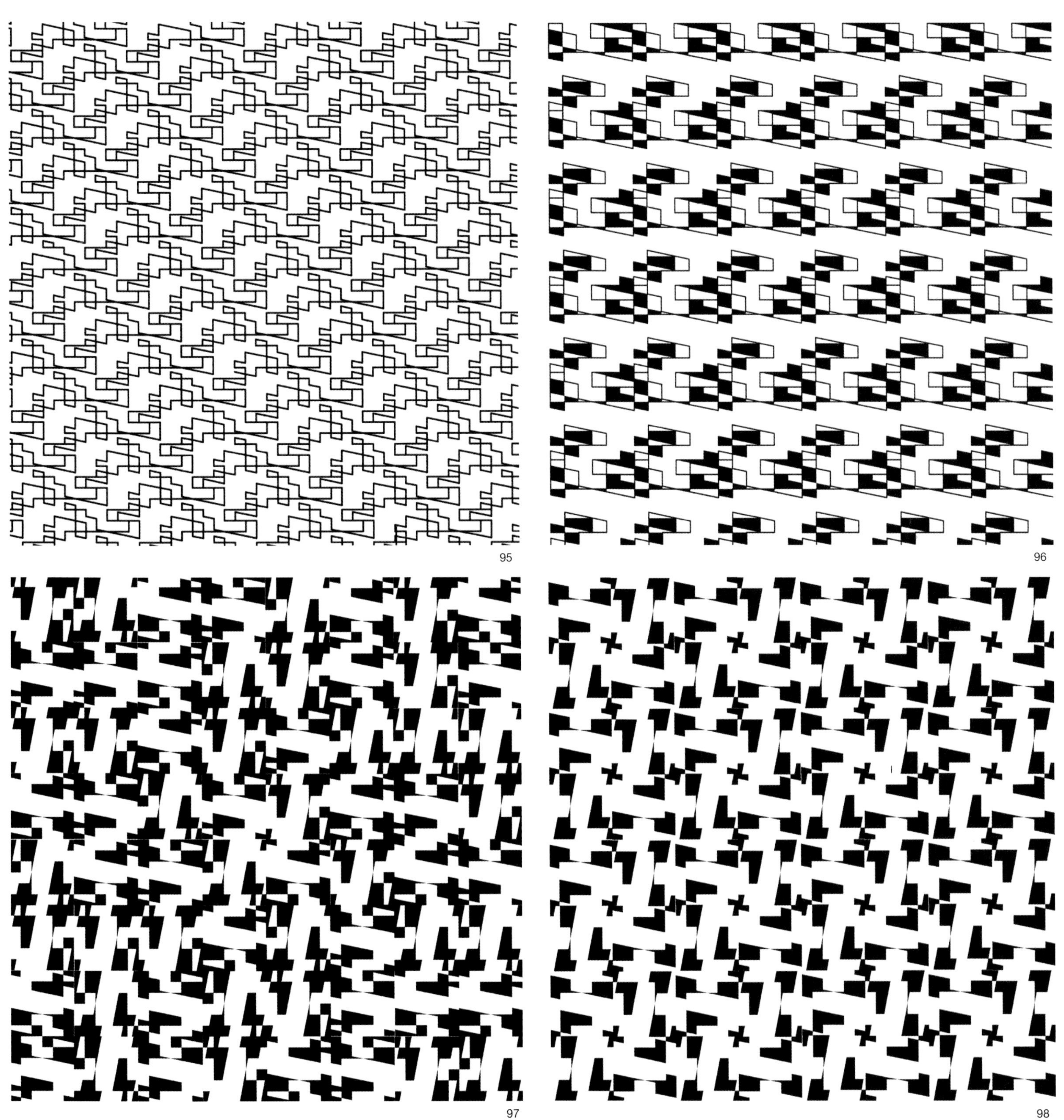

95 Original pattern created by the weaving of one continous line

96 Horizontally orientated variation of fig. 95 with filled areas

97 Variation of fig. 96 in a centralized configuration

98 muticentered pattern derived from fig. 97

99

100

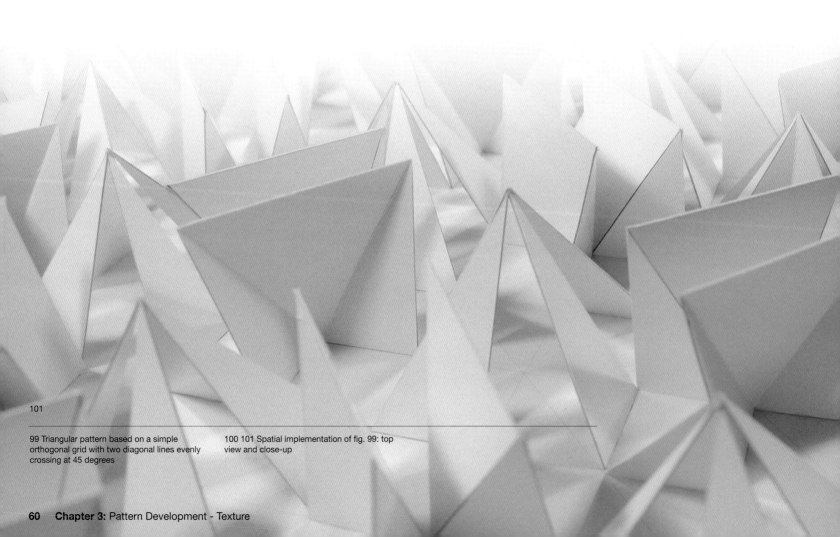

101

99 Triangular pattern based on a simple orthogonal grid with two diagonal lines evenly crossing at 45 degrees

100 101 Spatial implementation of fig. 99: top view and close-up

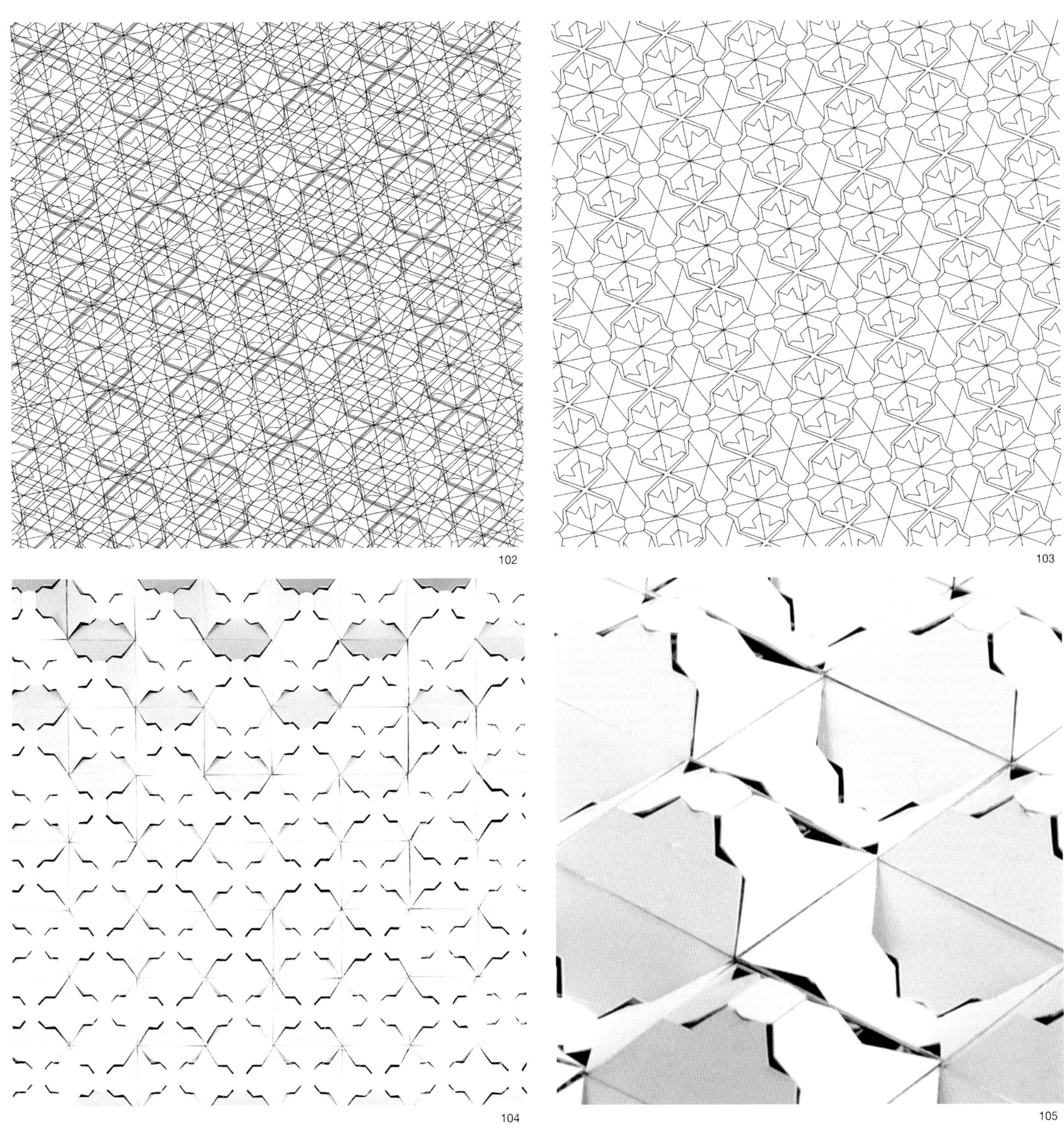

102 - 105 Pattern development from a two-dimensional grid to a textured spatial configuration

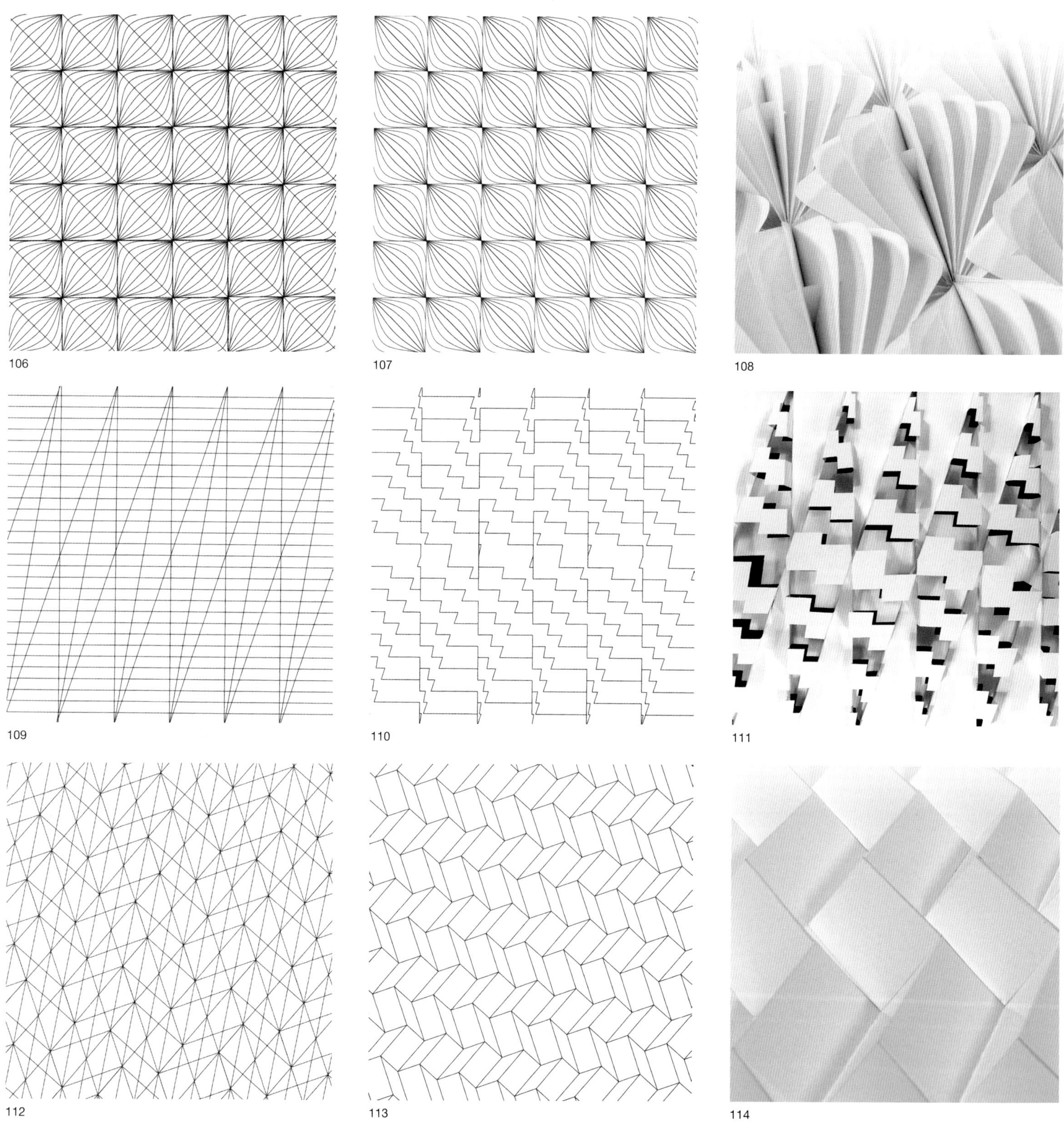
106
107
108
109
110
111
112
113
114

106 - 114 Different pattern developments
from two-dimensional grid to spatial texture

115 Conceptional sketch
116 Pattern of ellipsoid shapes and circles constructed on a grid

117 Derived pattern scaled down and without the grid

118 119 and 120 121 Pattern and resulting spatial development

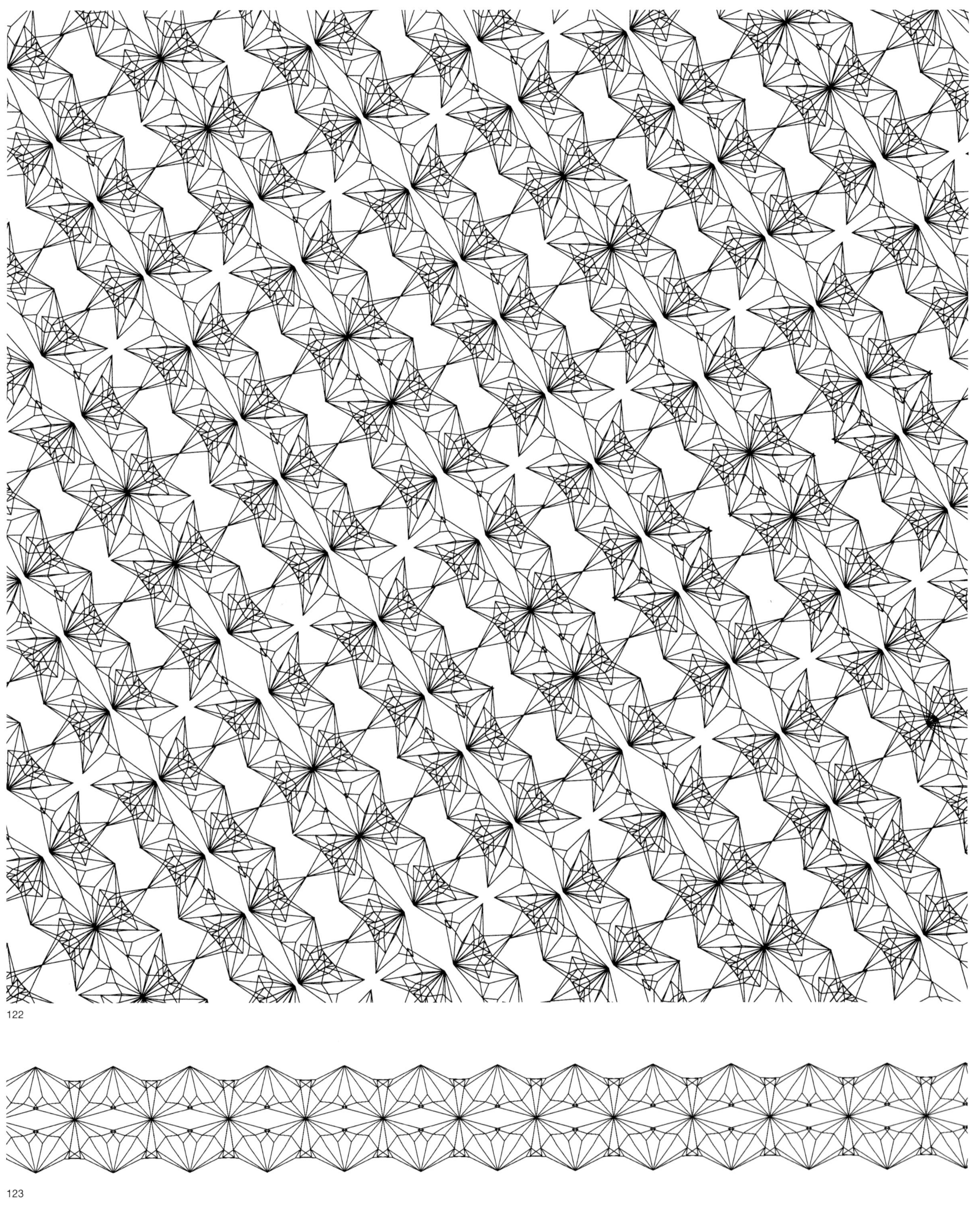

122

123

122 Pattern with floral appearance
123 Extracted strip from a variation of the above pattern

124-127 Pattern development from two-dimensional grid to spatial texture

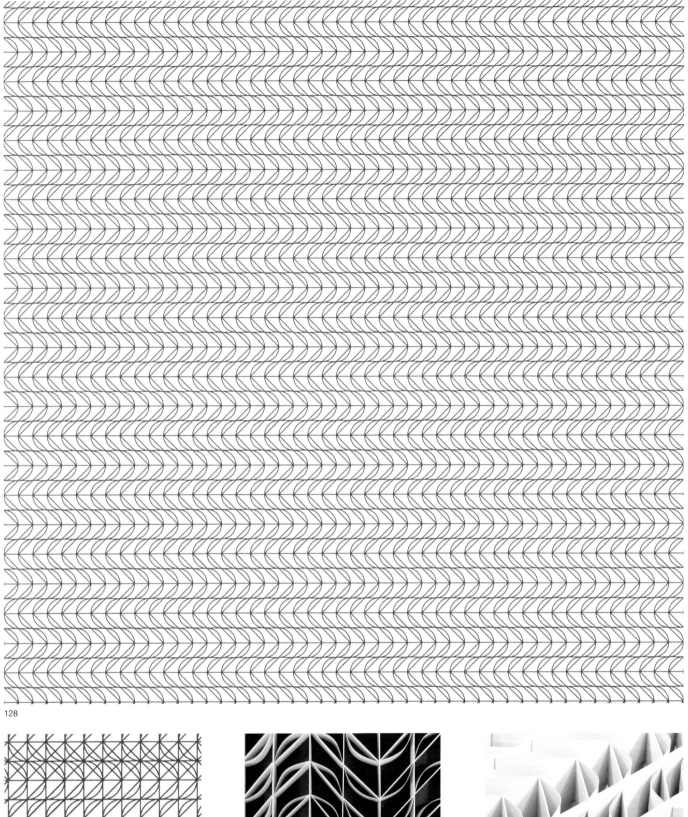

128

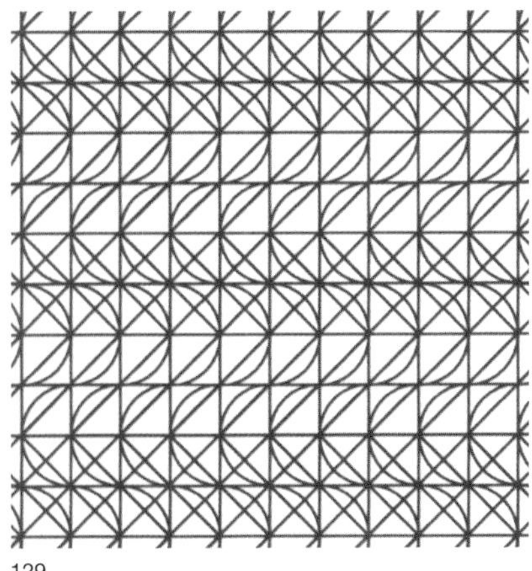
129

130

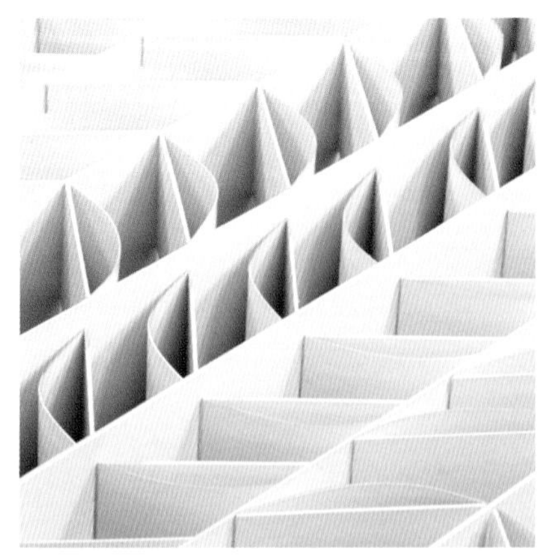
131

128 Pattern with an optical illusion: the seemingly converging lines are parallel in reality

129 130 131 Pattern development from a grid to a configured spatial texture

132

133

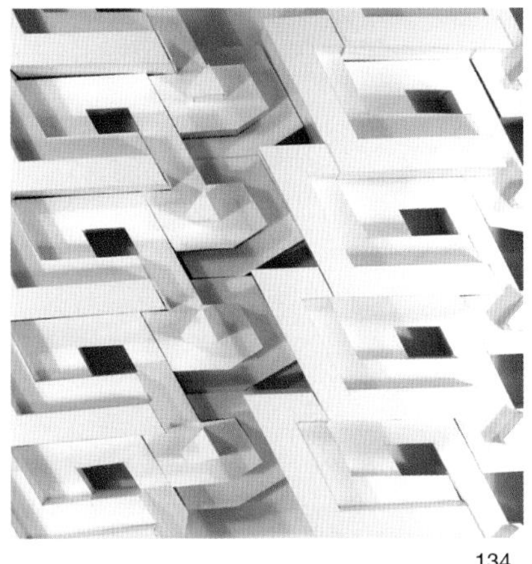

134

132 133 134 Differently scaled pattern development from a grid (fig. 133) to a configured spatial texture (fig. 134)

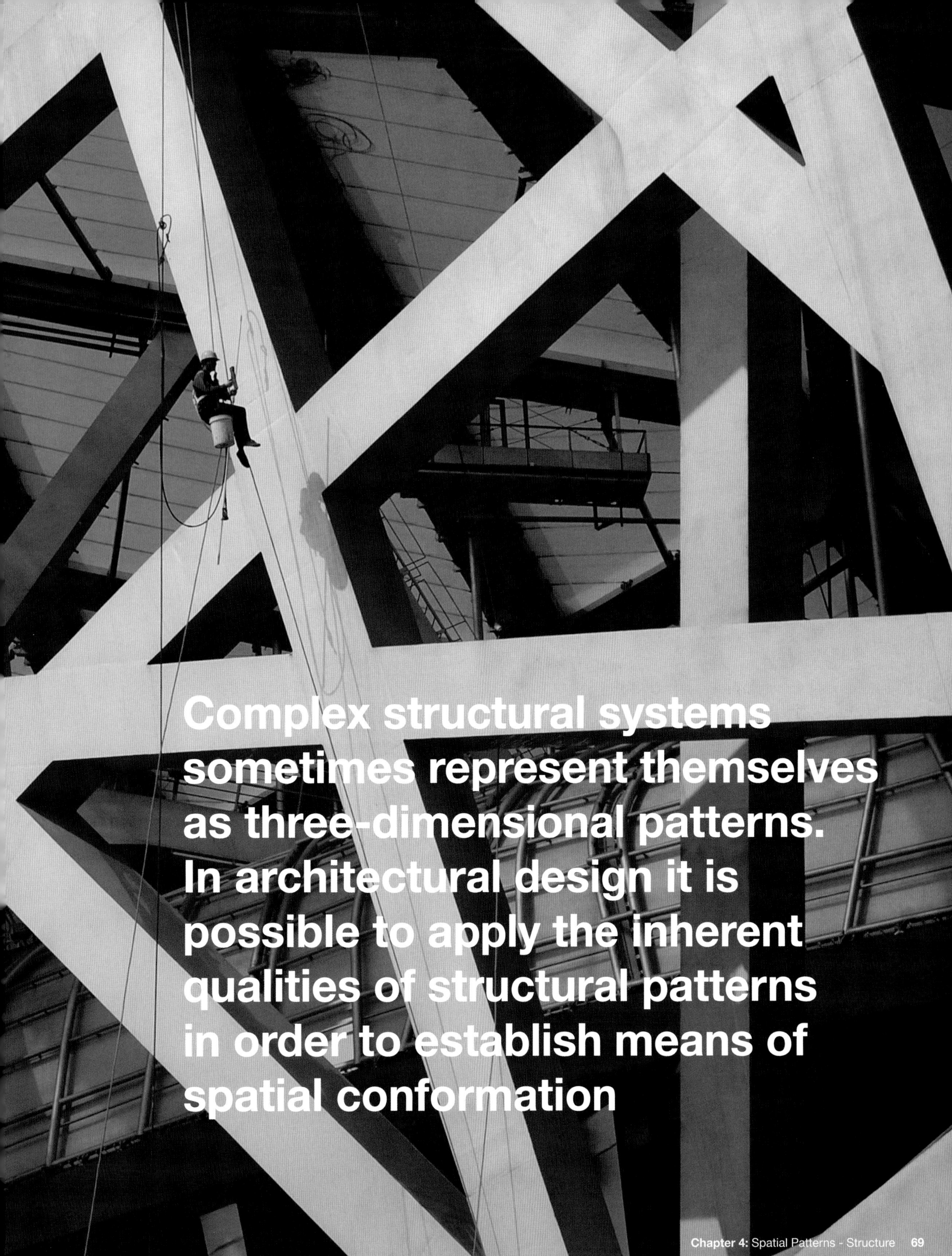

Complex structural systems sometimes represent themselves as three-dimensional patterns. In architectural design it is possible to apply the inherent qualities of structural patterns in order to establish means of spatial conformation

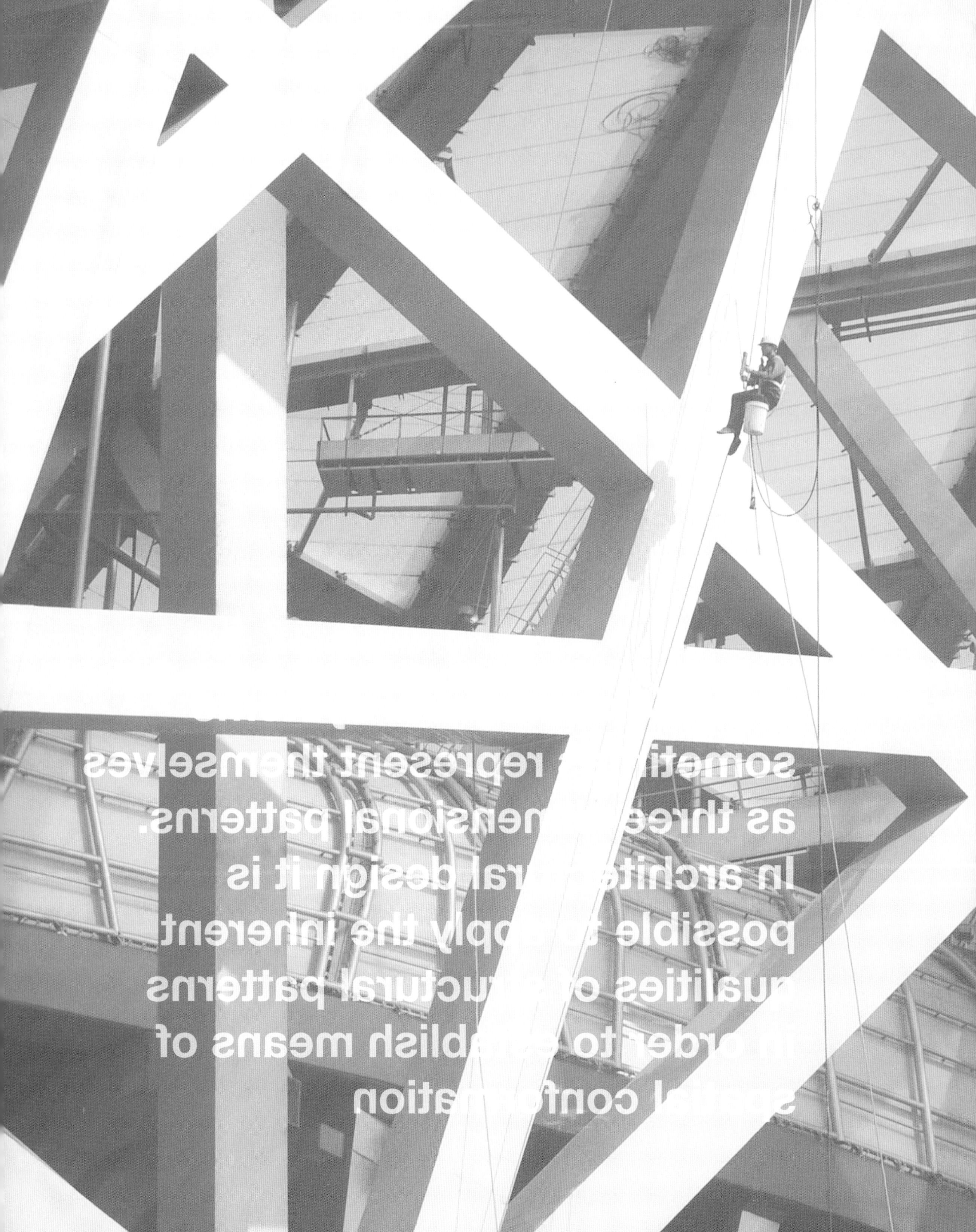

Chapter 4 : Spatial Patterns – Structure

texture vs. structure
spatial patterns
grids and matrix
formal entities
adapted modules
spatial modules

As a continuation of two-dimensional patterns and grids as surface textures, this chapter will focus on spatial grids, three-dimensional patterns and spatial structures.

Patterns, or ornaments, can be found in various architectural instances. They can emerge on a surface or in space, in an abstract texture, or even as structure. By definition, a texture is a mere surface characteristic that has the capacity to appear at most, in the form of a relief. A textural pattern as a surface entity in architectural design is more often a decorative element without primary tectonic function. (ref 4.1)

A structure, on the other hand, is three-dimensional by definition. Its attributes are continuous throughout its makeup, like the internal structure of a tree trunk for example. The tectonic characteristics of a structure can therefore materialize from a kind of three-dimensional texture. For example, if one uses the examples in the previous chapters as structural frameworks, structural patterns or structural ornaments begin to emerge.

An example of structural patterning can be found in the floor plans of Gothic cathedrals. Despite their rich ornamentation, the deep structure and columnar

Page 68 69: Olympic Stadium, Beijing, Herzog & de Meuron

4.1 An exception might be the slight ripple or tension ribs on aluminum sheets, that enhance the material's rigidity

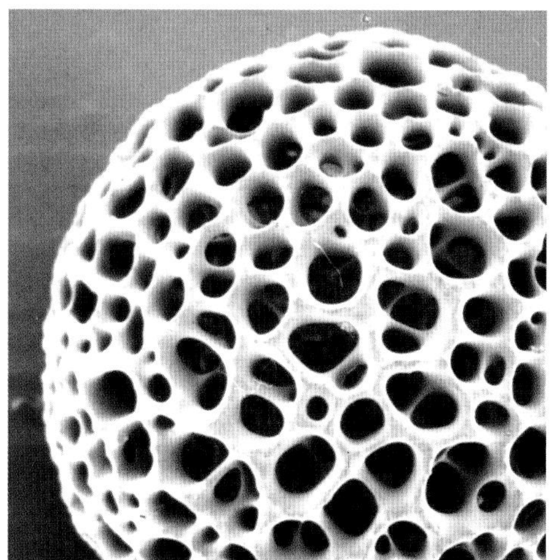
4.1 Marine microfossils

4.2 Espacio de las Artes at Santa Cruz de Tenerife, Spain. Herzog & de Meuron

4.3 Olympic Stadium Beijing, “Birds Nest”. Herzog & de Meuron

alignment within the otherwise symmetrical grid appear as a complex pattern. The built architecture is spatially analogous to the floor plan pattern, which is deeply connected with its ornamentation. The transformation of heavy walls into columns, beams and arches within Gothic architecture constitutes an ornamental tectonic. This phenomenon holds especially true for a vast array of pre-modernist architecture and can be found in many other architectural styles and epochs.

Modern spatial constructive systems sometimes also reveal themselves as patterns when abstracted in a floor plan or other types of spatial projections. In modernism, these patterns are mostly orthogonal in nature and can be expressed as grids or matrices that are deployed via repetitive or overlaid modular properties.

Contemporary architecture often combines the design characteristics and tectonic performance that are intrinsic to patterns to create increasingly ornamental architectural structures. The possibilities of digital methods challenge the conventional modernist practice of design by introducing an array of new constructive and material possibilities. As in many other instances, digitization has also resulted in an increase of complexity in the development of such structures. Construction, tectonics, and stability are in many contemporary cases impossible to understand or follow. Herzog and de Meuron’s National Stadium (fig. 4.3), created for the 2008 Olympic Games, is one of the most evident of recent examples. The design of its structure does not solely follow the modernist aim of revealing the tectonics of a building. Purely decorative and rigidly practical properties are combined into architectural structure that breaks free from the idea of form following function.

Designing sophisticated spatial structures is an important ability for archi-

4.4 CCTV Tower, Beijing. OMA

4.5 Façade element, Institute du Monde Arab, Paris. Jean Nouvel

4.6 National Aquatics Center, Beijing. PTW Architects

tects. In order to master multifaceted and diverse spatial connections in an aesthetically appealing and structurally sound manner, the design of patterns and their subsequent translation into spatial frameworks is vital.

Structural characteristics of various developed matrices can immediately be tested through the executions of small working models. The student examples in this chapter take the development of a two-dimensional pattern as a departure point to construct a three-dimensional structure.

In the assignment, the students were free to use an underlining grid or to develop the repetitive pattern through an additive method. An absolute precondition for the translation of the pattern into a three-dimensional model was the development of a module or a group of modules. Upon their completion, these components were analyzed in terms of their structural qualities and were subsequently optimized accordingly.

Lastly, the modules were constructed and combined into a spatial framework. Through repetition, modification or through an additive process, spatial frame structures with different appearances and properties were designed and constructed.

Within this process, one of the goals was to proliferate model constructions from initial patterns, so that the final design became a logical evolution and intelligent reflection of the inherent two-dimensional pattern characteristics. This working method resulted in a number of different outcomes, from a number of different approaches, leading to dialectical conclusions from ephemeral and fragile frames to rigid structures of highly static efficiency. These structures are often extremely ambitious objects that exhibit highly complex properties in need of further optimization in order to be transformed into feasible architectural possibilities.

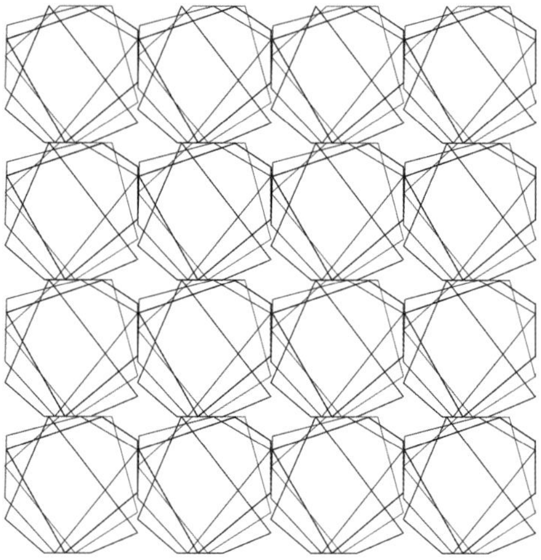

135

136

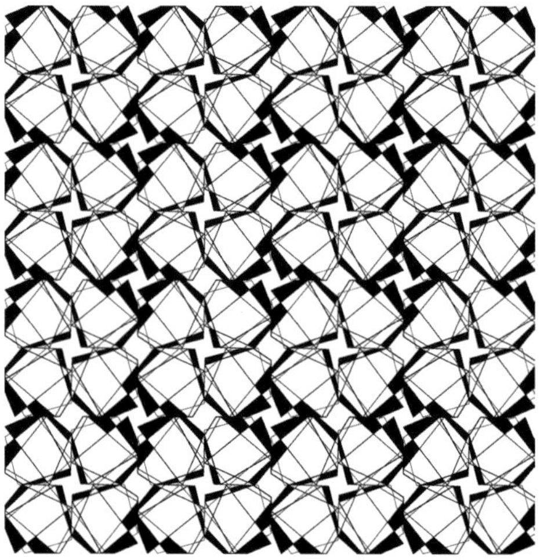

137

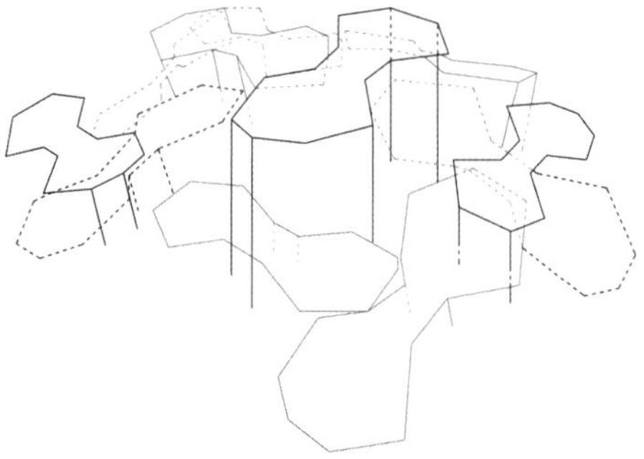

138

139

140

135 136 Densifying a pattern

137 138 Pattern and drawing of spatial module configuration

139 140 Single module and pattern derived from additive module arrangement

141

142

143

144

141 - 143 Preliminary pattern development

144 Model made of thin soldered copper wire evoking a strong ephemeral sense of fragility

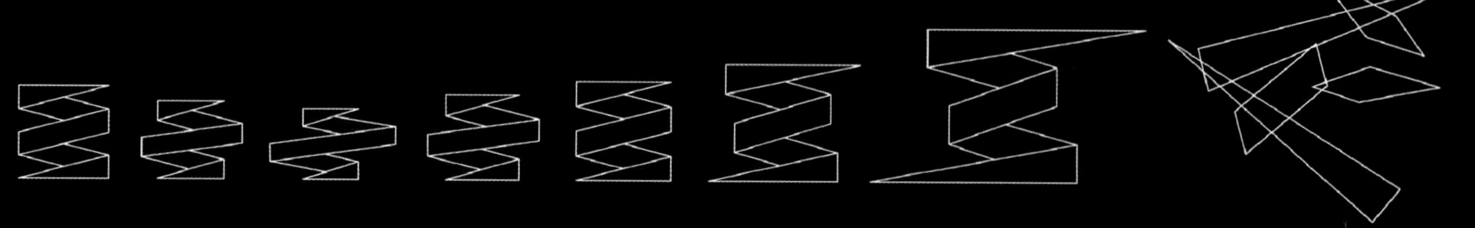

145

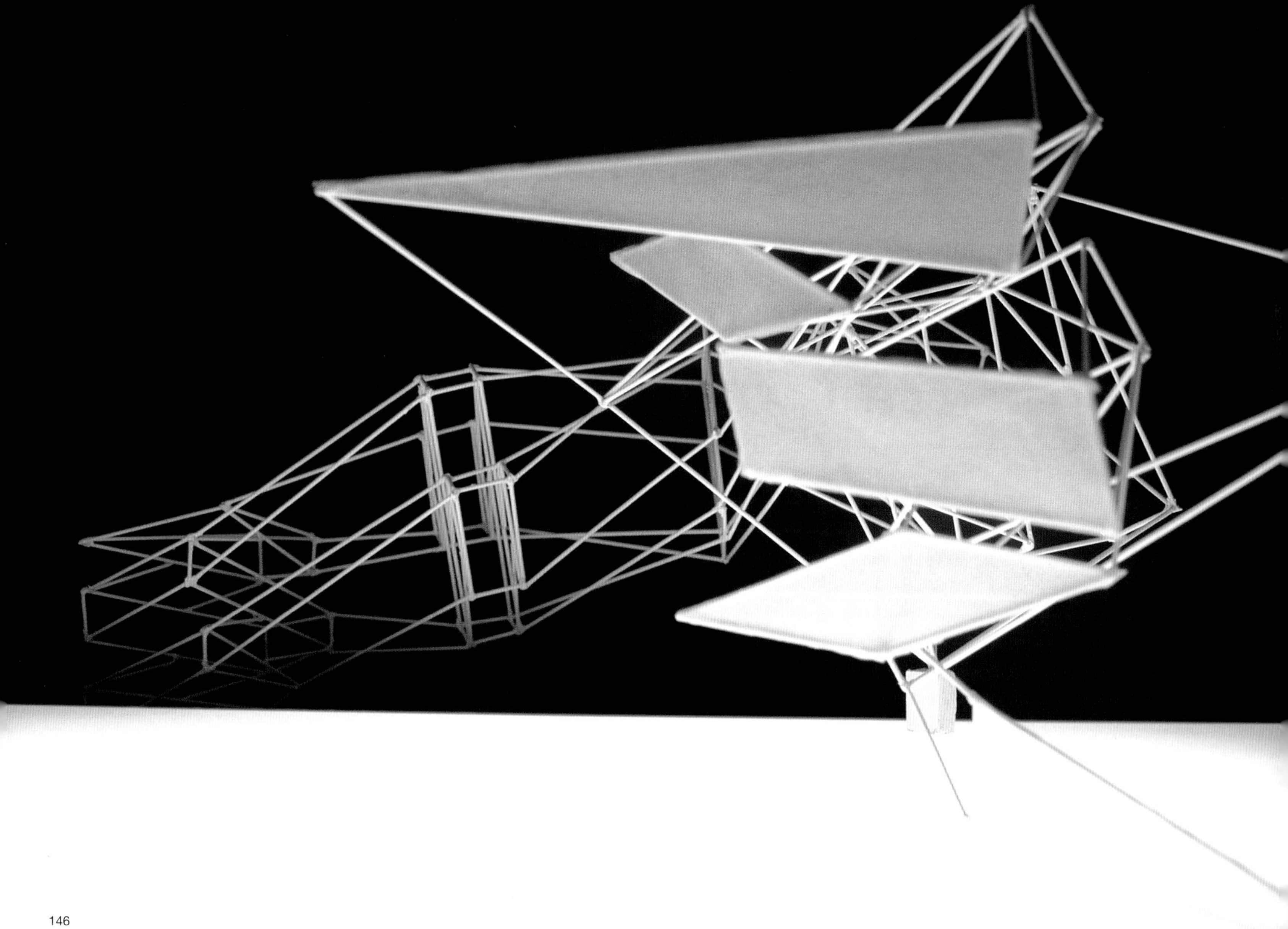

146

145 Morphological module studies
146 Wire model with partially closed surfaces

147

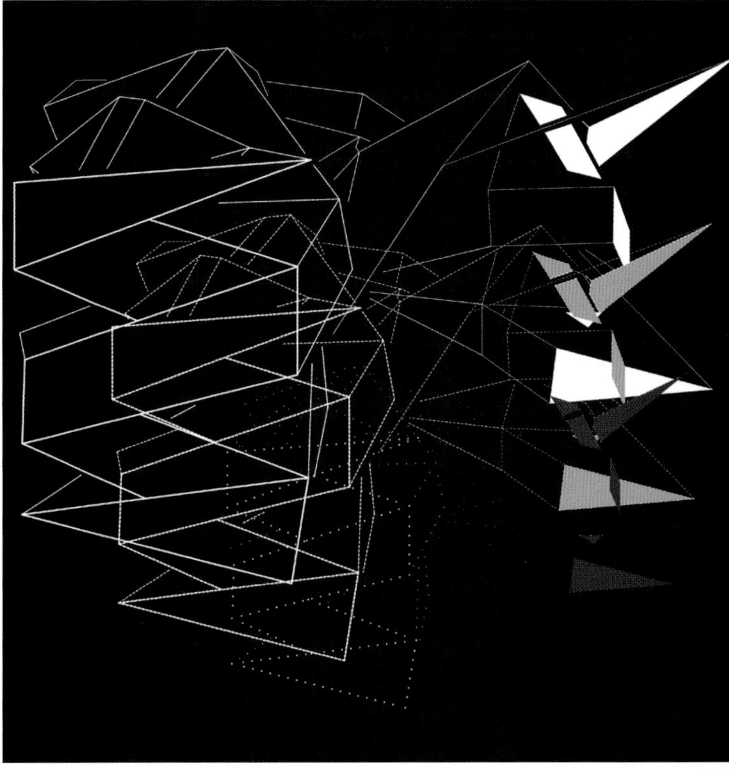

148

147 Initial two-dimensional pattern
148 Analytic depiction of model fig. 146

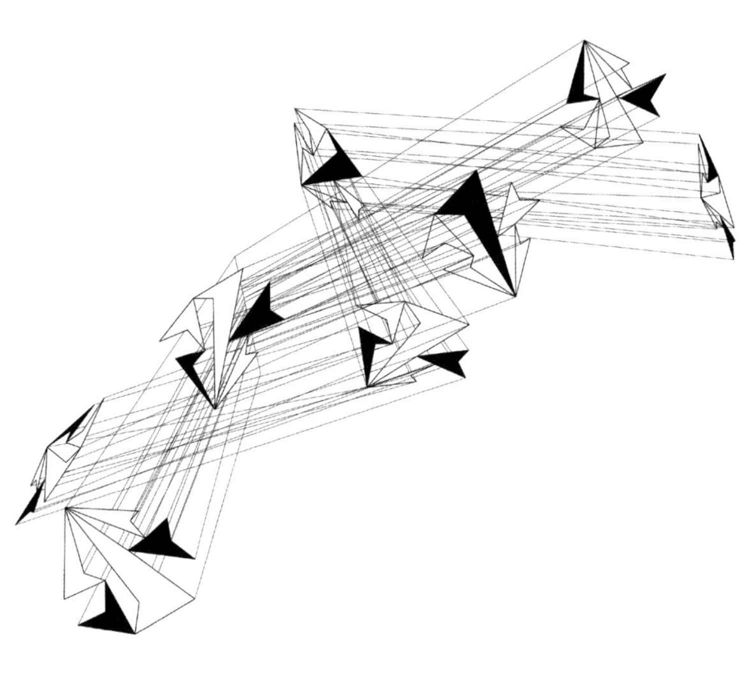

149

150

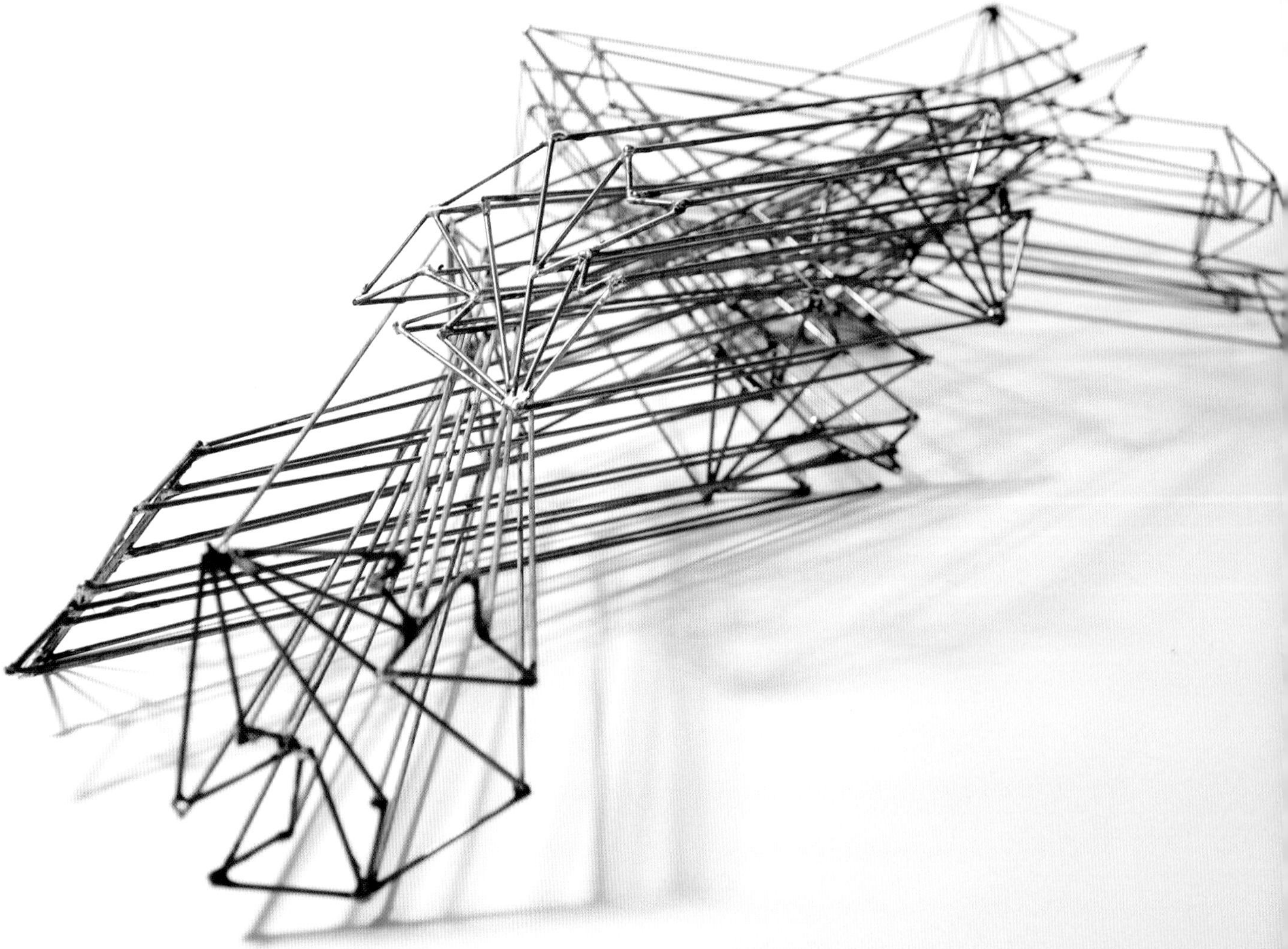

151

149 Digital sketch of spatial interaction between two-dimensional modules

150 Repetitive modular pattern with filled areas

151 Spatial tensions and dynamic interactions are created by accentuating the linear connection between displaced modules

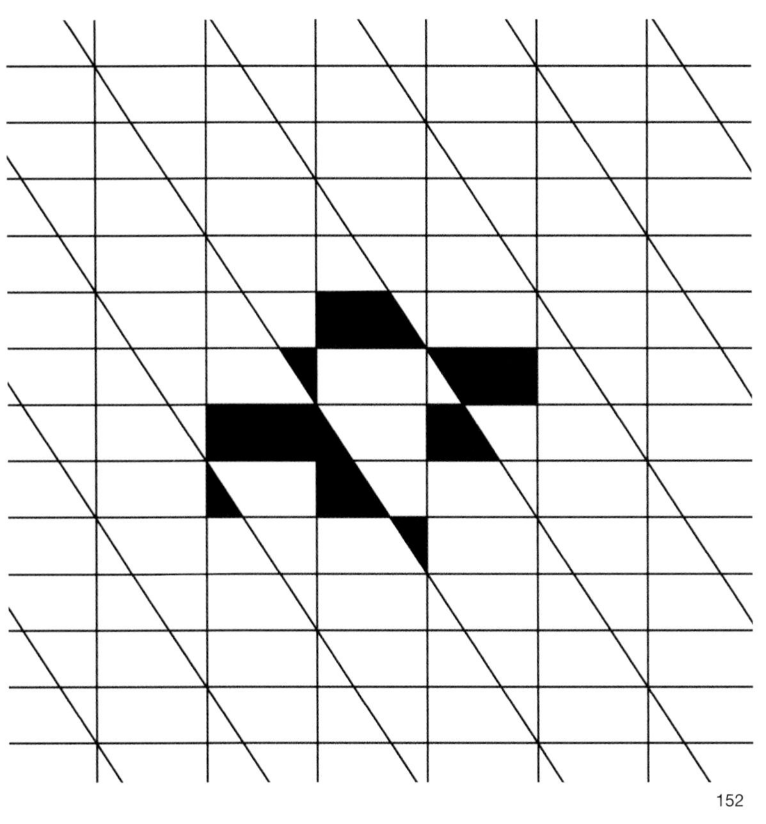

152

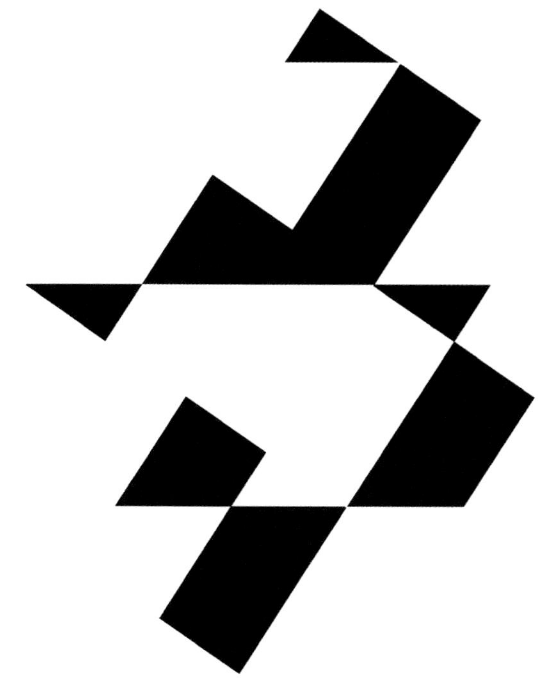

153

154

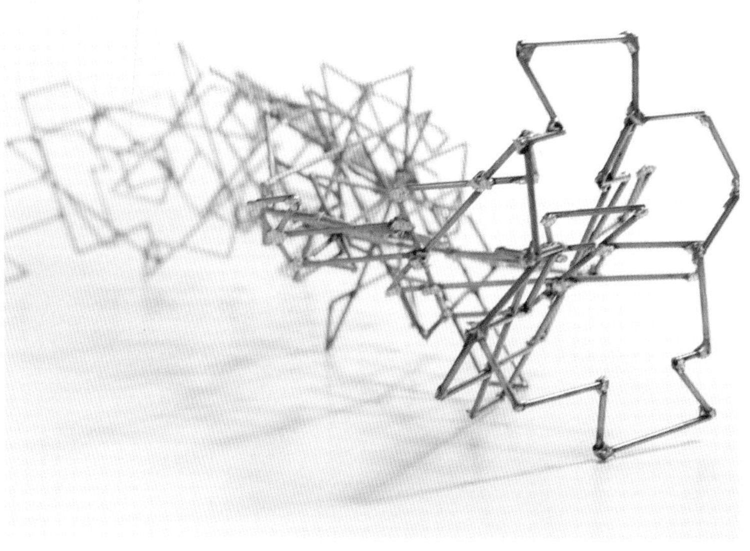

155

156

152 Grid and module
153 Single module

154 Diversified pattern derived by adding and overlapping the repeatedly rotated module (fig. 153)

155 Model derived from pattern and modules (fig. 152-154)
156 Analytical drawing of spatial module alignment

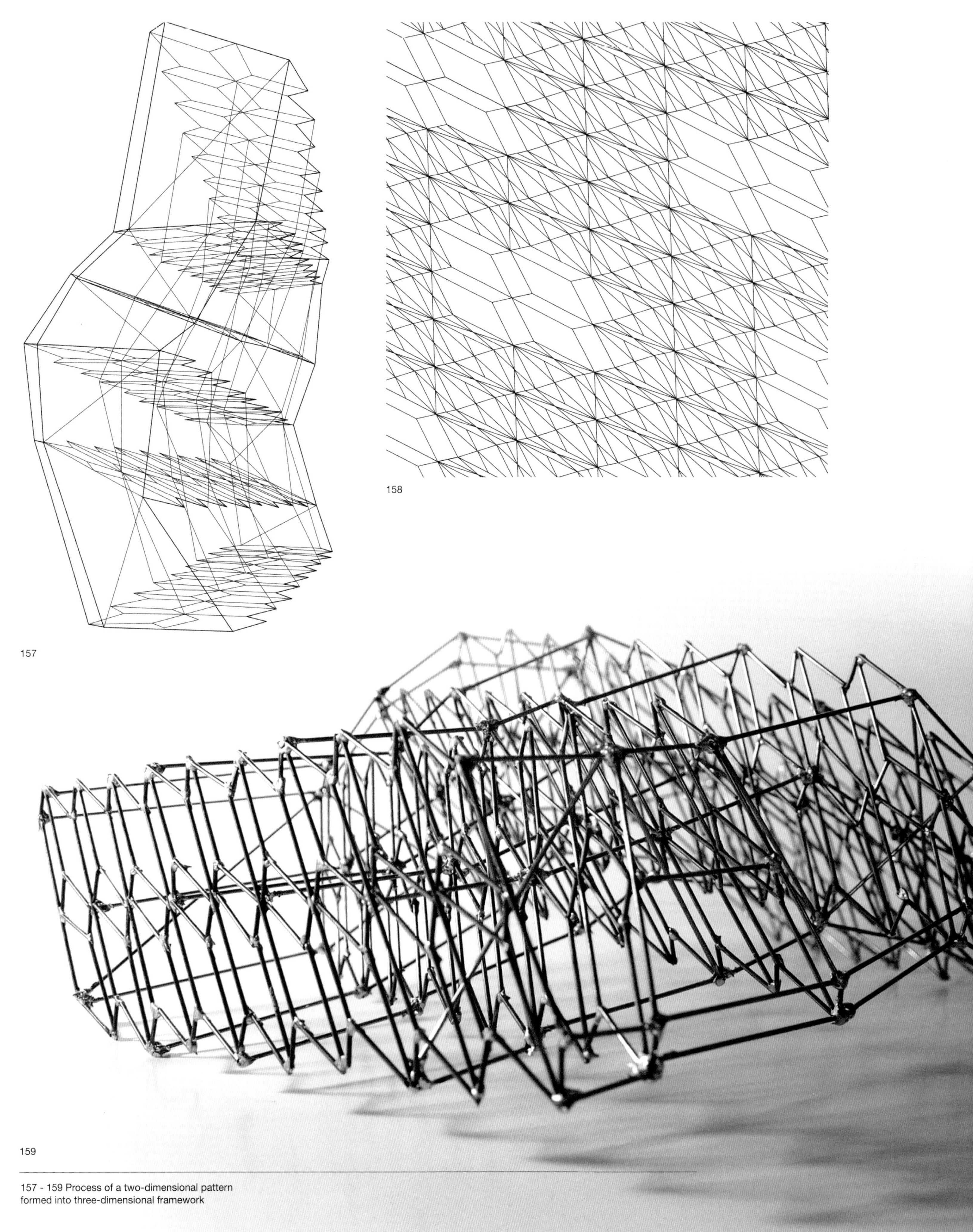

157

158

159

157 - 159 Process of a two-dimensional pattern formed into three-dimensional framework

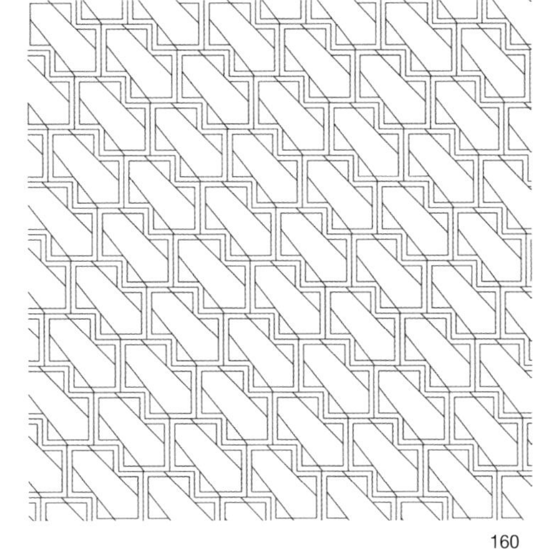

160

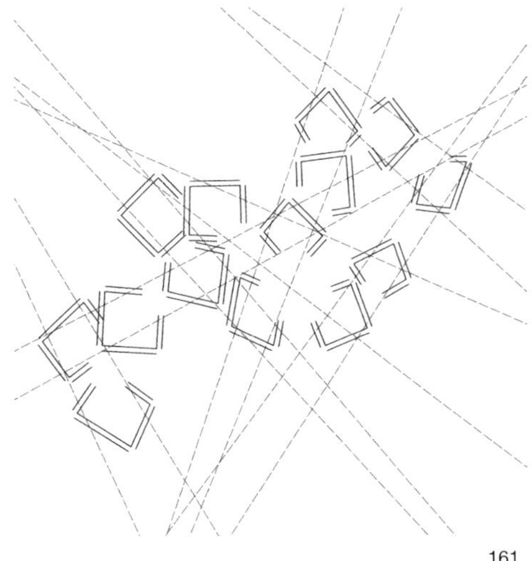

161

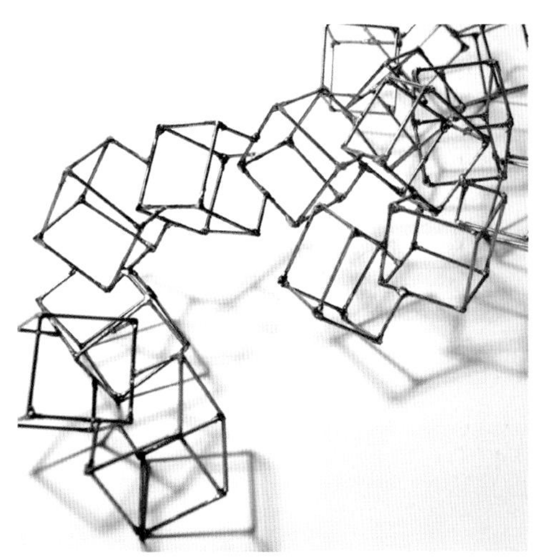

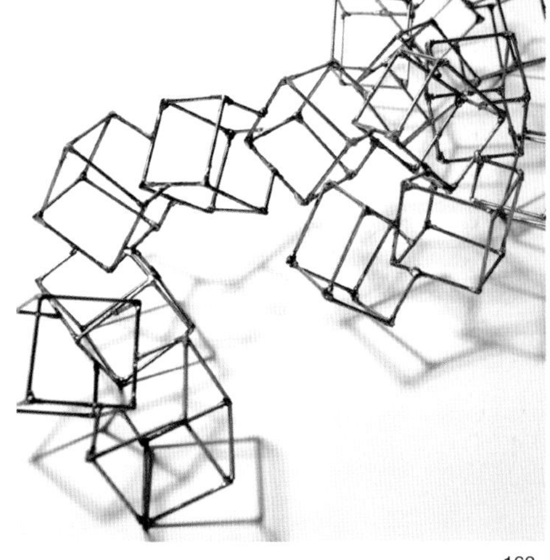

162

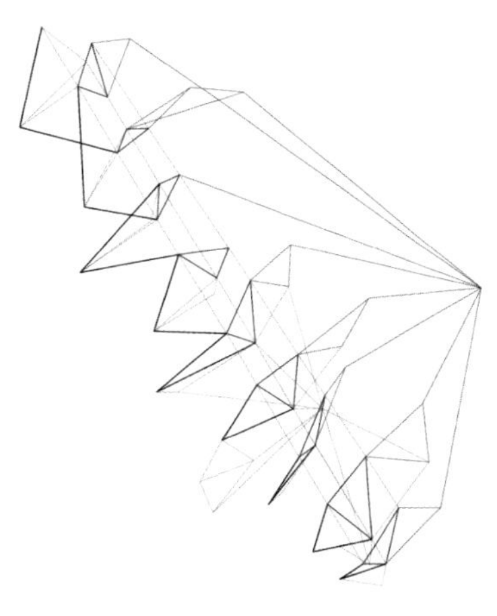

163

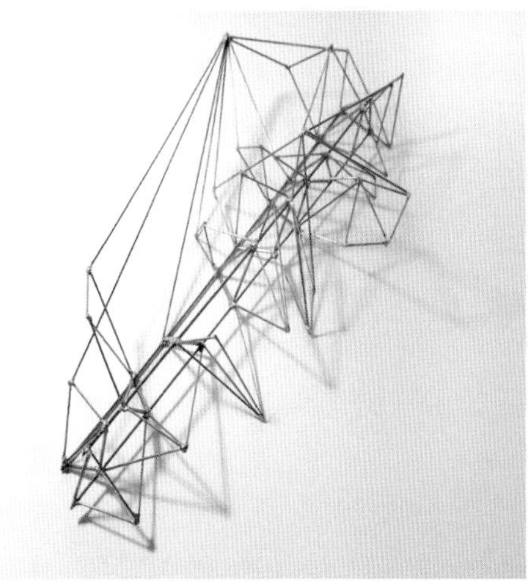

164

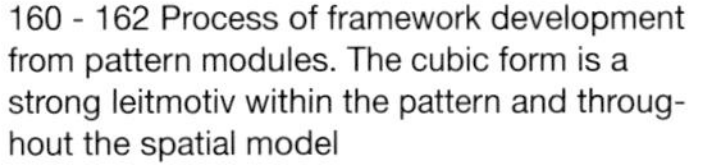

160 - 162 Process of framework development from pattern modules. The cubic form is a strong leitmotiv within the pattern and throughout the spatial model

163 164 Model and drawing showing the addition of different modules in a morphological process

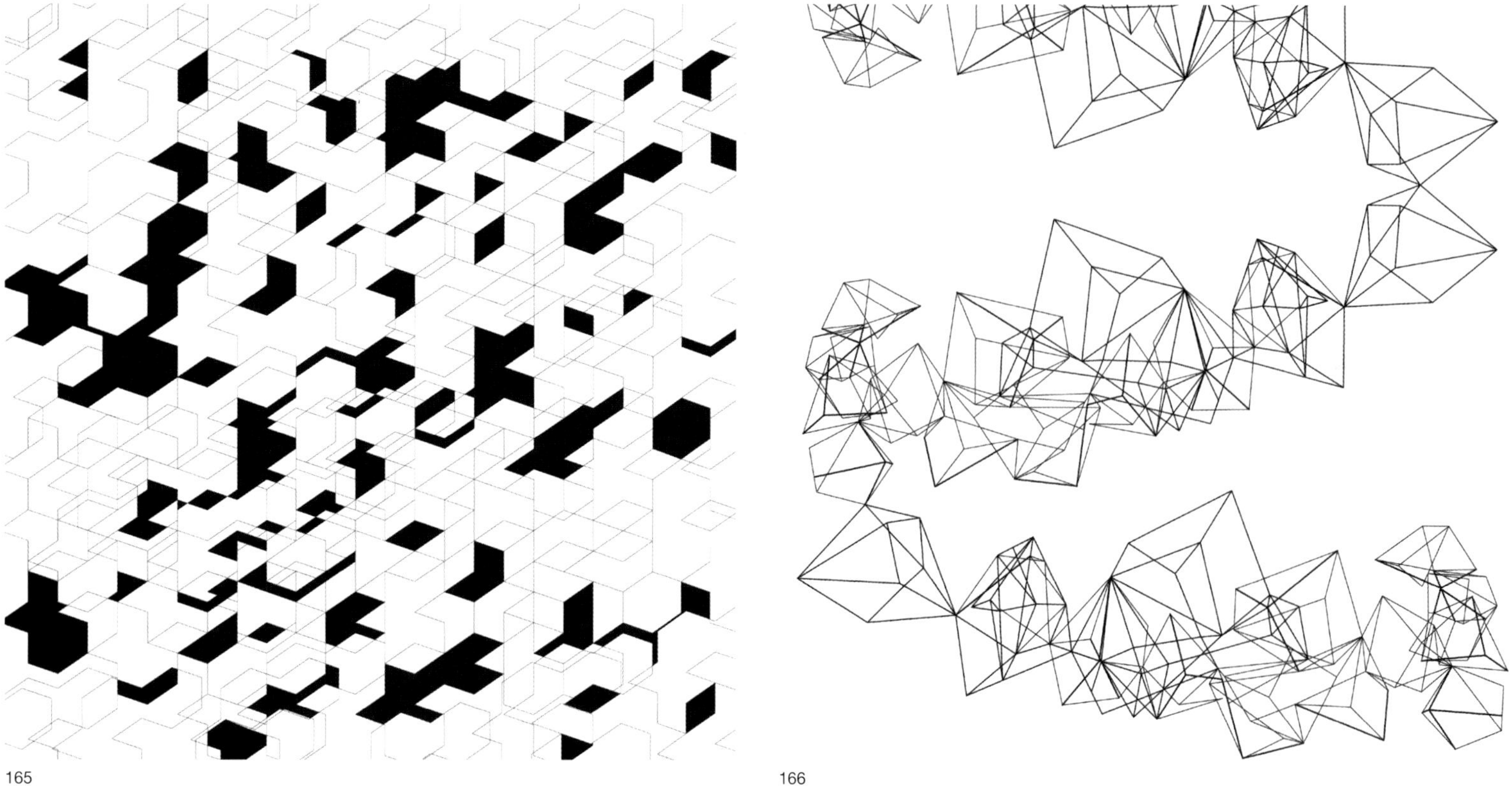

165

166

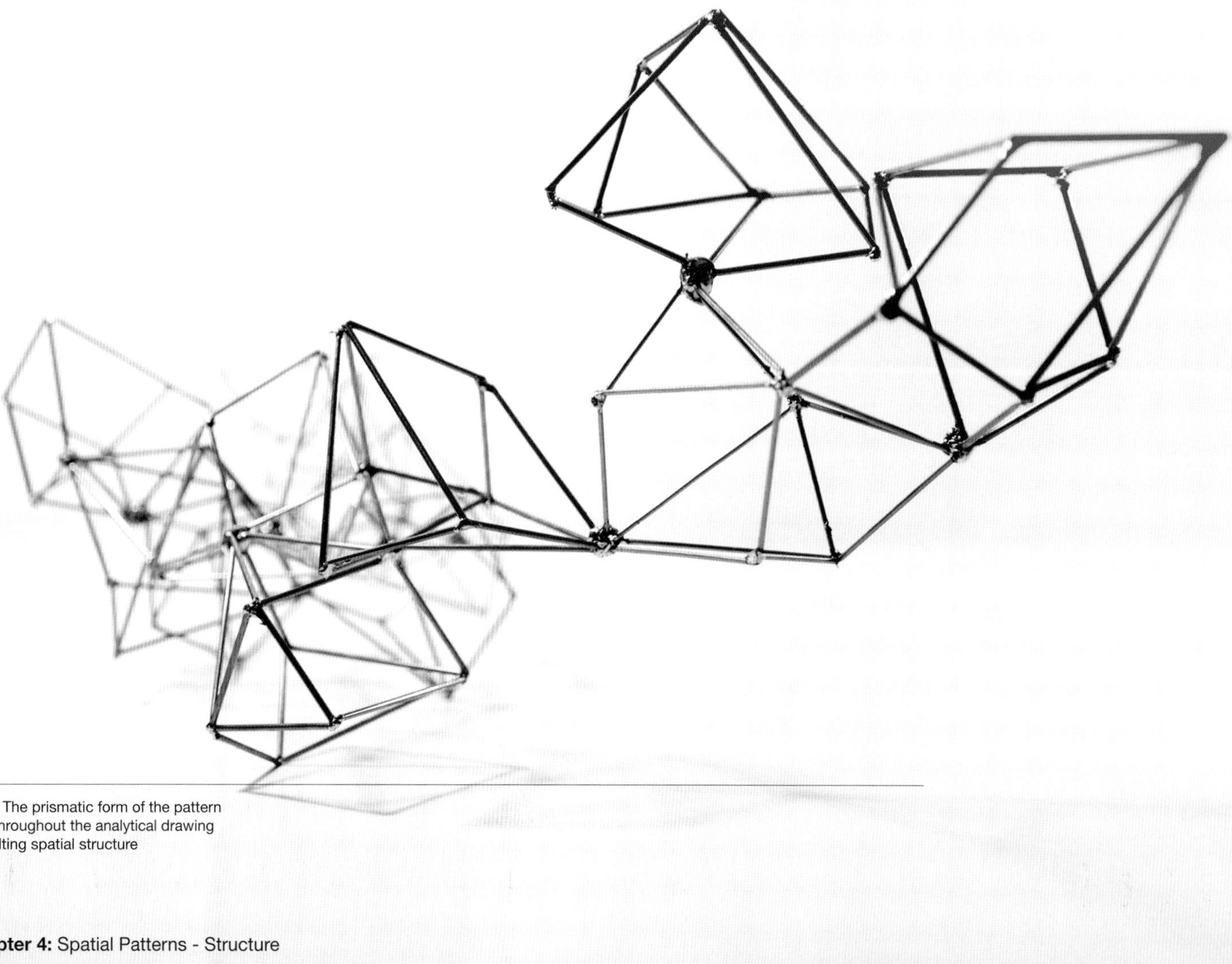

167

165 166 167 The prismatic form of the pattern is reflected throughout the analytical drawing and the resulting spatial structure

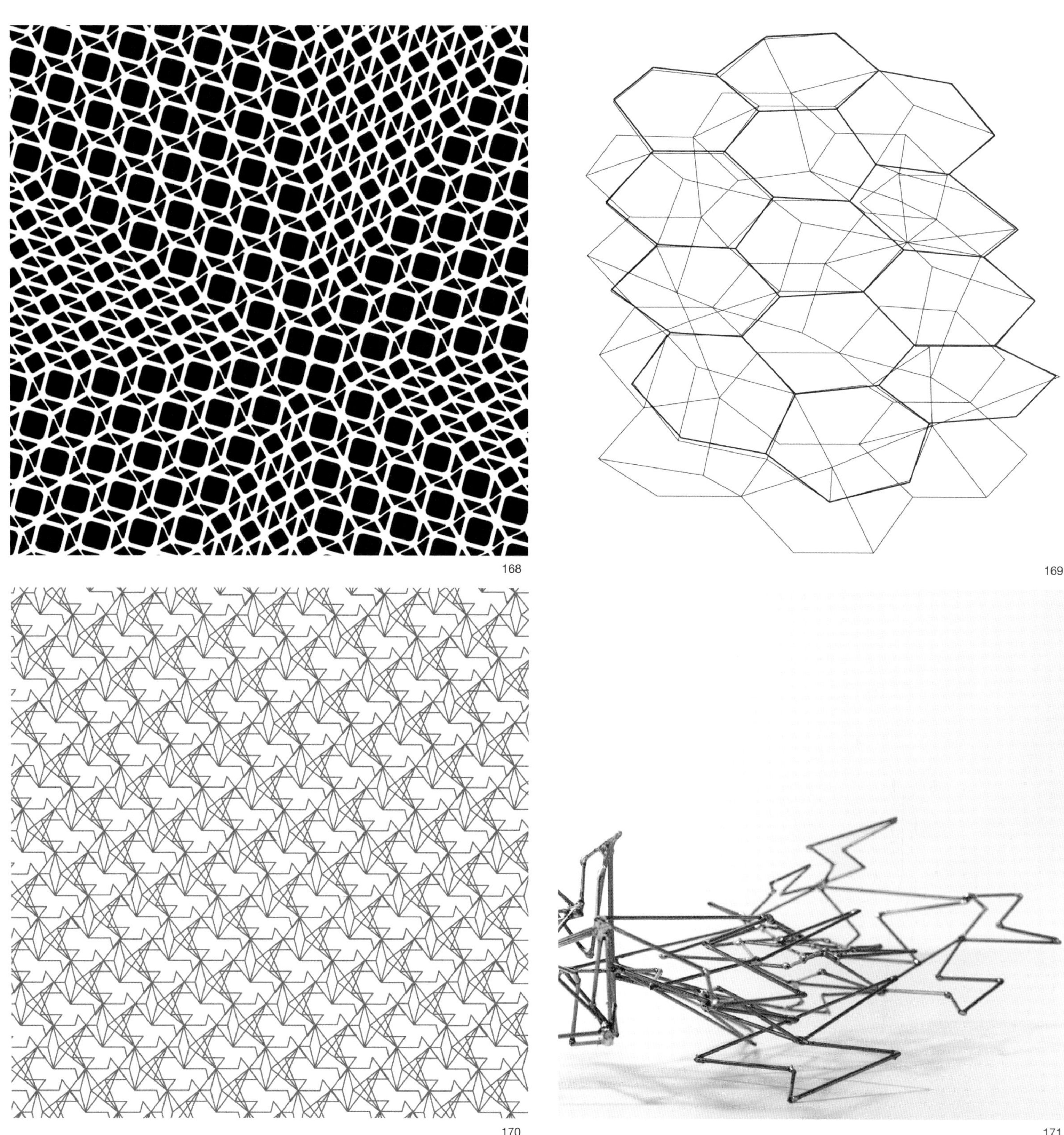

168 169 Cell-like pattern and drawing of resulting adaptive space frame structure

170 171 Filigree pattern and corresponding model

172

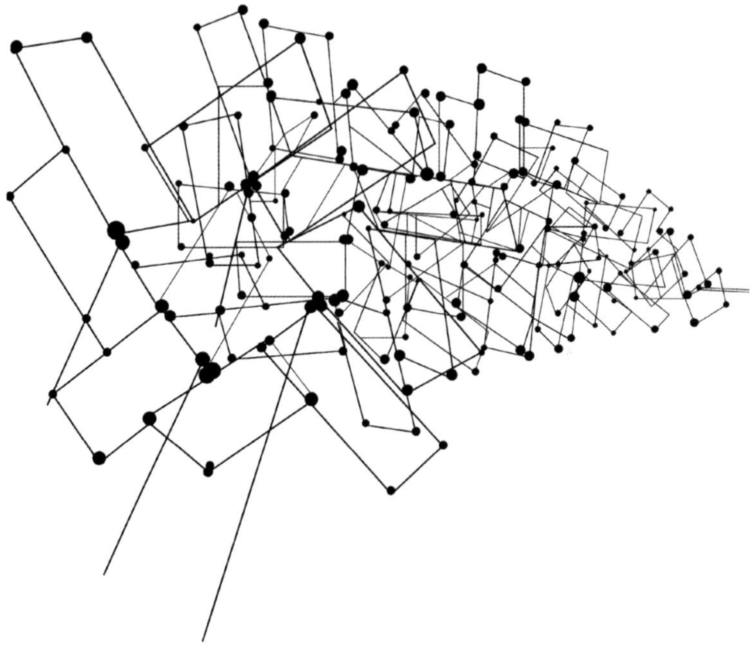

173

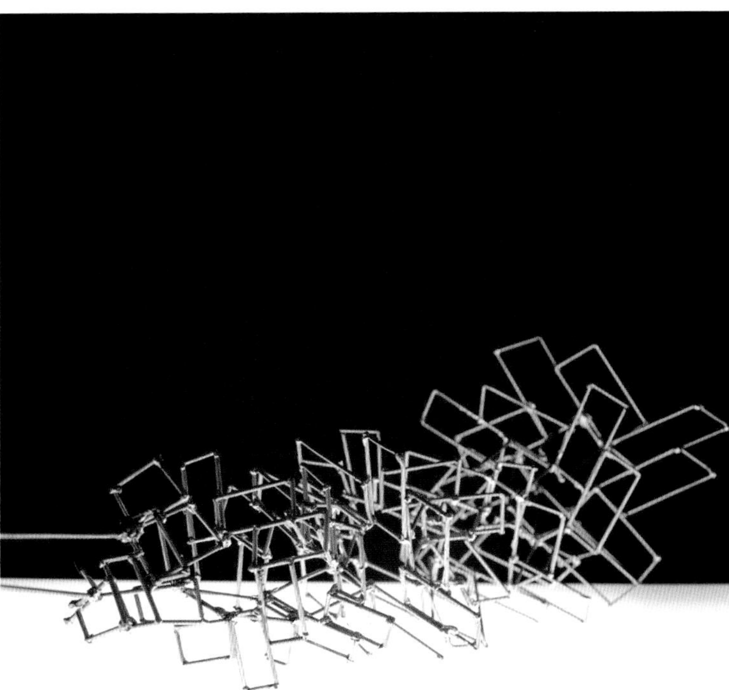

174

172 173 174 Process of a two-dimensional pattern that is rotated in space to form a three-dimensional framework

175 - 178 Differently scaled modules of the two-dimensional pattern are dispersed and rotated in space, their connections form a rigid and dynamic three-dimensional framework

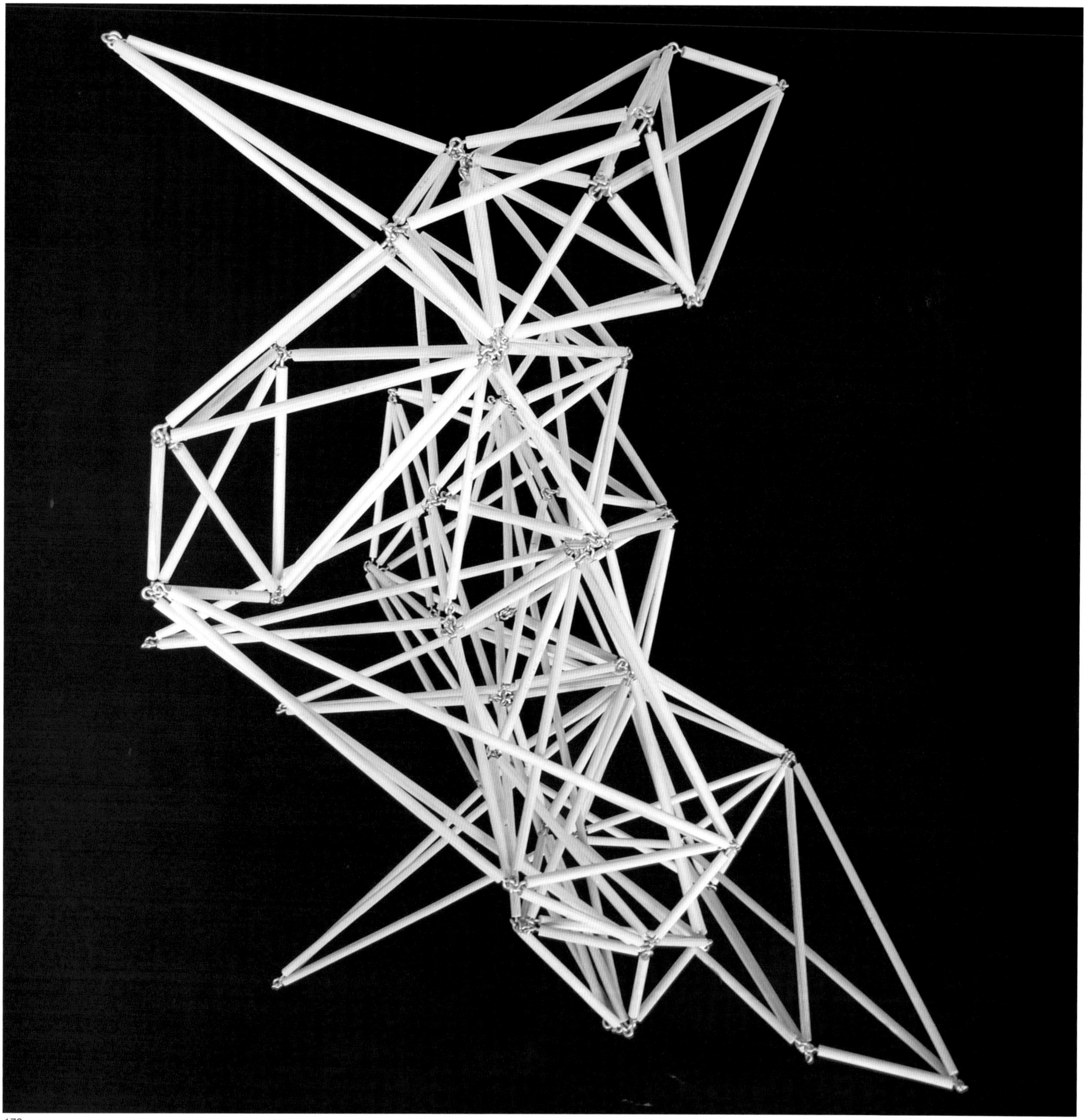

179

180

179 Wooden sticks connected via hooks and rings at their ends form a sound structure

180 Pattern development and definition of the module for the above wood structure

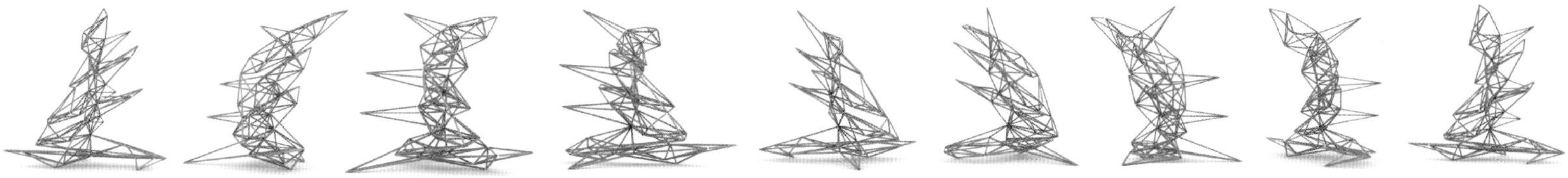

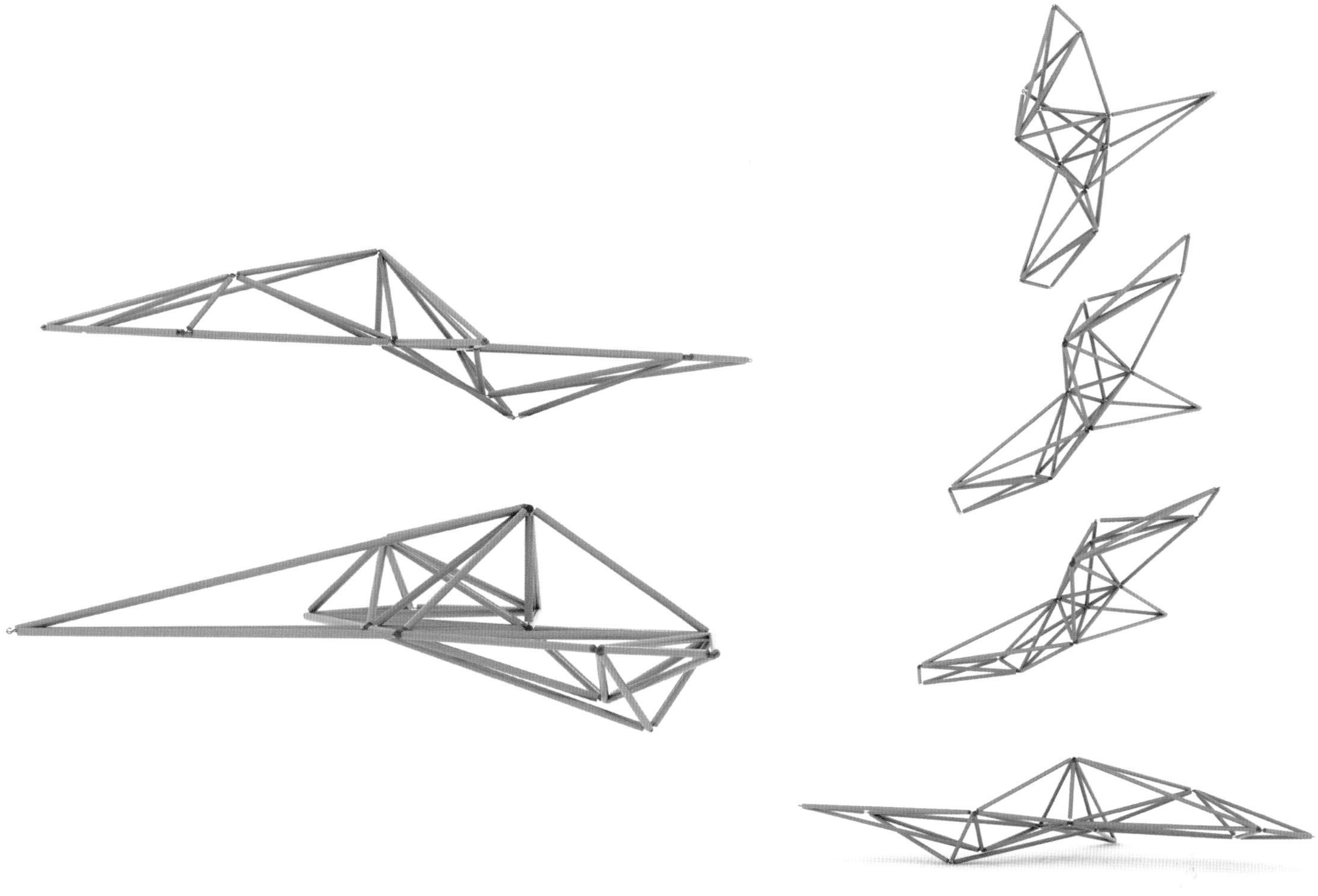

181

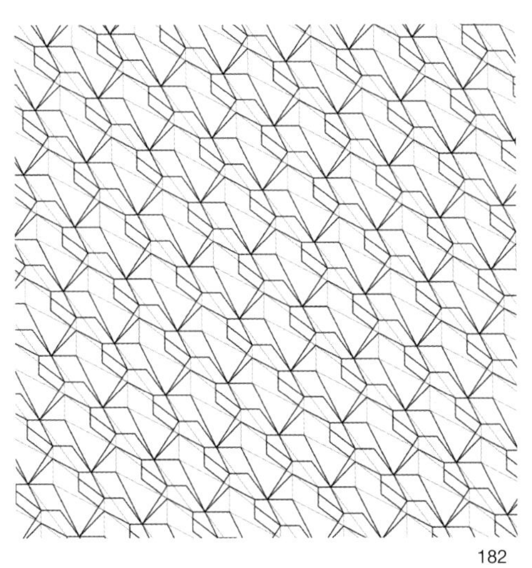

182

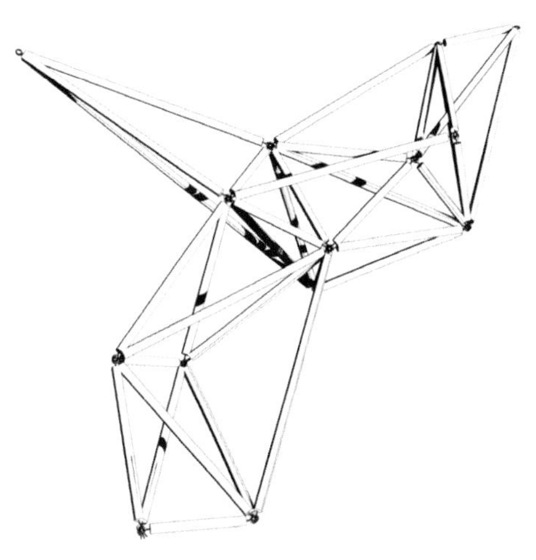

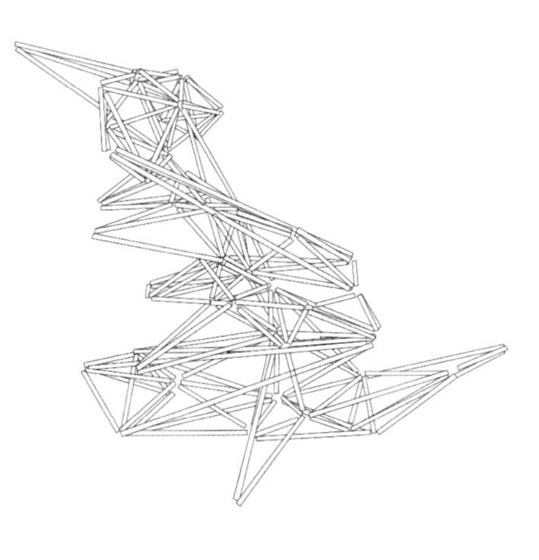

183

181 The sculpture is maily composed of three different modules
182 Developed pattern
183 Analytical drawings of the module and the final sculpture

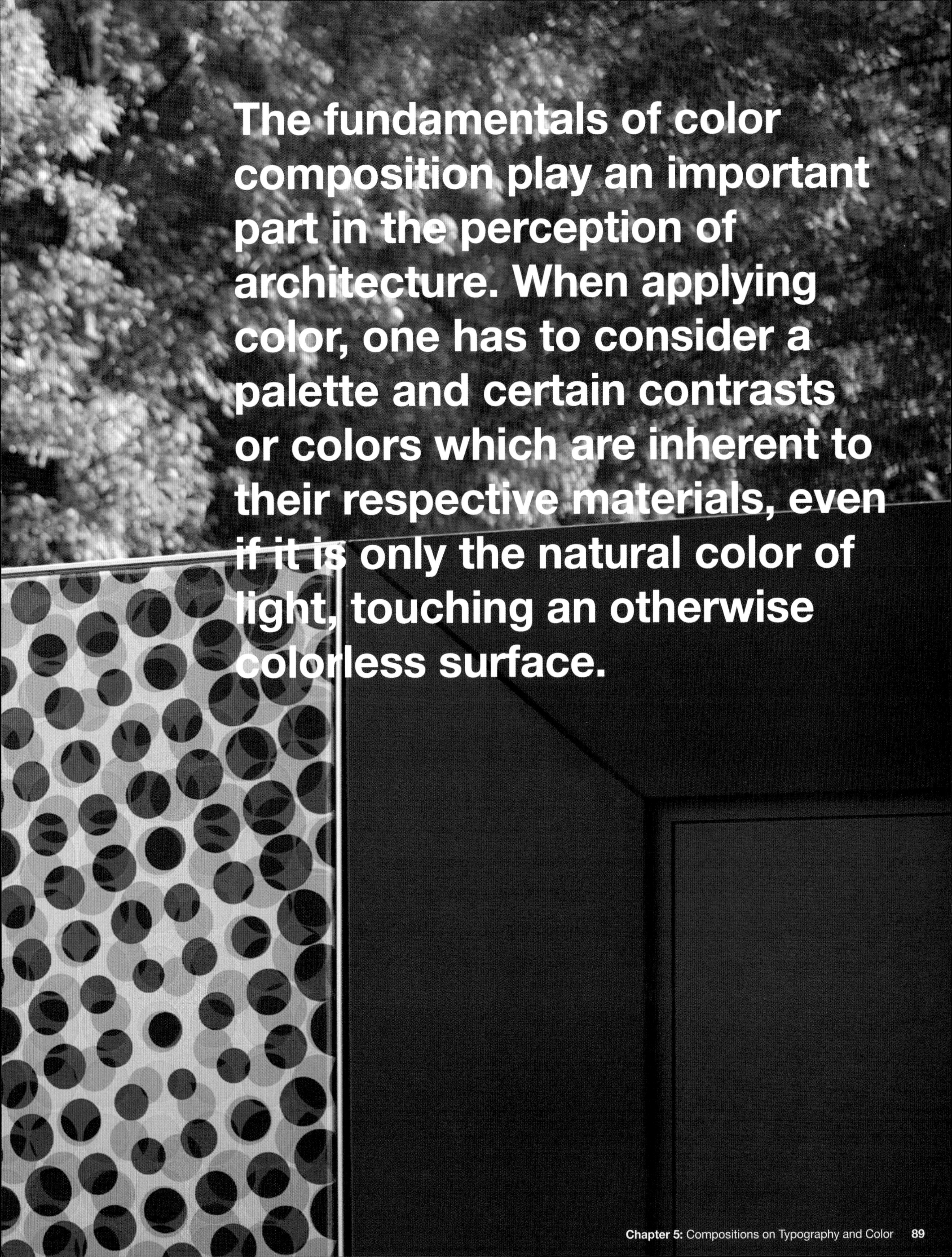

The fundamentals of color composition play an important part in the perception of architecture. When applying color, one has to consider a palette and certain contrasts or colors which are inherent to their respective materials, even if it is only the natural color of light, touching an otherwise colorless surface.

Chapter 5 : Compositions on Typography and Color

color palette

monochromatic use of color

color as concept

color effects

color theory

typography and architecture

psychological phenomena

composition theory

perception theory

Architectural design often restricts itself to a rigid and limited color palette. Despite color's ubiquitous presence in our built environment, it seems to play little role in architectural design education, when compared to form. The starting point of an architectural design oftentimes begins with pure, simple form, or a functional concept defined by the absence of color, eliminating potential distractions or uncertainties. In later design stages, however, a good command in applying the right color palette and choosing the right materials is not to be underestimated, as it can enhance design intent quite drastically.

The concept of polychromatic ornamentation of architecture has been well documented through the ages, beginning with the ancient world. (fig. 5.1) The scientific and cultural dimensions of these phenomena are too vast to be given a complete and thorough examination within the scope of this publication. This chapter, will focus on the beginnings of the modern movement of neoplasticism and de Stijl, the color theories of the Bauhaus school by Klee, Itten, Kandisky, and Albers, as well as the advancement towards contemporary architecture.

Today, the often sparse or monochromatic use of color can be interpreted as a sign of a contemporary perception of neutrality or timelessness. In addition to this existing proclivity, there are many other examples where color is used to achieve specific design objectives. In particular, throughout the architecture of Sauerbruch Hutton (fig. 5.4) , color is widely applied,

Page 88 89: CMYK House, Moers, Germany. MCKNHM Architects, Mark Mückenheim with Frank Zeising

5.1 Reconstruction drawing from 1883 illustrating the colour scheme of the entablature on a Doric temple

5.2 Ruhr Museum, Essen, Germany, OMA. The handrails resemble glowing steel and illuminate the spacious staircase

5.3 Public Library, Seattle, OMA. Escalators, elevators and stairs share a coloring in bright neon yellow, marking all circulation elements throughout the building

shaping their distinct architectural style. In the Seattle Central Library (fig. 5.3) or the Ruhr Museum in Essen, Germany, (fig. 5.2) for example, Rem Koolhaas uses color in a conceptual way to color code important iterating building elements such as circulation or entrance, to name a few.

The instances above illustrate the conceptual and perceptual importance of color schemes and combinations, rather than the meaning or appearance of one single color. In his work *Interaction of Color*, Josef Albers draws parallels to the reception of music and written text: "While we are reading, we do not see and understand single letters but the image of the word and its meaning, or when we are listening to music, we do not hear single tones, but the melody, that comes to life through harmonic interactions between the notes." Albers claims that the exploration of color perception only makes sense if we analyze its interrelation and concurrence. (ref. 5.1)

In addition to color, the examples in this chapter also illustrate the close relationship of architecture and typography, using perception theories to achive abstract compositions that are based on the Helvetica typeface family. Conceptually rigorous and visually harmonious composition has the capacity to transcend design fields. In the instance of typography, one can trace many shared roots and historical developments within the field of architecture: structure, proportion, aesthetics and function, taxonomy and rhythm. Parallel developments in architecture and typeface design are quite evident in recent design history.

5.1 Josef Albers: Interaction of Color

5.4 Museum Brandhorst, München. Sauerbruch Hutton Architects

5.5 WoZoCo, Amsterdam, MVRDV. Colored balconies at a housing project for the elderly

5.6 Public Street in Hongkong. The public space is no more framed by facades of the buildings but by signs, labels, characters and letters

In his book, *The New Typography*, Jan Tschischold maintains that modern architecture finds the expression of "the modern area" through the negation of the historic ornament. This conclusion refers to Tschischold's first visit to the Bauhaus, in which he met with László Moholy-Nagy, who in 1923 postulated a new and simpler language of form within the typography of the Bauhaus (ref. 5.2). The emergence of modern typography through the universal use of grotesque (sans-serif) typefaces can be traced throughout architectural modernism's beginnings; its close relationship to architecture is evident.

Much like architecture, typography with all its related references to the build environment is more accurately classified through epochs rather than by the ever-changing zeitgeist. Unlike design, which is significantly more influenced by fashion, typography shows a steadier development throughout history. Notwithstanding the short-term fads that can also be found in architecture, the use of sans serif typefaces around the start of the modern movement is consistent, illustrating the fact that the development of architecture and typography since their formative years in the early 20th century has been more or less parallel.

Typography also influences architecture. The Korean Pavilion at the Shanghai World Expo 2010 by Mass Studies, the Cottbus University library in Germany by Herzog and de Meuron, the Lentos Art Museum in Linz, Austria, by Weber Hofer Partner, and the Number House by Mitsutomo Matsunami, among many others, show a playful approach and attitude towards applying typography to architecture, or deriving

5.2 Jan Tschichold: Die Neue Typographie. Ein Handbuch für zeitgemäß Schaffende. / Jan Tschichold: The New Typography: A Handbook for Modern Designers. English reprint from the 1928 original

5.7 Graphic designer Chris LaBrooy combines typography design with architectural elements

5.8 Building-like interpretation of the Helvetica font by Chris LaBrooy

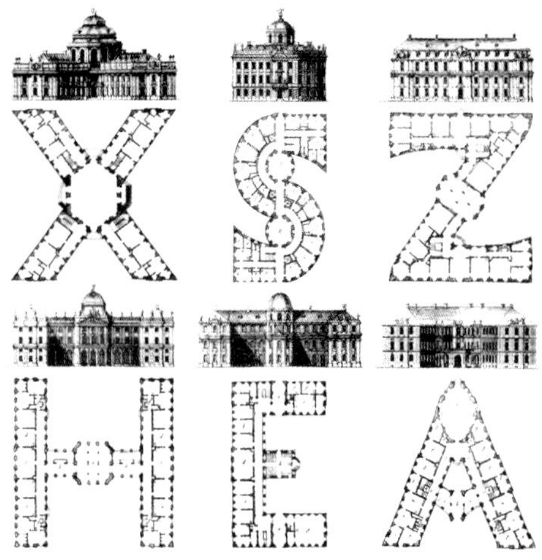
5.9 The architectural alphabet by Johann David Steingruber, 1773, still remains unbuilt

a building through a typographic archetype. To a certain extent, these contemporary buildings transport the "architecture parlante" of the French Revolution to a new, direct, and equally subtle level, where the house transforms into a kind of billboard while the actual function becomes abstracted.

Some of the works illustrated in the following chapter are based on design qualities that can be achieved through the composition of typography or typographic elements. These examples are based on an assignment initially developed by Professor Cord Bowen at the University of Houston, that was partially modified to accommodate color and typography fundamentals. Single letters or sometimes only partial elements of letters from the Helvetica typeface family were used to develop two-dimensional collages with a very high degree of abstraction. The intrinsic design qualities of the typeface were used in order to create a new quality of its own. The assignment departed from Bowen's version by requiring the students to incorporate theories of gestalt psychology into their designs. (ref. 5.3 / 5.4)

Principles of figure ground, pithiness, and reification, among others, were applied to activate the form-generating capacity of the students' imaginations, making the collages more deep and complex.

In the first step, students were asked to analyze the typography in order to form meaningful relationships between the letters of the typeface family. The second step was to develop a collage incorporating the laws of visual perception to highlight the intended impression through the theories of gestalt psychology. In doing so, the subtle

5.3 Willis D. Ellis / Kurt Koffka: A Source Book of Gestalt Psychology

5.4 E. Bruce Goldstein: Sensation and Perception

5.10 The Typography on the facade of the New York Times Building by Renzo Piano becomes a branding ornament

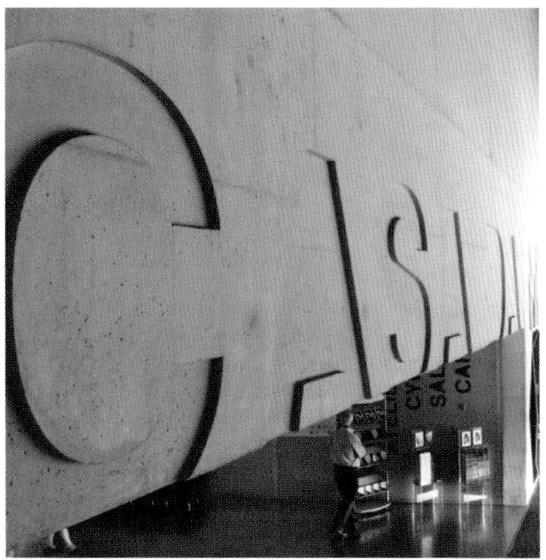
5.11 Type engrained into the concrete wall within the Casa da Musica, Porto. OMA

5.12 Neon text installation ‚Joanna (chapter one)' by Cerith Wyn Evans at the palazzo delle esposizioni, Venice Architecture Biennale 2010

nature of these theories emerged through increasing precision and further enhancement of the composition.

Perception theory is a good tool and resource for design didactics in architecture. For example, the typical architectural design process requires a constant shift in focus between various building components such as a wall, a beam, a window, etc., to achieve spatial definition. Within any given design procedure, a deeper sense of awareness of these shifting processes is initiated through the conscious use of applied gestalt psychology and the functional implication of the rules of perception.

Fundamental theories of gestalt psychology can therefore be applied to compositional tasks of various scales: from the development of urban block structures, with their resulting plazas and spatiality, to the design of a floor plan layout or façade. For example, the figure-ground relationship and the observation of void vs. volume or open vs. closed, helps in developing a harmonic composition whose totality of elements constitutes a given architecture.

The third and last step of the illustrated exercise deals with color and introduces the students to color composition theory by Johannes Itten and Paul Renner. (ref. 5.5 / 5.6)
This changes the black-and-white typography-influenced collage into a color composition that dwells on the combination possibilities and chord harmonics of color. The last examples in this chapter are color studies that are tailored towards imaginary façade applications instead of typography.

5.5 Johannes Itten: Kunst der Farbe

5.6 Paul Renner: Ordnung und Harmonie der Farben. Eine Farbenlehre für Künstler und Handwerker

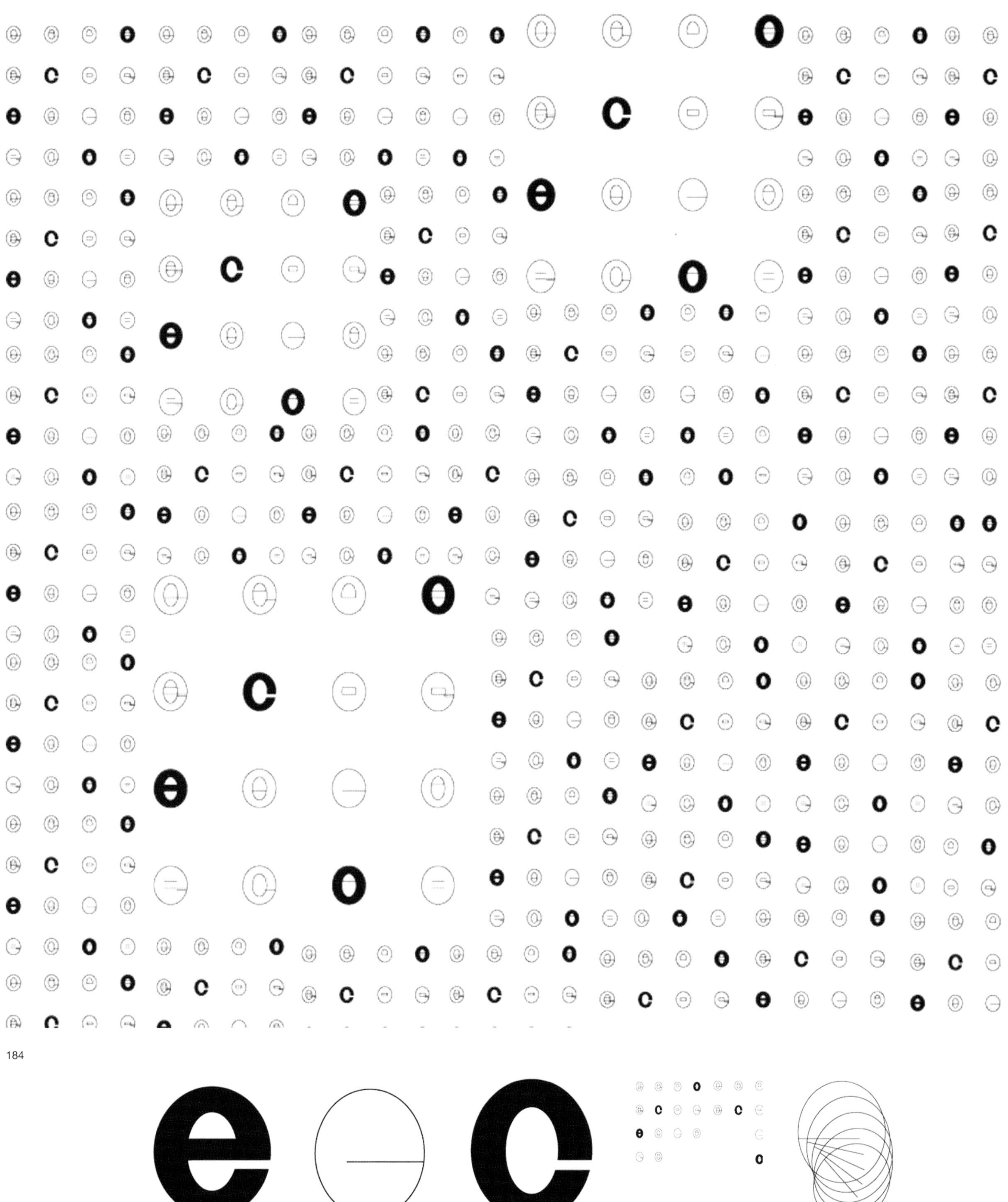

184

185

184 185 Analysis of the design potential and transformational pattern of the letter *e*

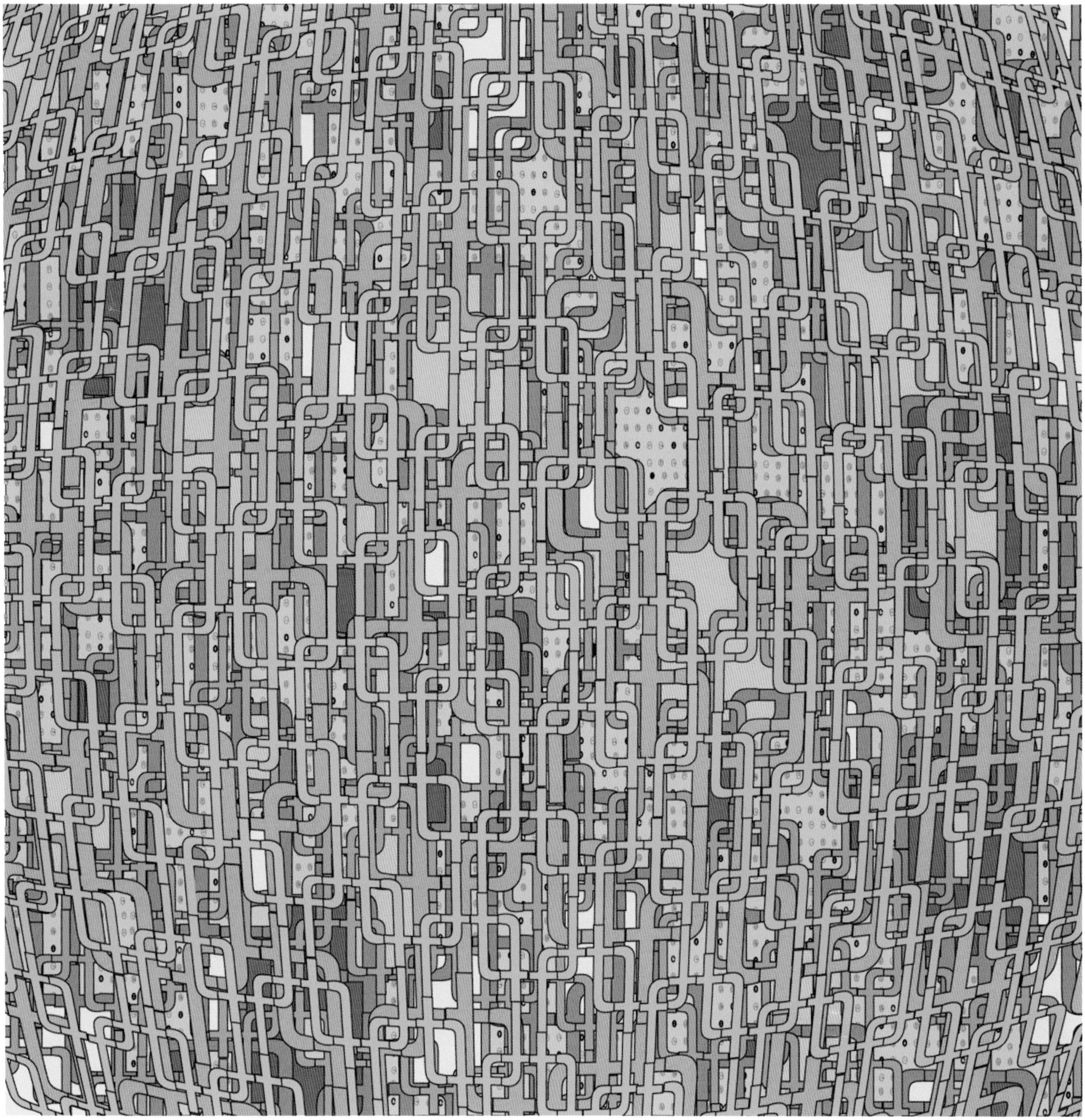

186

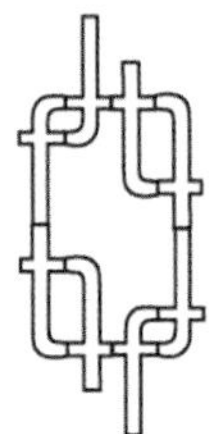
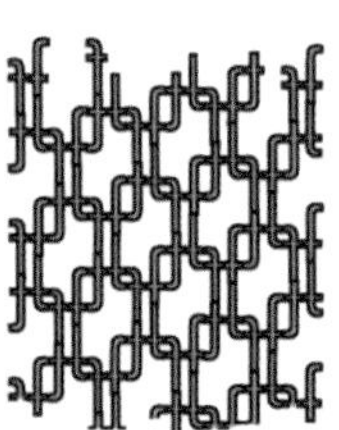
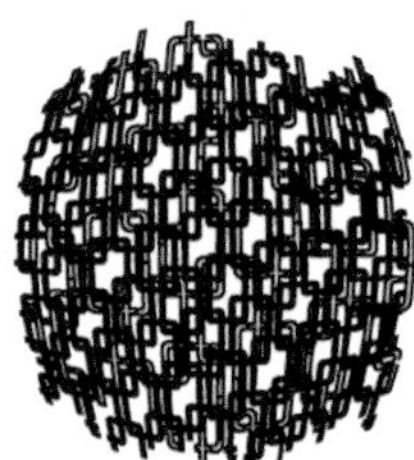

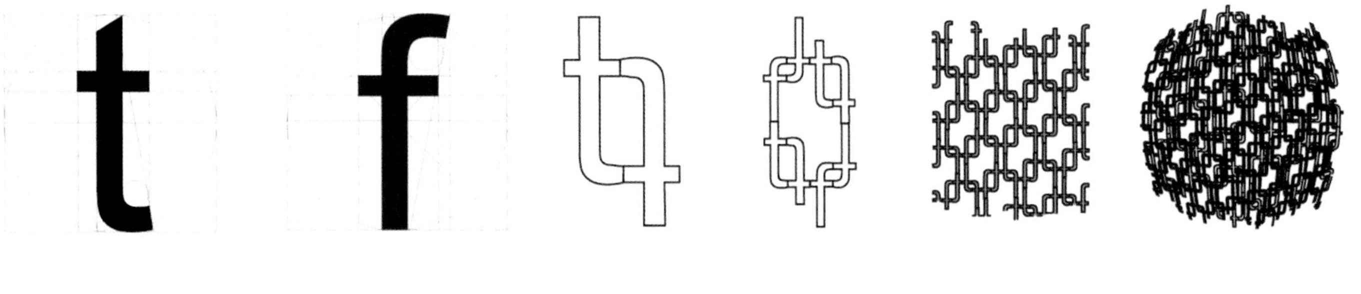

187

186 Staggered layers of different typography configurations in a variety of colors, evoke a sense of depth

187 Analysis of micro-typography characteristics and common attributes of the letter *t* and *f* results in an arrangement of both letters within in a pattern-like structure

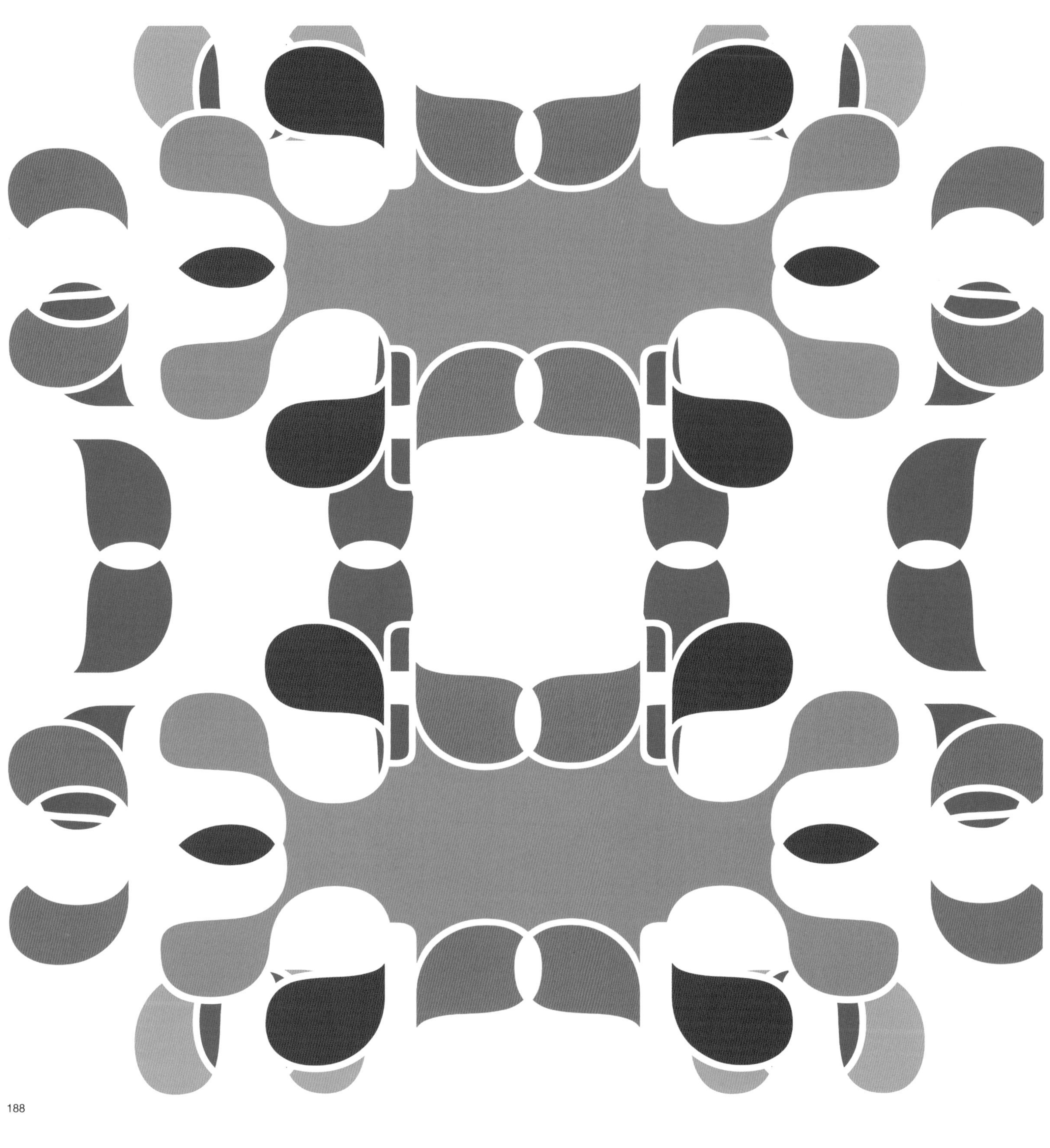

188

188 By filling the eye of the small letter *a* from the helvetica typeface and in choosing white color for the letters stroke, the notion of figure and ground becomes apparent colored ground areas turn into abstract figures

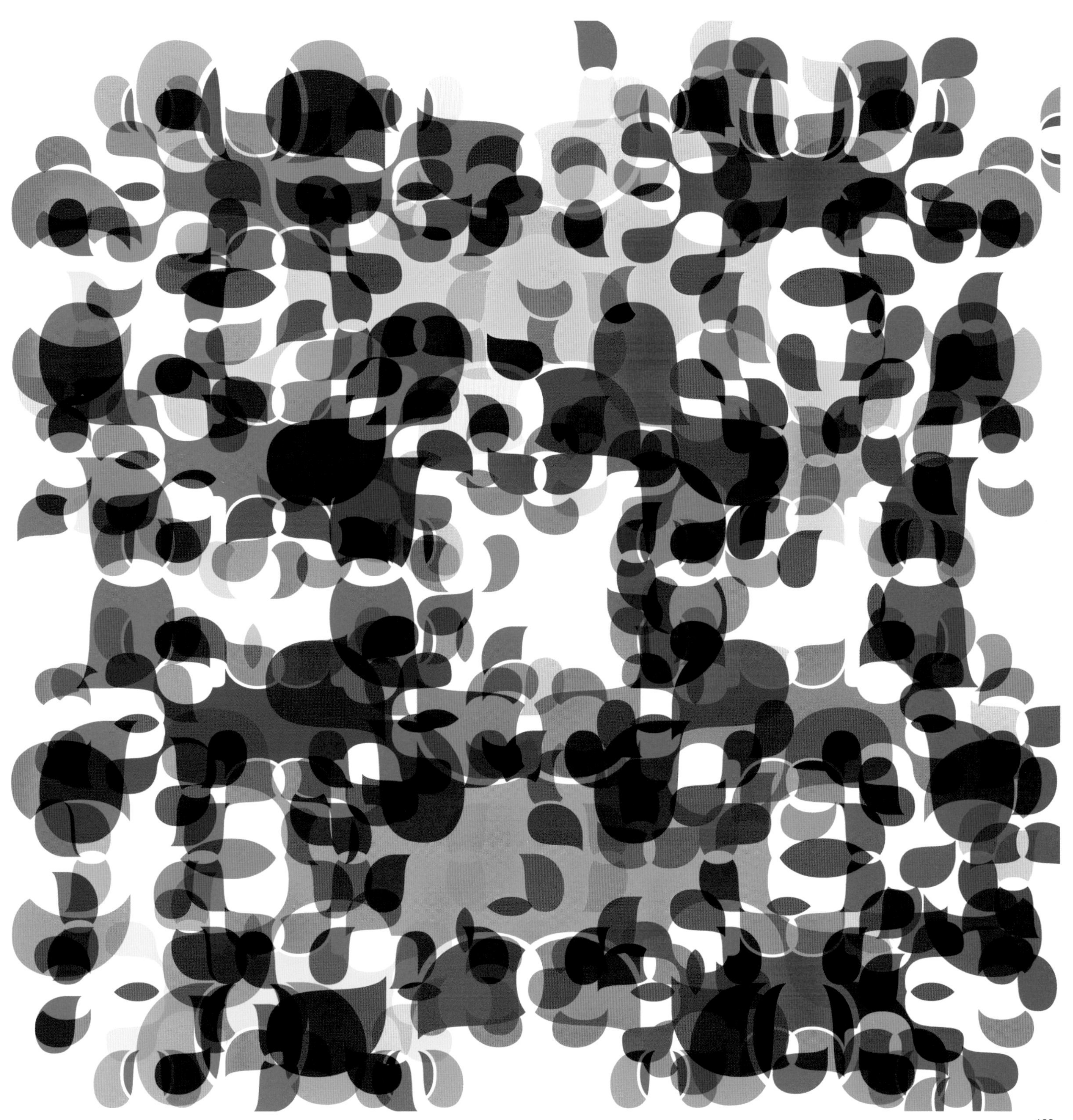

189

189 Graphical composition with superposition and transparent layering as a further development from fig. 188

190

191

190 191 Color studies and composition of desaturated light colors with changing color tonality graphic is based on repetitive circles inspired by radically abstracted analytical drawings that were derived from the letter *O*

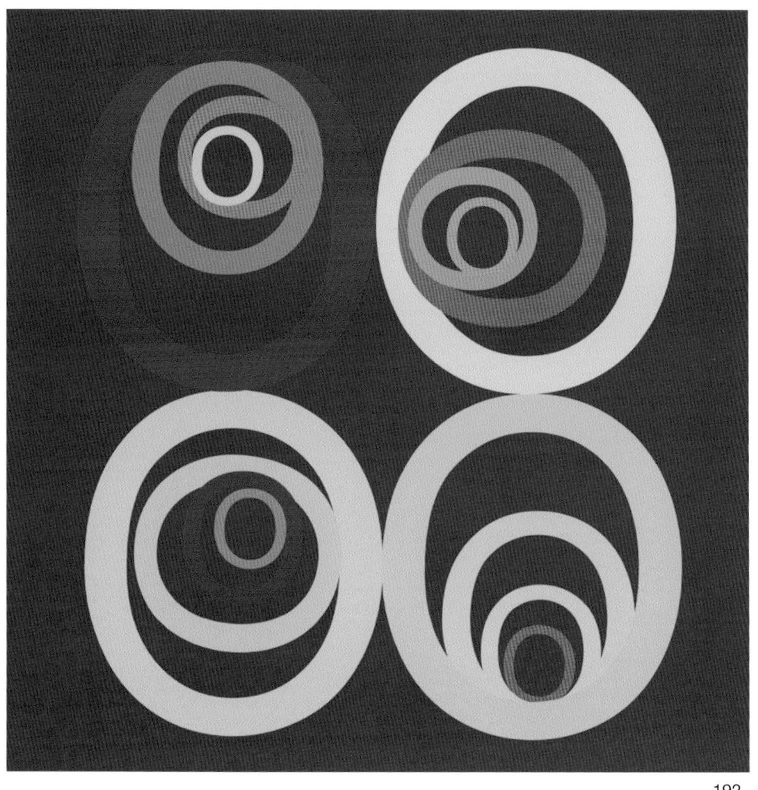

192

193

194

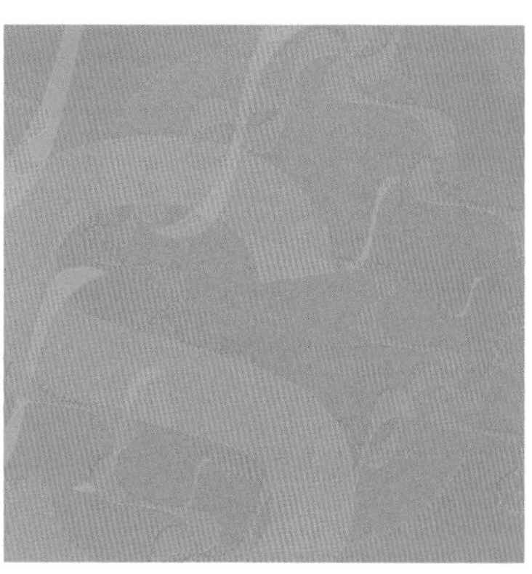

195

192 193 194 Different compositions and color contrast studies using the letter *O*

195 Composition and color studies with the letter *S*. The small curved shapes derive from the space in-between staggered and overlayed *S* letters

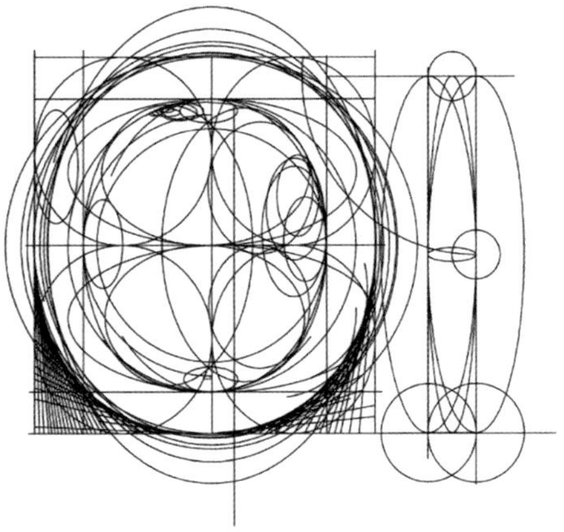

196

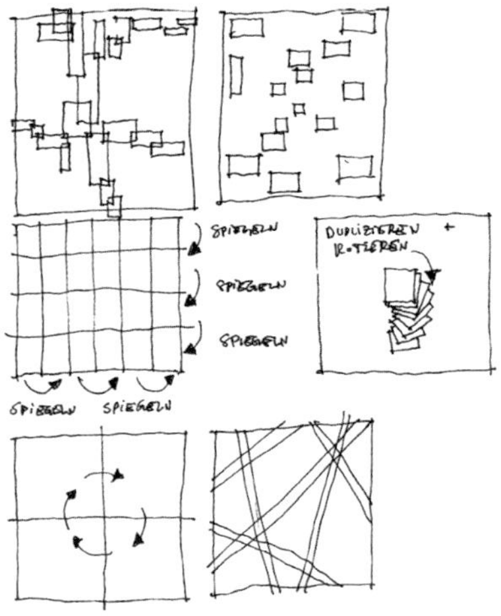

197

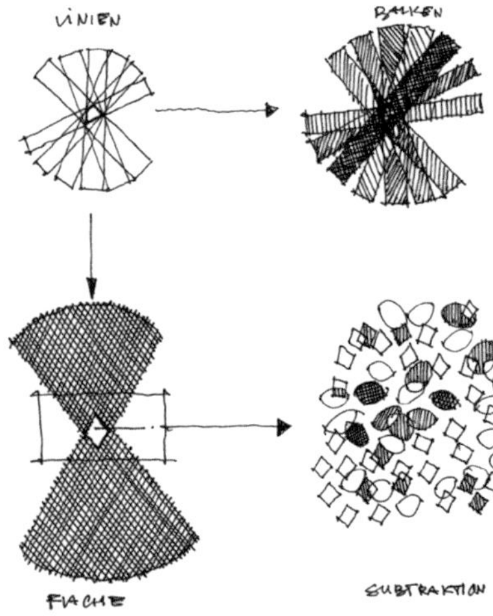

198

199

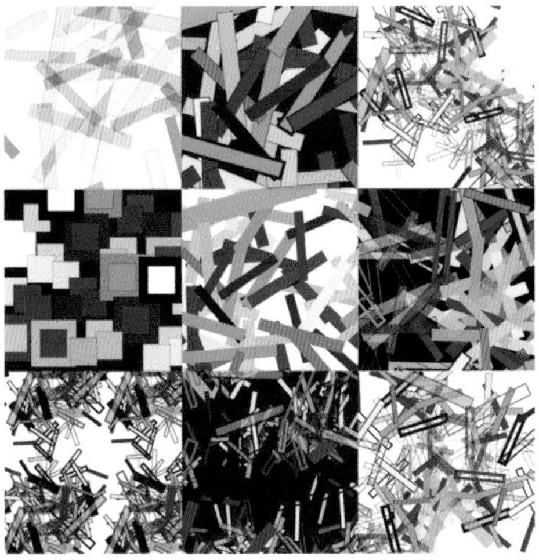

200

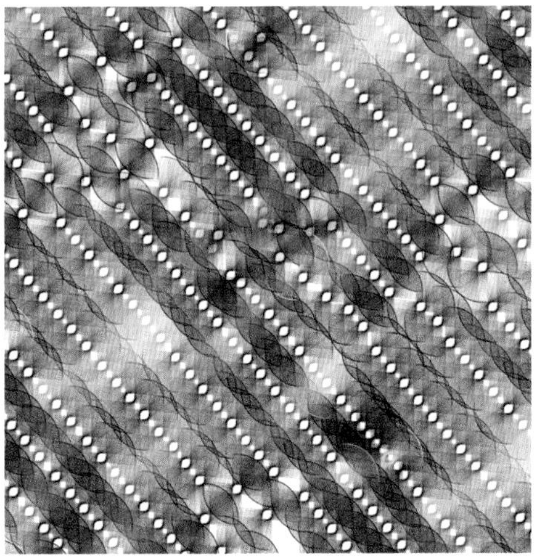

201

202

196 197 198 Analysis of proportion, composition and motion studies with the letter *I* decreasing its gestalt from typography into pure geometrical shape

199 Monochrome composition
200 201 Different color and composition studies

202 Final graphical composition with the letter *I* and slightly desaturated and darkened colors of a wide tonality

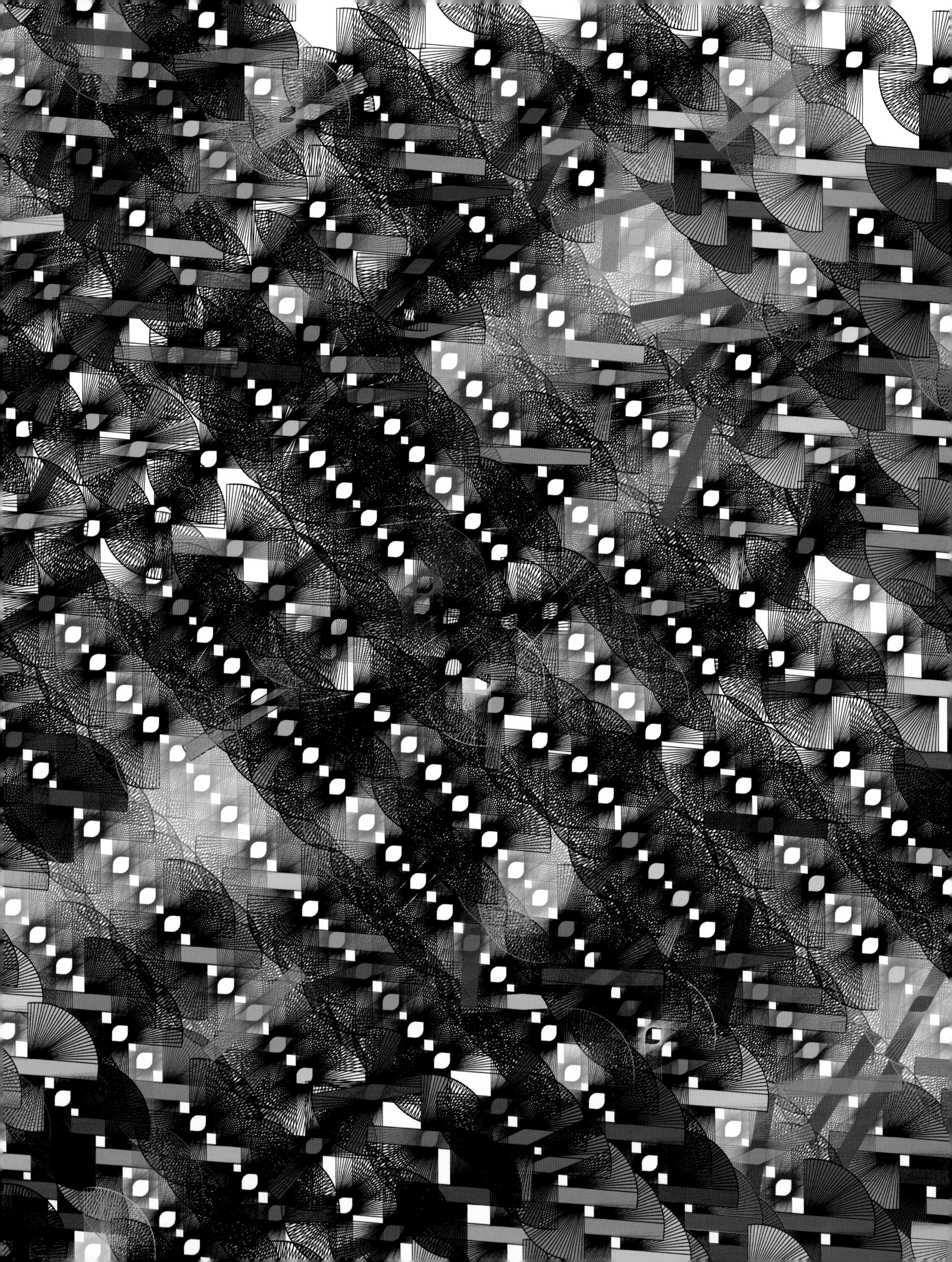

203

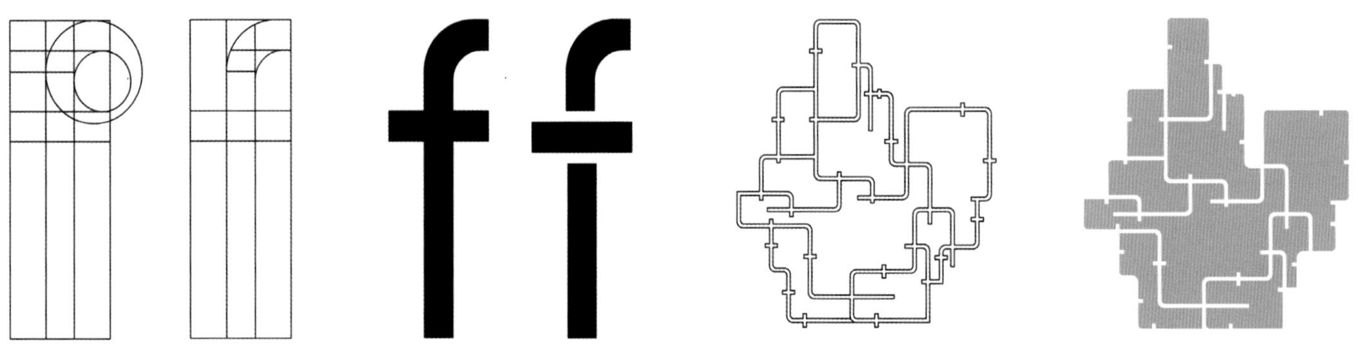

204

205

203 Study of the figure-ground principle

204 Anatomy of the letter *f*

205 Composition with the letter *f* where a new form arises from the ground figures when chains of letters are linked together

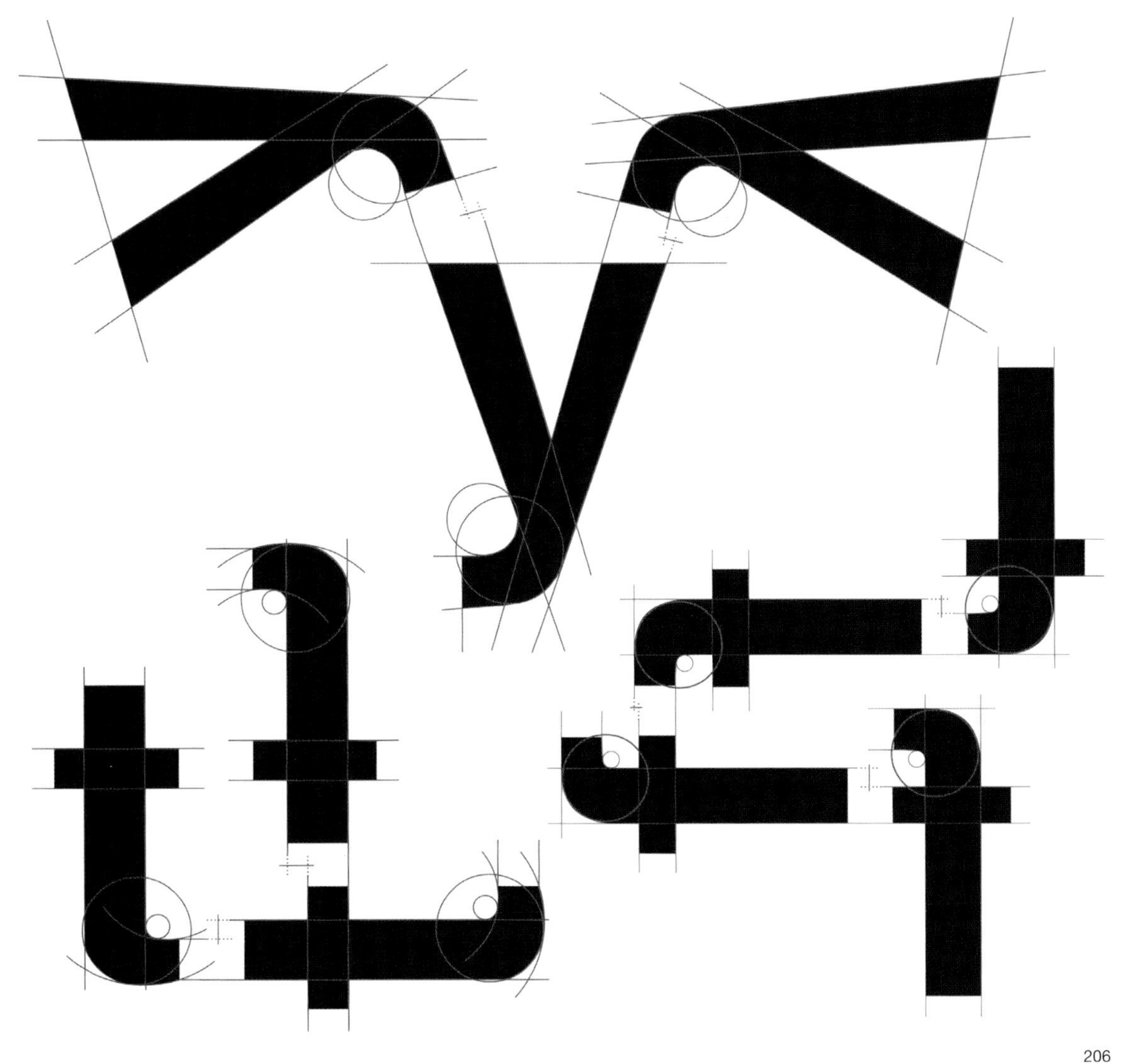

206

207

208

206 Analysis of the proportions and diameters of the letter *f* and *y*

207 208 The letters *f* and *y* joined together to form a fractal pattern

209

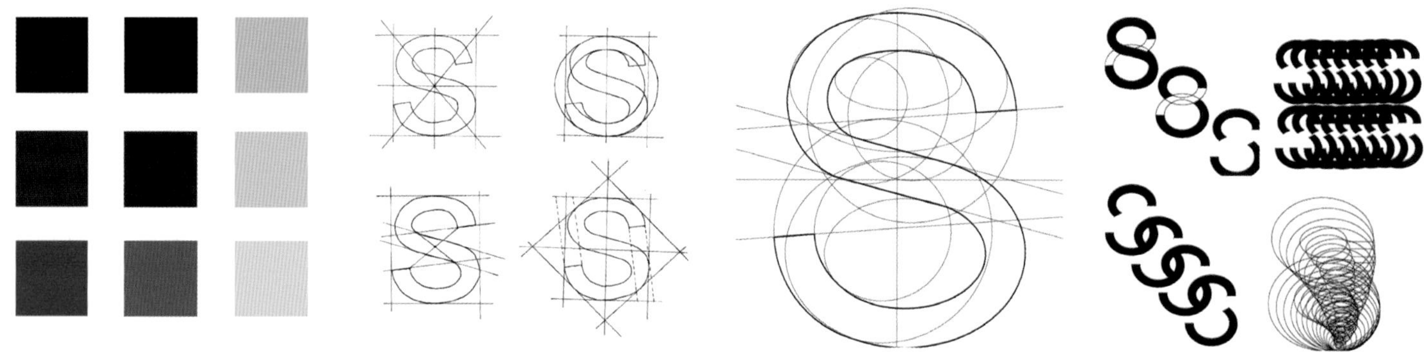

210

209 Abstract montage from combinations of the letter *S* using a confined field of view, superimposition with different transparencies, and a color scheme that is derived by lightened and darkened tones in a complementary palette

210 Geometrical analysis and design study of the letter *S*

211

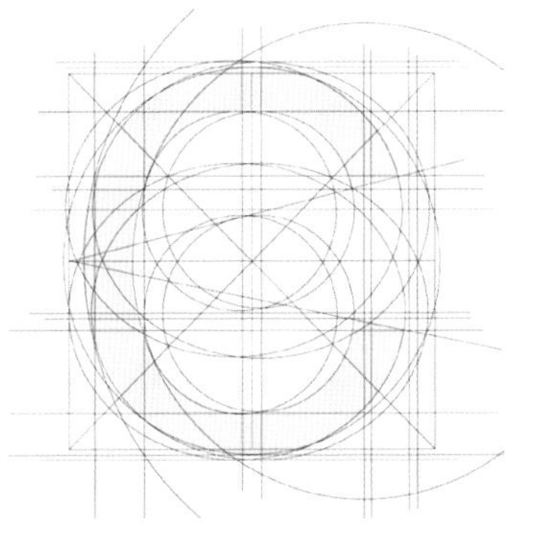

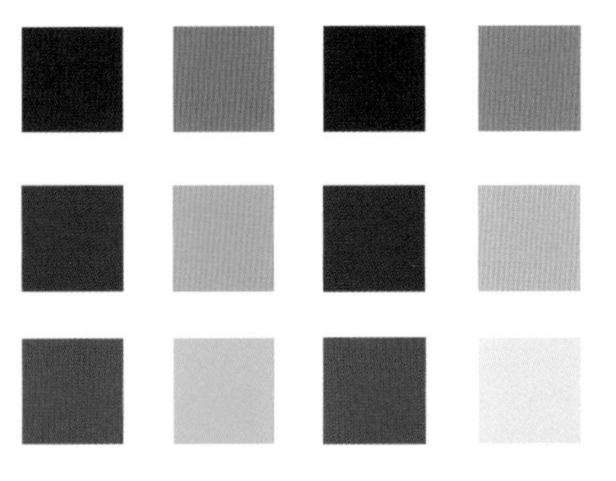

212

211 The dark background, the use of layered transparencies, and the graduated tone value of the grouped *C* letters within this composition evokes a mysterious effect

212 Proportion analysis and configuration study

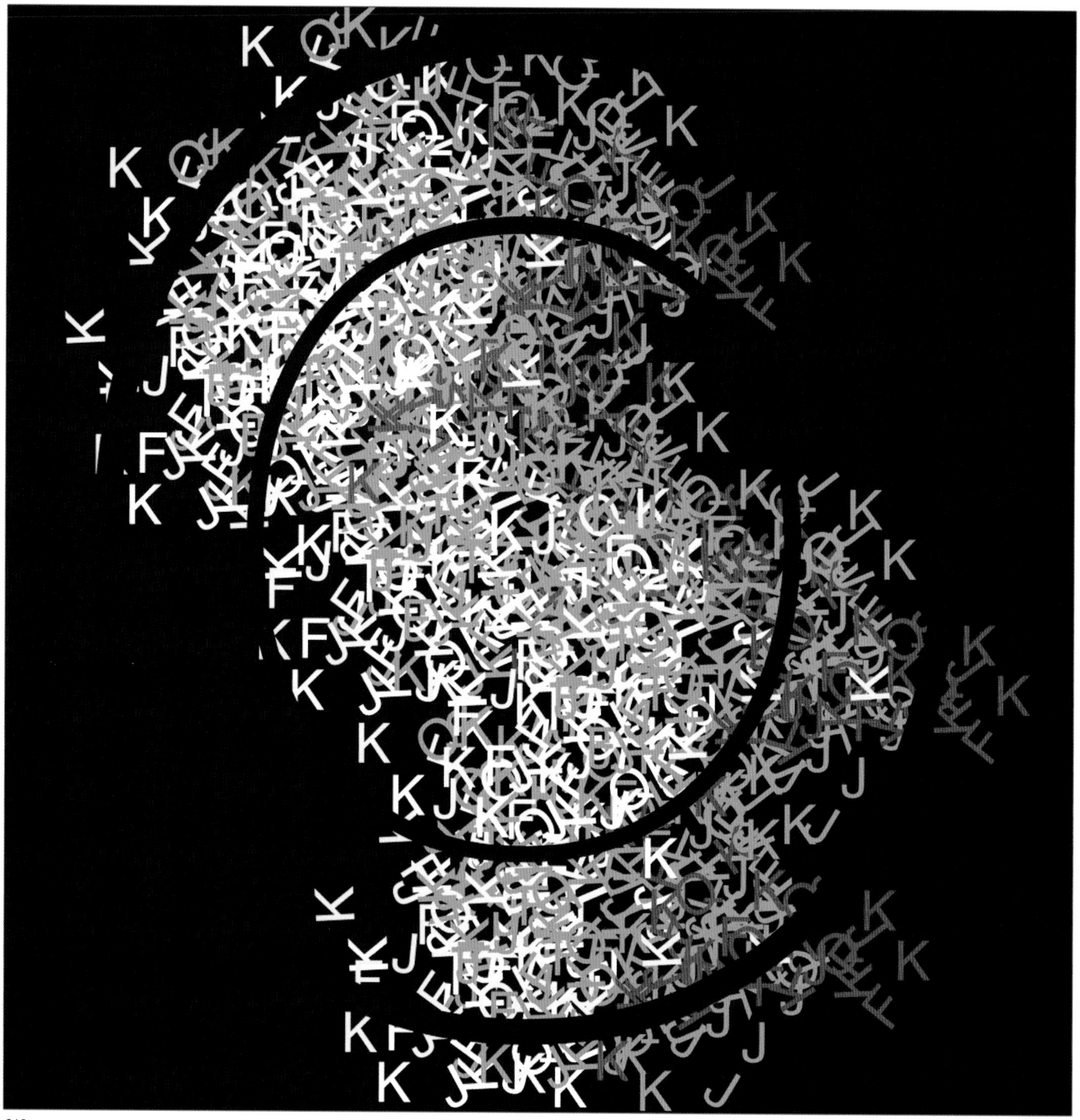

213

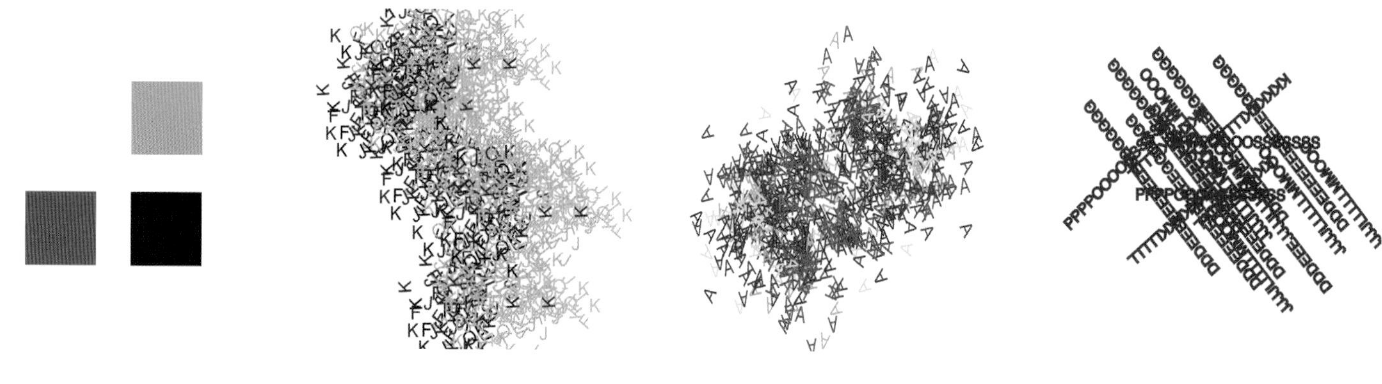

214

213 Random superposition of the letters *F*, *J*, *K* and *Q*. The large outlines that are superimposed on top and the color scheme of two colored tones (red and light yellow) that are matched by two none colored (grey and black) add up to the quality of the composition

214 Color and composition studies

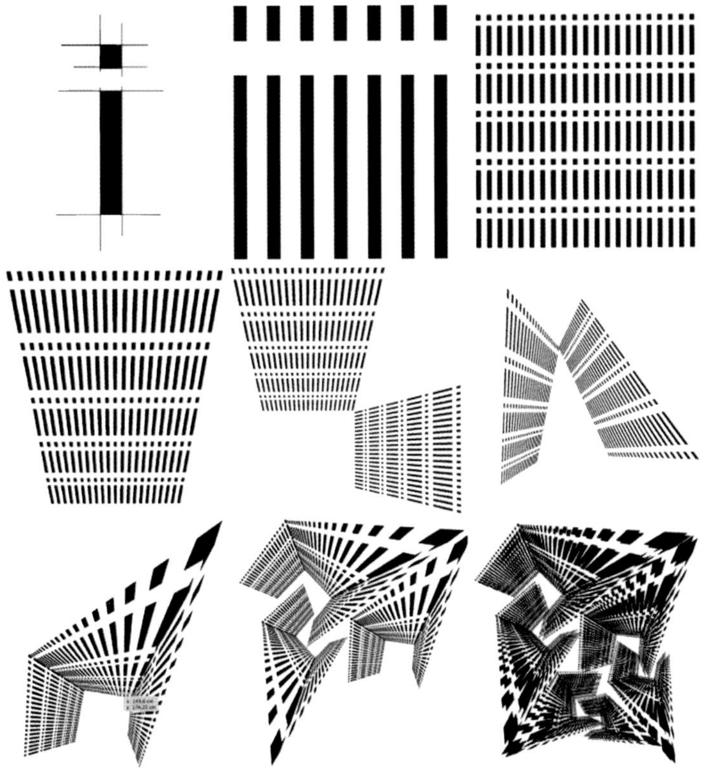

215

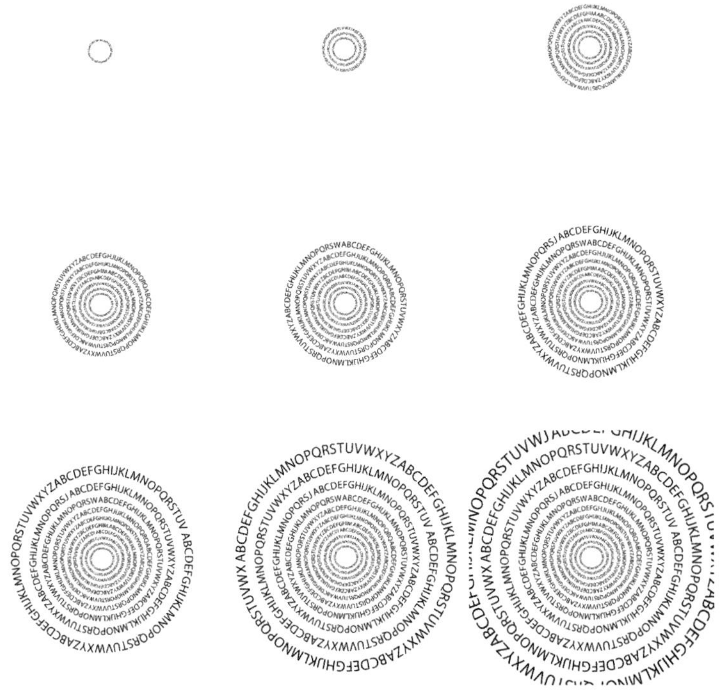

216

217

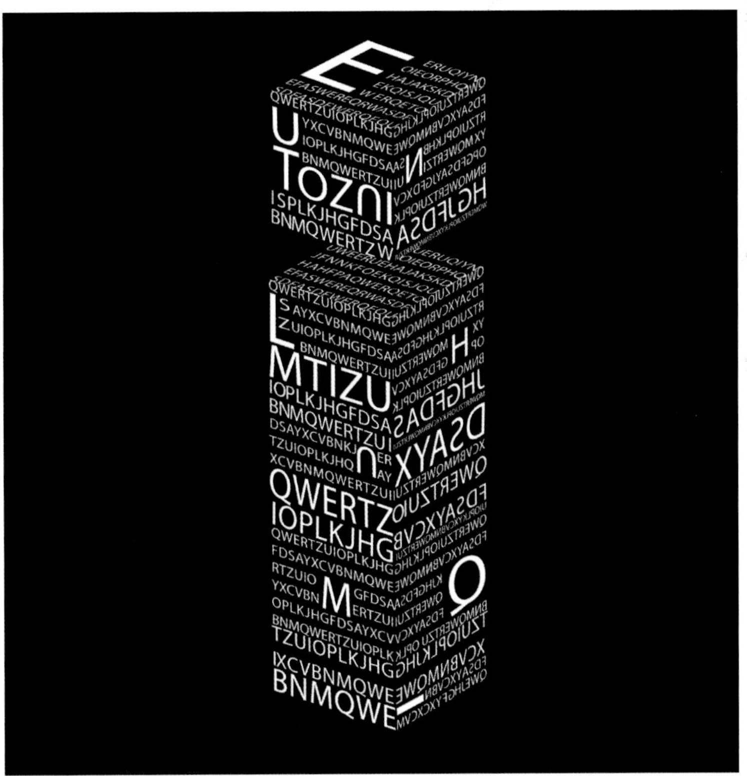

218

215 Composition and motion studies using spatial projections

216 Radial typeface arrangement

217 218 Typography used to texture geometrically aligned surfaces eventually depicting an axonometric object

220

219

219 Composition using the letter *p*. Repetition and radial arrangement evoke an image of a seemingly fractal geometry together with a gradient two-tone color palette that is changing from light to dark tones

220 Studies on the additive configuration possibilities of the letter *p* and the number *9* applying fractal principles

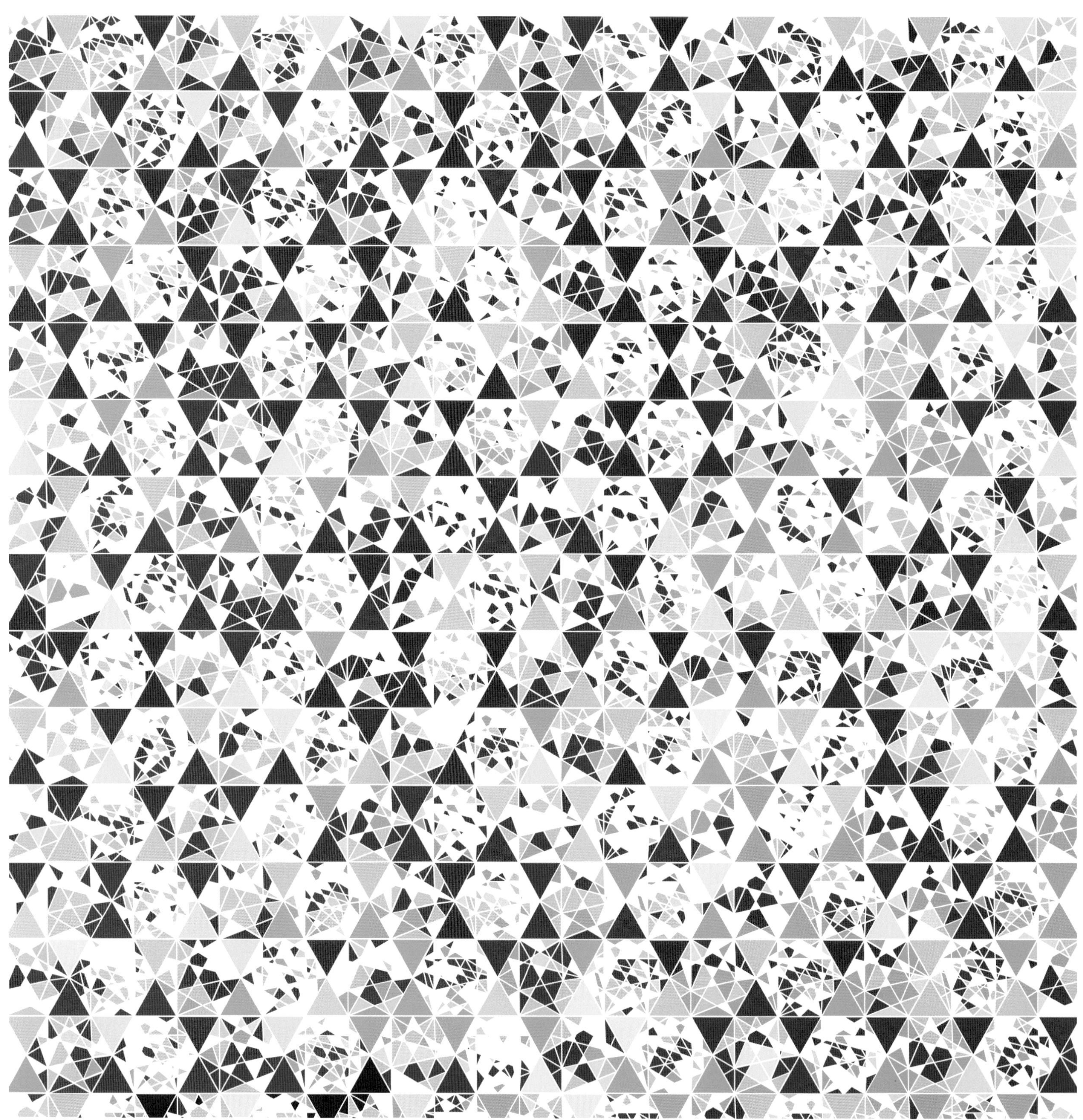

221

221 Composition based on a regular pattern in the front and an irregular pattern in the background. The color palette is using an alternating hue angle and darkened or slightly diminished saturation levels

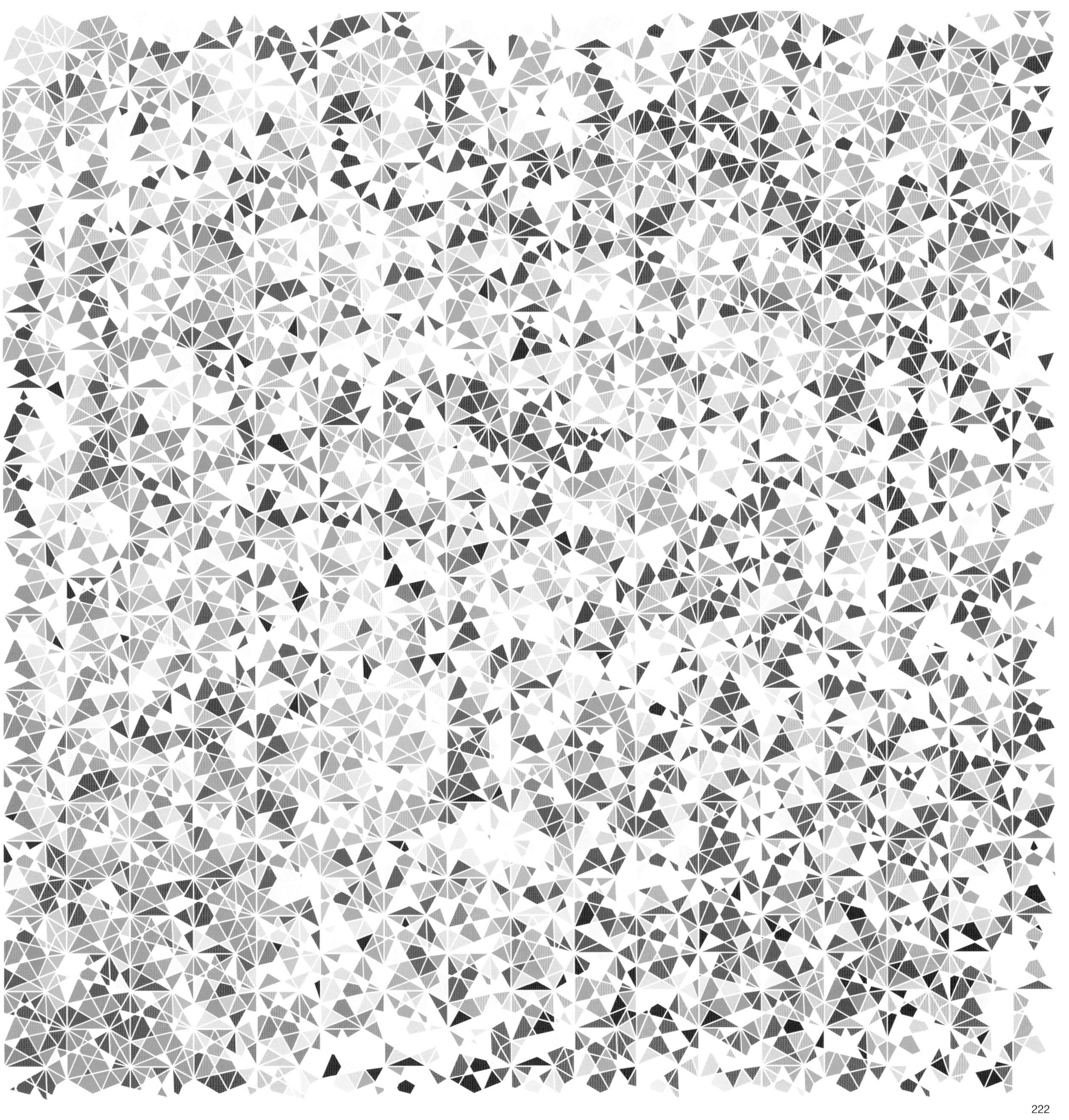

222

222 Fragmented color arrangement based on a grid and module construction. Compositions like this can easily be imagined in an architectural context or within a number of building applications

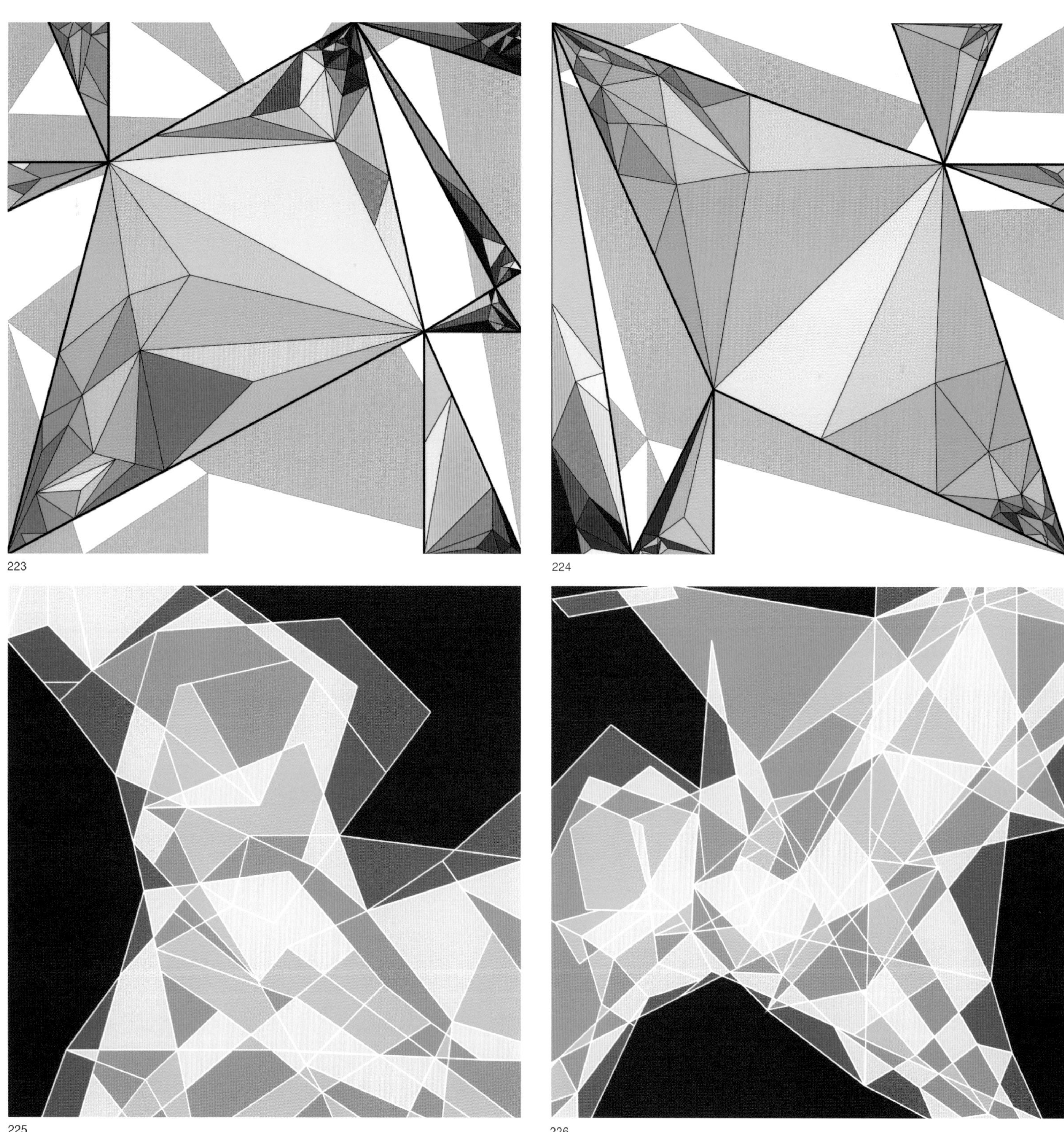

223 224 Diptych composition applying the simultaneous contrast by Johannes Itten in using complementary colors of red and green. Together with light, almost yellowish tones, the color composition is bridged and leveled out. A foreground background spatial effect is created, using greyish greens

225 226 Diptych composition using a limited green palette that changes from a yellowish tone to a cold green with parts of blue

227

228

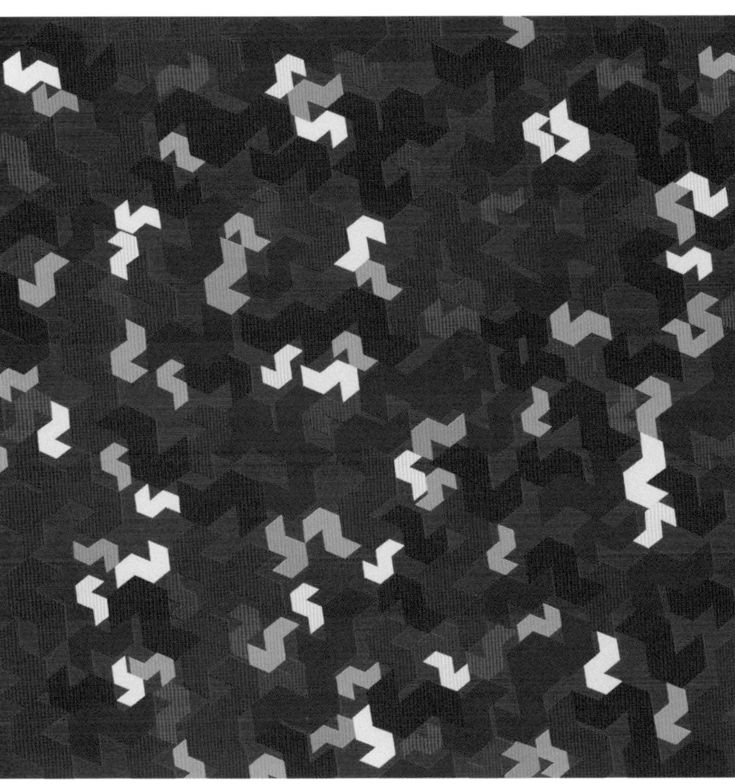

229

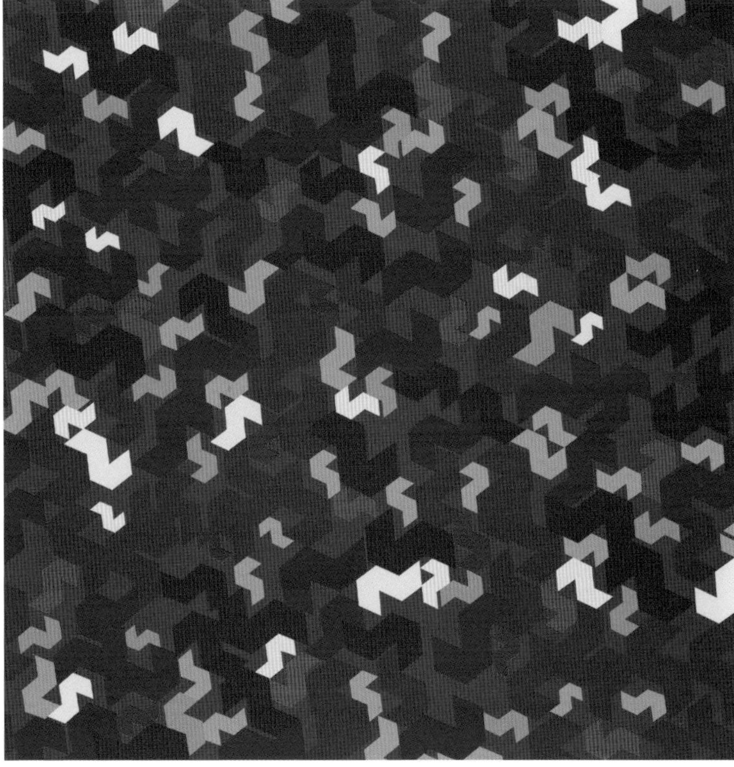

230

227 228 Diptych composition using changing hue angles for a widespread color palette added shadows evoke a sense of depth and architectural application

229 230 Diptych with an inverted background within the color scheme

231

231 Color composition applying the use of primary and secondary colors while introducing darker tones through transparencies

The fundamental laws of composition can best be explained in a two-dimensional environment where basic entities develop into complex arrangements when theories of perception are incorporated. Eventually, the qualities from a two-dimensional surface transform into three-dimensional space, from a floor-plan or section into build form.

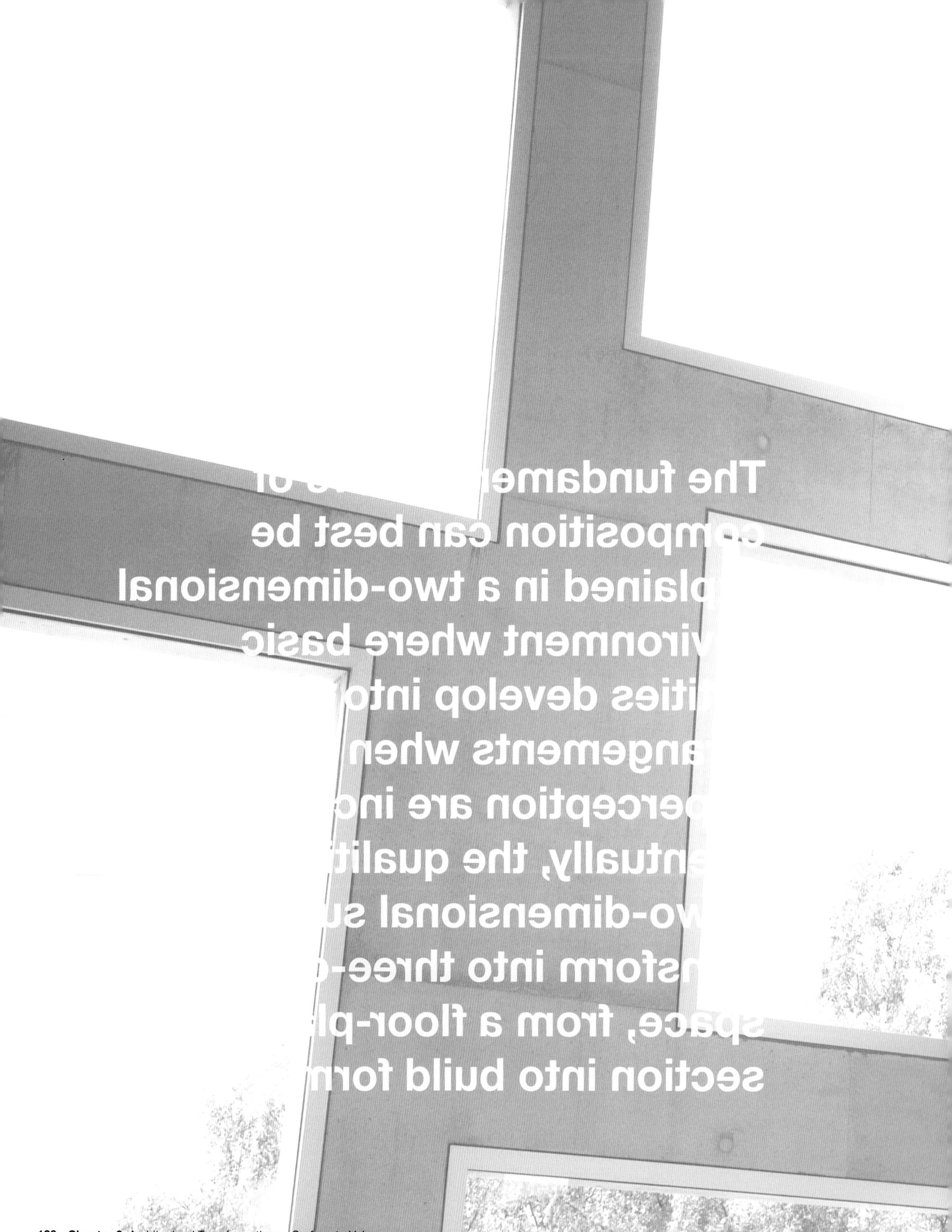

The fundamen... of
composition can best be
plained in a two-dimensional
vironment where basic
ities develop into
angements when
perception are inc
ntually, the qualit
wo-dimensional su
nsform into three-
space, from a floor-pl
section into build form

Chapter 6 : Architectural Transformations – Surface to Volume

non-physical space

space defined by surface

psychological phenomena

perception of space

virtual space

spatial perception vs. spatial design

By mathematical definition three-dimensional space, within a Cartesian grid that extends horizontally by the x and y axes, emerges by introducing the third coordinate, the z-axis. Within architectural design, however, space can also be experienced, manifested and structured through two-dimensional surfaces. Because human cognition and human experience are of spatial nature, the z axis is constantly implemented and programmed into our perception of space even if it is physically absent. For this reason, a two-dimensional surface, initially defined by three or more points or lines, has the potential to be perceived as a place, plaza, or space. Based on these spatial boundary conditions, the surface is an important tool in architectural design.

The play of two-dimensional surfaces and the virtual spatiality that a floor plan or the surface of a plaza evokes in our perception constitute an open space in ways similar to a physically enclosed volume. This "surface-defined space" is the simplest defined space—the first origin of physical space. This kind of space is initially not enclosed and its vertical expansion is potentially infinite. One could describe this space as nearly virtual: despite its surface definition and its ability to be described by laws of perception and design, it is a manifestation of one's imagination. Therefore, the space defined by two-dimensional surfaces cannot be described in a mathematical sense but through its spatial effect in our spatial experience.

"Real space" is derived through the physical manifestation of the z-axis, resulting in a comprehensible description of such a space. Advanced spatial

---

Page 118 119:
Zollverein School, Essen, Germany.
Kazuyo Sejima + Ryue Nishizawa / SANAA

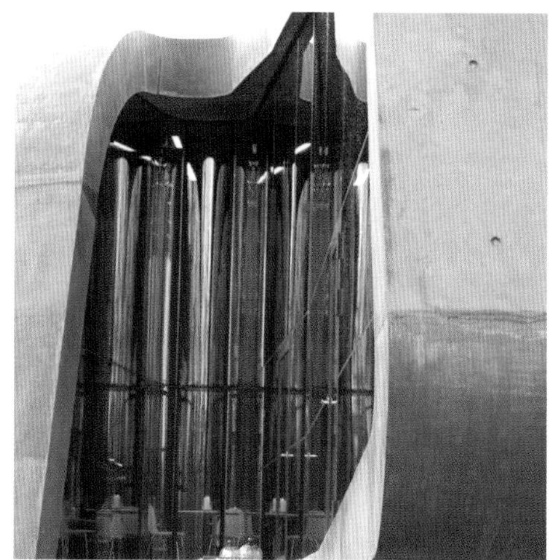

6.1 Reflections within the bended windows of the Ordrupgaard Museum extension in Charlottenlund, Denmark, evoke irritations within the perception of space and shape. Zaha Hadid Architects

6.2 Detail Porsche Museum, Stuttgart, Germany. Delugan Meissl Associated Architects

6.3 Staircase Museum Küppersmühle, Duisburg, Germany. Herzog & de Meuron

thinking and cognitive transformation from surface to volume and vice versa are elementary abilities in learning architecture and architectural design. Considering the various scientific definitions of space, contemporary spatial concepts have the potential to transcend both space and time.

Vilém Flusser describes the invasion of the virtual space into our living environment, dissecting outdated terms of public and private space that are used to describe the uncertainty and the existence of these intangible spatial models. Flusser concludes that the integration of virtual space as a place for "previously inconceivable activities" is obligatory and that within architectural design, it is mandatory to implement these new spatial modes, as geometry itself is no longer capable of describing the space that we experience as our current living environment. (ref. 6.1) This spatial philosophy gives rise to another point of view that influences spatial design in addition to traditional geometry and the "topology" propagated by Flusser, that is expanding its boundaries into the more scenic and sensual aspects of architecture.

The examples in the following chapter employ surface transformations and spatial conversions, which are based on a variety of the previously introduced design techniques. In the assignment, students produced a number of analytical drawings that led to the production of two-dimensional collages, which were based on a variety of architectural precedents. Similar to the typography assignment in the previous chapter, students were encouraged to elaborate on specific architectural characteristics of their choosing.

The harmonic proportions and the design qualities found in the preceding examples give a good foundation for the subsequent, more complex collage work. Due to the concreteness of architecture, a higher level of abstraction was applied to the student examples.

Through the formatting and simplification of the architectural examples into a two-dimensional analytical drawing of

6.1 Vilém Flusser: „Räume" (in Heidemarie Seblatnig (Hg.): außen räume innen räume.)

6.4 Detail Casa da Musica, Porto, Portugal. OMA

6.5 Detail De Kunstlinie Theatre and Arts Centre, Almere, Netherlands. Kazuyo Sejima + Ryue Nishizawa / SANAA

6.6 Detail Kunsthaus Graz, Austria. Peter Cook and Colin Fournier

forms and shapes, a transformation of perception emerges, which influences the translation from a spatial object into a drawing typology. The two-dimensionality of the object's depiction leads to a new reinterpretation of the precedent that in itself evokes a certain spatiality, which has the potential to generate new characteristics.

The goal of the assignment was to engage into a process of abstraction that exceeds the more concrete character of the original architecture, thereby deriving new graphic, compositional, architectural, and spatial qualities.
For this reason, some of the works concentrated on the spatial allegories and scenic qualities of the analyzed architectural elements. Also, much like the examples in the previous chapters, the works show the application of laws of graphic configuration, perception theory, and color composition.
In a second step, the assignment, took the two-dimensional processing described above into a three-dimensional computer model that lead to design arrangements, composed of spatial configurations achieved through the remodeling, sampling or quoting of architectural elements from contemporary and historical building precedents. The methods applied in this assignment and design work are intended to train spatial thinking and awareness. They help to exercise harmonic spatial compositions with the incorporation of scenic aspects, and to further develop incisive spatial characteristics of known architectural examples into new spatial configurations. Considering Flusser's questioning of Cartesian space, the works pick up on the threshold relationship of spatial perception and spatial design. The examples in this chapter therefore start to open ways of thinking that transcend graphic composition or already known traditional spatial qualities, in order to blur the boundaries of conventional spatial definition into to a scenic virtuality.

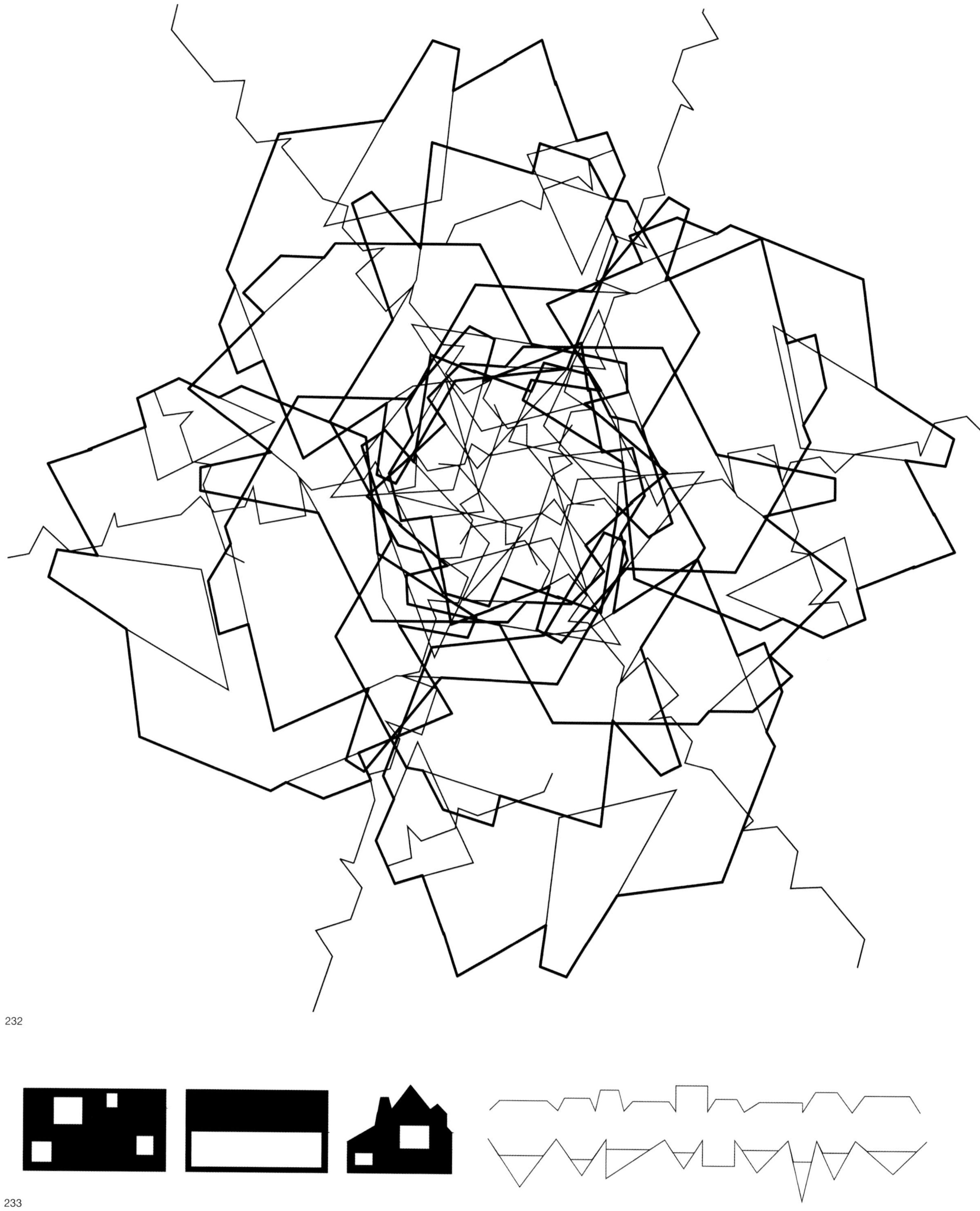

232

233

House Bierings
Architects: Rocha Tombal Architecten / Ana Rocha, Michel Tombal
Location: Utrecht, The Netherlands
Project year: 2008-2009

232 Rotated outline of transformed projections

233 Figure-ground analysis and transformation drawings

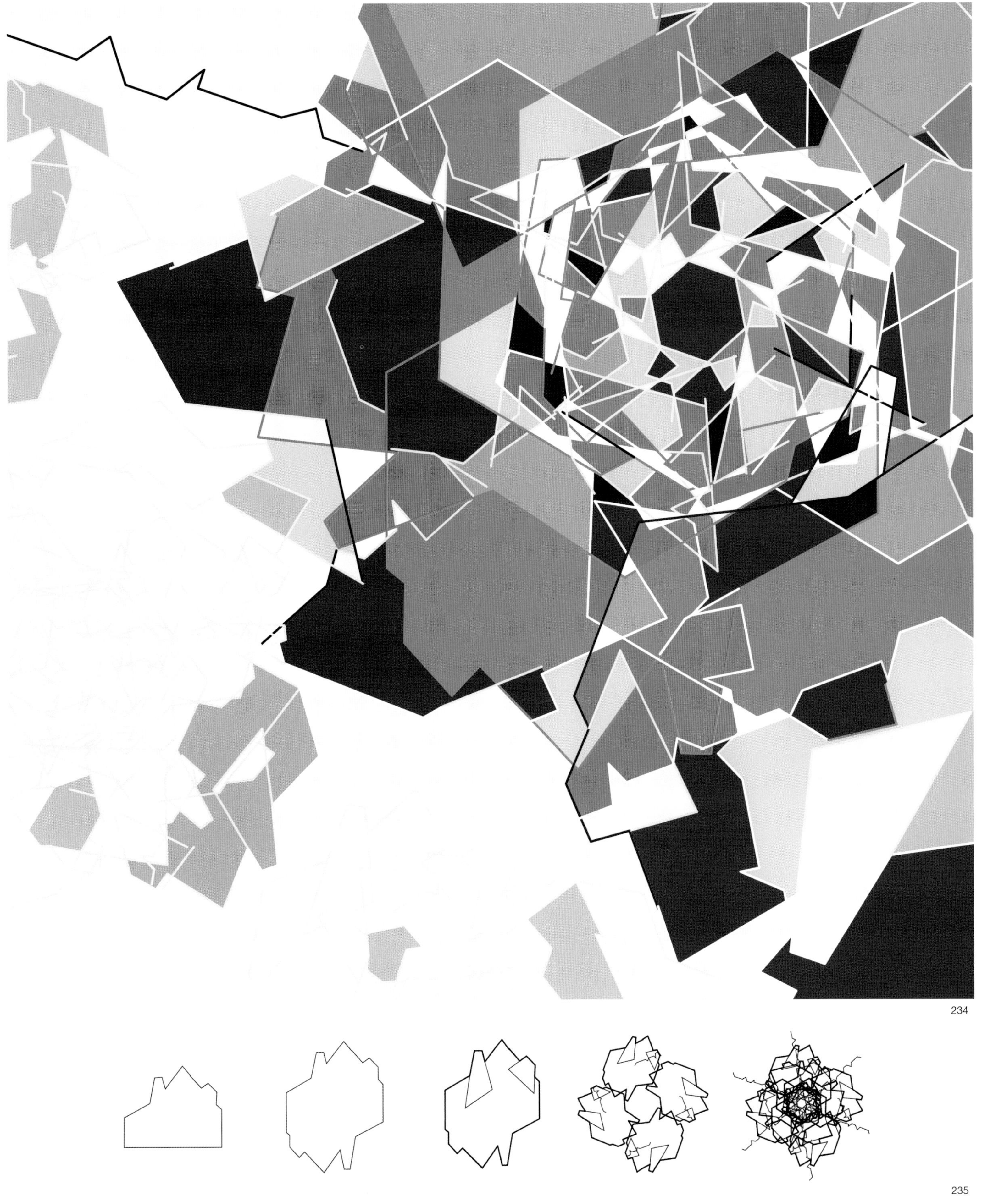

234

235

234 Advanced composition based on fig. 232 and on the results of selected analytical drawings based on house Bierings

The color palette uses desaturated tones of a green/blue and brown/red with changes in lightness

235 Mirrored duplicate of an abstracted elevation generates a new form that is then rotated and copied for a central arrangement

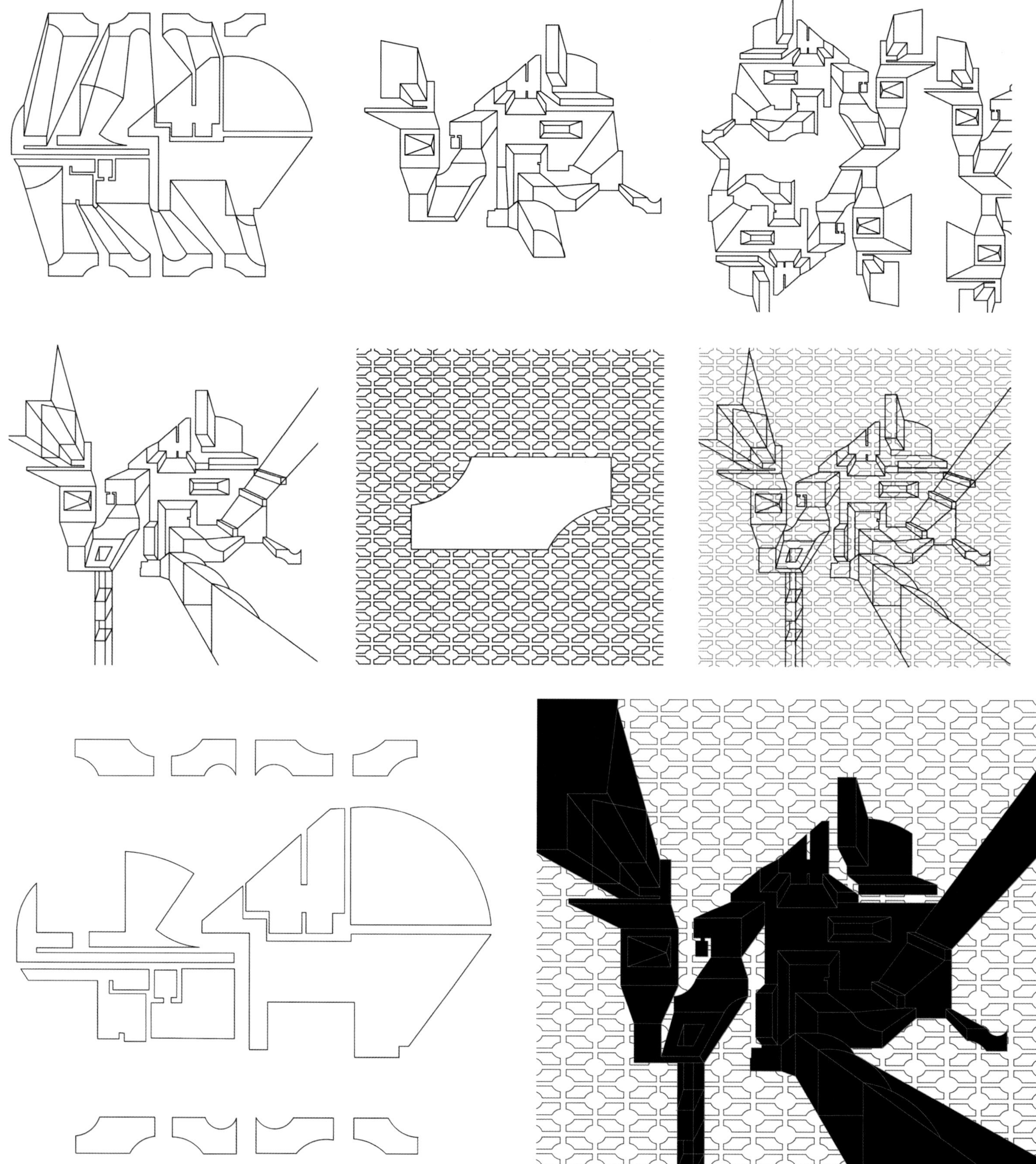

236

237

View House
Architects: Johnston MarkLee & Diego Arraigada Arquitecto
Location: Rosario, Argentina
Project year: 2004-2005

236 Experiments on deconstruction and transformation based on projections of the View House by Johnston MarkLee

237 Relief model of final composition with a cold to warm color contrast

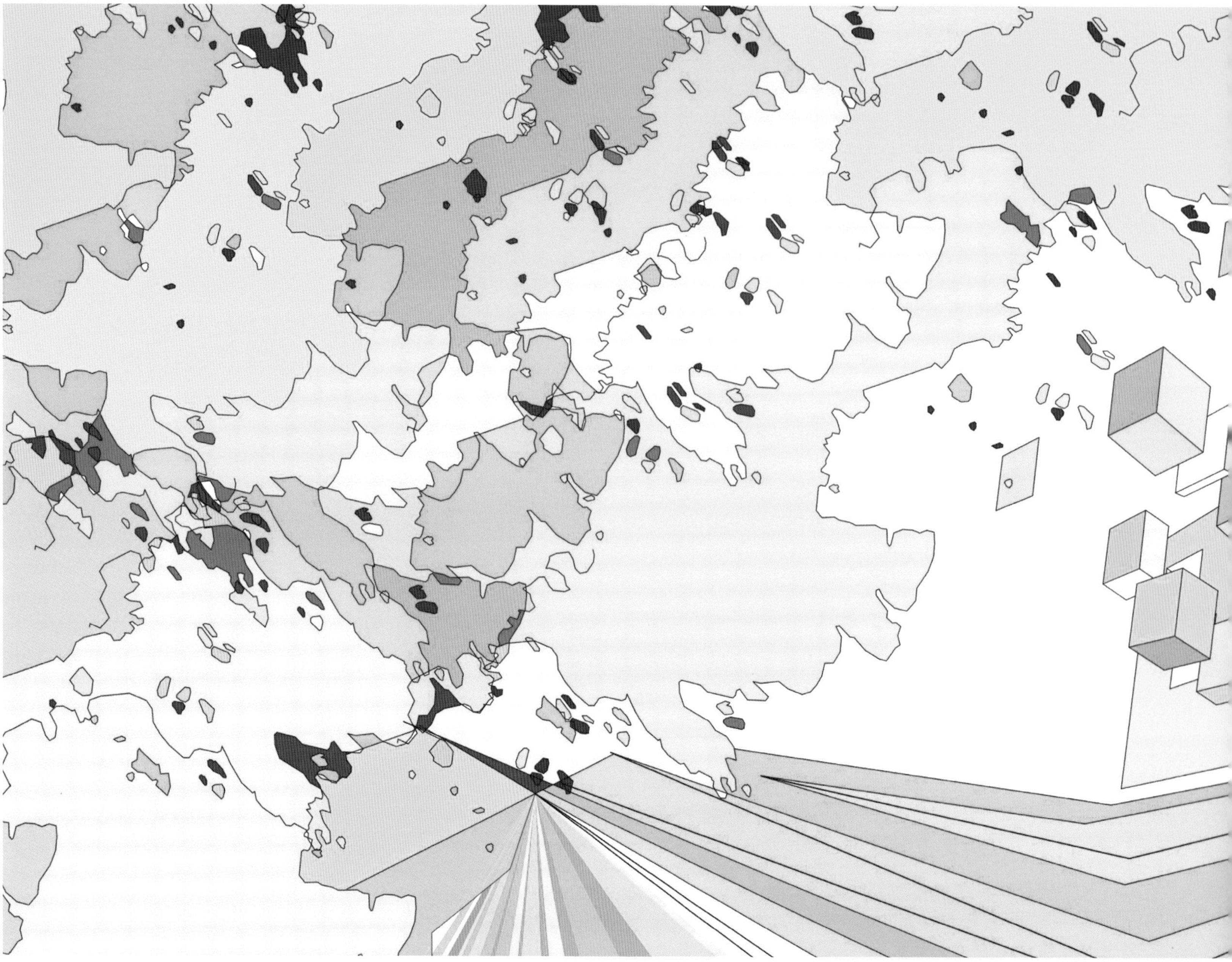

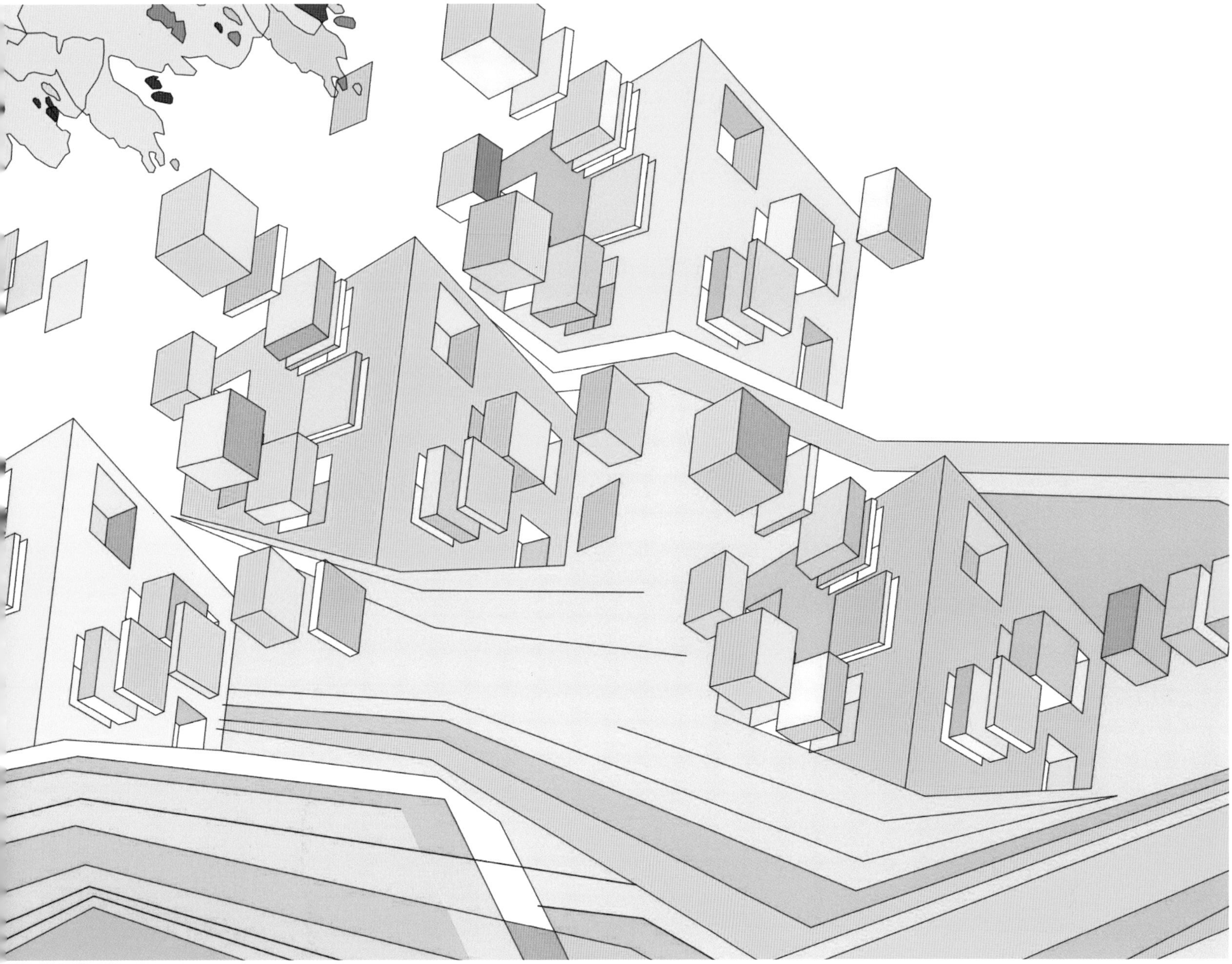

238

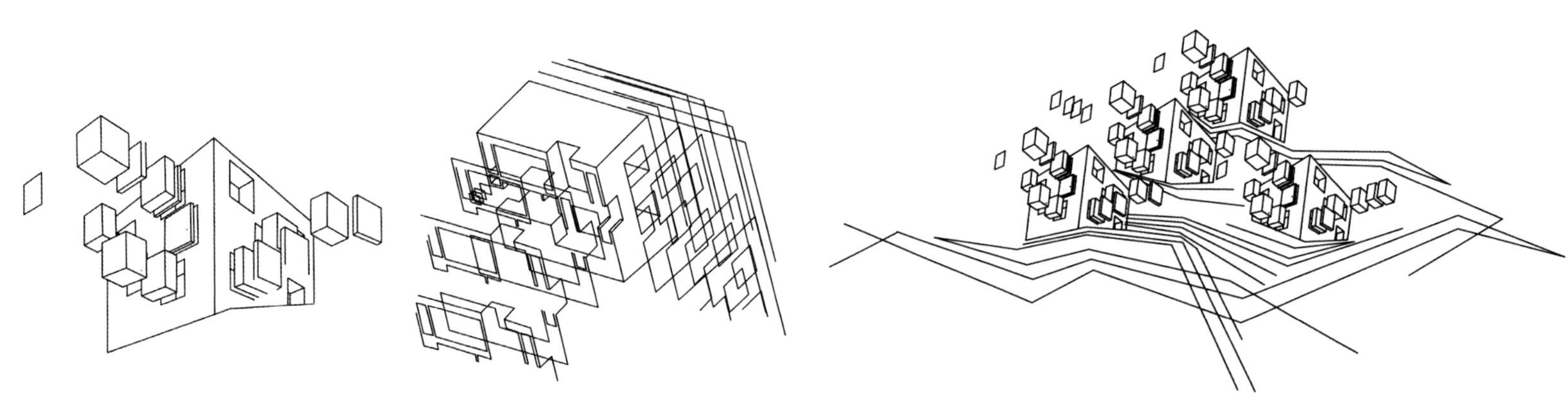

239

Poli House
Architects: Pezo von Ellrichshausen
Location: Coliumo peninsula, Chile
Project year: 2004-2005

238 Composition after the analysis of the Poli House. The image uses a cool color palette with mainly consistent lightness

239 Different parts of the house are taken, analyzed and tested for their graphic design potentials

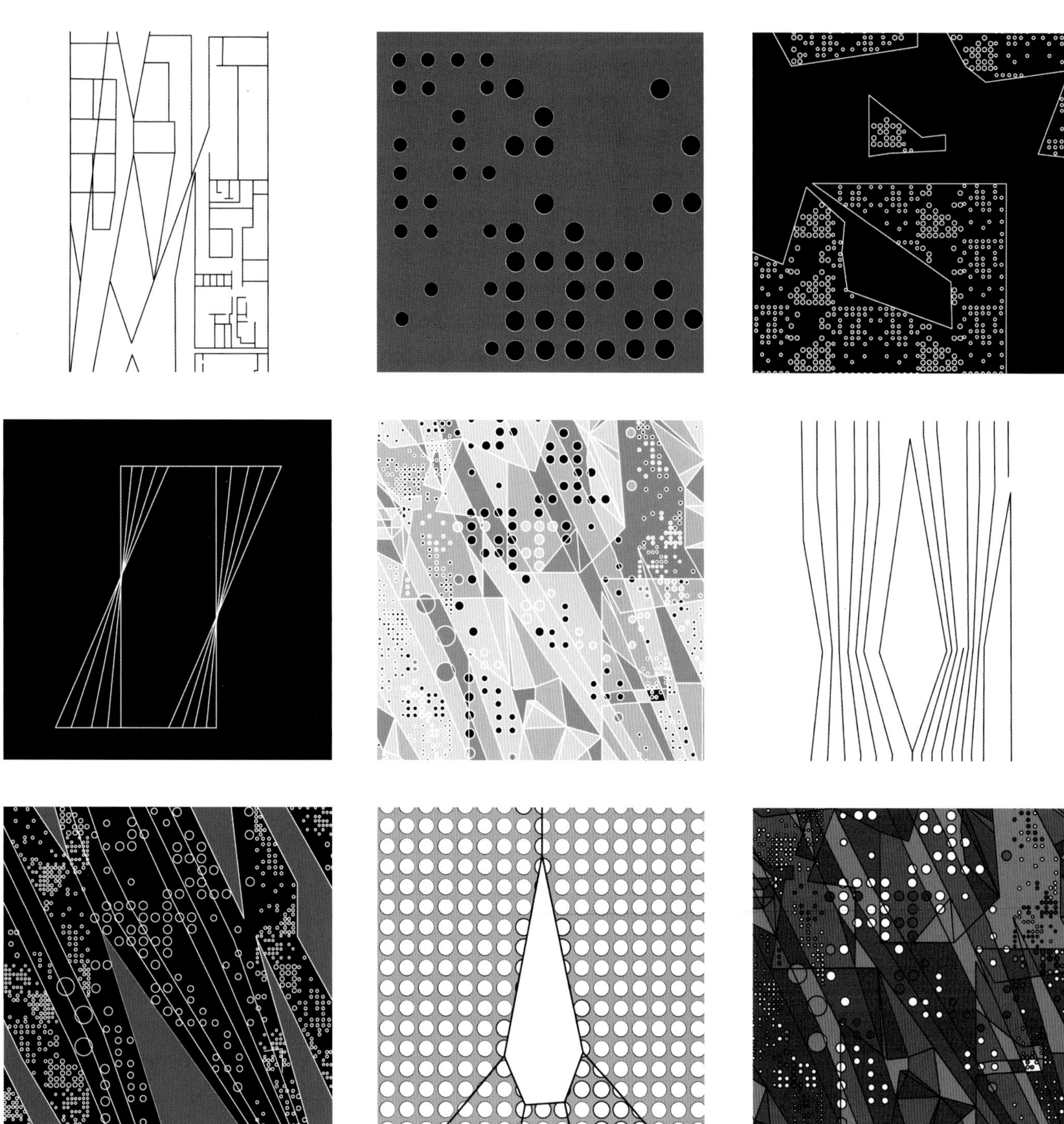

240

240 Formal analysis of the buildings design components establishes a dialectic context as a starting point for the collage in fig. 241

241

241 Collaged relief based on altered and transformed design elements of the De Young Museum by Herzog & de Meuron

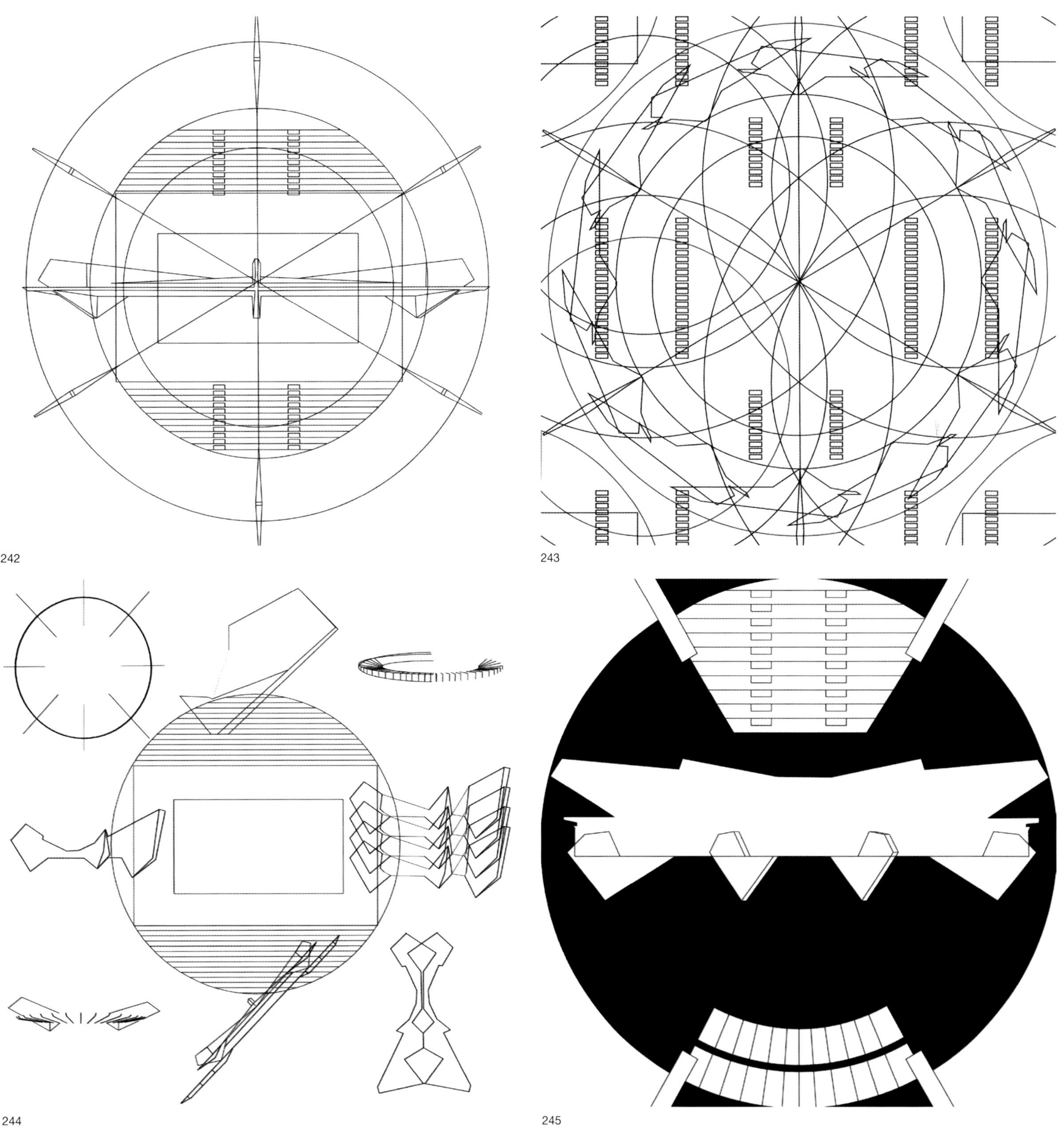
242
243
244
245

246

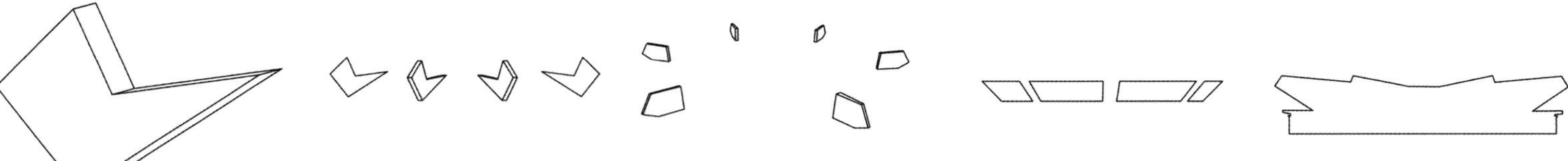

247

Paulistano Athletics Club
Architects: Paulo Mendes da Rocha
Location: São Paulo, Brazil
Project year: 1958

241-247 Analysis and synthesis. Removal, dissection, and reconstruction of structural building components into a new graphic spectrum

248

249

Poli House
Architects: Pezo von Ellrichshausen
Location: Coliumo peninsula, Chile
Project year: 2004-2005

248 Perspective composition of exterior wall elements with a desaturated and partly darkened palette of secondary colors: green purple and yellow

249 Preliminary studies to fig. 248

250

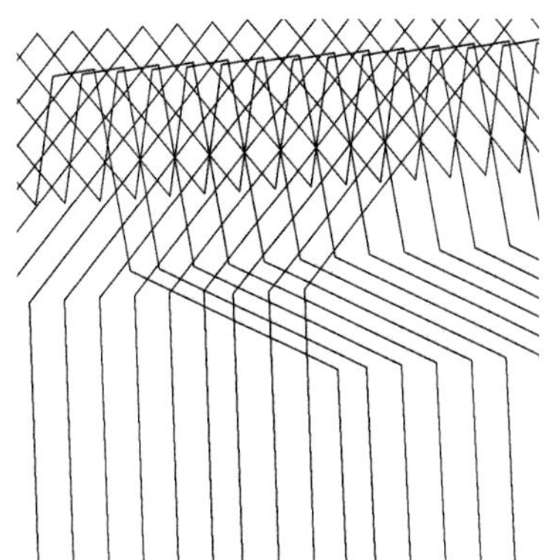

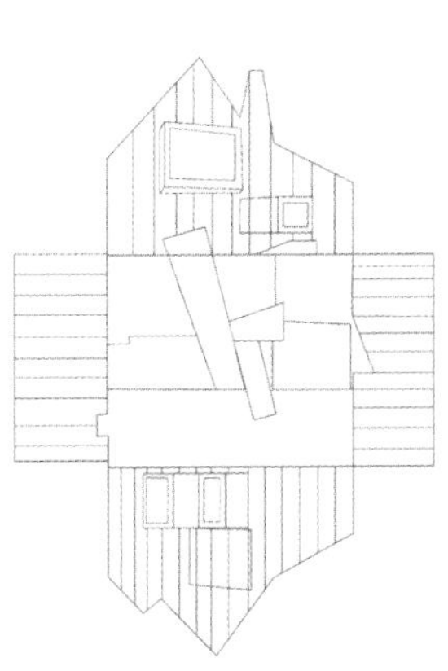

251

House Bierings
Architects: Rocha Tombal Architecten / Ana Rocha, Michel Tombal
Location: Utrecht, The Netherlands
Project year: 2008-2009

250 Spatial collage addressing the concise and irregular shaped dormers of the House Bierings. The center piece has a monochromatic color scheme in a greenish blue that rests on a very light yellow ground giving it a contrasting look in a cooler tonality

251 Analytical an progress drawings

252

253

de Young Museum
Architects: Herzog & de Meuron
Location: San Francisco, California
Project year: 2005

252 Deconstruction of the sententiousness of the de Young Museums tower

253 Preliminary studies to fig. 252

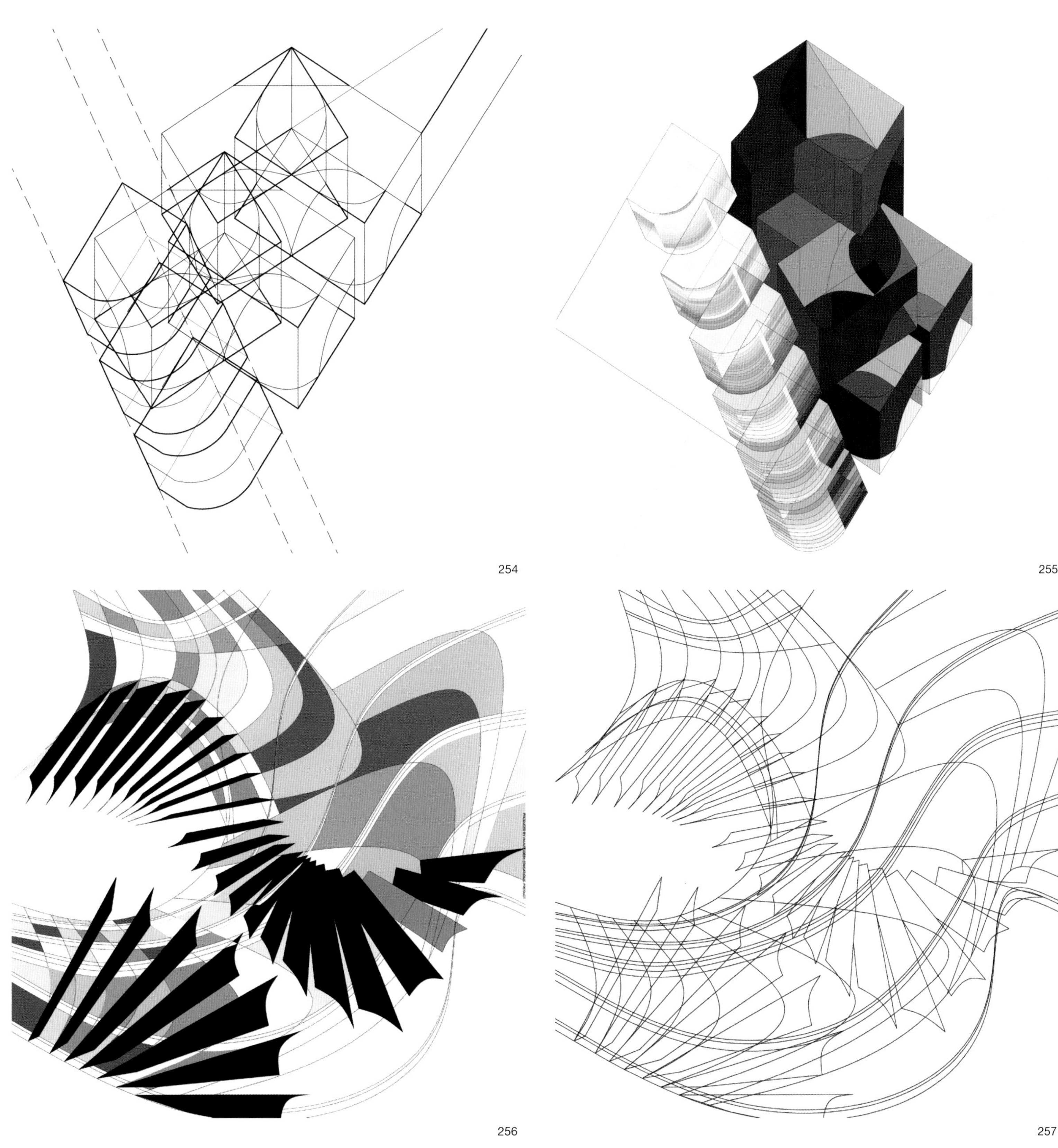

254 255 Abstract axonometric composition of the View House (p. 126) using a cold color palette with lighter and darker shades

256 257 Composition inspired by the roof of the Olympic Stadium, Munich, 1972. Gunther Behnisch with Frei Otto

259

260

261

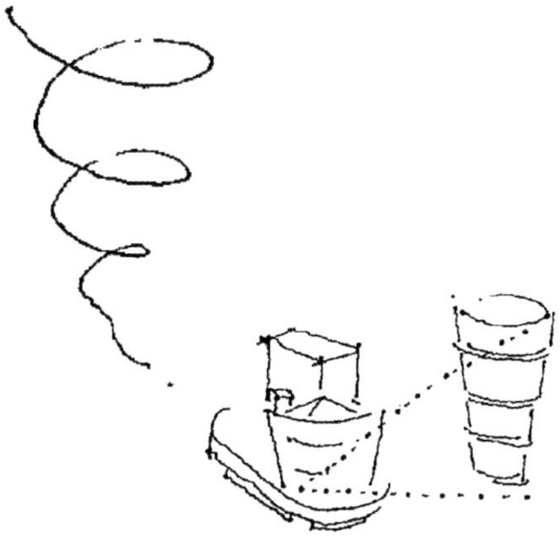

262

263

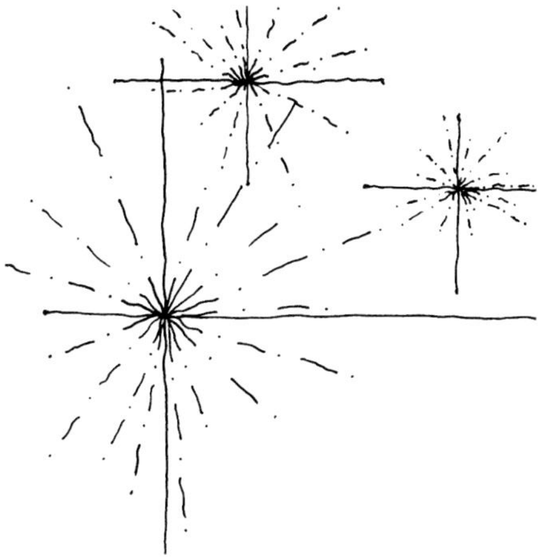

264

258

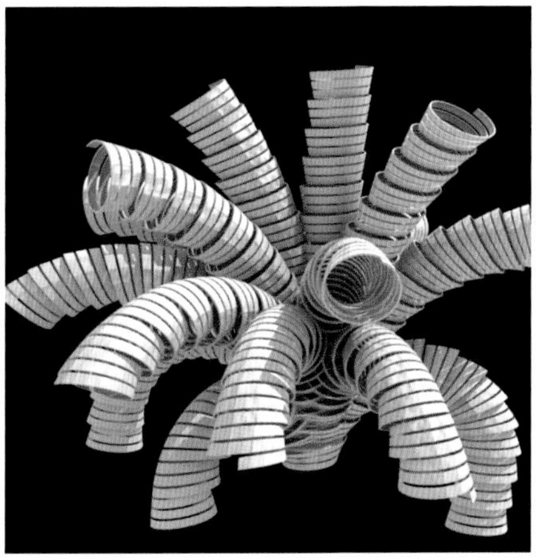

265

266

Guggenheim Museum
Architects: Frank Lloyd Wright; George Cohen
Location: New York
Project year: 1959

258 Spirals within spirals 3D metamorphosis of the Guggenheim Rotunda computer rendering

259 - 266 Preliminary studies

267

268

269

270

Guggenheim Museum
Architects: Frank Lloyd Wright; George Cohen
Location: New York
Project year: 1959

267 Swarming behavior, grouping and different densities tested on multiples of the Guggenheim rotunda

268 269 270 Different stages of transformation and deformation

271

272

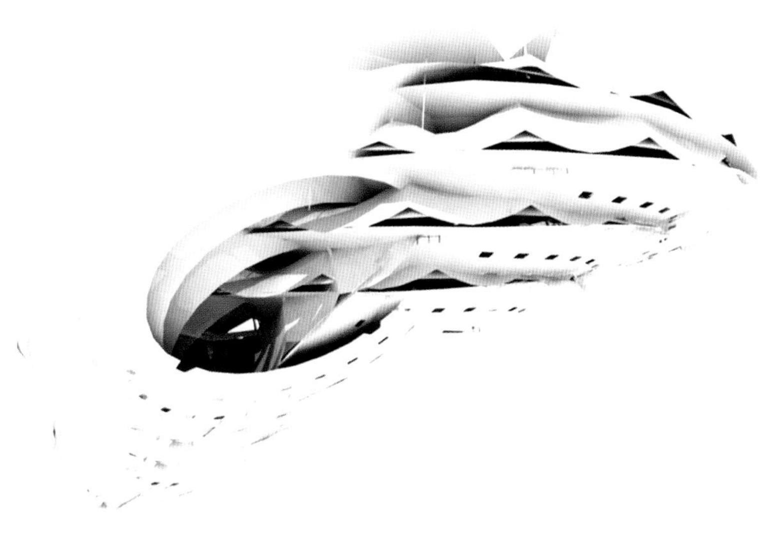

273

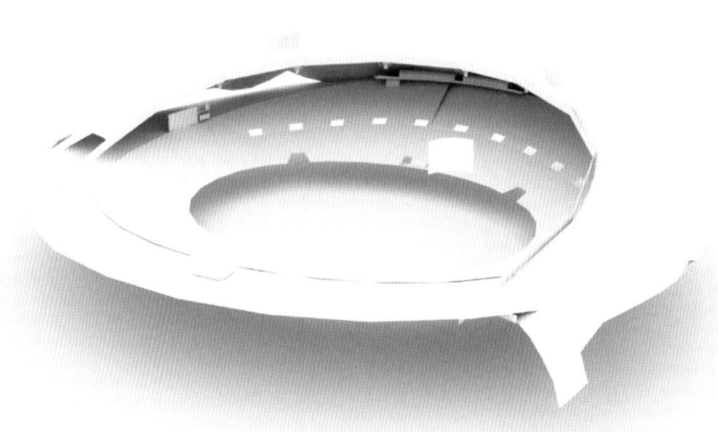

274

Olympic Stadium
Architects: Gunther Behnisch with Frei Otto
Location: Munich Germany
Project year: 1972

271 272 273 Different collages composed with transformed and dissected roof elements of the Olympic Stadium

274 3D model of simplified stadium

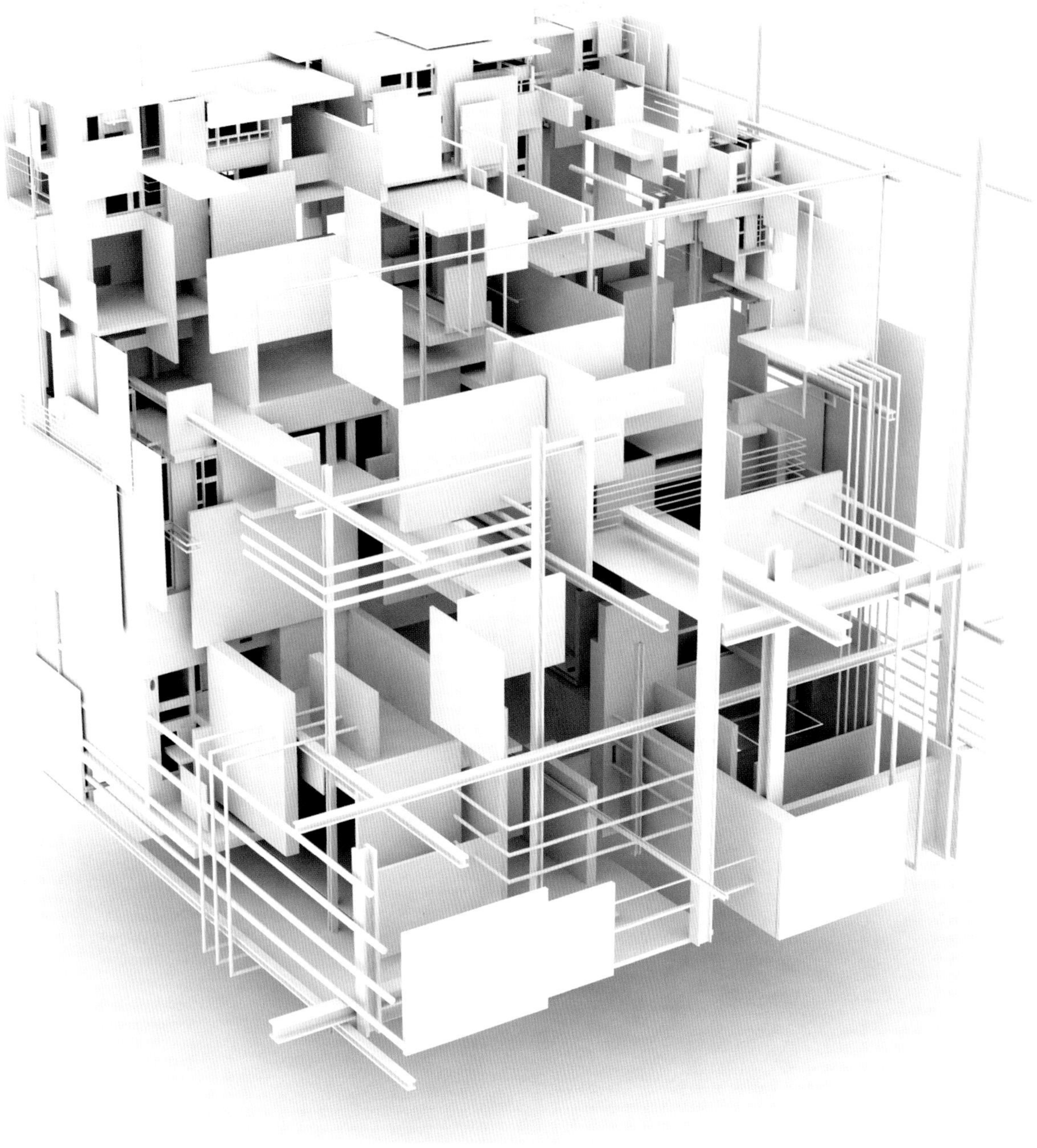

275

276

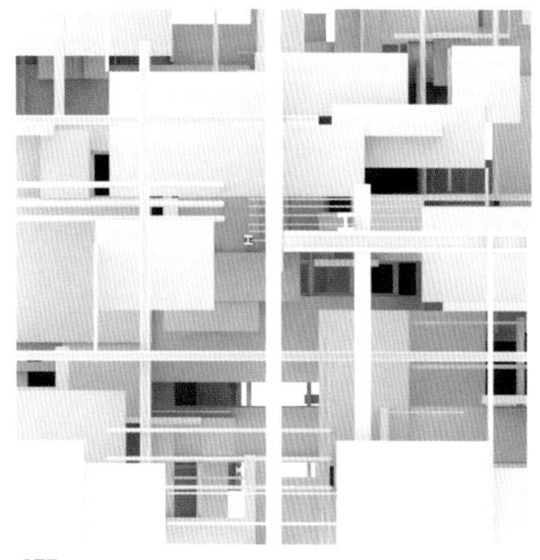
277

278

Rietveld Schröder House
Architects: Gerrit Rietveld
Location: Utrecht, Netherlands
Project year: 1924

275 Collage confined within an imaginary cubic border utilizing structural elements of the Rietveld House

276 277 278 Close-up renderings of the new spatial configurations

279 Exploded spatial collage

280

Tizio table lamp of Artemide
Architects: Richard Sapper
Project year: 1972

280 Deformation of the Tizio lamp: Displaced segments within the 3D model create a fascinating dynamic. A seemingly mistake becomes a deliberate design decision

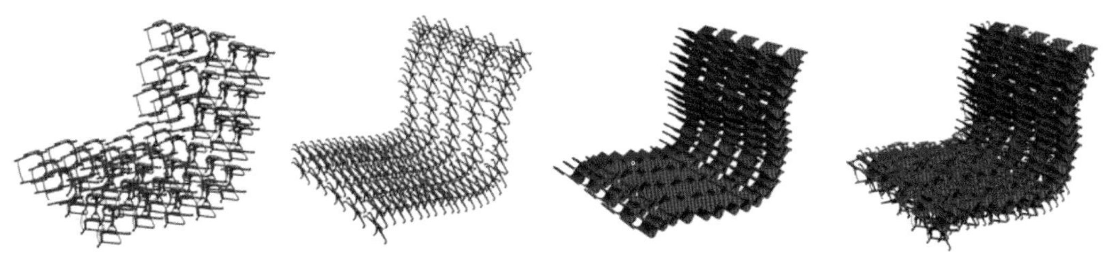

281

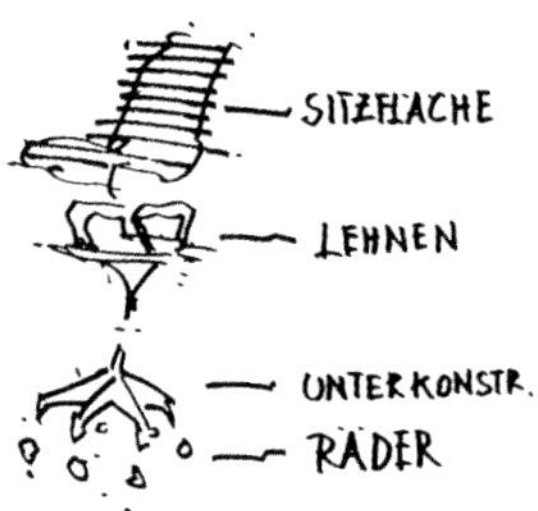

282

283

Eames Chair (80087)
Architects: Charles and Ray Eames
Project year: 1958

281 Additive clustering of Chairs into a new, self similar shape which corresponds to the original seat of the Eames Chair

282 Dissection of the chair

283 Agglomeration of Eames Chairs into a highly energetic bundle

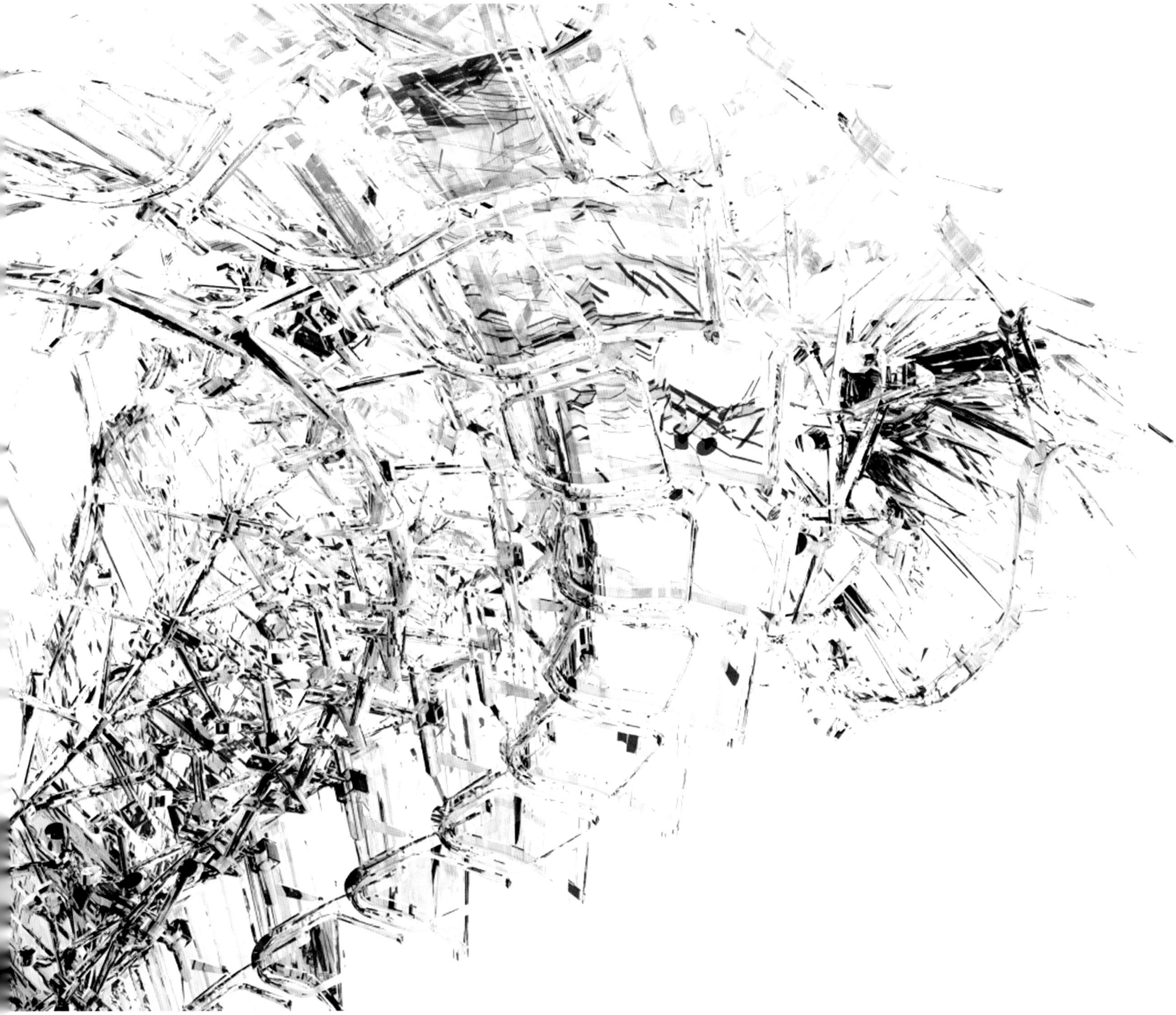

284

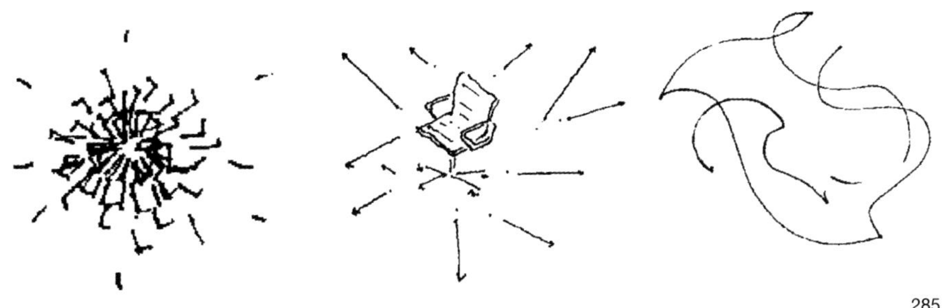

285

284 Crystalline computer rendering of a composition of Eames Chairs using transparent model parts

285 Conceptual sketches, studies on dynamic and motion

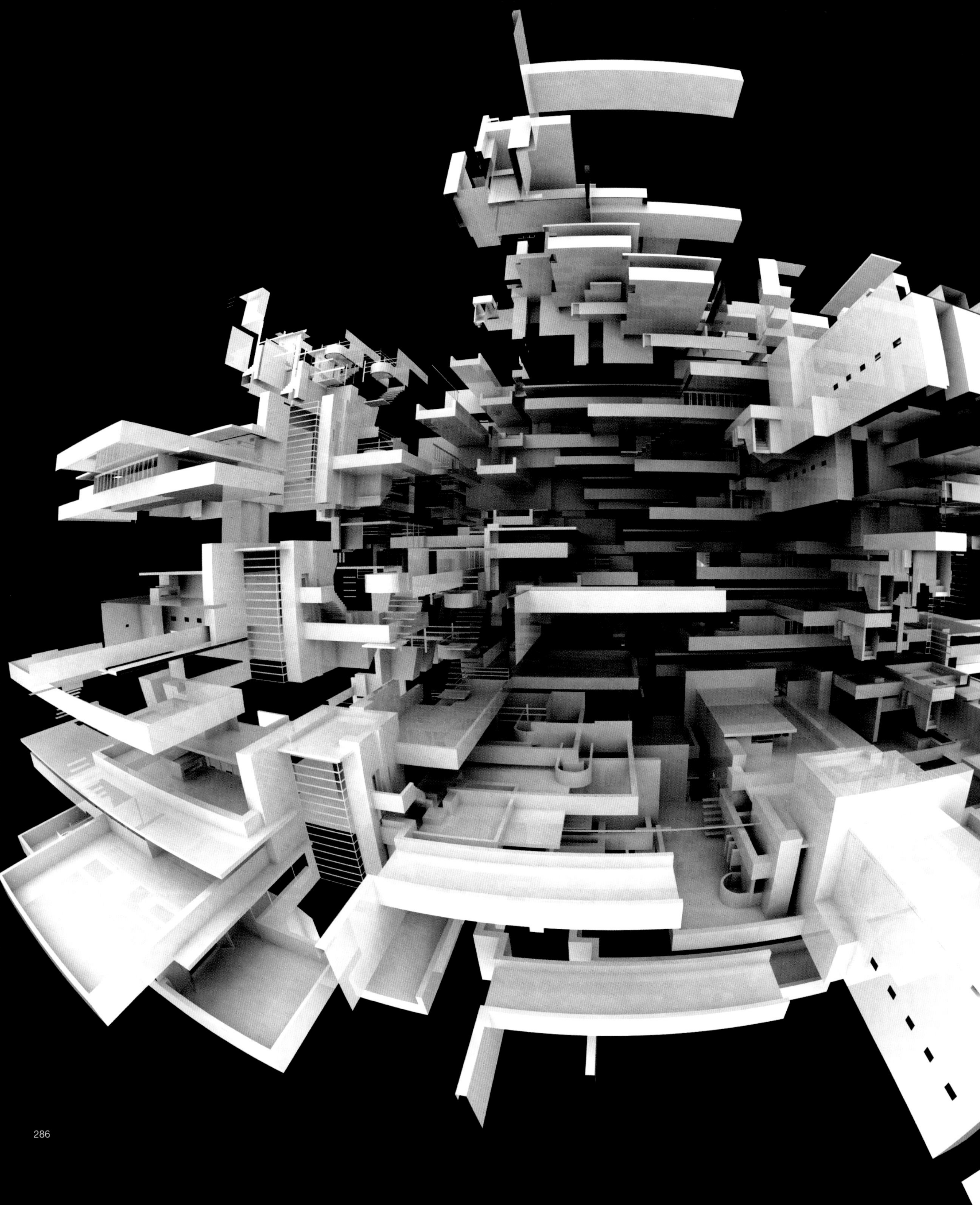

286

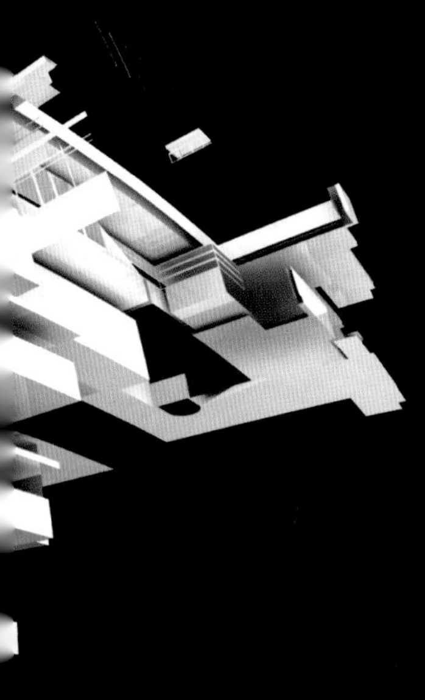

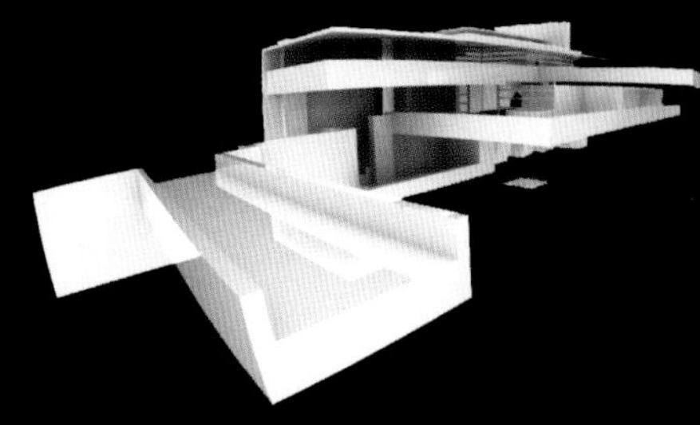

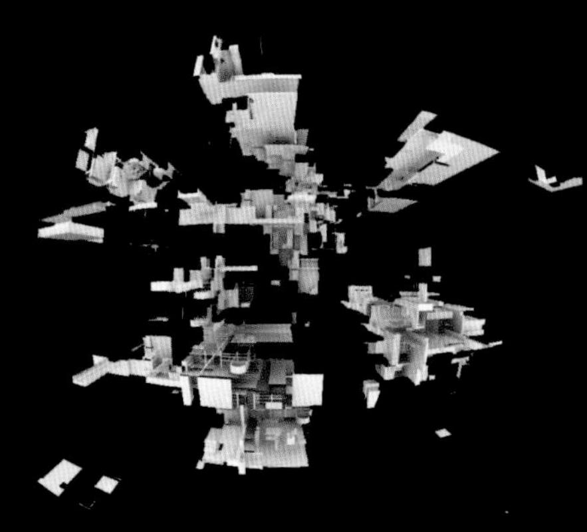

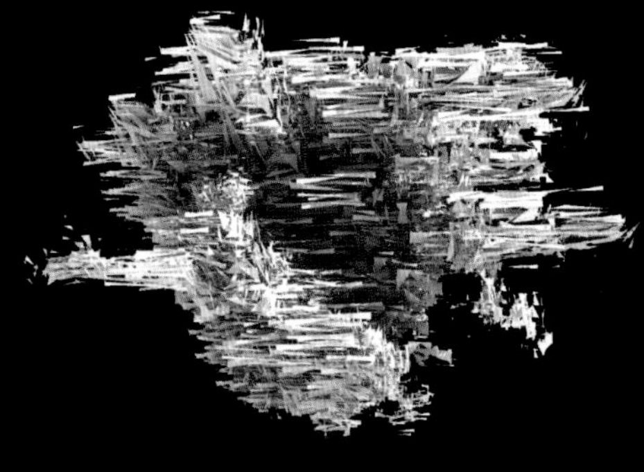

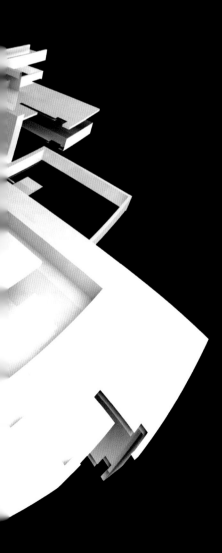

287

Falling Water House
Architects: Frank Lloyd Wright
Location: Ohiopyle, (Bear Run), Pittsburgh, Pennsylvania
Project year: 1935 - 1937

286 Fallingwater Spatial reconstruction rendered with fish eye projection

287 Dissections and spatial reconstructions using different elements of the Fallingwater house

288

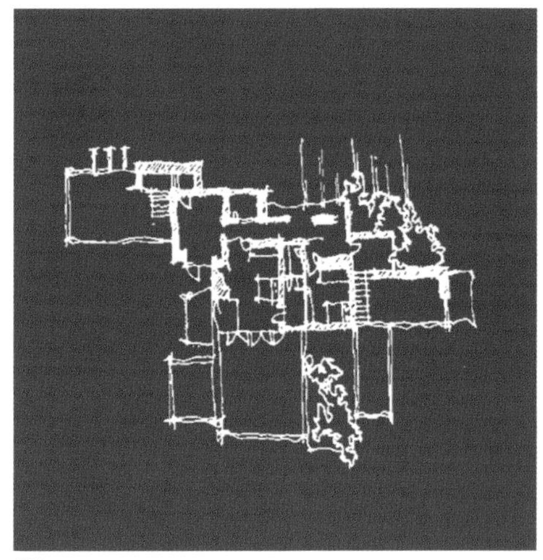

289

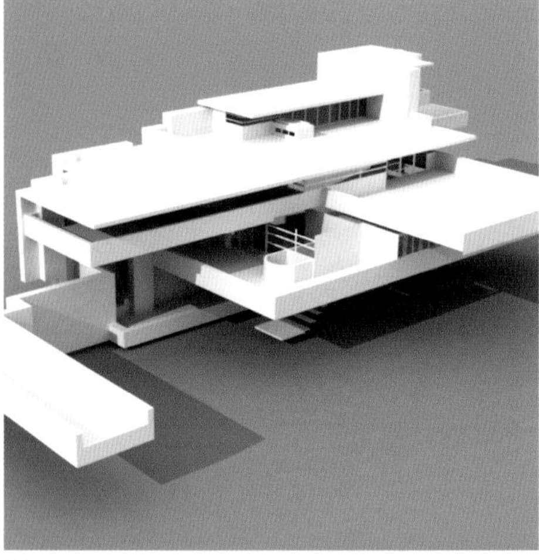

290

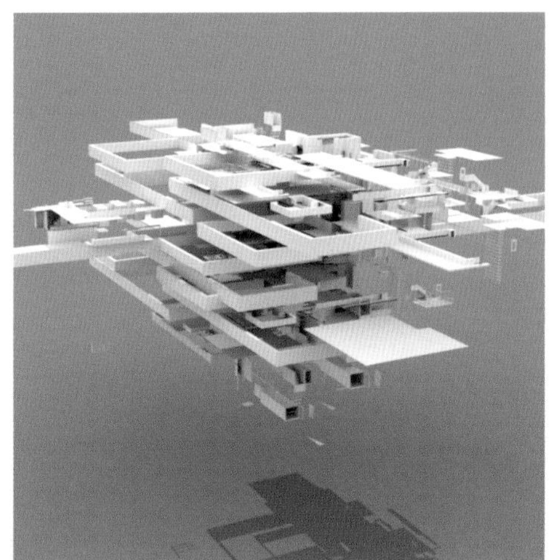

291

292

293

294

288 289 Sketches
290 Simplified 3D model of the Fallingwater house showing the most characteristic elements that constitute its formal appearance

291 and 292 Elements that are strongly attributed with formal qualities of the house are combined into a new object of different appearance and similar qualities

293 The alternating use of floor slabs and stairs within this 3D collage dissolves spatial limits and boundaries

294 Detail rendering of final collage

All architectural endeavors are targeted to the creation of space. The cultivation of spatial design abilities starts with very basic elements that develop a certain complexity within the design process.

Chapter 7 : Volumetric Alterations

generation of space

conceptuality

additive design

subtractive design

application of proportion theory

contextualization

The fundamental goal of any architectural endeavor is the generation of space and volume that can be utilized for human activity and occupation. In architectural design education, the concern is to process a defined spatial program into a higher order or concept that at the same time considers a complex set of circumstances from usage, to genius loci, to tectonic considerations. At its best, this way of thinking produces solutions in which the architecture has an inherent abstract concept. The concept provides an overall meaning to the architecture and also possibly indicates poetic and intellectual qualities that might be specific to the particular architectural solution.

Within the abstract design of space, the incorporation of these conceptual notions can also play a role in spatial definition. This can be the reaction to a context, a certain perception and idea of space itself, or a rigorous application of specific design methods that are thematically and abstractly connected to the given design task. The assignments that produced the student work illustrated in this chapter derive from spatial programming and are limited to an abstract processing of a circumscribed volume: a visual conception that had to be derived by an additive and / or subtractive spatial composition process.

The first chapter describes the method of addition as an important two-dimensional design technique. In a spatial three-dimensional environment, this principle is translated into a method in which architectural constituents are positioned in relationship to one another in order to create a space. In the case of a subtractive design method, the spatial entity is a mass that becomes sculpted by the designer. This can be either achieved through an expedient spacing and breakup of a given volume, or through free form modeling and subtraction.

Additive compositions can be found in numerous architectural examples. Again, looking at the floor plan of the Aachen Cathedral (fig. 7.1), the many additions throughout the centuries can be seen as an additive arrangement of space and structure. The resulting complex and multifaceted space emerges with much more complexity than the simple additive operation that

Page 153 154:
Final Wooden House, Kumamoto, Japan, Sou Fujimoto Architects

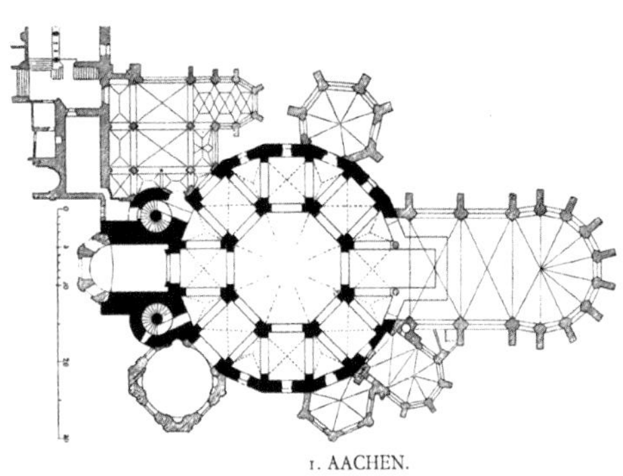

7.1 The additive evolution of the Aachen Cathedral is clearly visible in the floor-plan that shows the various building extensions es they were executed through time

7.2 VM Houses, Copenhagen. BIG Architects

7.3 New Museum, New York. Kazuyo Sejima + Ryue Nishizawa / SANAA

initially constituted it might suggest. More recent examples like the VM House by Bjarke Ingels, with its collating sequence of "Leonardo DiCaprio balconies" (fig. 7.2) on the southern side of the building, achieves a spatial and visual surplus value that grants the architecture a very specific recognition factor. SANAA's New Museum in New York City is based on the simple addition or stacking of volumes that is heightened through the abstraction of its expanded metal façade (fig. 7.3).

In modern architecture, the subtractive editing of a volume is a theoretical contemplation for architects, as architecture in practice is most always a process of assembling building parts, not a sculptural endeavor. In this respect, a purely subtractive design can be constructed only in theory, as a void cannot be physically removed from a given architecture. However, there are some outstanding examples of subtractive design in pre-modern architecture that illustrate the fundamentals of subtractive design and construction. These precedents include Abu Simble, the city of Petra, and the well-known monolithic churches of Lalibela in Ethiopia, all carved out of solid rock in a subtractive construction technique. In modern and contemporary architecture, there are various examples of built projects that conceptualize the process of subtraction through a highly unusual building process. The Temppeliaukion church in Helsinki's Töölö quarter by the architects Timo and Tuomo Suomalainen (chapt. 2, fig. 2.5), carved into its foundation rock in 1969, exemplifies the subtractive process of both design and construction. The Brother Klaus Field Chapel, near Mechernich, Germany designed by Peter Zumthor (fig. 7.5), and built through an archaic construction process in which a mound of wood was covered with rammed earth and burned to form its interior, also clearly illustrates this concept.

Finally, "The Truffle" in Costa da Morte, Spain, created by Ensable Studio, employs a similar technique to Zumthor's, using poured concrete over a stacked heap of straw and a cow eating up the straw after the concrete is cured, to generate a cave-like architectural space. These examples are unbelievably atmospheric and poetic cases of high architectural quality that show the great potential of this design technique if conventional modes of construct-

7.4 Natural substraction through water. Antelope Canyon, Arizona, USA

7.5 Bruder Claus Field Chapel, Mechernich, Germany. Peter Zumthor

7.6 Schaulager / Laurenz Foundation, Basel, Switzerland. Herzog & de Meuron

ing buildings are abandoned. Many more examples can be identified when regarding subtraction solely as thought process or abstract conception, and not as literal subtractive architecture. The Therme Vals Hotel by Peter Zumthor, Simmons Hall at Massachusetts Institute of Technology by Steven Holl, the architecture of Claudio Silvestrin, and also John Pawson, are only a few examples of architectural works designed with a subtractive concept in mind.

Throughout the sample works that are shown in this chapter, students were required to learn from their own experience to initiate a simple spatial design process that incorporated various architectural design tools including models, sketches, and computer programs. The rapid switching between different tools was intended to turn the development and optimization of a given design task into a natural process.

As part of the abstract assignment, a given volume had to be produced by a subtractive or additive strategy. In the first step, the process had no formal regulations except that the students were required to engage in a morphological selection process by choosing a base structure from a series of working models, which they later sequentially optimized by using drawing and three-dimensional computer modeling. Many of the works shown simultaneously incorporate both design techniques. This first step was then further manipulated by the application of various proportion theories like the Fibonacci series and the golden section. (ref. 7.1 / 7.2)
In the second step, students learned about the meaning and rules of proportions and their application within spatial compositions. The goal of the assignment was not the repetition of knowledge but rather the applied understanding of the importance of proportion theory in architectural design. The works do not directly apply the generation of architectural space but the abstract design of a volume.

Some of the works show photomontages that intend to bring the volume into a post-rationalized context, in an effort to understand the scenic and experiential potential of their architectural designs in the built environment. The ultimate goal was for the students to be able to evaluate their own design work, and to transfer this evaluation into a context that supports the concept of their design and ideas.

7.1 P. H. Scholfield: The Theory of Proportion in Architecture

7.2 Gyorgy Doczi: The Power of Limits: Proportional Harmonies in Nature, Art, and Architecture

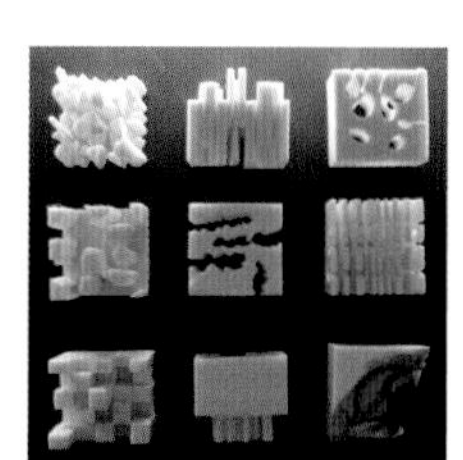
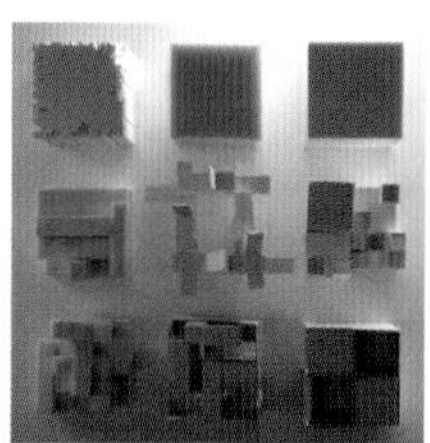

295

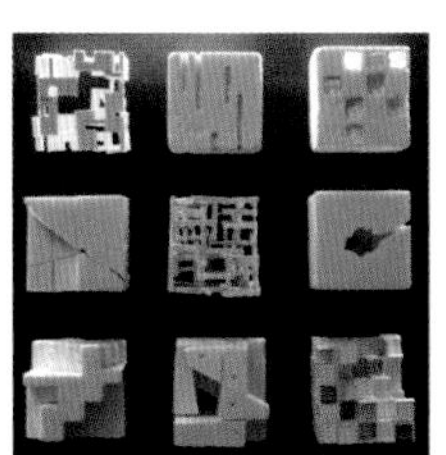

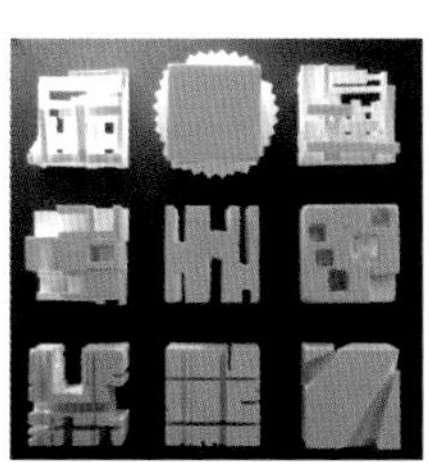

296

295 296 Working models of studies on subtractive and additive design methods

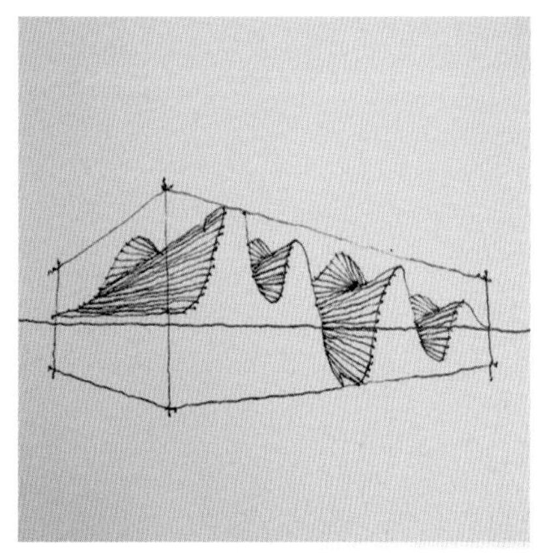

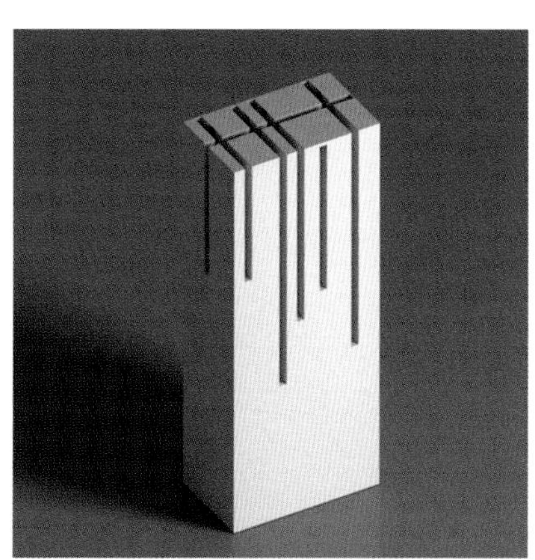

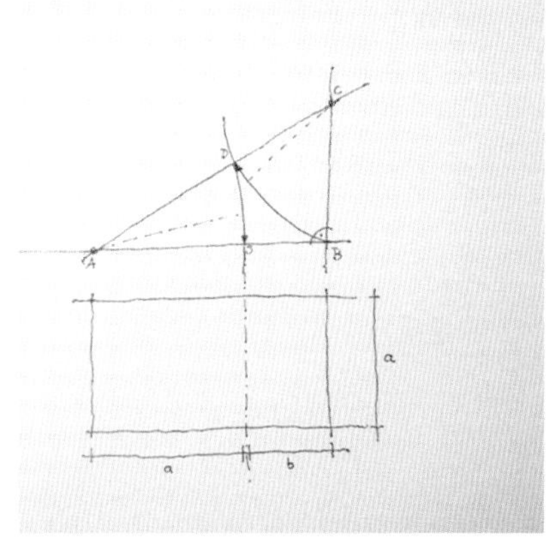

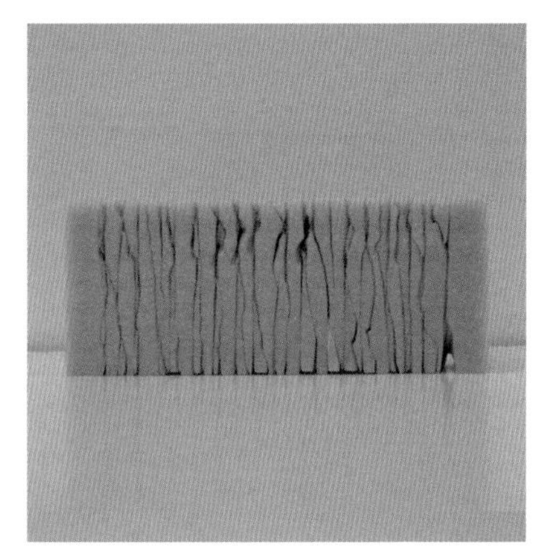

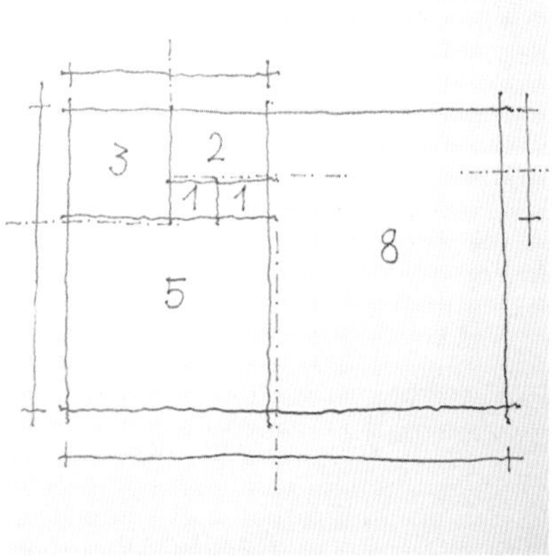

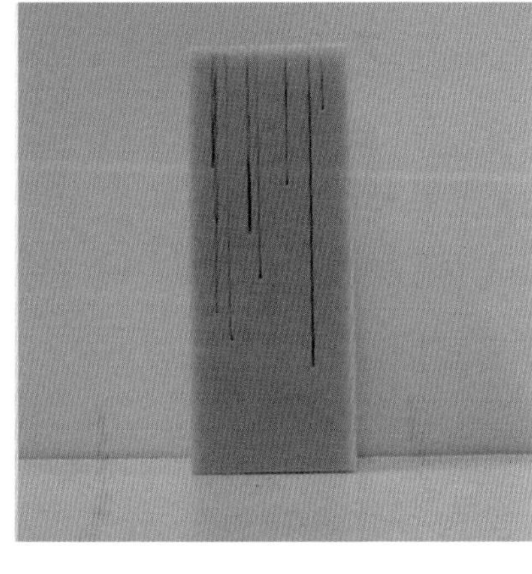

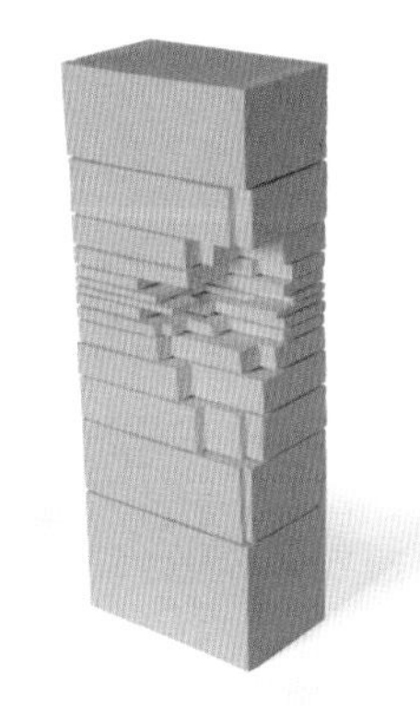

297

297 Different study models, sketches and renderings of subtractive design strategies on a rectangular solid incorporating rules of proportion (Fibonacci and Golden Section)

298

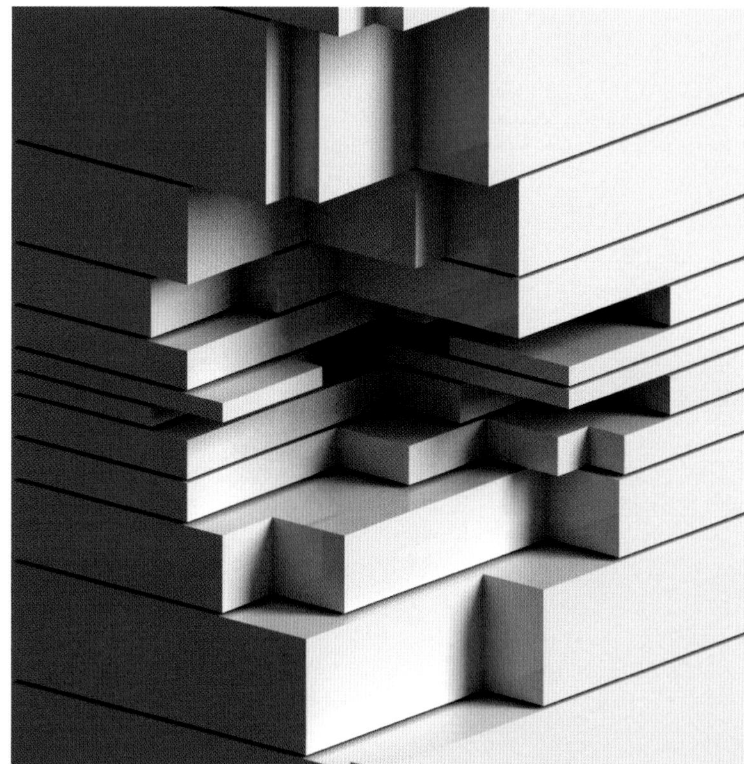

299

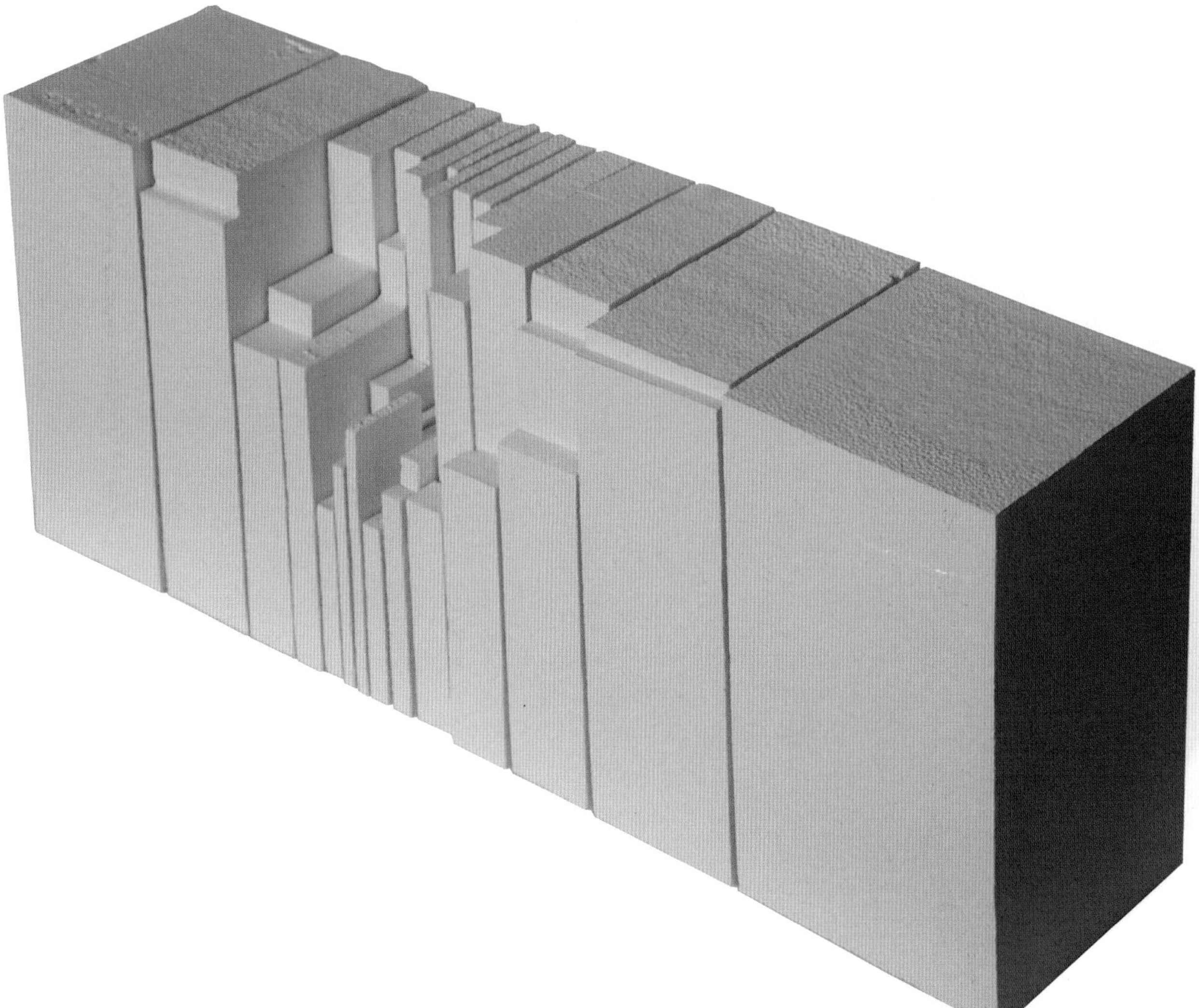

300

298 Embedding the cube into an urban context via a photomontage, determines its scale and dimensions

299 Close-up view
300 Physical styrofoam model

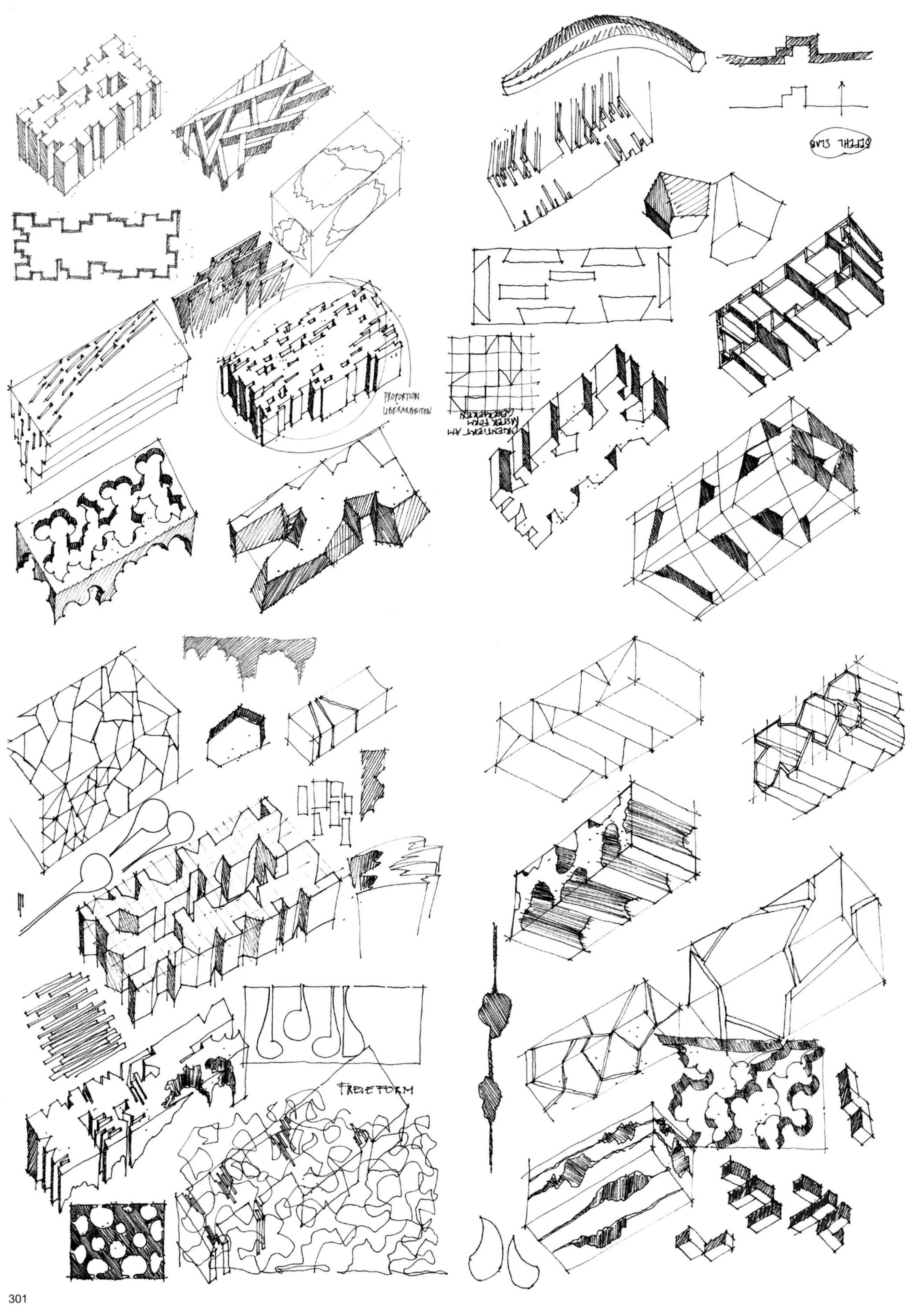

301

301 Conceptual sketches showing a number of different design ideas for a subtractive approach that that is leading to a sculptural solution

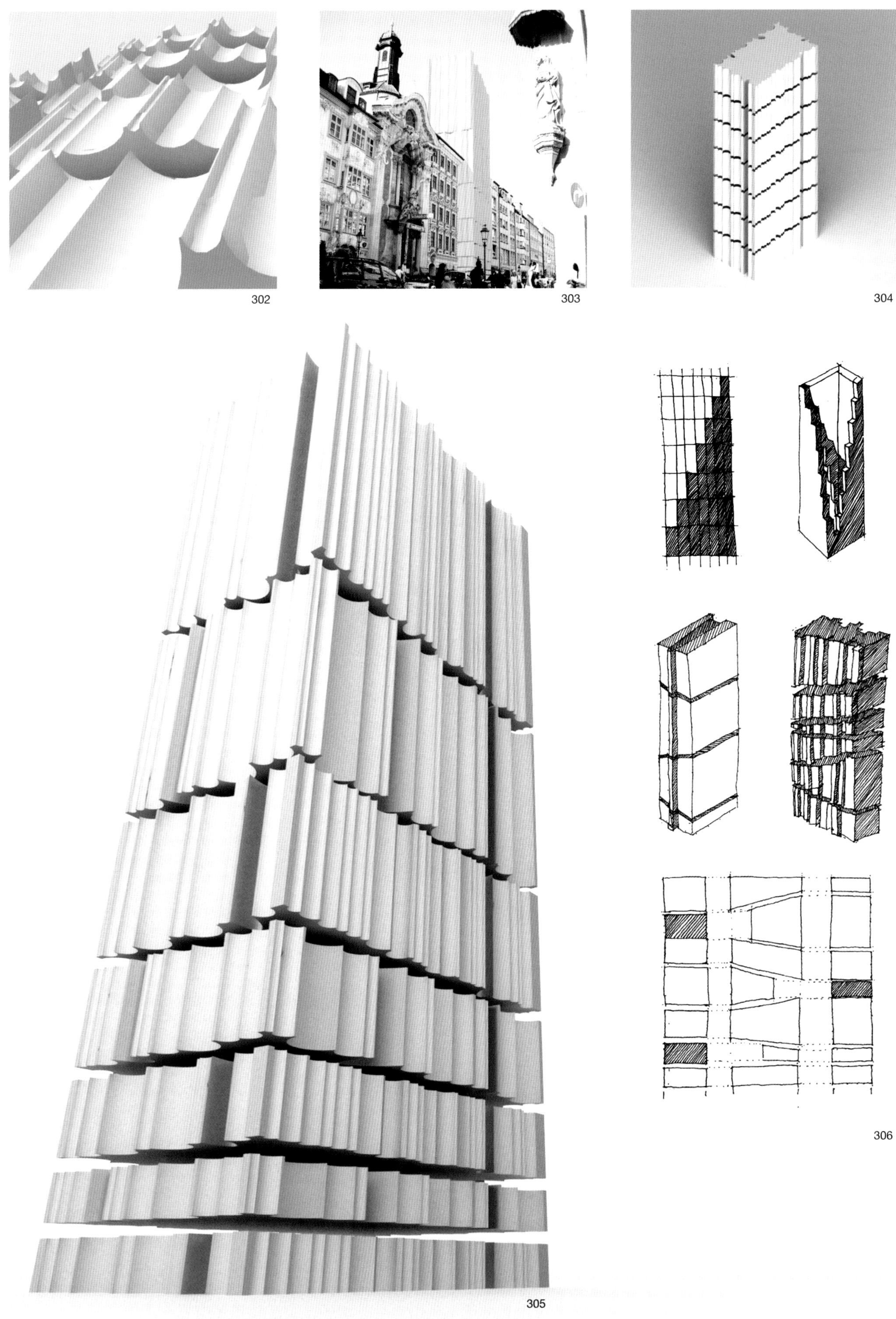

302 The subtractive operation of horizontal cuts subdivide the cubic volume. The undulating surface stimulates the external appearance

303 304 Different perspective renderings of the cube in fig. 305

306 Design development sketches showing different subtractive operations

307

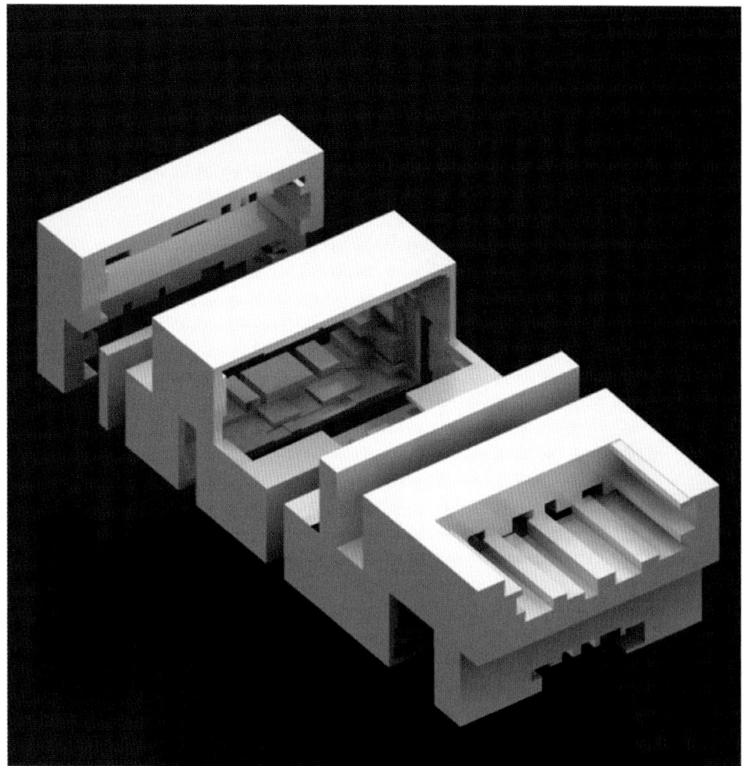

308

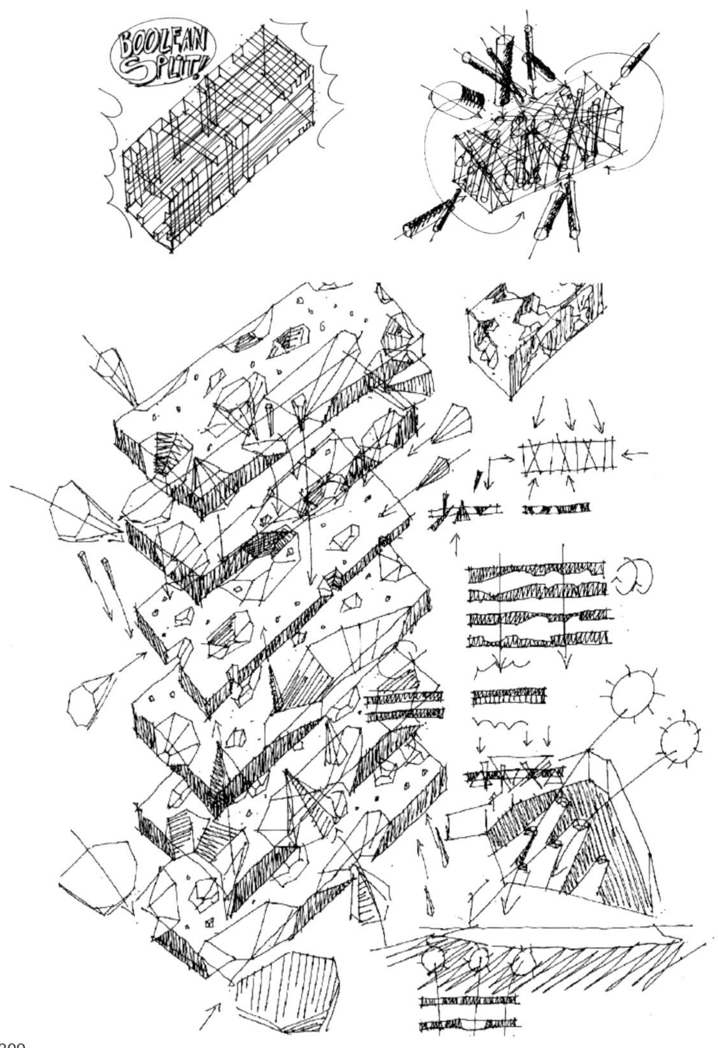

309

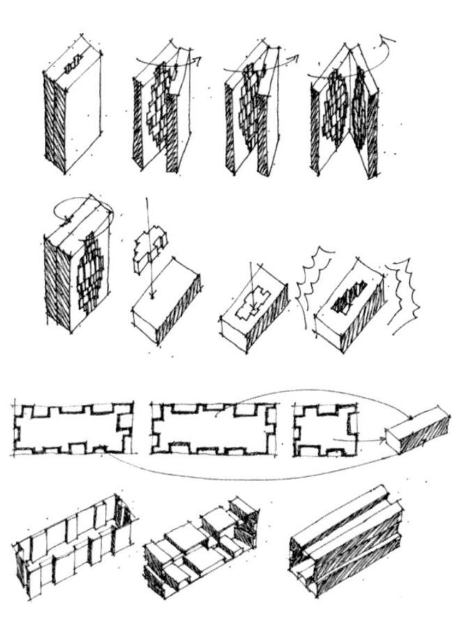

310

307 308 Volumetric sculpture. Advanced design development from the model in fig. 310

309 Hand sketches displaying the process of a boolean operation

310 Hand sketches showing the process of inverting the relationship between inside and outside which is the concept on most of the operations in this design work

311

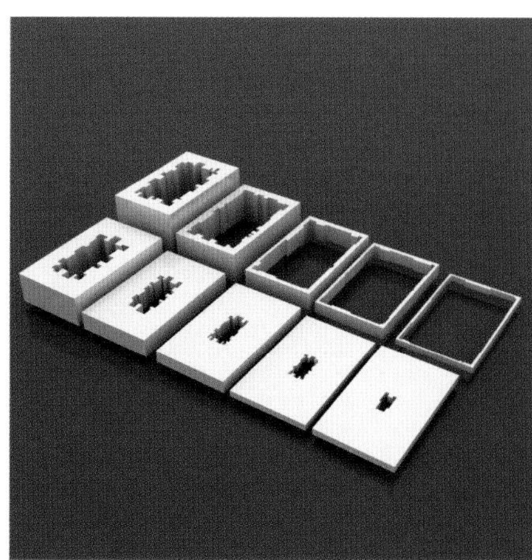

312

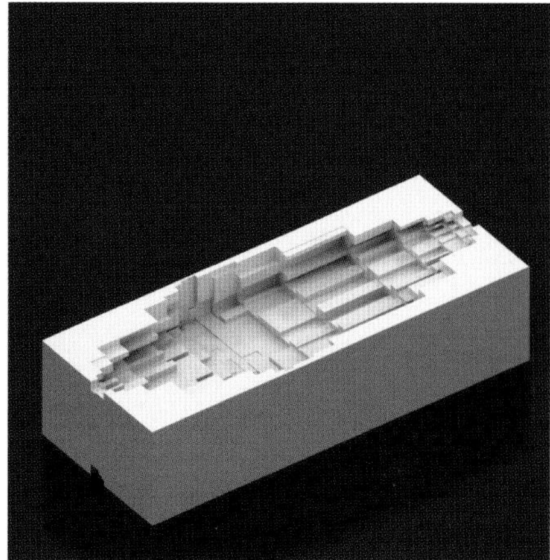

313

314

315

311 The laser-cut cardboard model illustrates the concept of varying inside and outside space relations through a cross-section of the sculpted volume

312 Digital model of fig. 311 cut vertically into slices of different spatial properties

313 Completed model from fig. 311
314 315 Digital and physical model details

316

317

318

319

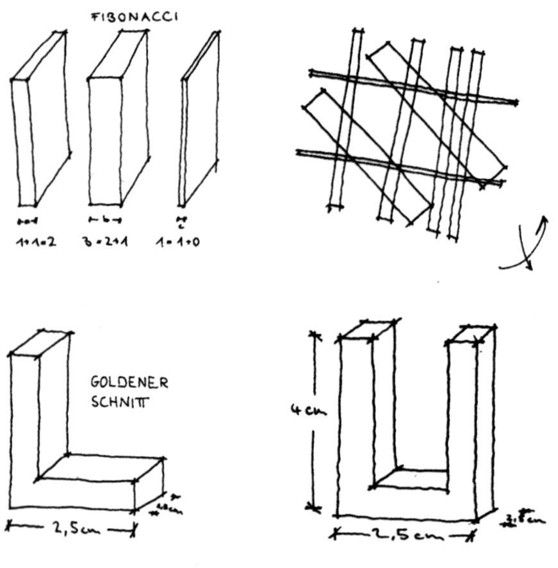

320

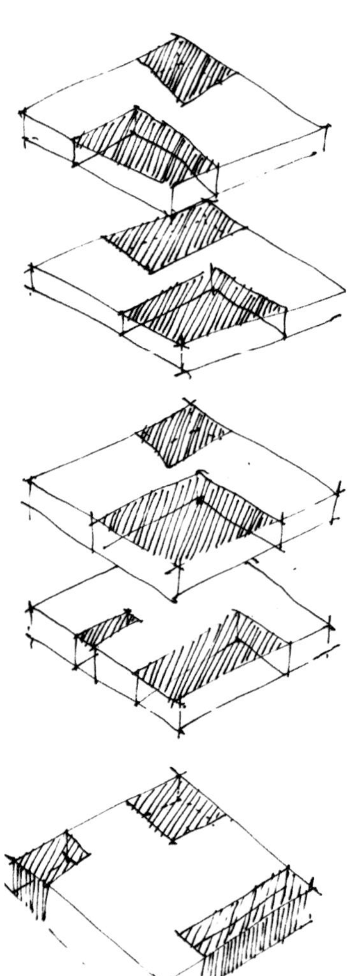
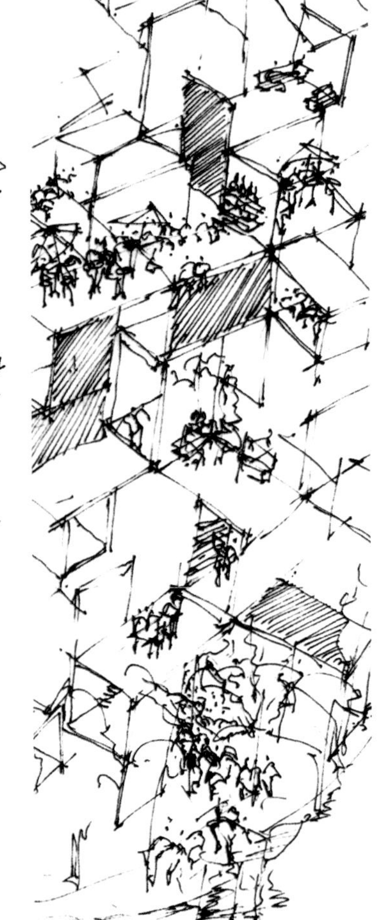
321

316 317 318 Similar design themes with different proportional ratios and densities

319 320 Design development sketches and proportional studies
321 Design studies with a subtractive approach on the left and additive design on the right

322

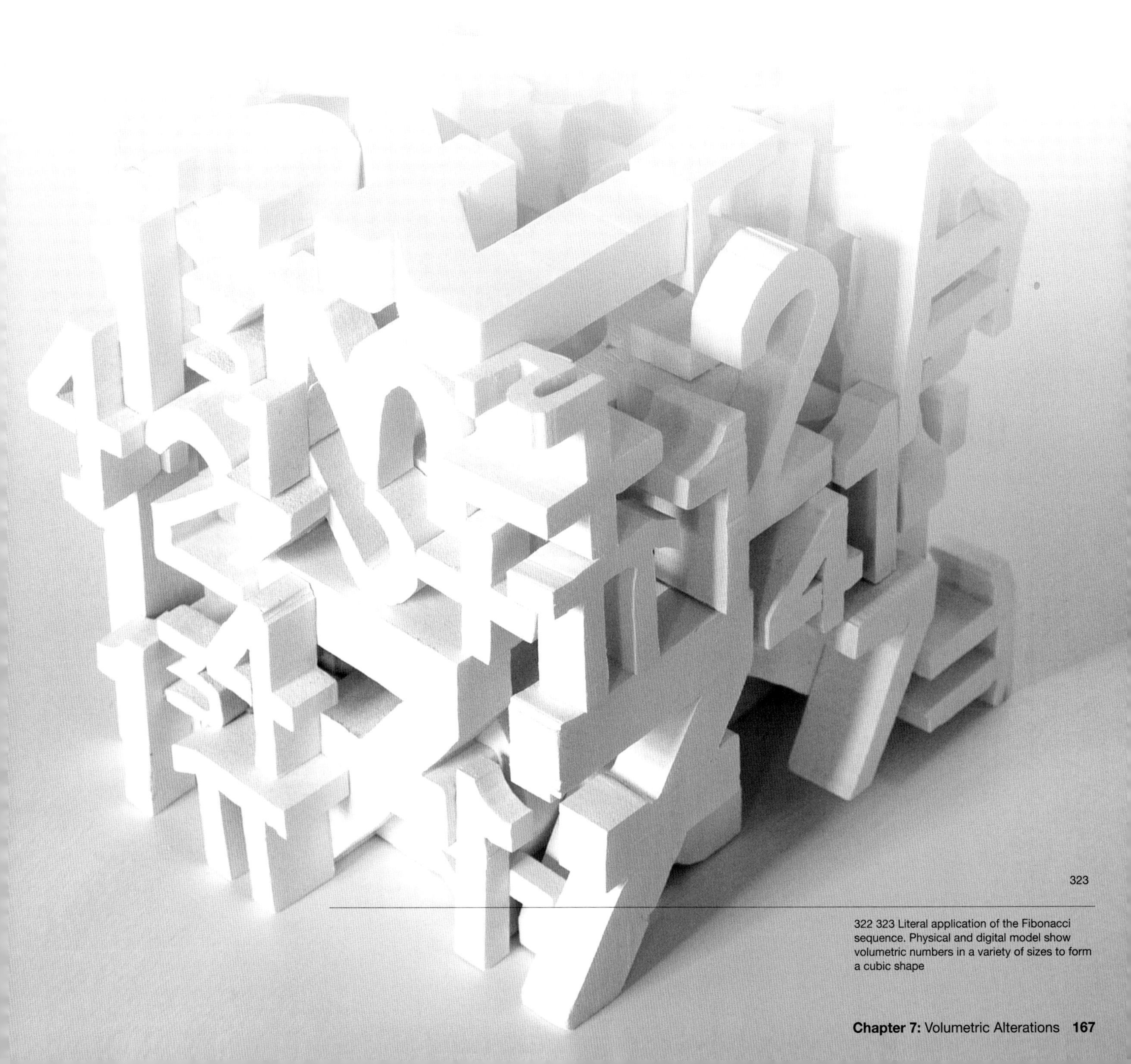

323

322 323 Literal application of the Fibonacci sequence. Physical and digital model show volumetric numbers in a variety of sizes to form a cubic shape

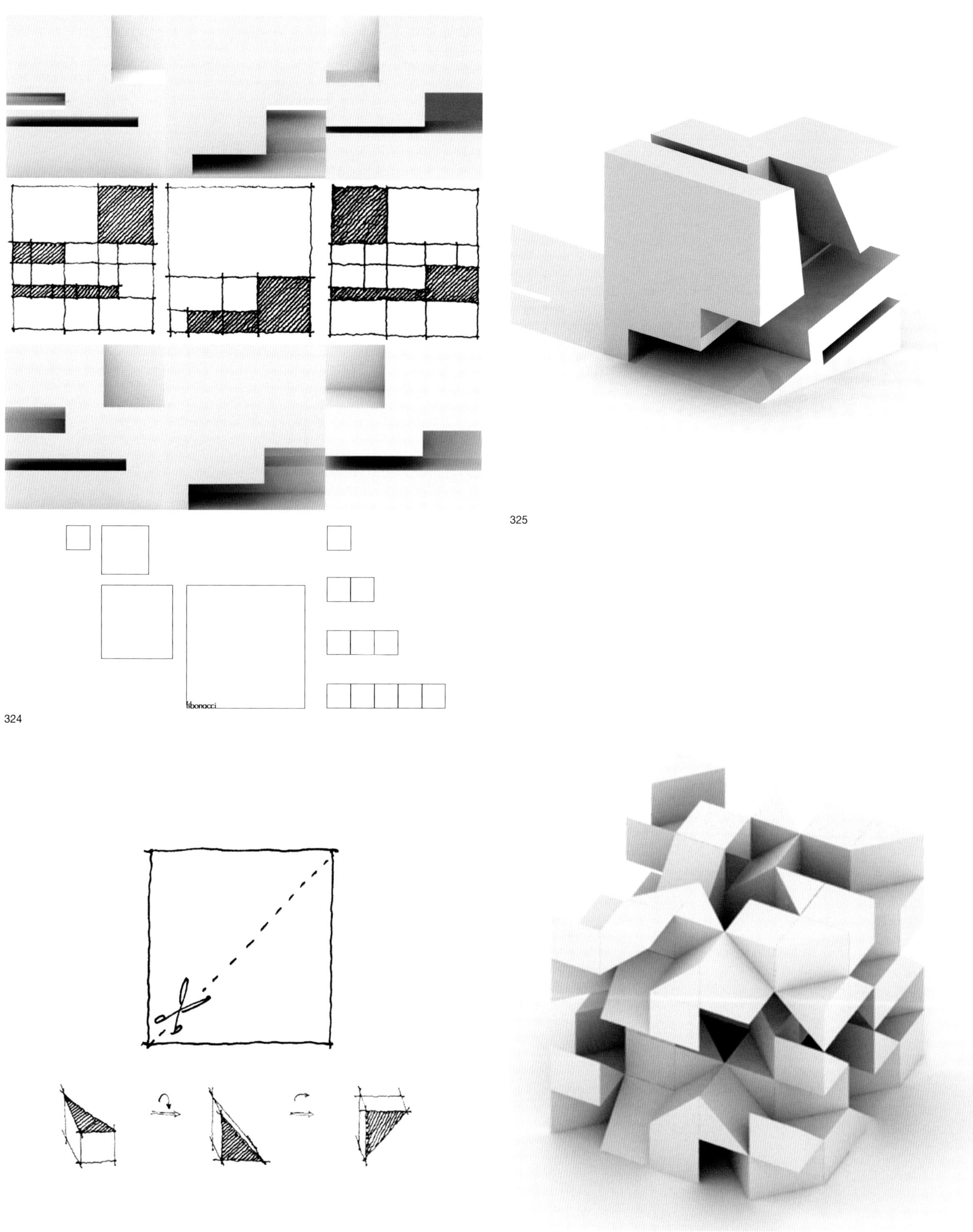

324 Elevation studies of different proportions
325 Cube on the basis of fig. 324

326 Triangular modul
327 Cube consisting of a single triangular module in altered orientations and alignments

328 The rectangular solid is split up by random diagonal cuts thus leaving some elements detached
329 Conceptual sketch
330 Same volume then fig. 327 but before proportional revision
331 Photomontage into an urban surrounding

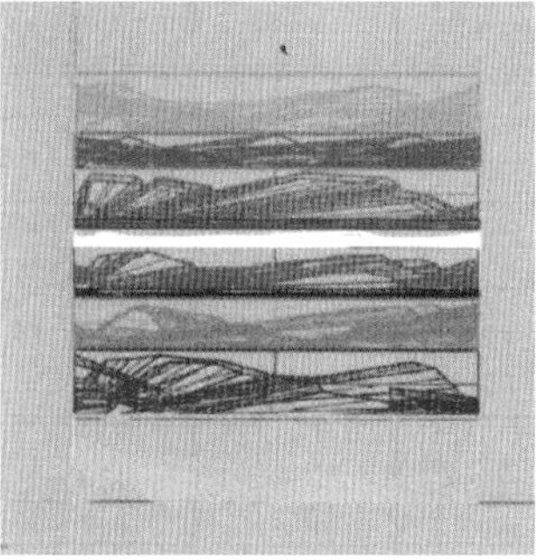

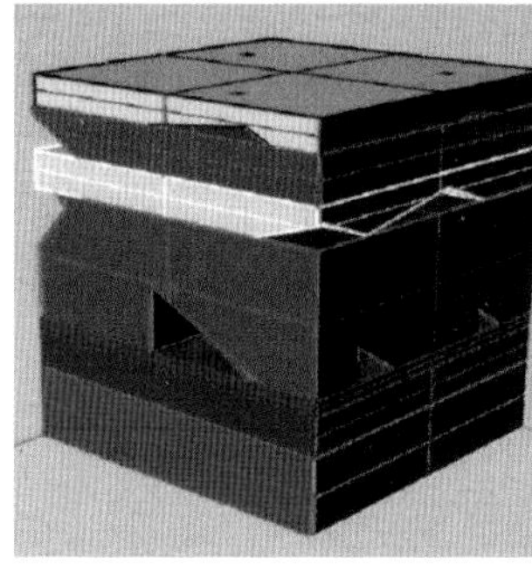

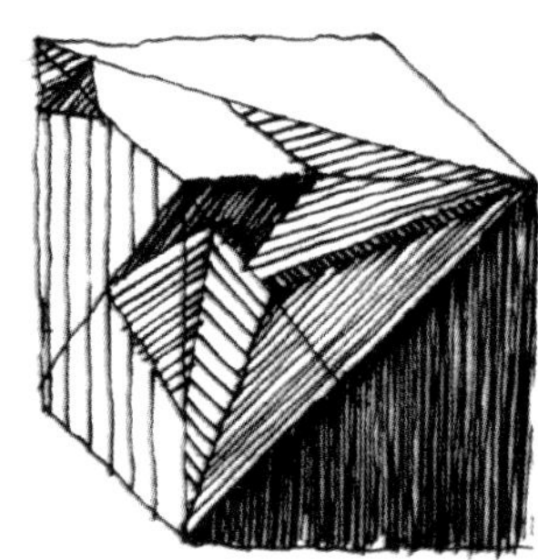
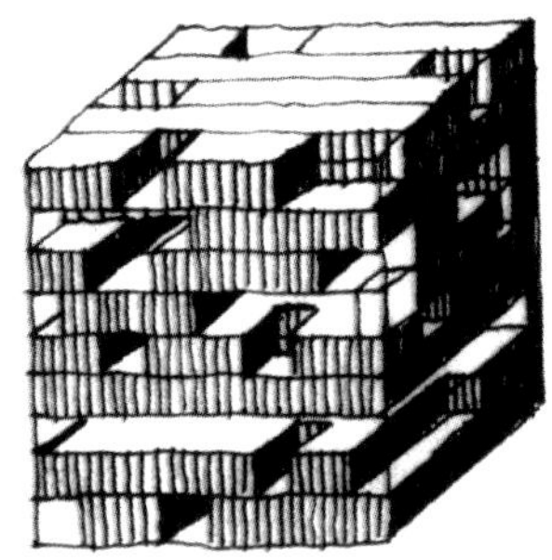
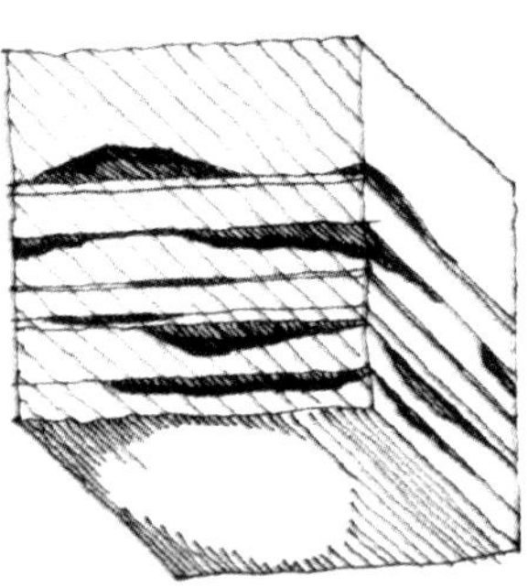

332

333

332 Design process through hand drawings and intermediate digital steps

333 Horizontal layering of amorphously modulated sections that are even towards their top

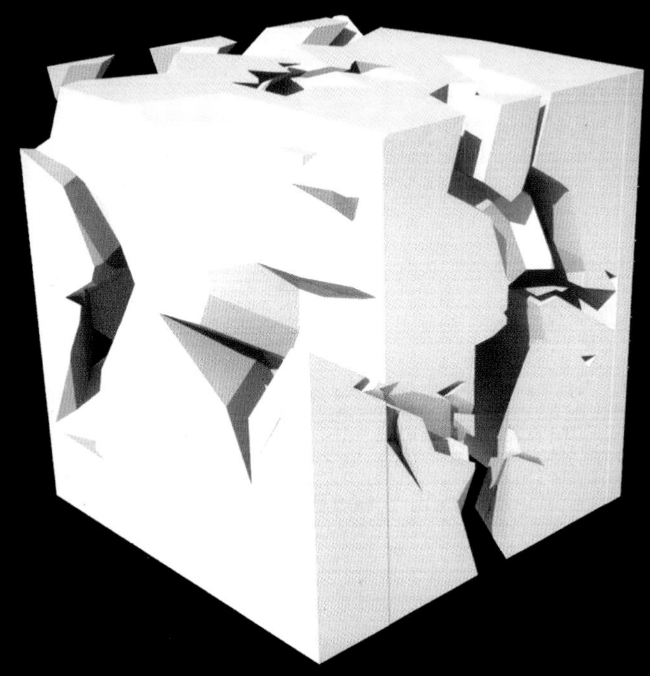

334

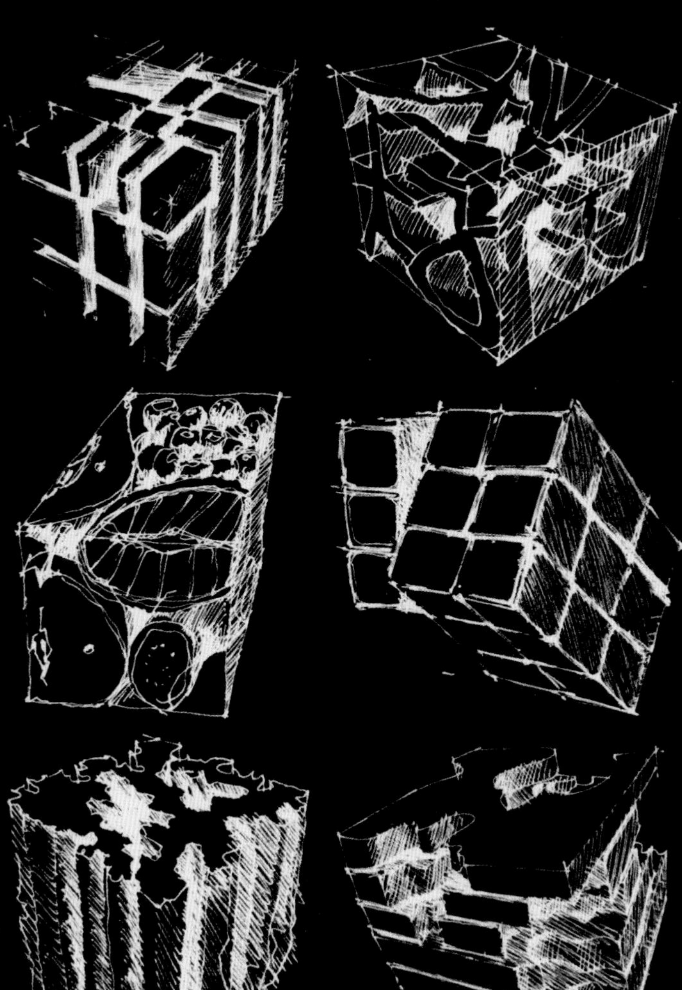

335

336

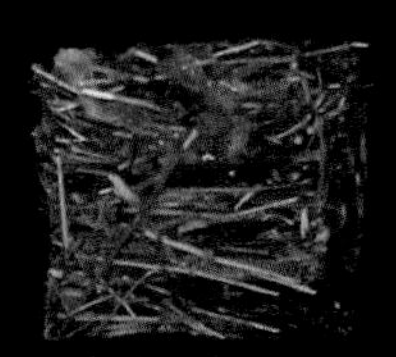

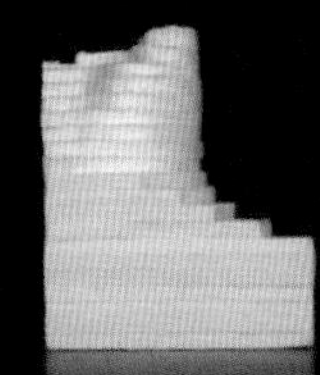

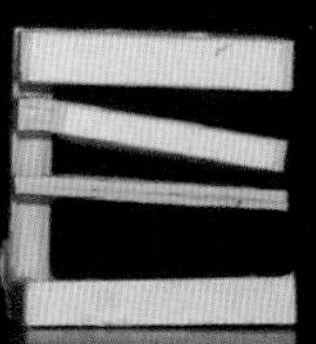

334 Organic structure
335 Study sketches on subtractive and additive design strategies

336 Working models of different design approaches

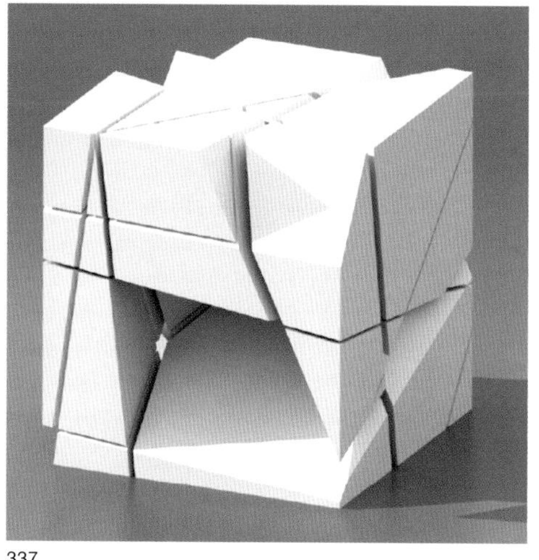
337

338

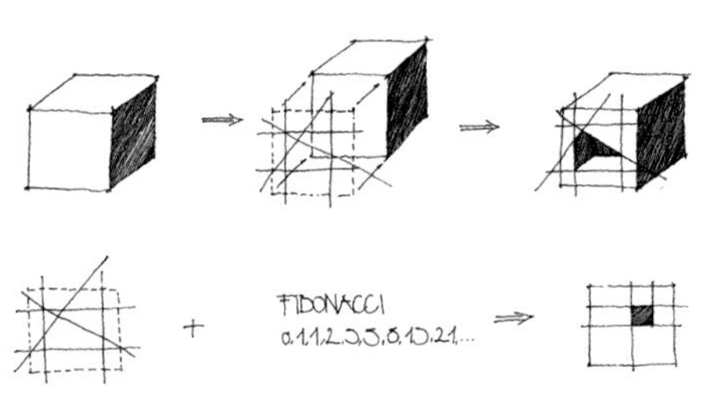

339

340

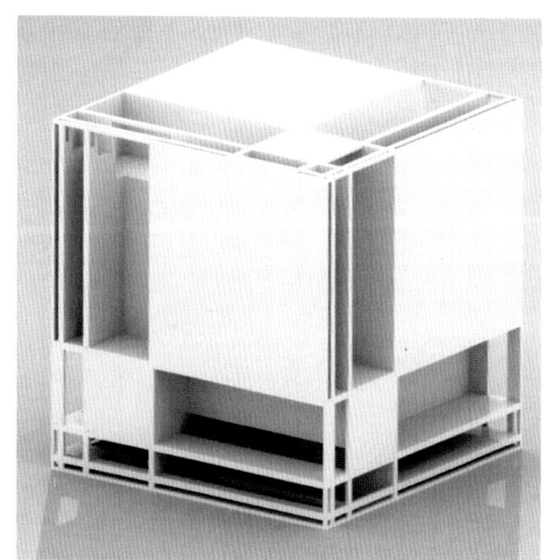
341

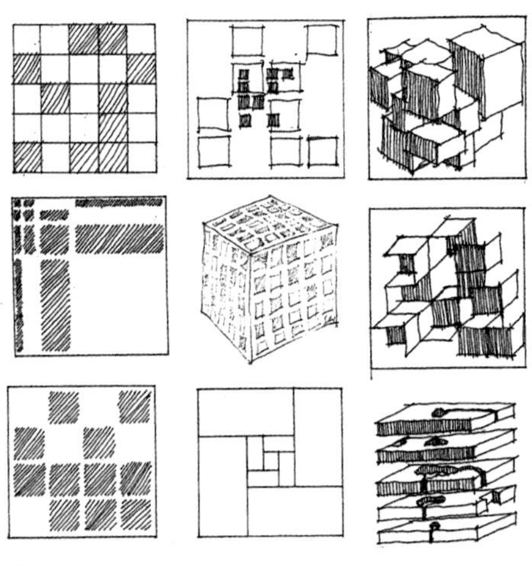
342

337 338 339 Intuitive design and redesign according to proportional theories

340 341 342 Spatial cube design before and after proportional editing

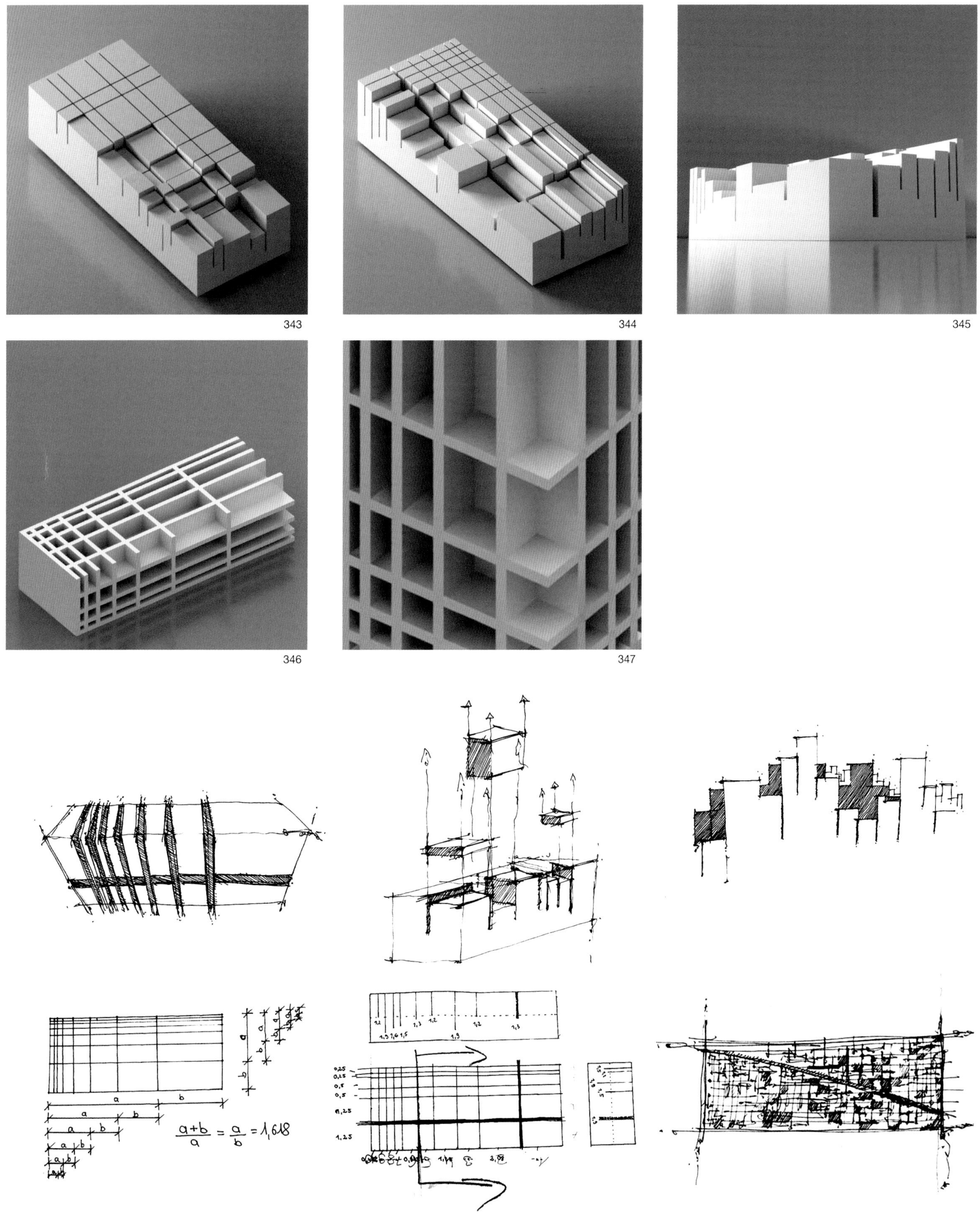

343 344 Before and after the implementation of the Fibonacci Sequence
345 *Pedestrian* perspective of fig. 344

346 347 Spatial structure derived from the negative form of fig. 343

348 Sketches of various proportional and conceptional studies

349

350

351

352

349 350 351 Corroded cuboid evoking the image of insect or shotgun like piercing

352 Design sketch of core module

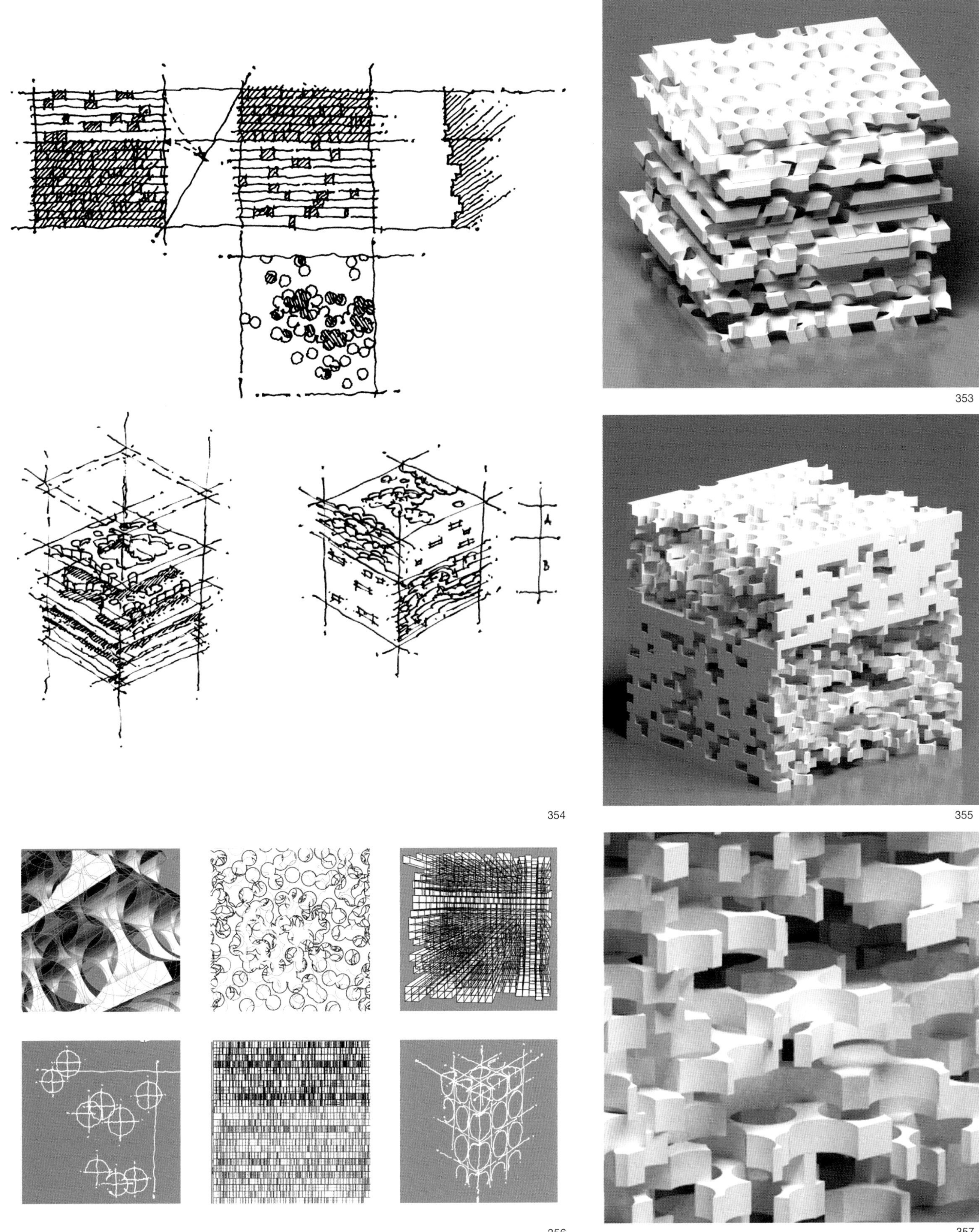

353 A hybrid in between an additive an subtractive design strategy: stacked slabs with randomly punctured round holes form an interesting cube

354 Sketches showing the design process of fig. 355

355 Further development of fig. 353: façades are arranged in correlation to the golden section

356 Intermediate process images

357 Close-up view revealing the interesting spatial structure

358

359

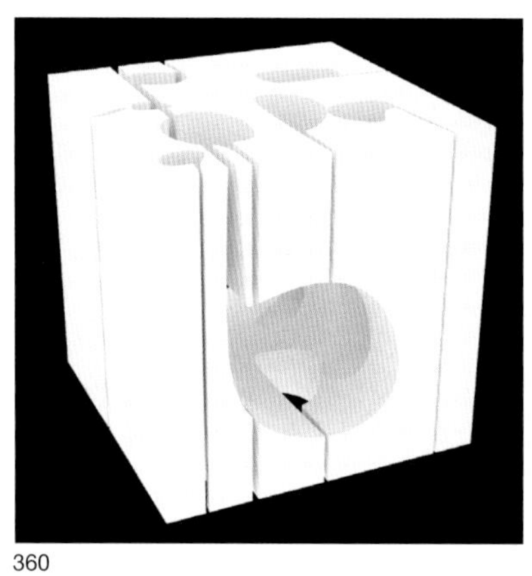

360

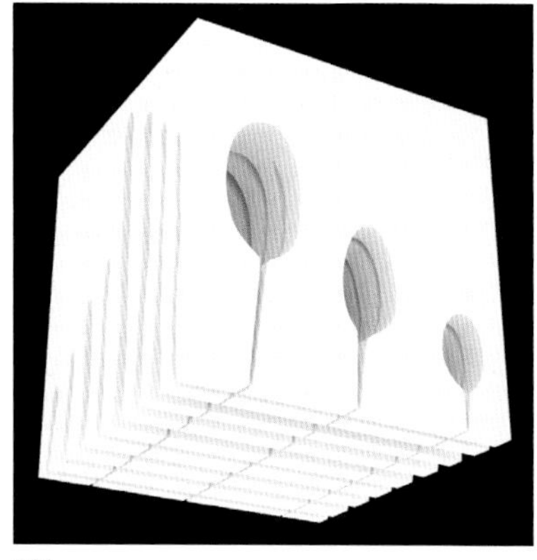

361

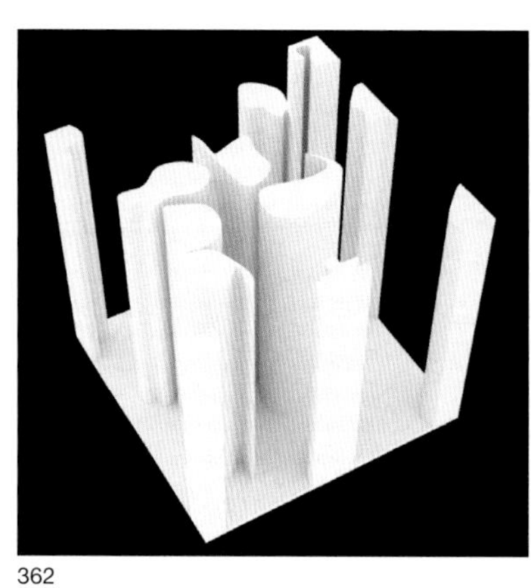

362

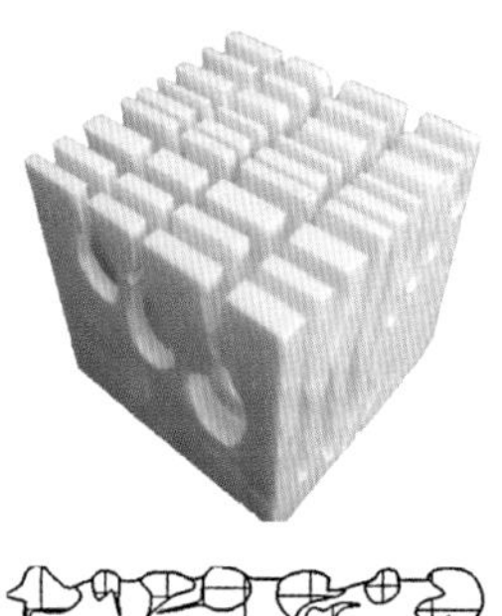

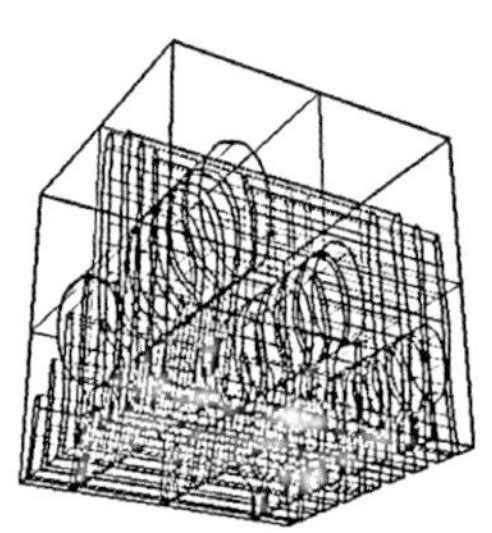

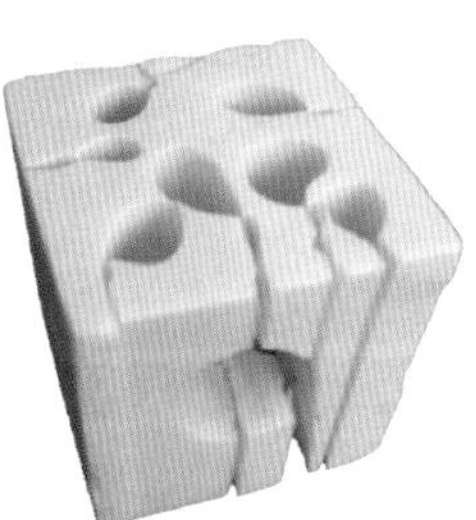

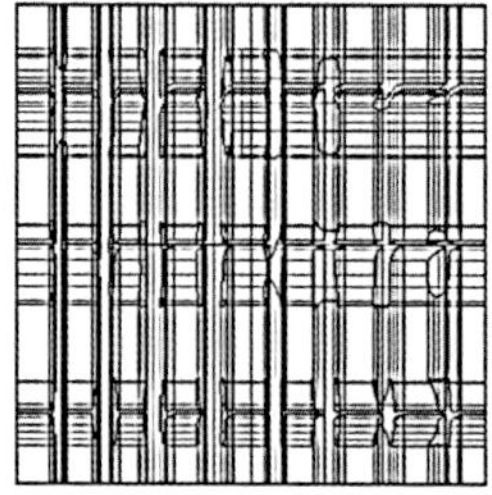

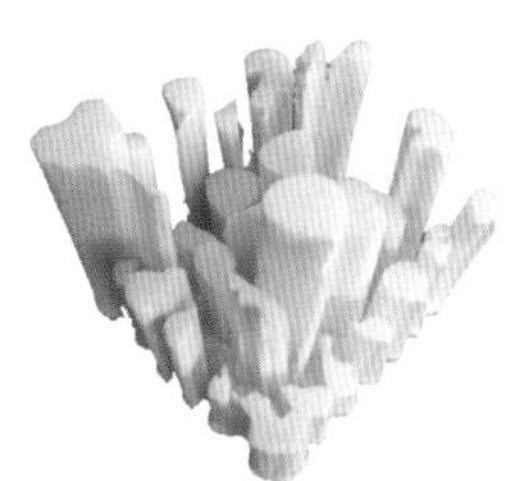

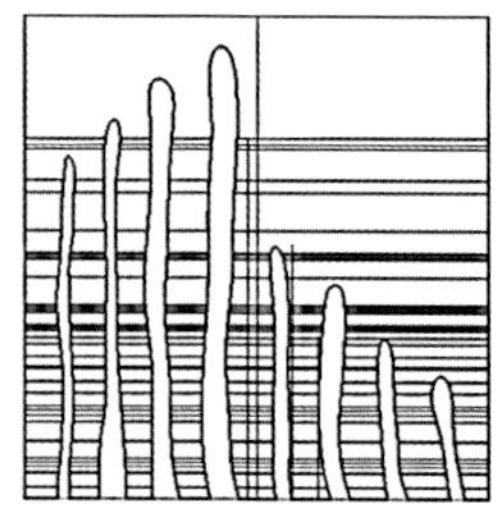

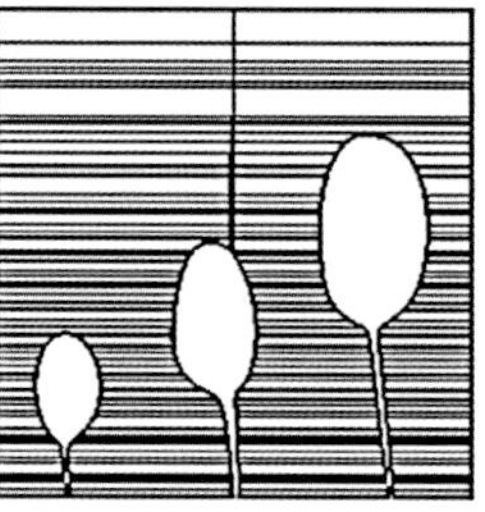

363

358 Subtractive design, physical clay model

359 Joining of self-similar structures with variations in height, density and proportion optimizes the design quality of the overall configuration

360 361 Renderings of subtractive cube before and after proportional revision
362 Base of fig. 359
363 preparatory steps for fig. 359 - 362

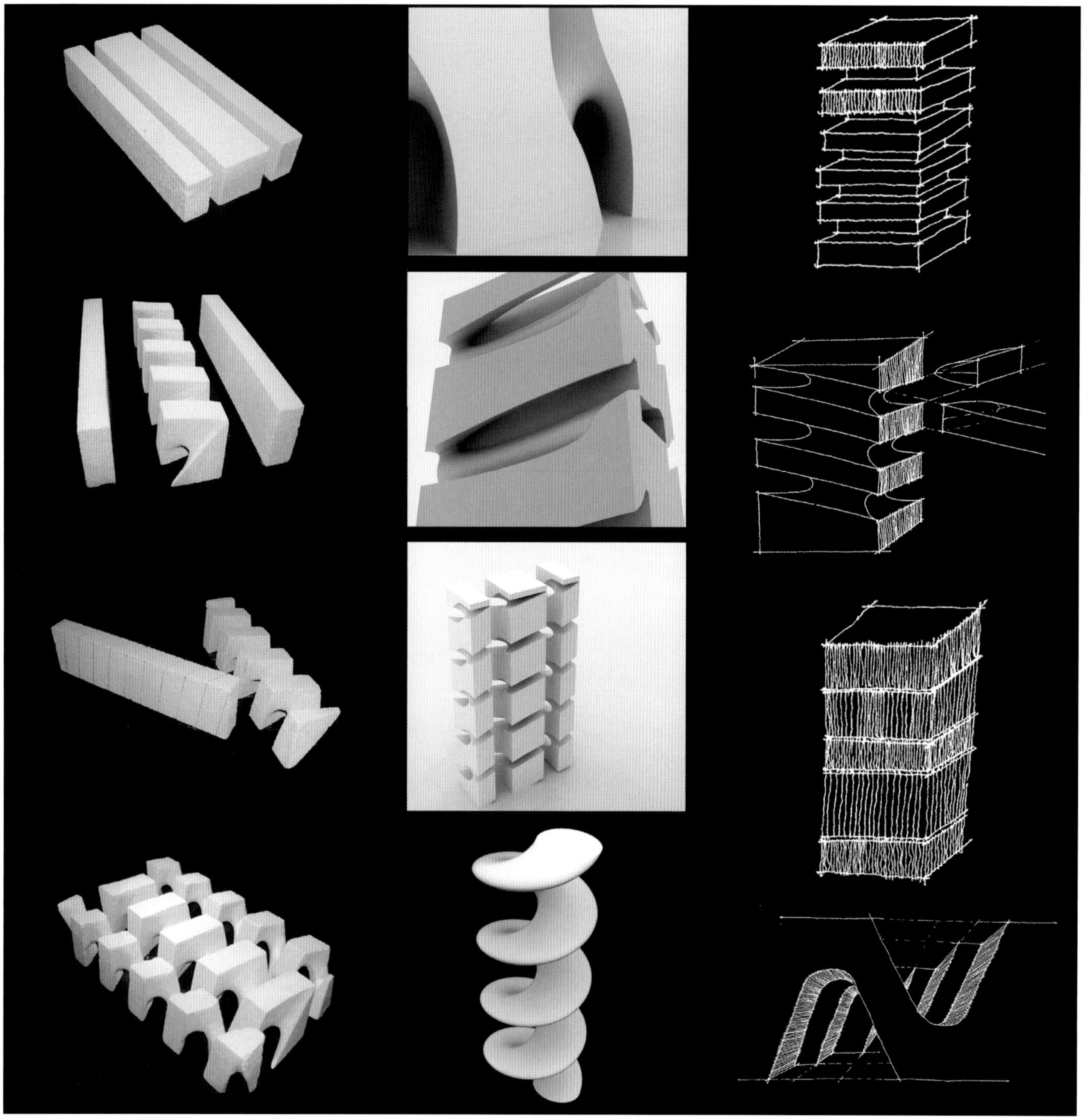

364

365

366

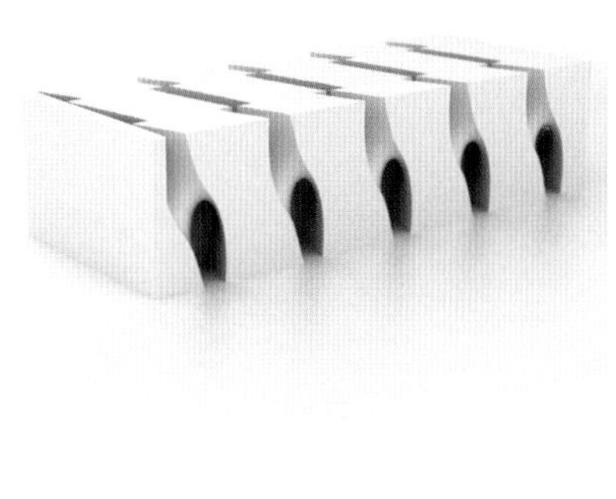

367

364 Studies on the boolean intersection of a spiral-shaped volume and a rectangular solid using various media: physical modell, digital model and drawing

365 Photomontage: Scale and context provide a first image where a concrete architectural implementation becomes conceivable

366 367 The same spatial configuration is perceived much differently depending on vertical or horizontal positioning

368

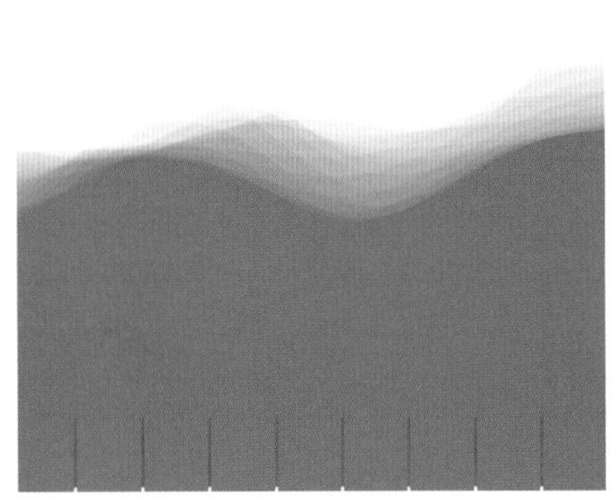

369

370

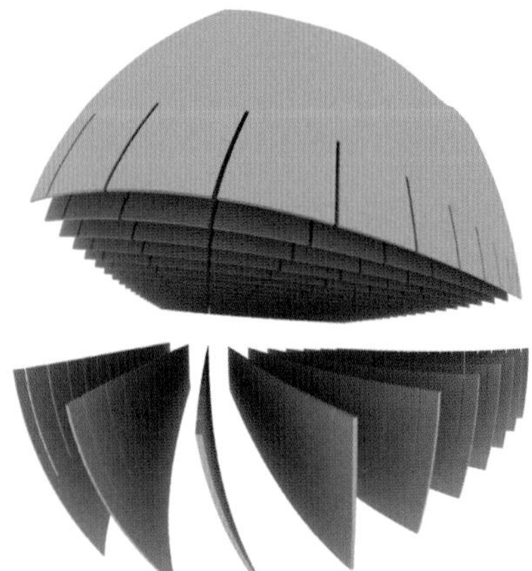

371

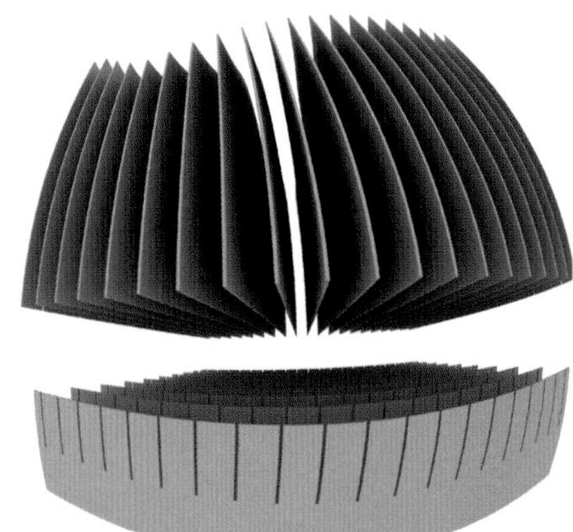

372

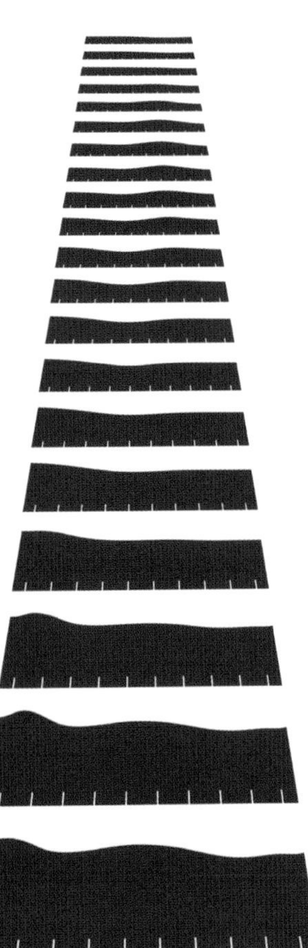

373

368 Fractured shape
369 Blurring of staggered layers evokes depth effect in elevation

370 Topographic landscape design
371 372 The fish eye effect allows to frame a specific view within the exploded model

373 Array of planes

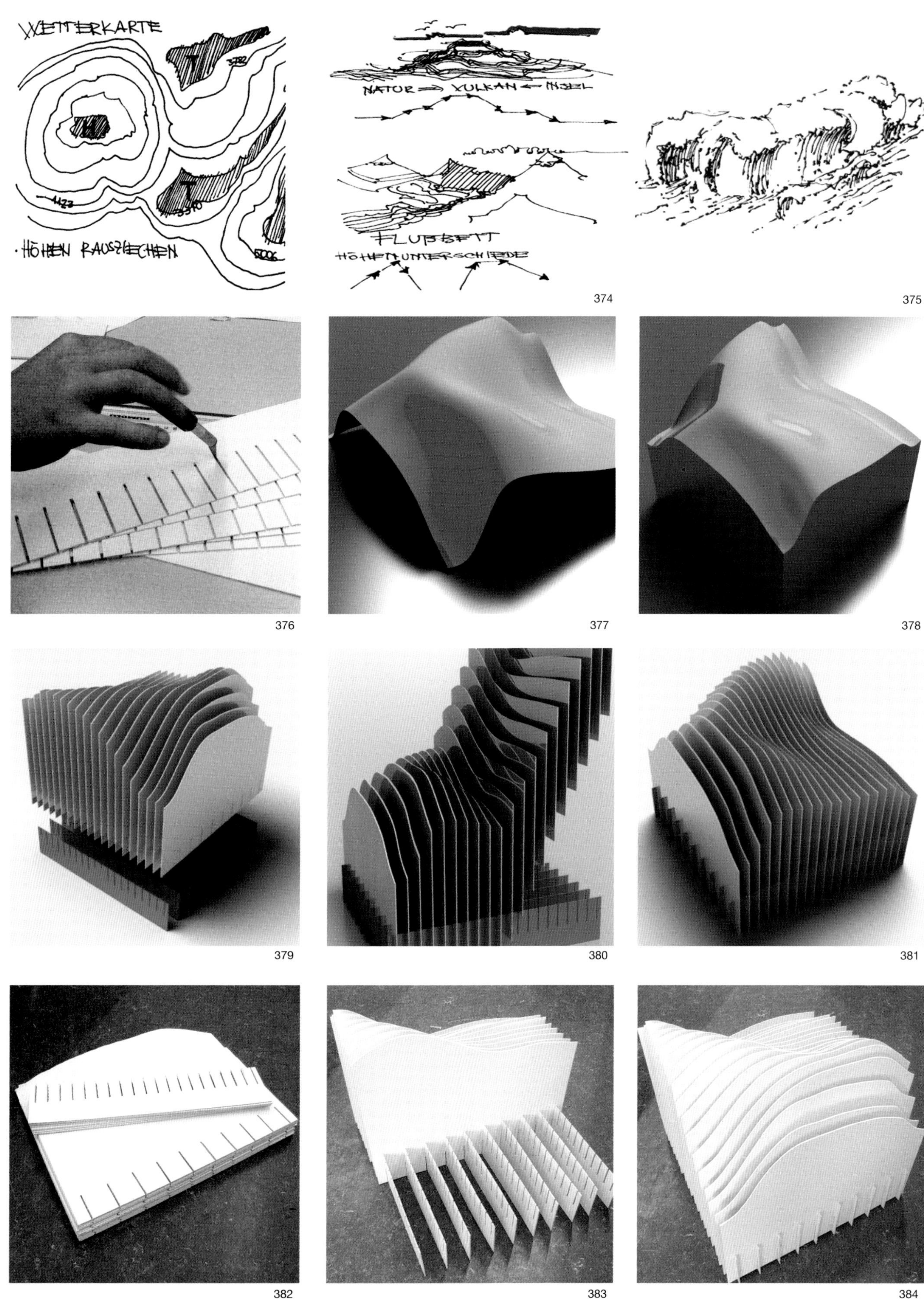

374 375 Sketches of sources of inspiration for the design of curved surfaces

376- 384 Digital and manual production steps

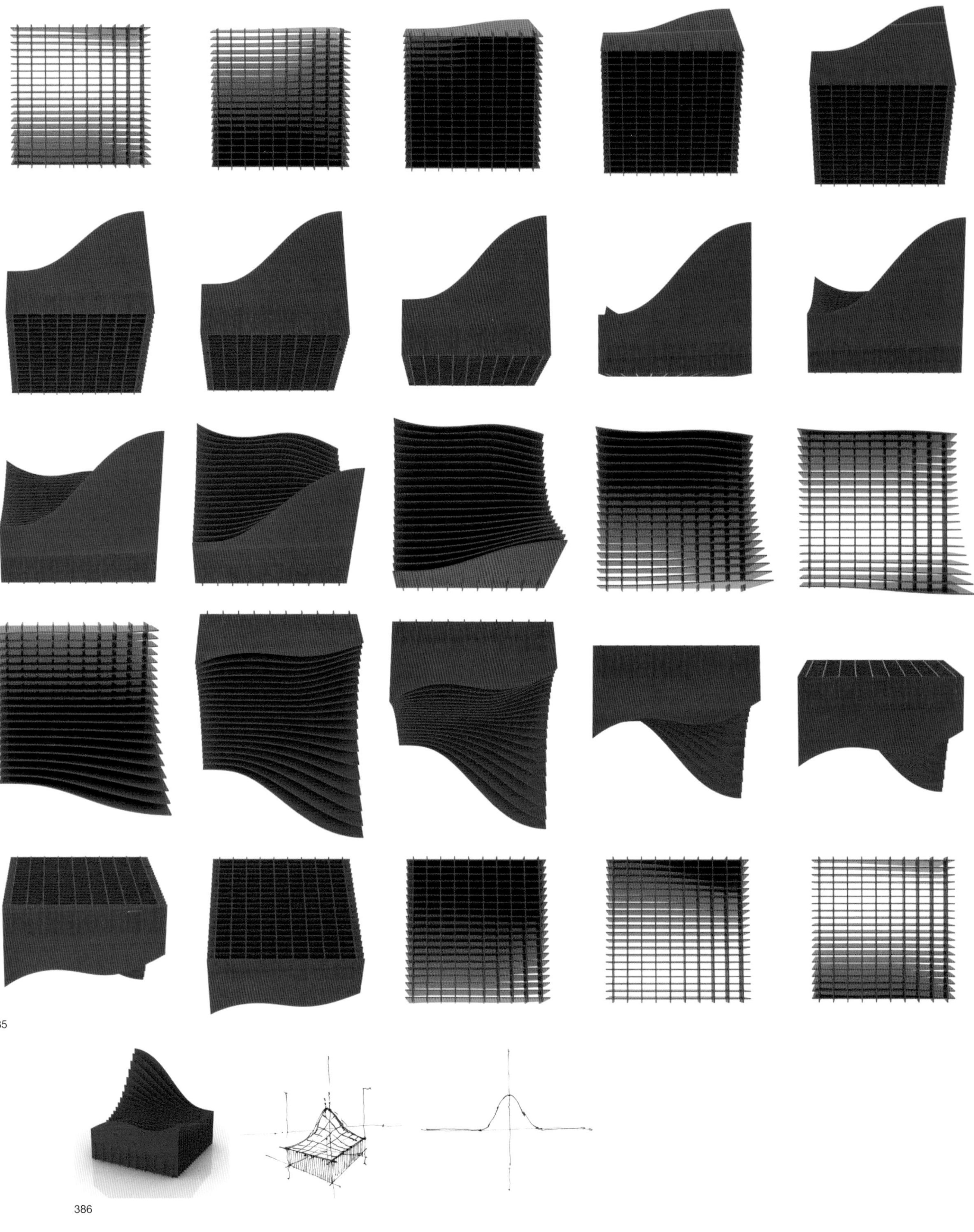

385

386

385 Series: Rotatiing spatial element structured by a regular grid pattern
386 Perspective and conceptual sketches

387

388

389

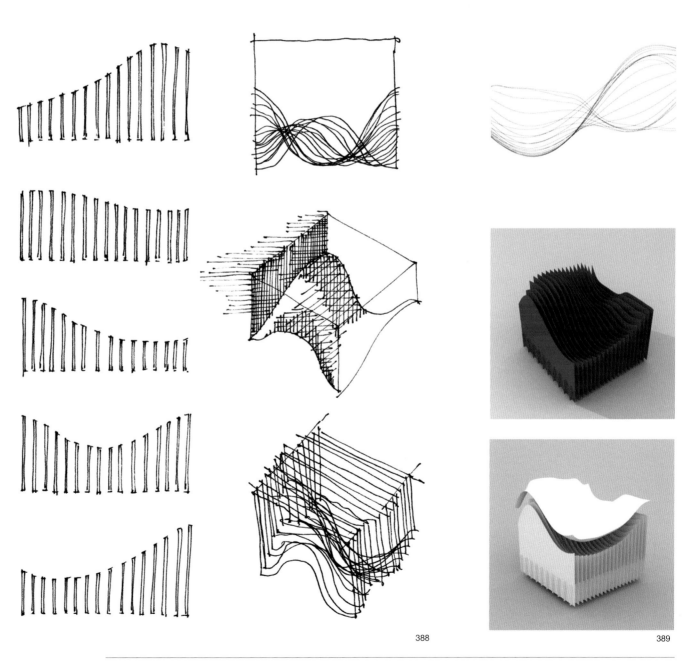

387 Initial concept sketch

388 389 Development of a double curved topography in section and perspective

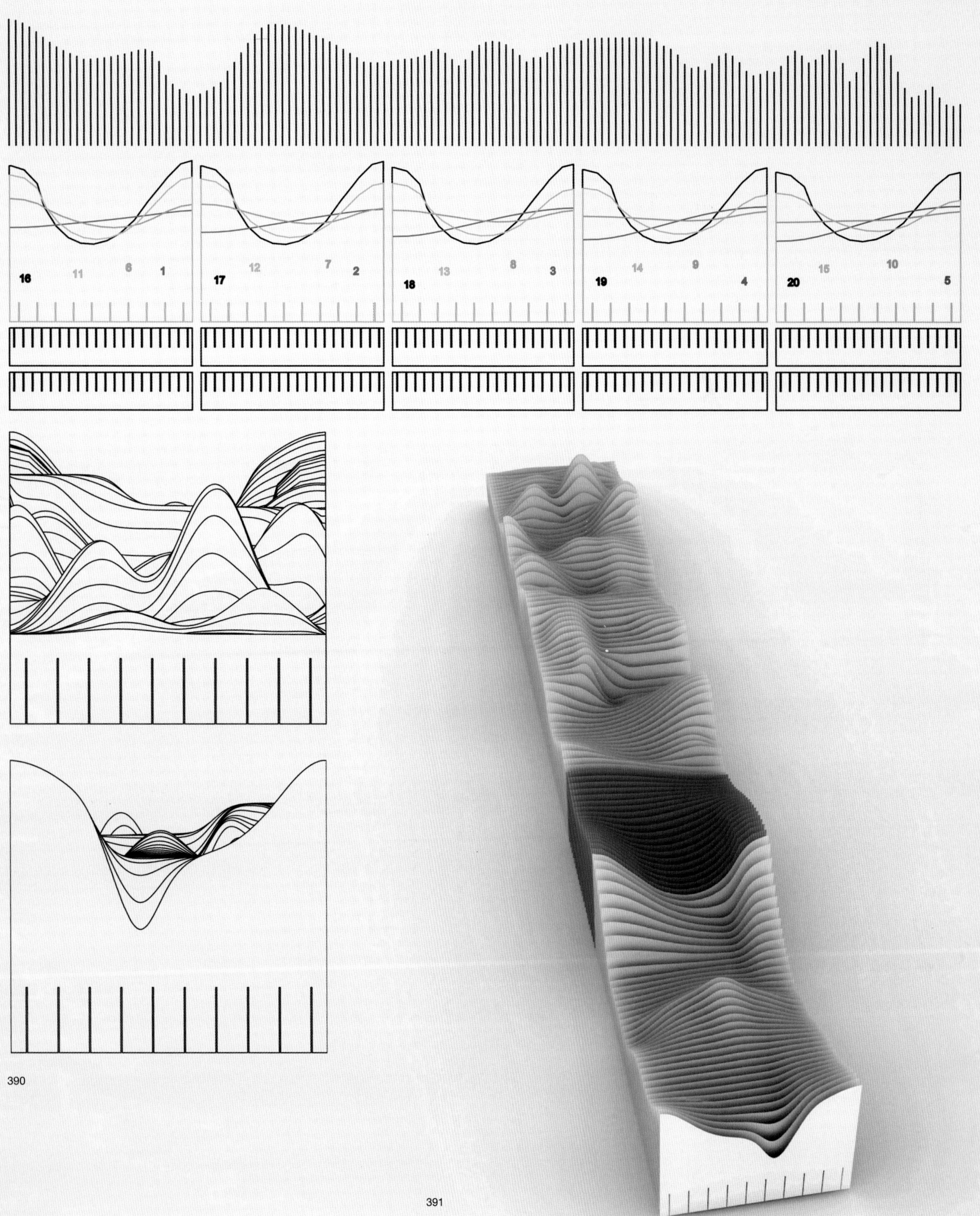

390 Digital templates for fig. 391
391 Digital model of completed sectional topography

392

393

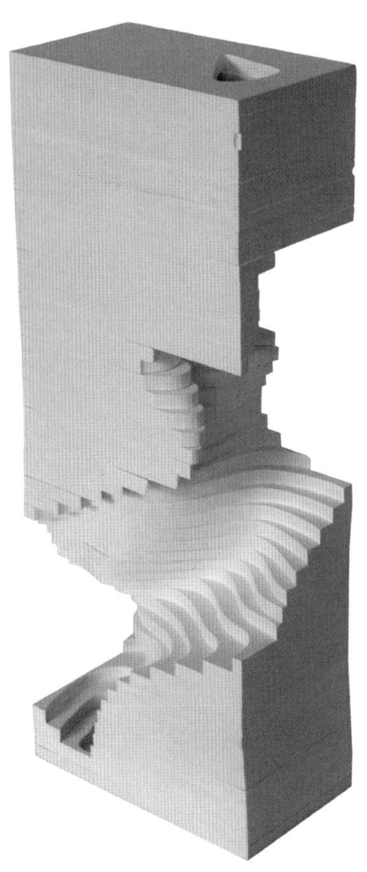
396

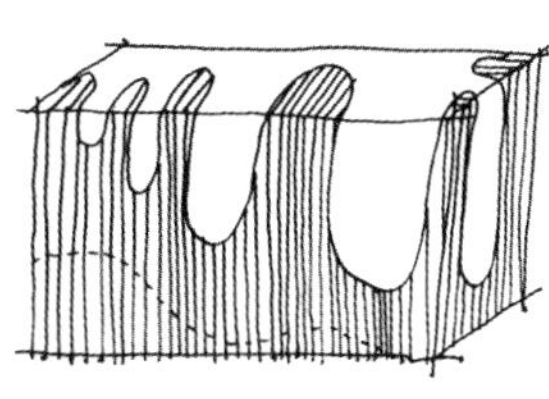
394

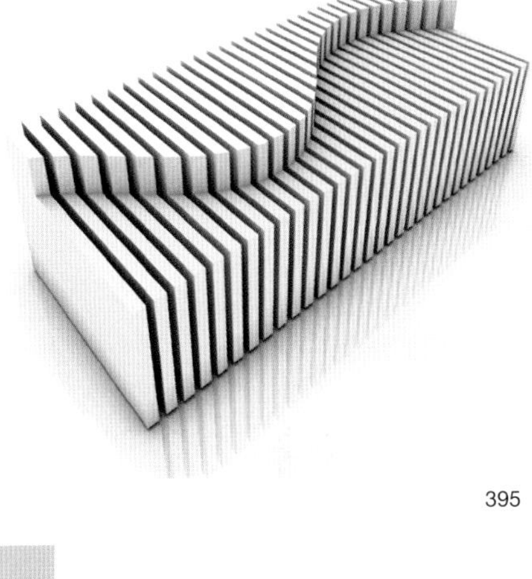
395

397

398

392 393 Studies on dynamic space entities by rotating slabs along an axis

394 395 Preliminary design studies for the sculpture in fig. 396

396 397 398 Physical and digital model of layered slabs that were a subtracted by a curved solid form a sophisticated flowing space

399

400

399 Color coded templates and physical model
400 Layered cardboard creating a dynamic landscape

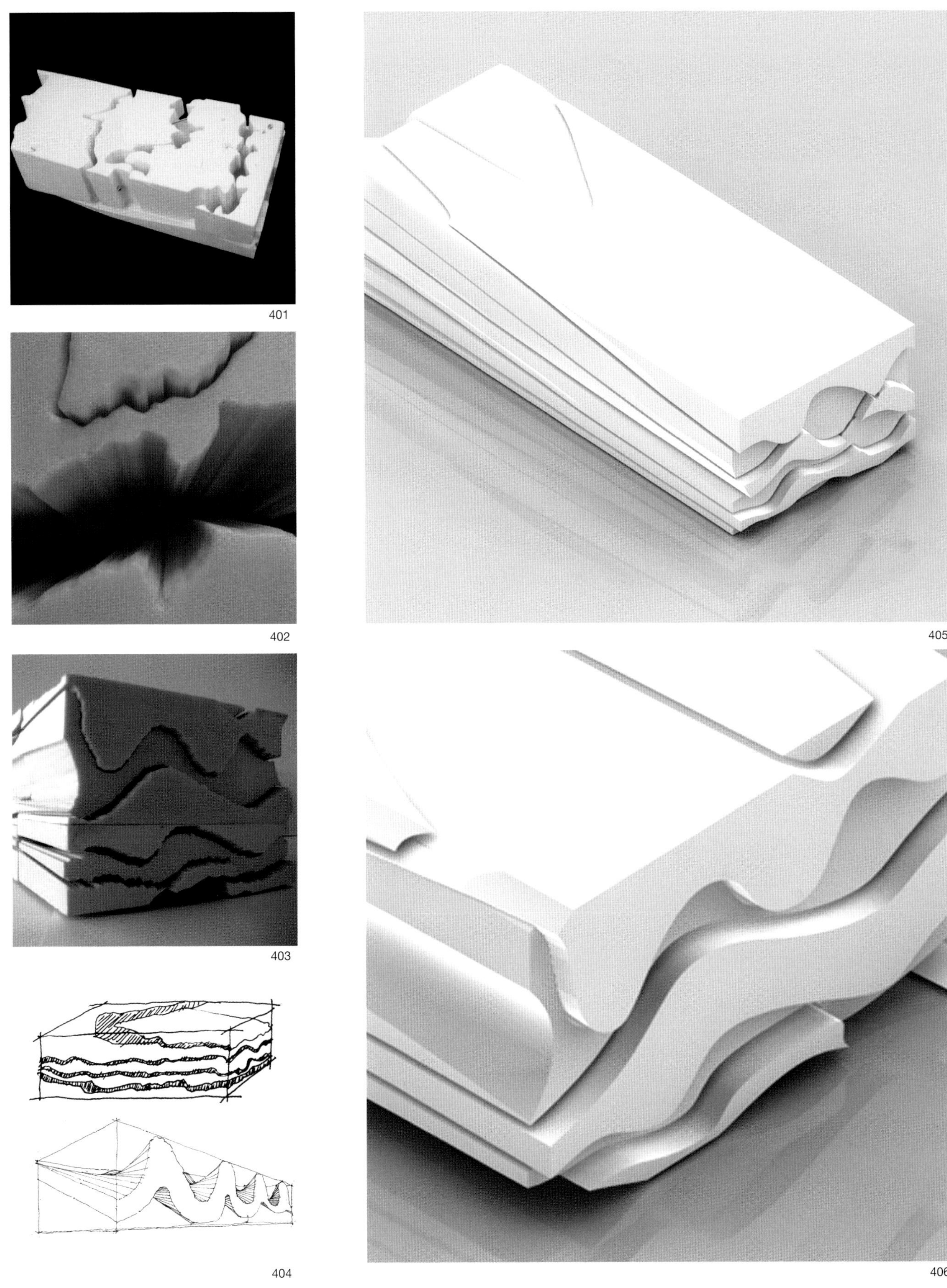

401

402

403

404

405

406

401 402 403 Styrofoam models with morphed cleft

404 preliminary considerations

405 406 Rectangular shape split into successive biomorphic sections

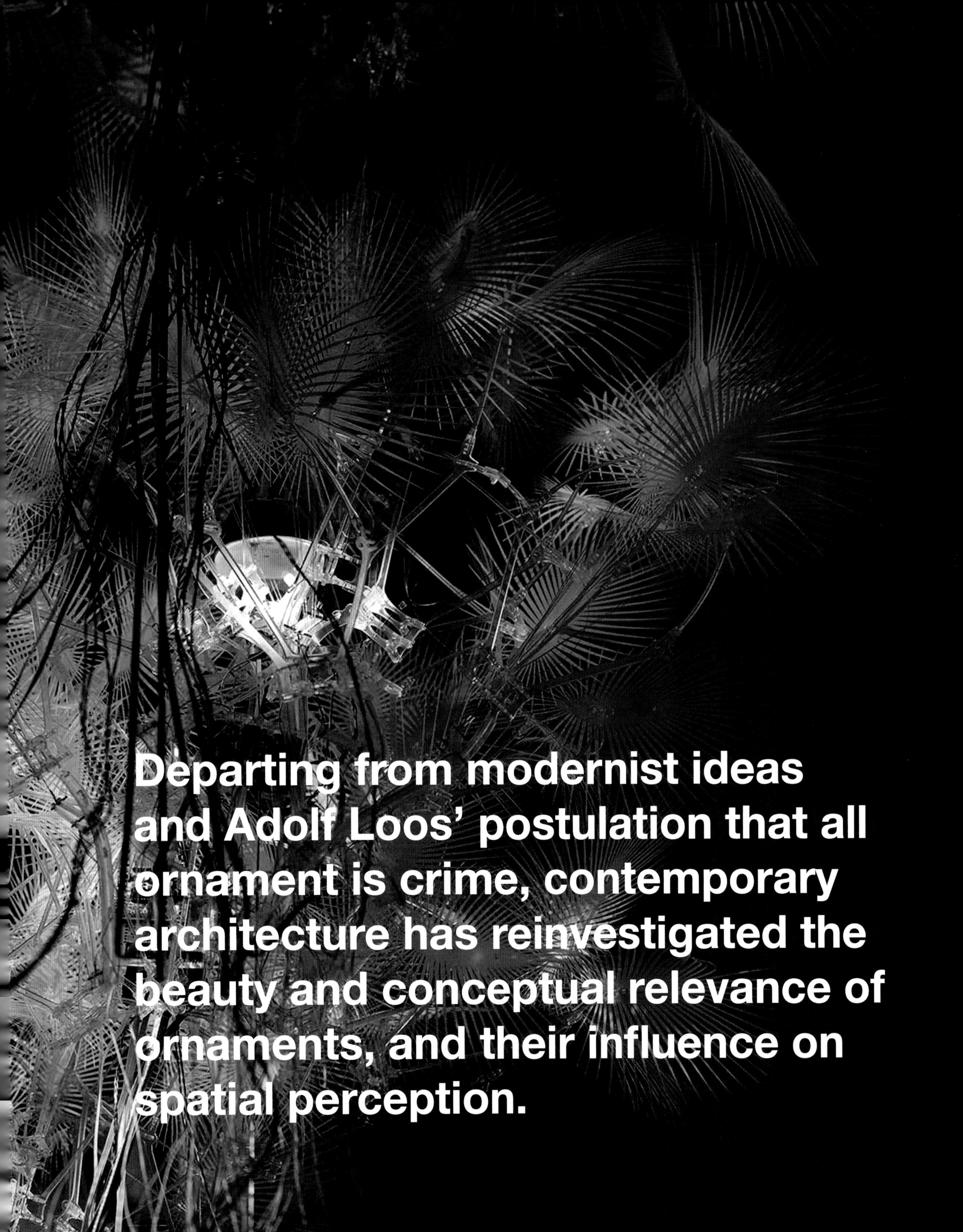

Departing from modernist ideas and Adolf Loos' postulation that all ornament is crime, contemporary architecture has reinvestigated the beauty and conceptual relevance of ornaments, and their influence on spatial perception.

Chapter 8 : Spatial Ornaments

Revisiting the Crime of Ornament

by Tobias Klein

ornament and crime

cultural and social context

mass customization

digital fabrication techniques

art and craftsmanship

narrative qualities

ornamental systems

A little over 100 years ago, Adolf Loos wrote his seminal work titled *Ornament and Crime* (ref. 8.1), a text that banned the "immoral" ornament from architecture and gave passage to a generation of admirers of Loos' "passion for smooth and precious surfaces" – a generation of modernism in architecture. Loos argued that the energy and material required to decorate an object and render it fashionable or belonging to a time and taste was a waste, and preferred to focus on the functions of the object itself, detaching it from a cultural and social context. This manifesto became one of the foundations of modernism, characterized by white rendered surfaces; a deniability of origin or cultural context and connotation in the surface.

Today we have entered an age in which technology and methodology in architecture have rendered outdated most of the rational production-base arguments that led to modernism's rejection of the ornament. Once seen as a wasteful and decadent byproduct of "truly functional" design, the mass customization of today's architecture via methods of three-dimensional software and modelling, as well as the fabrication techniques of laser cutting, CNC milling and three-dimensional printing, have led to a revival of ornamentation and hence an engagement with contextual, narrative and culturally embedded tectonics.

The emergence of computer-aided design is a key player in stretching artifice to its

page 187 189:
Hylozoic Ground by Philip Beesley.
Installation at the Venice Architecture Biennale 2010

8.1 „The evolution of culture marches with the elimination of ornament from useful objects" Adolf Loos: Ornament und Verbrechen / Adolf Loos: Ornament and Crime: Selected Essays

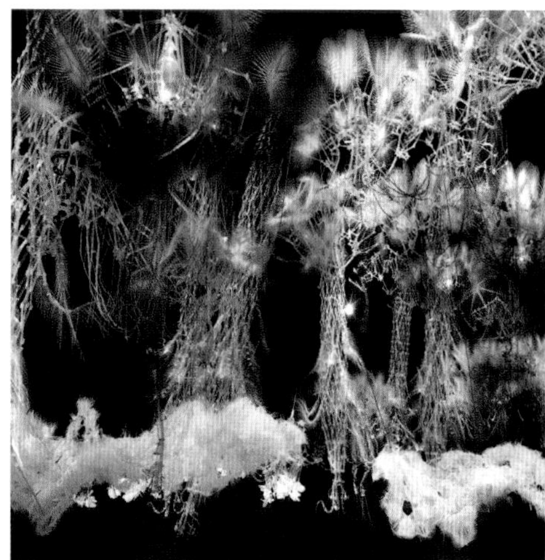

8.1 Hylozoic ground. Spatial installation by Philip Beesley. Mexico, 2010

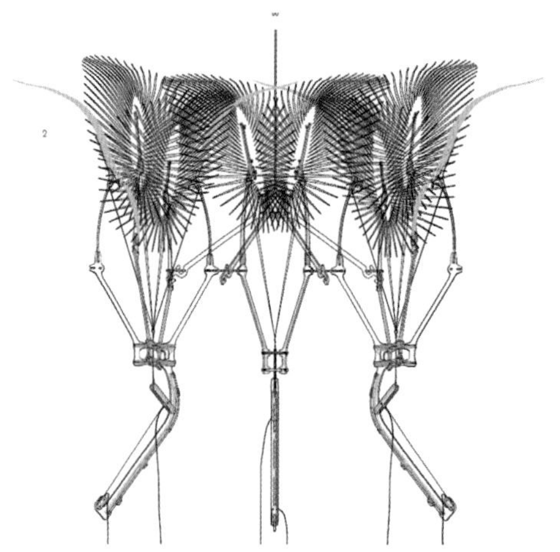

8.2 Hylozoic ground, elevation of filter cluster assembly

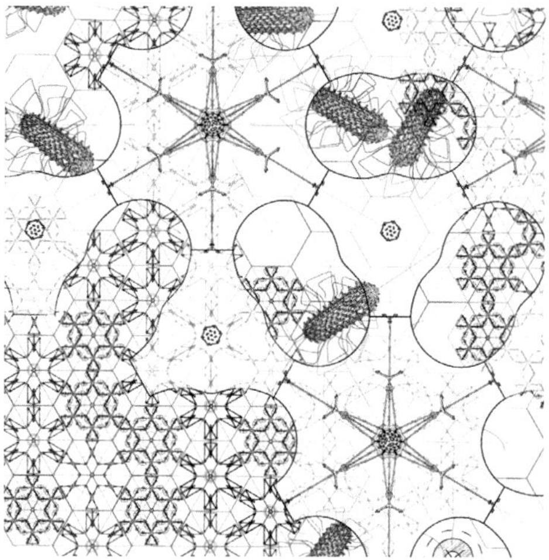

8.3 Hylozoic ground diagrammatic plan, Philip Beesley, Canadian pavilion. 12th International Architecture Exhibition, la Biennale di Venecia, Venice, 2010

extremes, leading on the one hand to a parametric, process-driven, generative architecture, and on the other, to a new role of architects as creators, and craftspeople, able to reunite architecture as an interplay between techne (art) and poiesis (craftsmanship). These architects work and operate within a CAD/CAM liberated environment but are not solely and epistemologically interested in a parametric accountancy of the computational potential, manufactured customization and efficiency driven optimization. Their interests lie in the cultural amalgamation between tool and idea, embedded in specifics of site and narration.

The ornament is one of the only elements in architecture in which forms and ideas, narrations within architecture, can create an identity of place and contextualization, ranging from the romantic to the grotesque, the critical to the illustrative. Within the European tradition, these range from an innocent rose petal pattern to an assemblage of weaponry – a demonstration of might and power – to the ecclesial ornamentation of the great baroque churches and their voluptuous counter-reformative glorification.

One example of this metamorphosis between artifice, biological systems, symbols, and the use of ornament as a contextualizing tool in architecture, is the work *Contoured Embodiment* created by Ben Cowd and myself, exhibited in London's Royal Academy Summer Show in 2009. The work consists of an interpretation of the Dome of Sir Christopher Wren's St. Paul's Cathedral in London. *Contoured Embodiment* was inspired by a fascination with Catholic Iberian Baroque, an excess of ornament, organic spatial exuberance and the scale-less implementation and rhetoric of symbolism, allegory, and narrative explored through the Sacred Heart. Developed from Magnetic Resonance Imaging-generated body data

8.4 Window to the Partal. Alhambra Granada, Spain

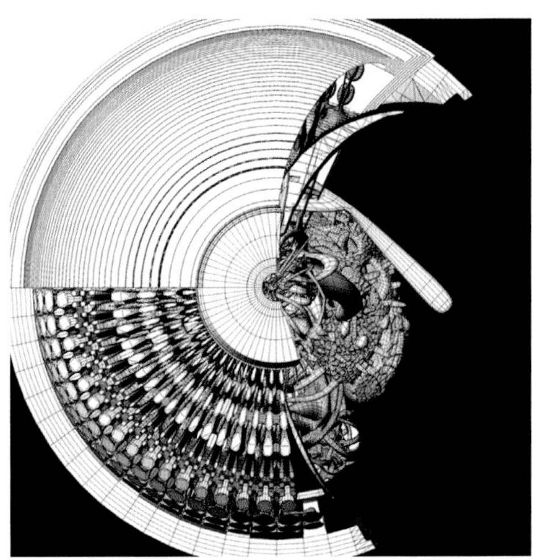

8.5 Drawing of a speculative reinterpretation of Sir Christopher Wren' St Pauls Cathedral, Tobias Klein. London

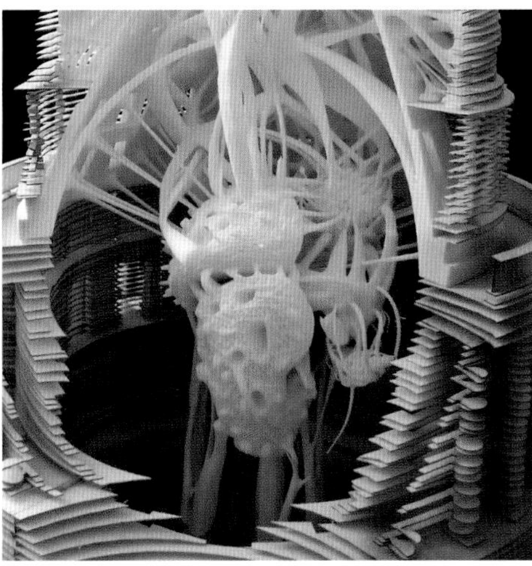

8.6 Physical model of speculative spatial intervention inside the Dome of Sir Christopher Wren' St Pauls Cathedral, Tobias Klein. London

and inserted into St Paul's Cathedral, space is sculpted viscerally and digitally, utilizing adjacent properties as constructive and symbolic interpretation; exaggerating sublime illumination and baroque illusion through the interruption of views and distortion of natural light by a complex layering of skins, veins and arteries.

On the other hand, the Islamic pattern, devoid of narration and pictorial elements, incorporates mathematical precision and repetition as a religious cultural value – famously portrayed by Owen Jones and analyzed by Keith Critchlow (ref. 8.2 / 8.3), and best seen in the elaborate two- and three-dimensional works of the Alhambra (fig. 8.4). The ornament allows a virtual instance to influence an actual functional design and place it into a conversation that ranges beyond the mere physicality of a building, referencing a larger context.

With an equal precision and atmospheric quality the new ornament allows an emerging of natural and artificial systems in this amalgamation of non-pictorial narration and hybrid transgressions. One example that emerged from the debate of ornamental systems bridges mechanized and biological elements: the mass-customized reactive pattern landscape *Hylozoic Ground* by Phillip Beesley, exhibited at the 12th Venice Biennale (fig. 8.0 - 8.4 / ref. 8.4).

8.2 Lit.: 1. Hrvol Flores, Carol A. Owen Jones: Design, Ornament, Architecture & Theory in an Age of Transition

8.3 Keith: Critchlow: Islamic Patterns

8.4 Beesley, Philip. Hylozoic Ground: Liminal Responsive Architecture

407

407 408 Ornamental details of physical models

408

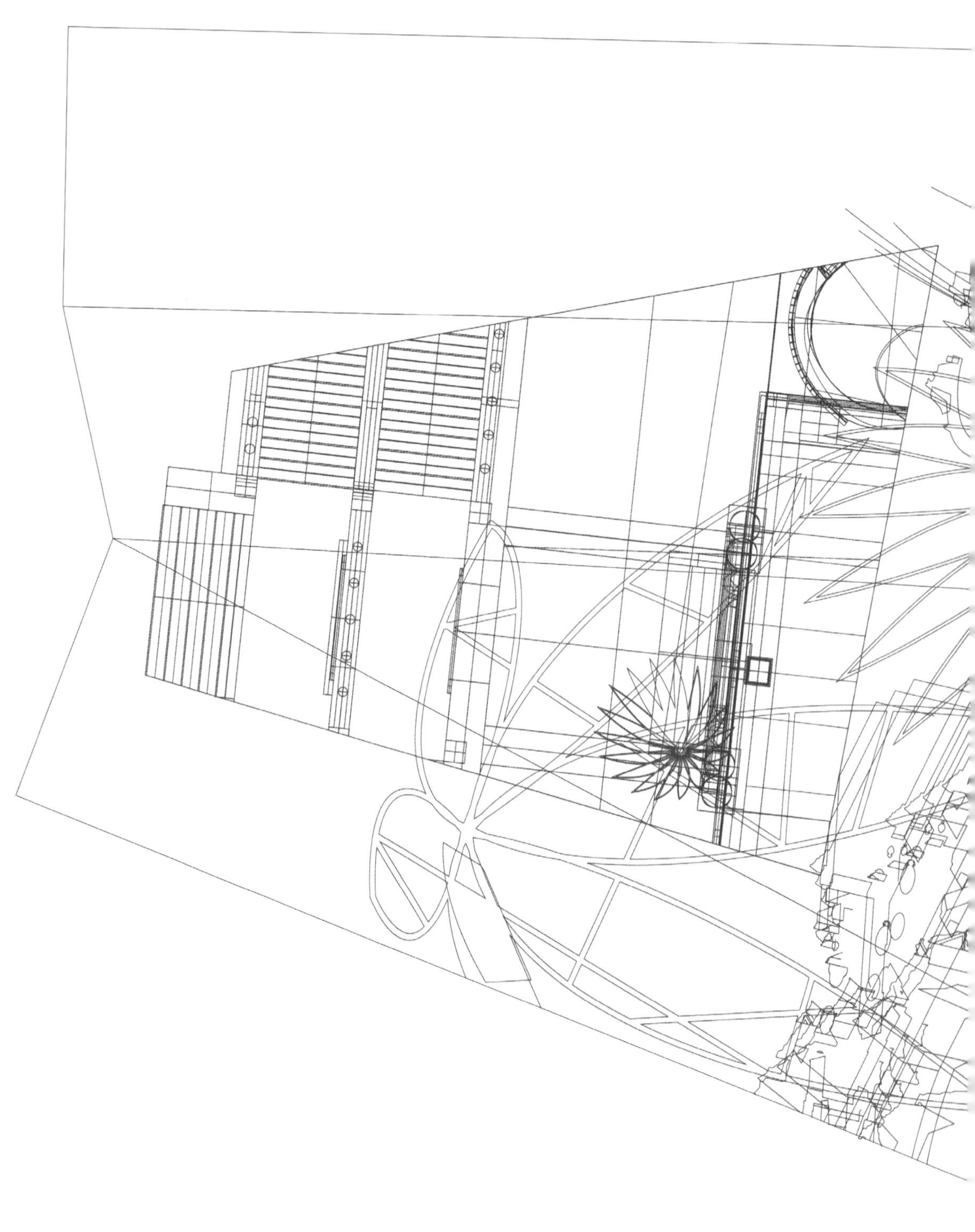

409

409 Interpolation of planimetric views from 3D models of three different Bavarian churches displaced according to the movement of the Foucault pendulum

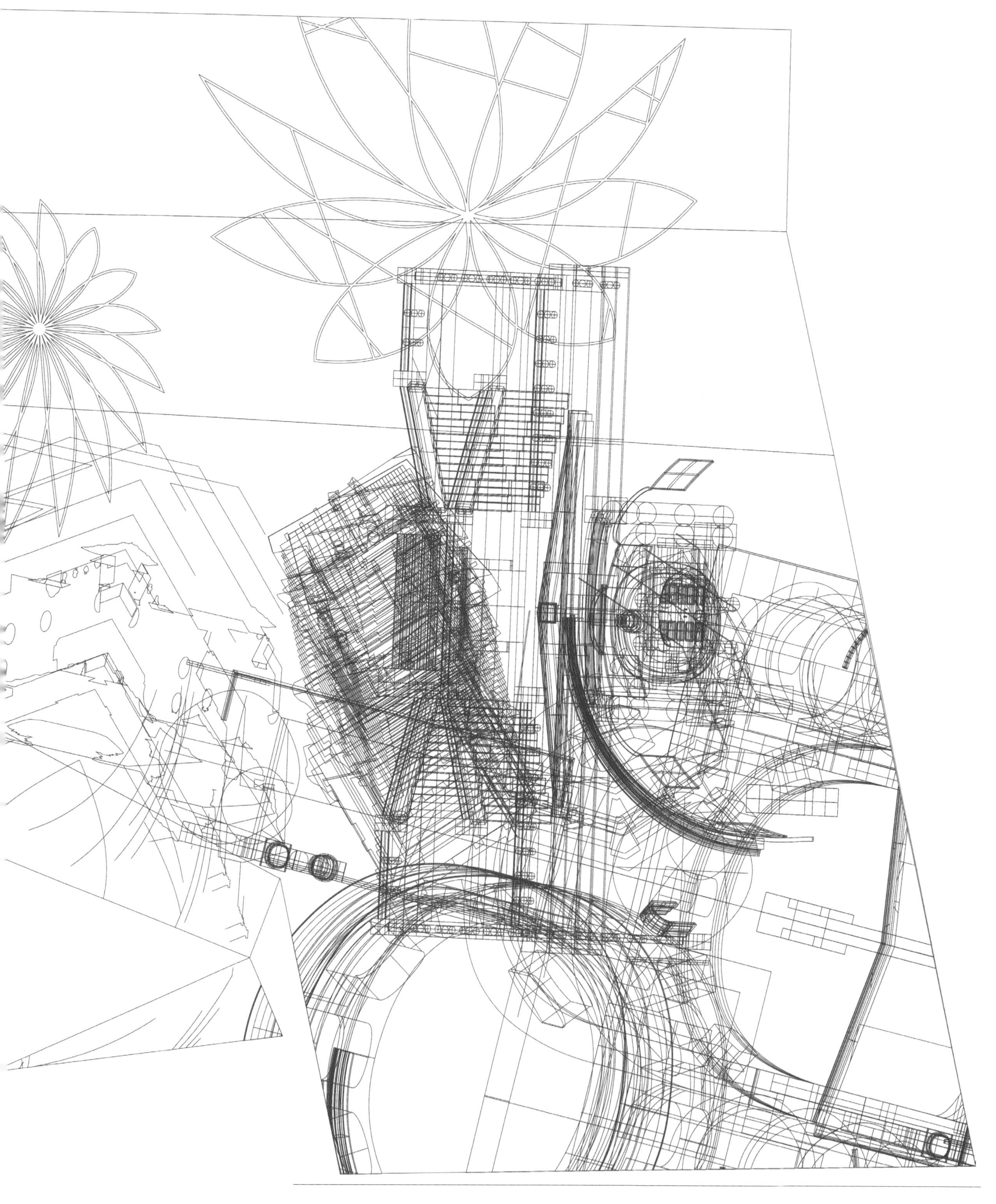

410

411

412

410 - 412 Physical model of interpolated drawing from fig. 409: the churches are freed of their function and transform into animated spatial objects with random references towards their origin

413

413 Morphological study models of different spatial ornamentation

414

414 Detail of final model from fig. 413

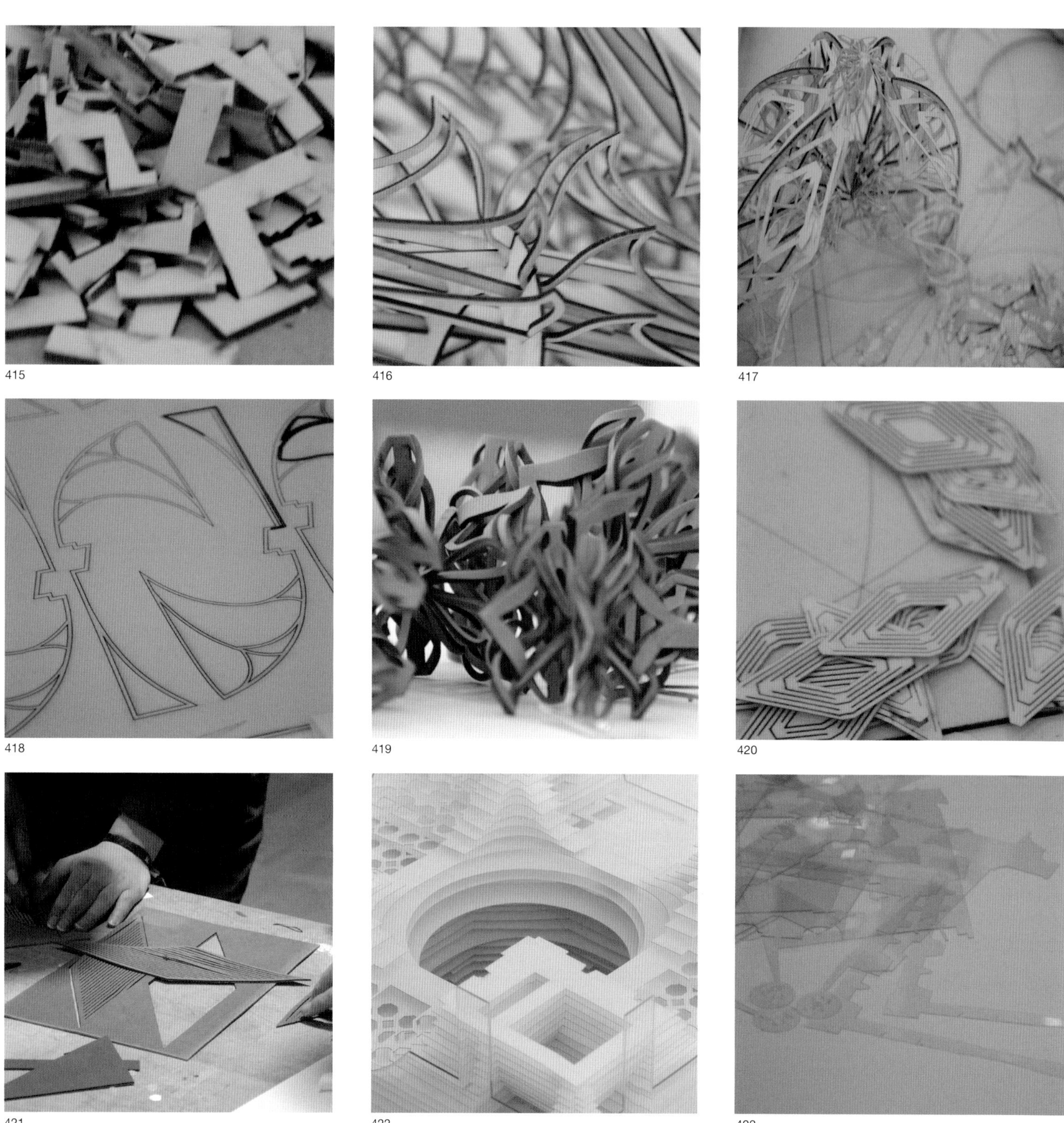
415 416 417 418 419 420 421 422 423

415 - 424 Different stages of the model building process

424

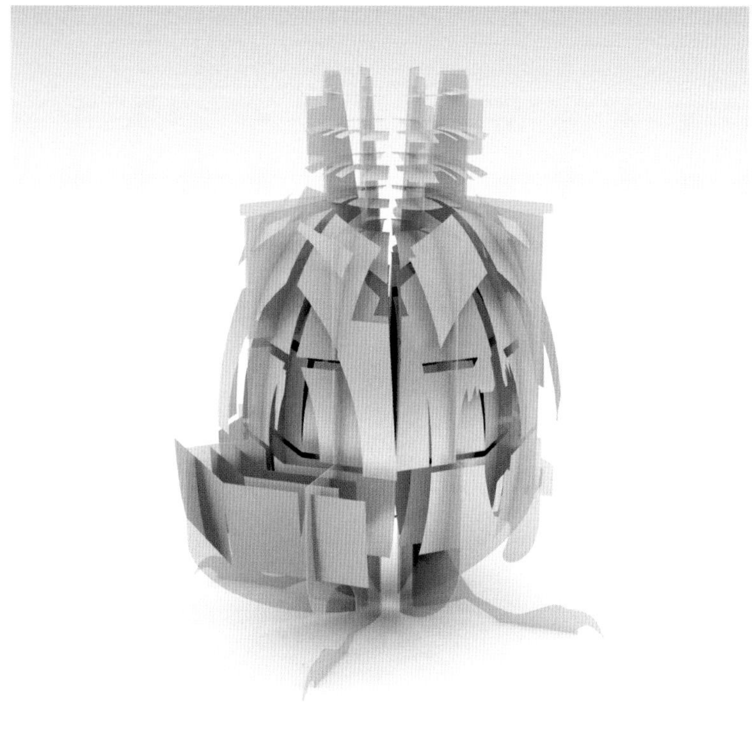

425

426

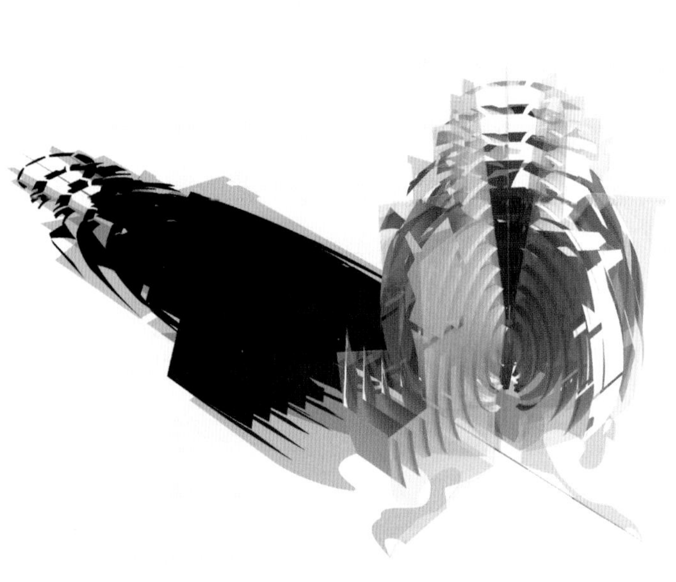

427

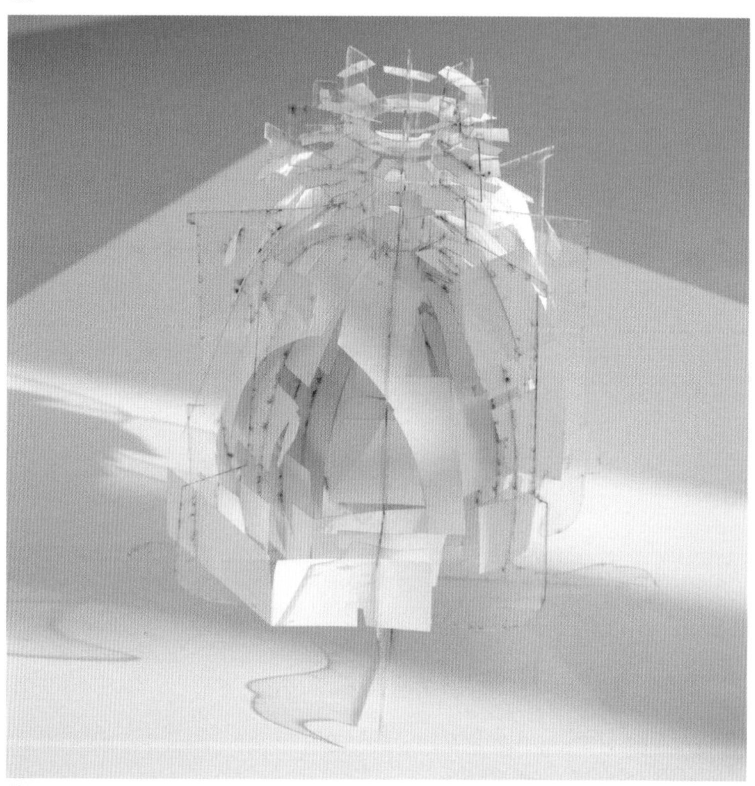

428

425 - 428 Physical and digital models showing different stages of the process described by fig. 429 and fig 430

429

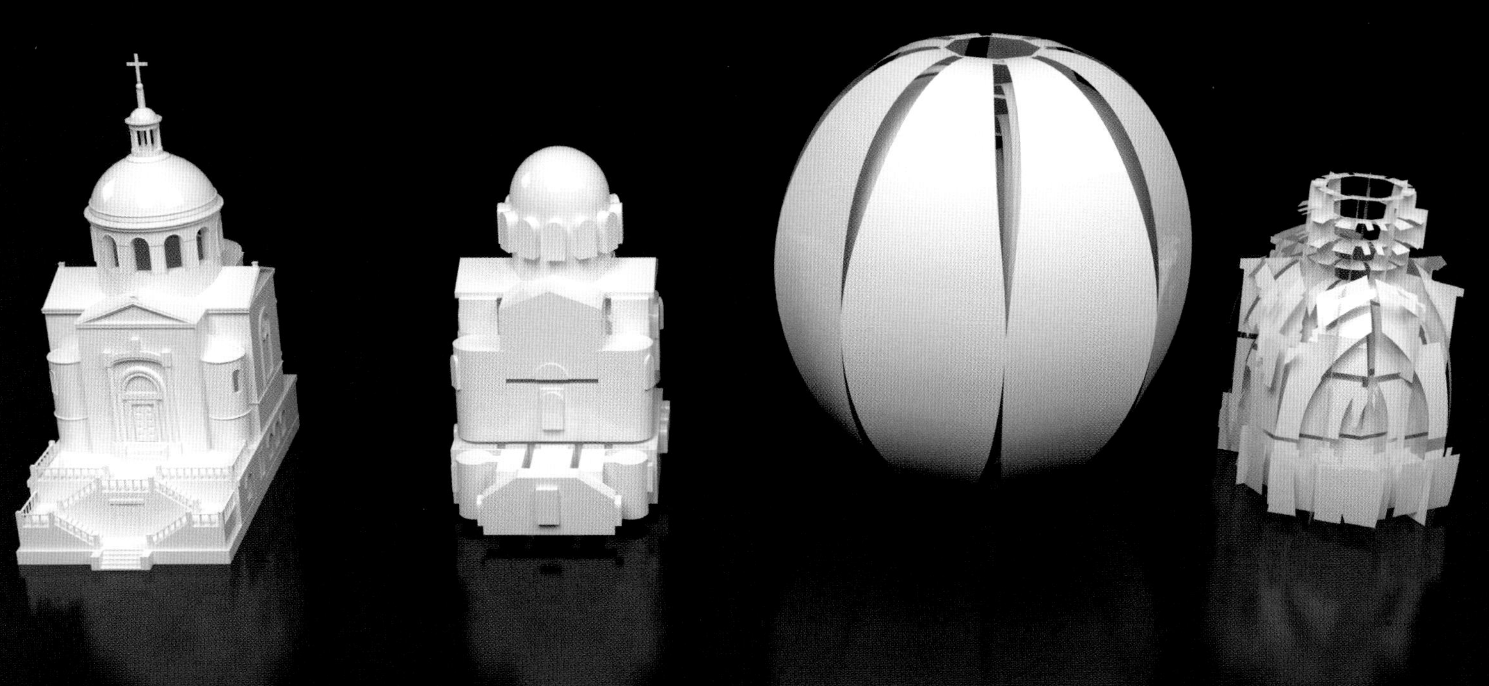

430

429 430 The inner volume of a classical Bavarian church is build as a positive and then sliced by onion skin like sections that are layered in a spherical realm surrounding the heart of the church, redefining the spatial impact of the given architecture

An effective method in creating a form or further developing a design is to apply tracing, mapping, or notation techniques to a design process. These methods allow for a more conceptual design approach, which can be closely related to the investigated subject.

An effective method in creating a form or further developing a design is to apply tracing, mapping, or notation techniques to a design process. These methods allow for a more conceptual design approach, which can be closely related to the investigated subject.

Chapter 9: Tracing, Mapping and Notation

tracing and drawing

design by trace

referencing by trace

notation

tracing the virtual

three dimensional trace

conceptualization

The act of tracing is deeply rooted in the architectural profession. Starting with the traditional representation of sketching and drawing, the act of transferring a physical or imagined spatial condition onto paper for the deeper understanding and analysis of that space can already be seen as an early act of tracing. The translation of space through drawing can also be seen as an act of meditation that is catalytic in nature. In addition to the drawn transfer of the observed subject, the act of tracing begins with the personal insights of the observer and the transformations these insights will instigate. Through the use of transparent or sketching paper, the act of tracing a plan to morphologically develop and improve a design is a natural and important process of any creative activity. New insights and ideas are often stimulated by the act of tracing. The spatial and material layering of architectural qualities reach out far into the reception of architecture itself, through the method of tracing, spatial perception with all its complexities can be thoroughly investigated and derived.

If an architecture or building is the final manifestation of a design process distinguished by constant advancements of optimized variants, then the act of tracing within this process can be understood as a natural characteristic of architecture itself. In addition to the design process, the physical manifestation of architecture through light and shade, as well as the spatiality that is manifested by the casting of shadows, are also related to tracing.

Architecture and our designed environment are too complex and multilayered to be merely analyzed for aesthetics and formal characteristics. The built environment and its spatiality are characterized by varied expressions of life, situations, atmospheres, motions, and phenomena, which are able to transgress physical boundaries and neutrally observable special characteristics. If one consciously follows this observation, the importance of tracing processes in architectural design methods becomes evident: Through tracing, designers can develop modes of perception that open up the possibility

page 204 205:
Art Installation at the Venice
Architecture Biennale 2010

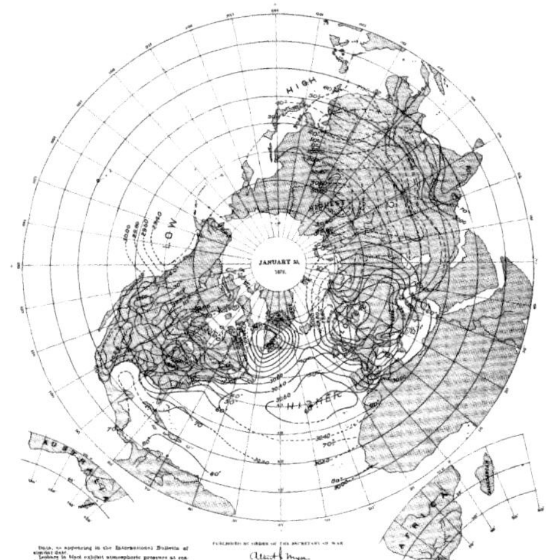

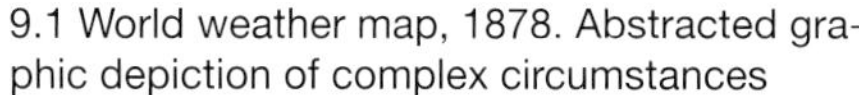

9.1 World weather map, 1878. Abstracted graphic depiction of complex circumstances

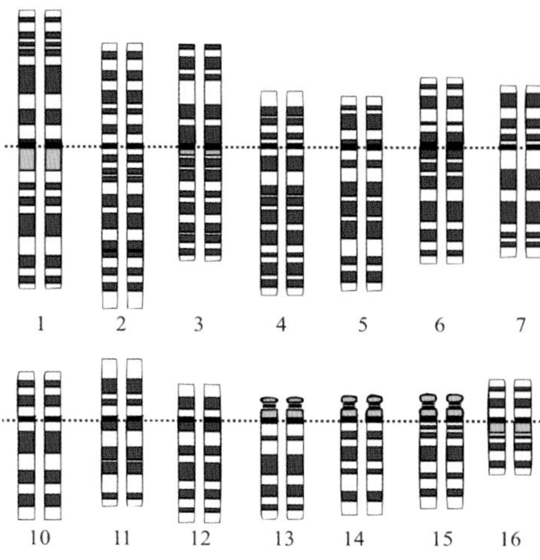

9.2 Down Syndrome Karyotype. The karyogram is an abstract graphic display of genetic analysis

for more complex spatial experiences. In this context, tracing can also be understood as quoting or referencing. Architecture, if not generic, always refers to a certain context: for example, the surrounding urban or natural environment, the content, the function, the usage, or the historical significance of a site. Throughout the development and the design of architecture, multilayered references can help to link an architectural design to its place. Because of these connective relationships, the architecture becomes more tangible, specific and contextualized. A visitor can relate to this kind of architecture through the realization of these connections. The architecture then has a human dimension, which from their links can be integrated into the intellectual or experience context of the spectator.

The layering of different connections and references to possible interpretations of a built environment allows for a multidimensional reception of architectural space within its cultural and intellectual context. This also relates to Vilém Flusser's earlier discussed claim on the incorporation of virtual space into the design of human habitation. (ref. 9.1)
The technique of tracing helps to develop and incorporate such references, bringing them into the design process to develop a complex layered spatial experience that surpasses the basic ordering of inside and outside or public and private. Tracing also allows one to elucidate processes that do not always fit into the traditional categories of beauty and classical design, enabling a contemporary examination of the built environment. Rem Koolhaas argues that the idea of a single aesthetical system can be disregarded to develop a new form of perception, where beauty can be seen through different systems. He compares the beauty of universally appealing historic city centers like Prague's or Paris' with the need to find beauty in wilder, more accidental, and more contemporary urban complexes. (ref. 9.2)

At the beginning of this chapter, the technique of tracing was described as a process. This process naturally takes place through a linear time sequence.

9.1. Flusser, Vilém: „Räume" (in Heidemarie Seblatnig (Hg.): außen räume innen räume)

9.2 Koolhaas, Rem / Kuhnert, Nicolaus: Berlin, Offene Stadt, in: Lettre International Nr. 18

9.3 Aircraft contrails tracing time and space into the sky

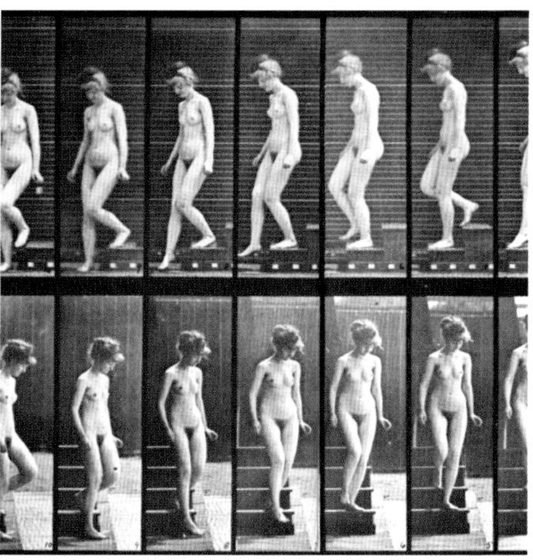
9.4 „Woman walking downstairs“ Eadweard Muybridge, 1901

9.5 Osaka city subway map

Tracing is able to visibly diagram space and movement, as well as the perception changes of these phenomena within a certain timeframe. The well known photos of Étienne-Jules Marey and Eadweard J. Muybridge, (fig. 9.4) as well as the famous painting "Nude Descending a Staircase, No. 2" by Edward Duchamp illustrate this space-time relationship. The sequence of movement in these depictions corresponds to tracing, visualing the inhabited space of the depicted subjects. In the work of Wolfgang Weileder, buildings that are partially erected and almost simultaneously taken down are documented through multiple exposures and time-lapse photography, showing the potential of tracing where spaces emerge on the interface between physical manifestation and virtuality. (ref. 9.3 / 9.4)

The dynamic relations between space and time can be integrated into the design process through tracing, mapping, and notation. This method leads to spatial solutions that establish a link between their use and their varied configuration by making each condition spatially visible. Another example from the arts is the work of Rachel Whiteread. Her larger spatial castings, where an architectural void becomes solidified, allows a different perception of spatial sequences and wall reliefs that evoke an imaginative reflection on the virtuality and lapse of time of habitable spaces. The casting technique can therefore be regarded as a three-dimensional trace. (ref. 9.5)

Tracing, mapping, notation and casting as design methods are acts of transformation that are informed by various design parameters. These techniques are therefore a form of analog parametric design in the truest sense of the word. The works in this chapter show different approaches that were generated using tracing, mapping, and notation techniques, expanding the meaning of these designs. The use of such parameters and design systems in these relatively abstract works can easily be applied to more concrete architectural examples.

9.3 Miria Swain, Michael Stanley. Transfer: Wolfgang Weileder

9.4 Matzner, Florian. Wolfgang Weileder: House- Project

9.5 Mullins, Charlotte. Tate Modern Artists: Rachel Whiteread

431 Champs-Élysées, Paris: Areal view with non-hierarchical tracing of the roads

433 434 Abstraction of fig. 481 and development into a regular pattern

435 Resulting model from process illustrated in fig. 431 - 434 where different light conditions increase the prismatic spatial effect

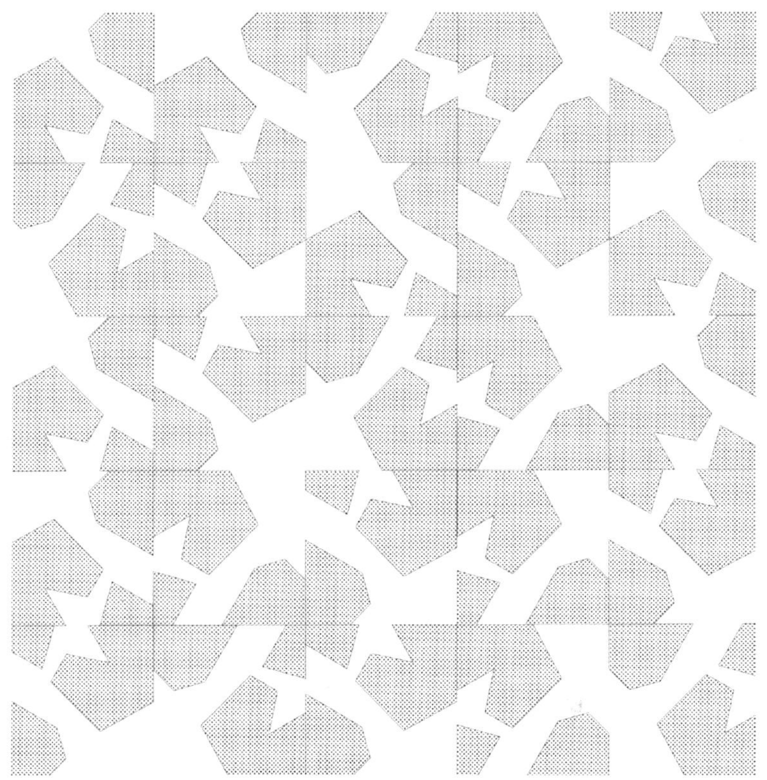

436

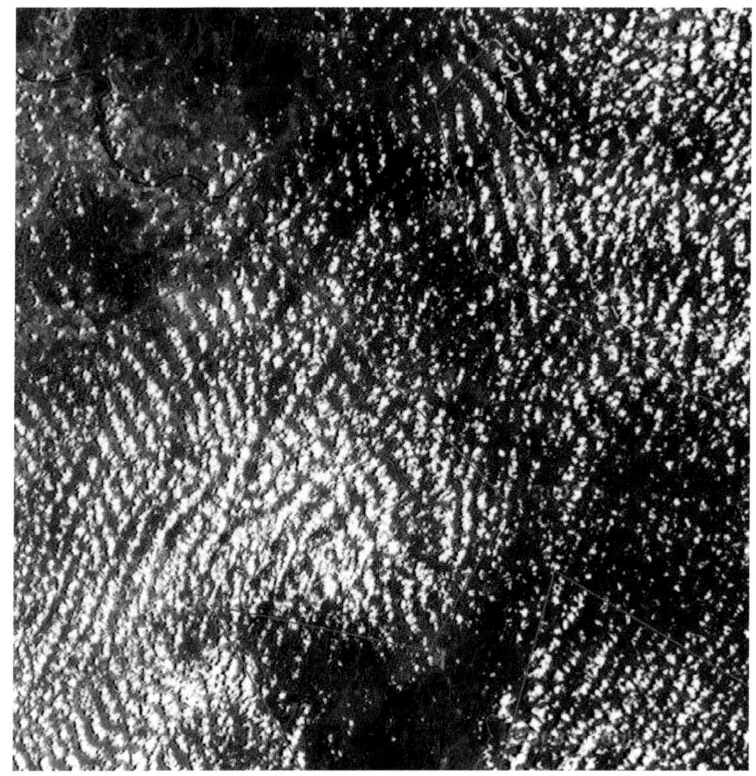

437

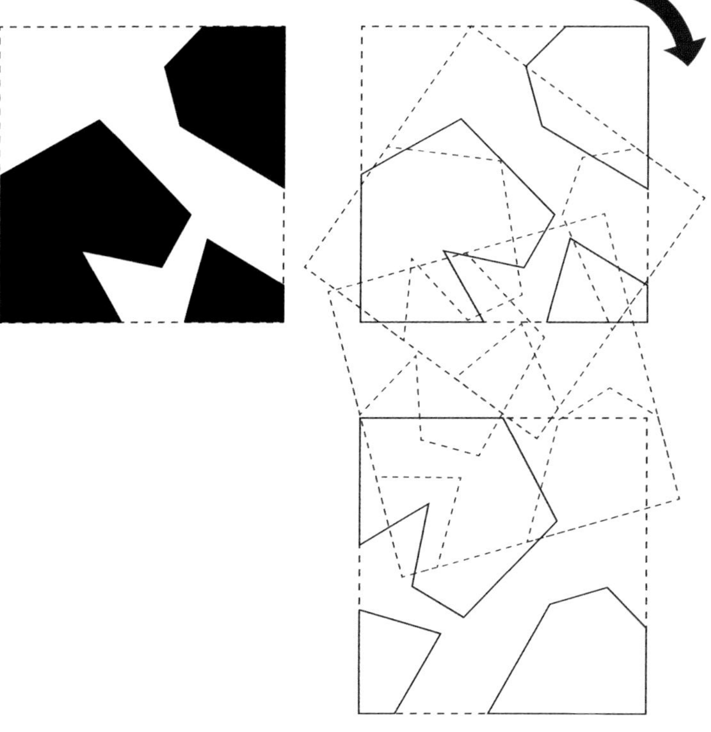

438

436 437 Pattern development: Traced areas of lighter and darker densities in an image are assembled to form an interesting irregular pattern

438 Altered module for pattern composition of fig. 436

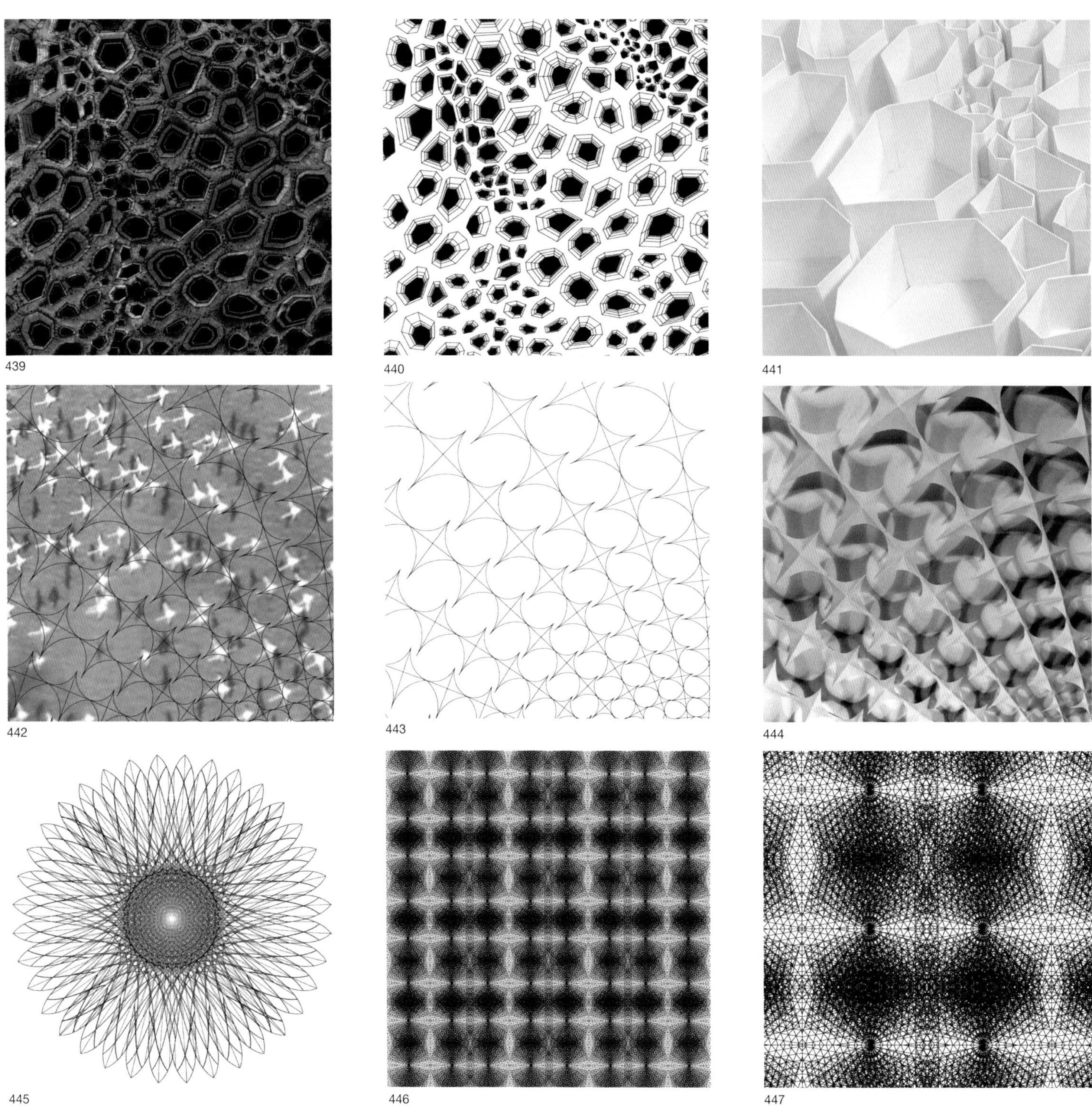

439 440 441 Tracing from an image of a coral structure to a spatial design with irregular polygons

442 443 444 Flock of birds as the source of an abstract tracing process that leads to a poetic spatial model

445 446 447 Emergent pattern derived from the abstract representation of a blossom with perfect symmetry in fig. 445

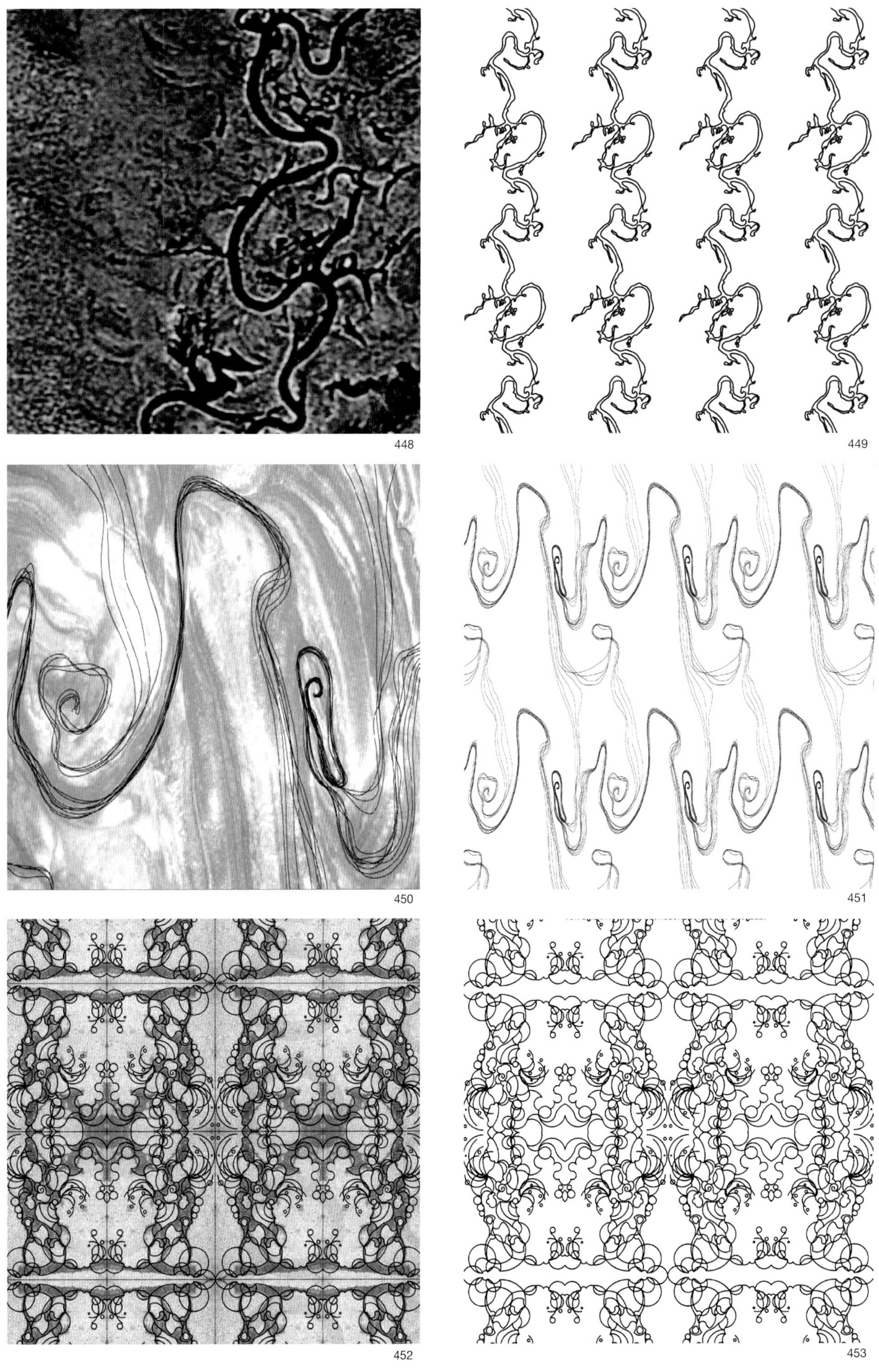

448 449 The repetition of a traced meandering river leads to an ornamental pattern

450 451 The tracing of a viscous liquid, in this case a close up image of milk foam on a cafe latte, results in a dynamic pattern structure

452 453 Traced water spots on partially wet asphalt lead to ornamental figures that through duplication and mirroring seem to resemble baroque ornamentations

454

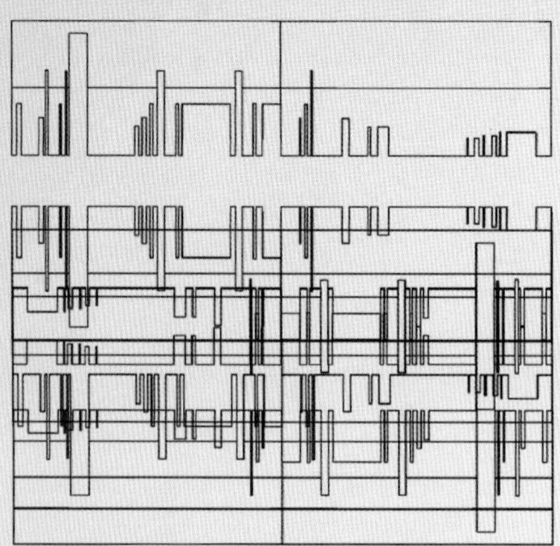

455

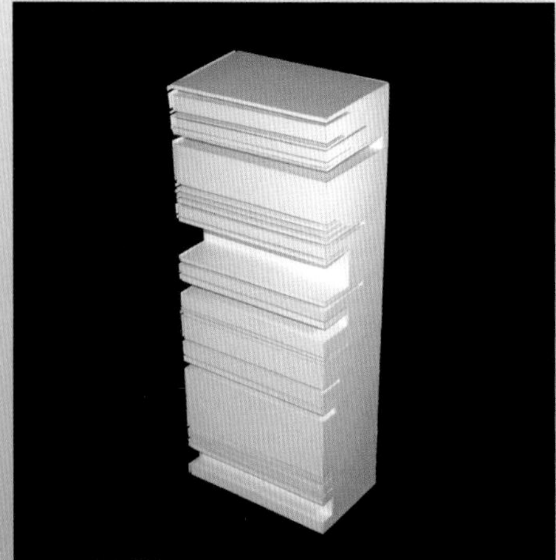

456

457

458

454 Notes of an ABBA song
455 Graphical 2D notation drawing of the songs tune

456 457 Physical models based on the notation of fig. 455

458 Rendering of the spatial transformation of Music: Voids cut out from the volume reflecting the notes of the ABBA song

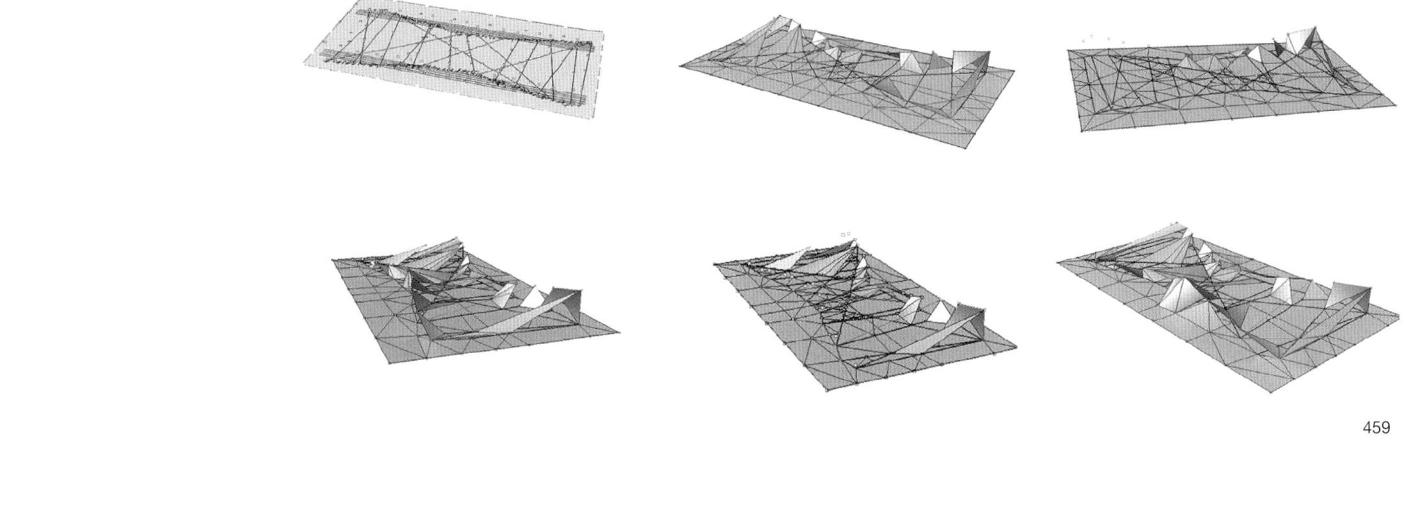

459

460

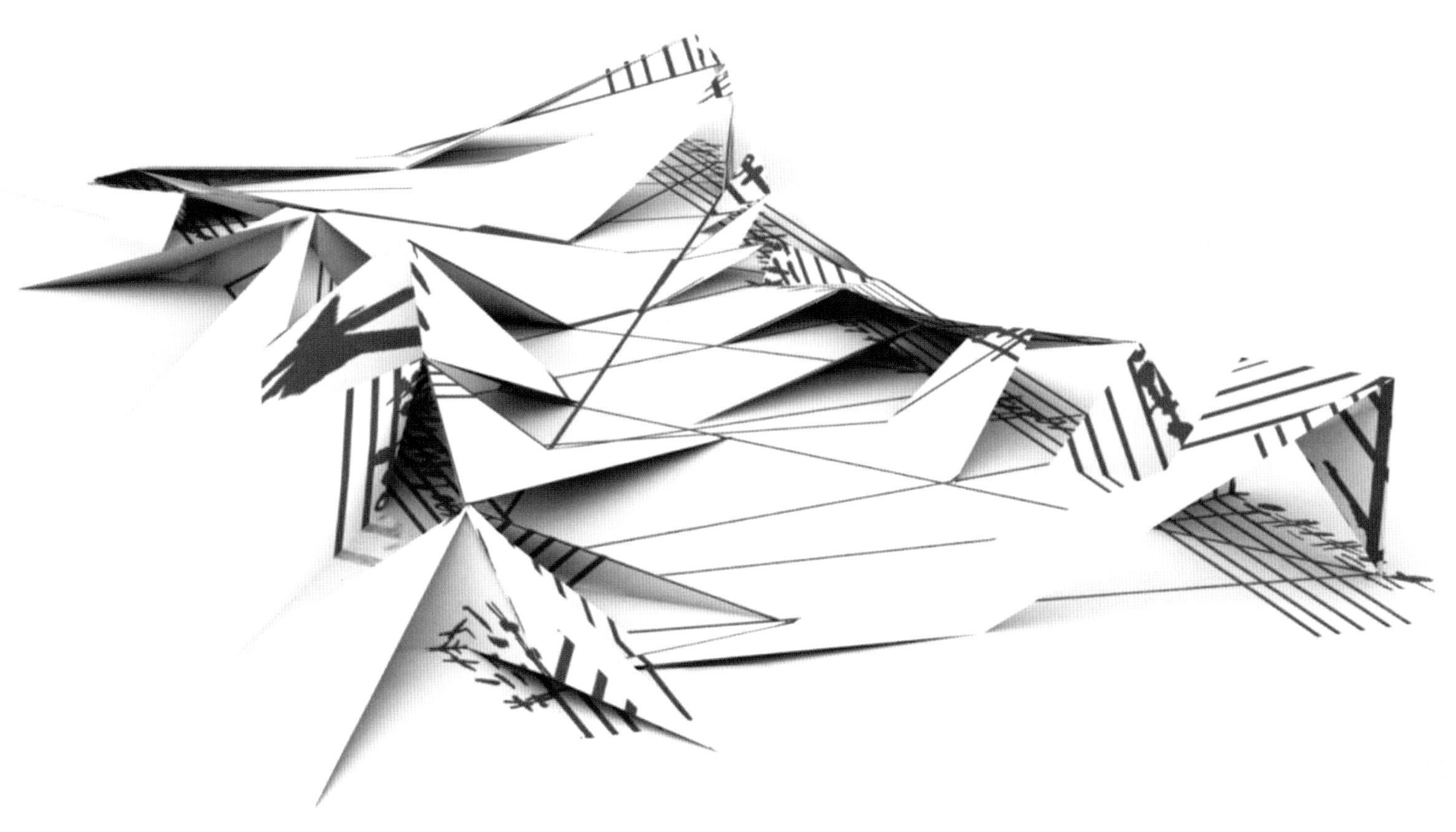

461

459 Folding morphology displaying a different musical notation of instrumental relations within the score

460 conceptual sketches showing these relations

461 Rendering of final fold with a texture mapping of the notated song

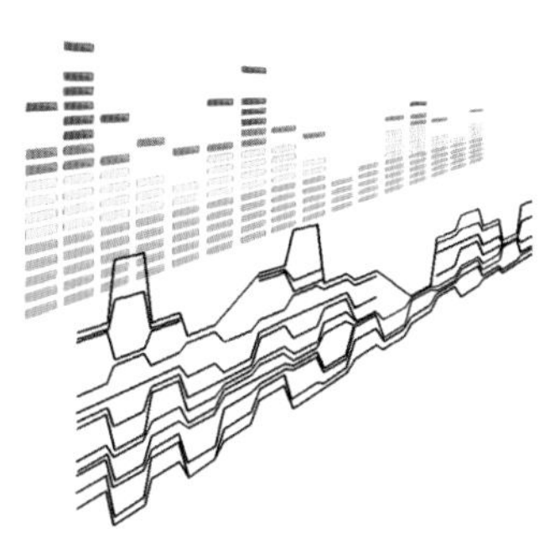

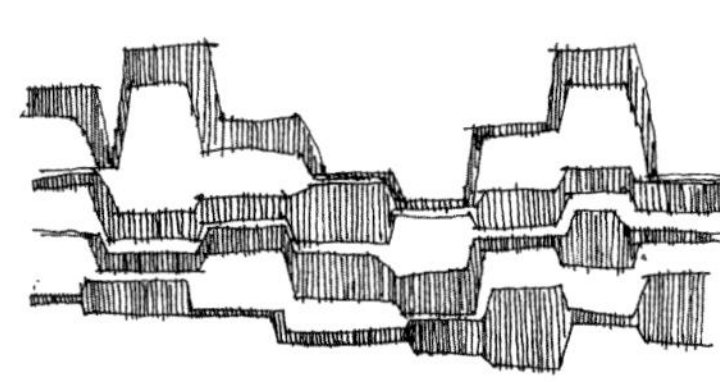

462

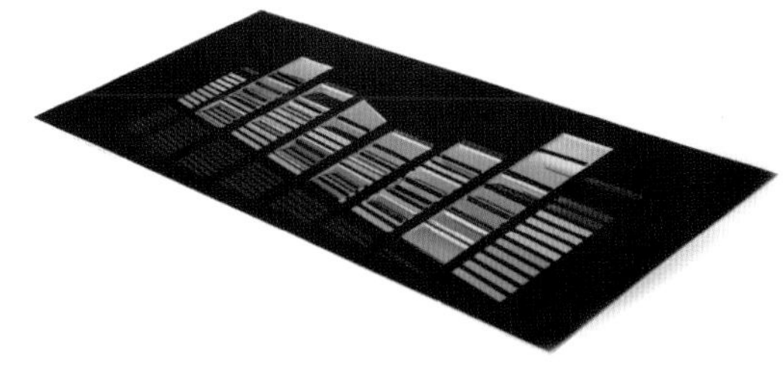

463

464

462 Notation of the amplitudes of an equalizer and conceptual sketch
463 Model with perforated notches

464 Digital model in side view, where the two-dimensional notation of fig. 462 becomes a three-dimensional representation of an equalizer. The spatial deflection is interconnected to the amplitude of the equalizer

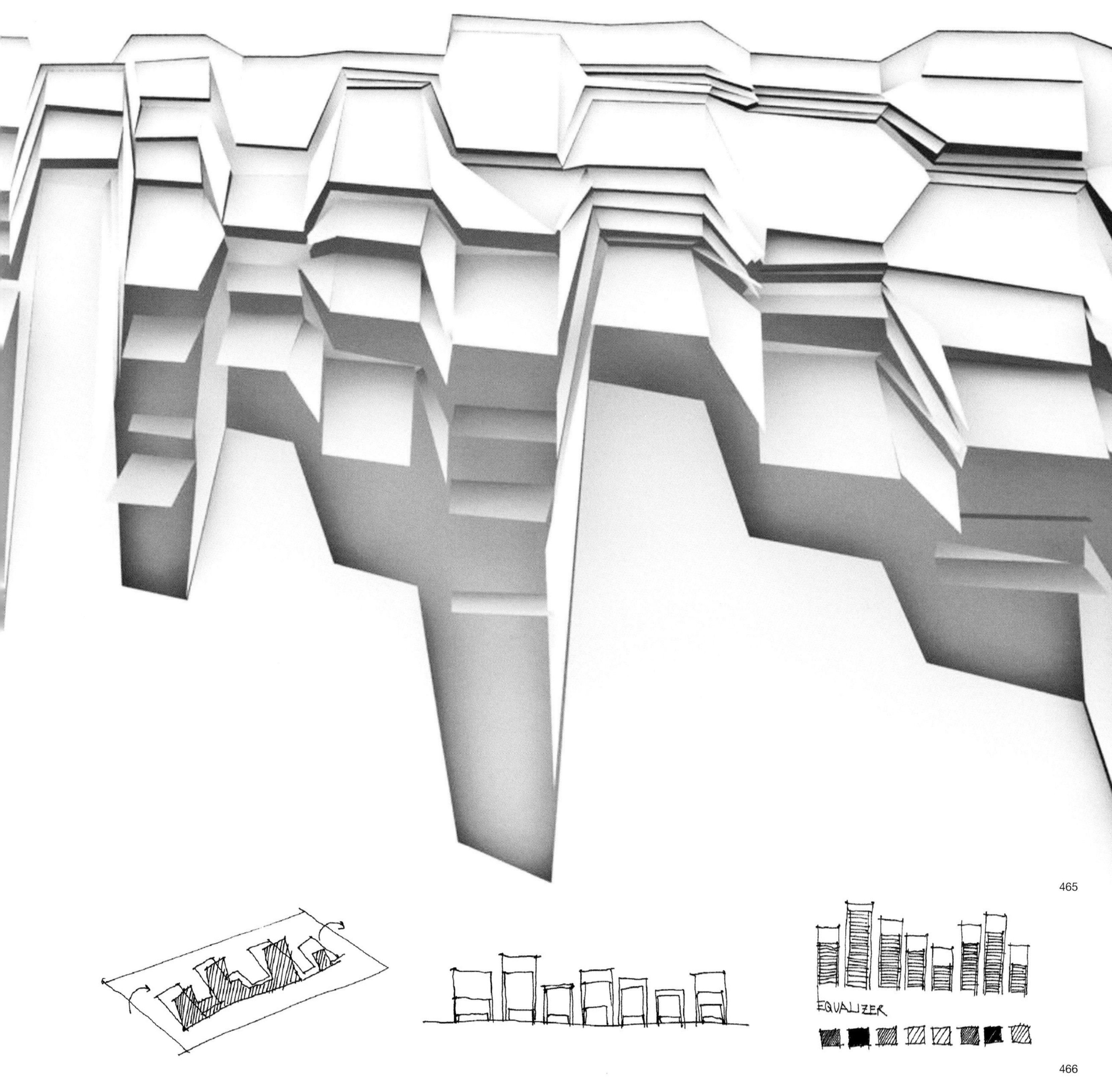

465 Top view of digital model in fig. 464

466 Design development sketches illustrating the process from initial notation to final spatial implementation

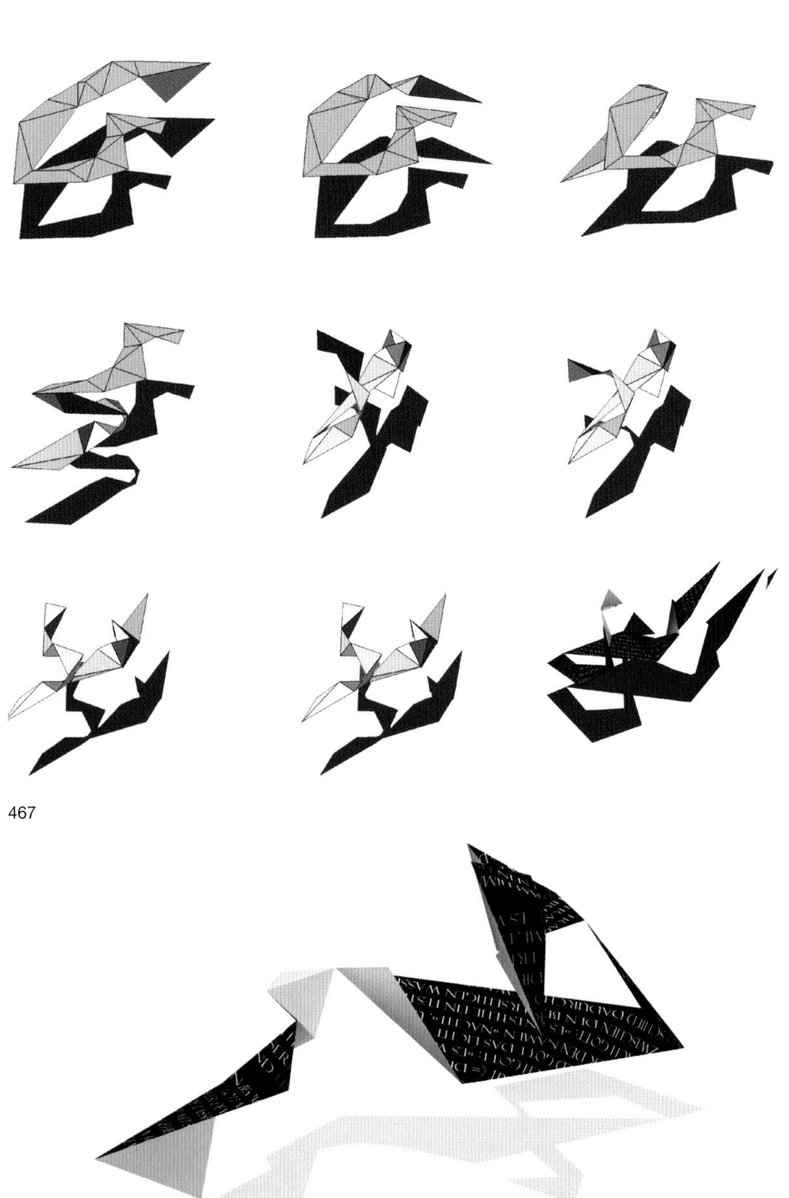

467

468

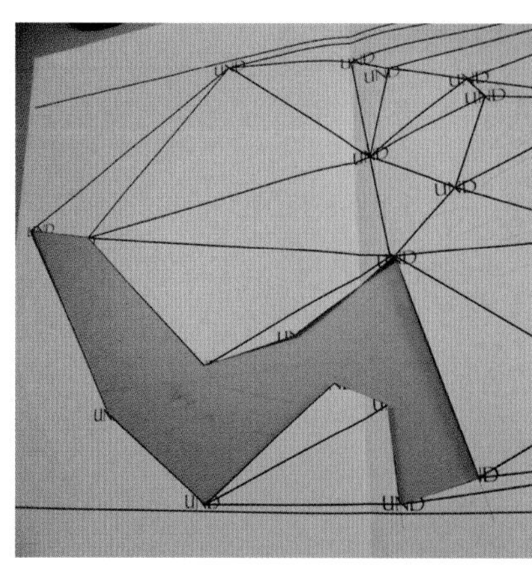

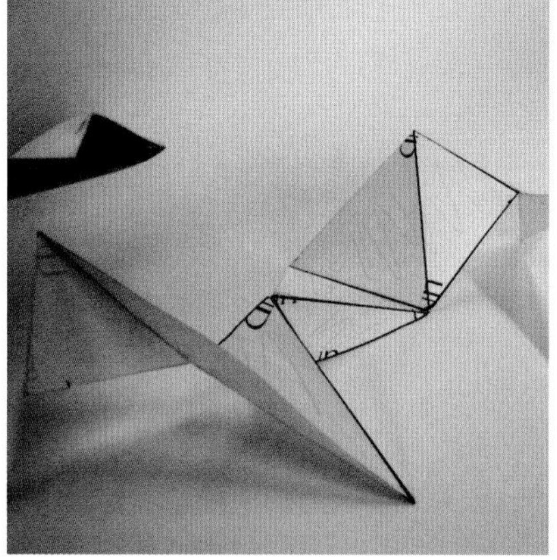

469

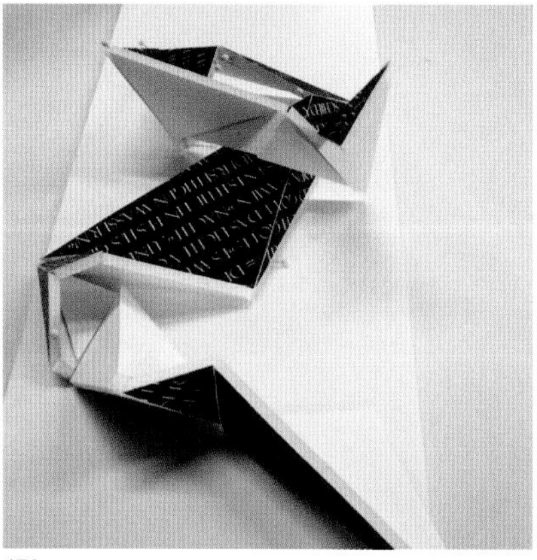

470

467 - 468 Folding morphology based on the analysis in fig 469 where the analyzed texture is used as a mapping on the upper surface

469 Spatial analysis of relations within a text: Recurring words in a text are highlighted and connected.

470 Physical model based on the process in fig. 467 - 469 connections within the text are spatially simulated by threads

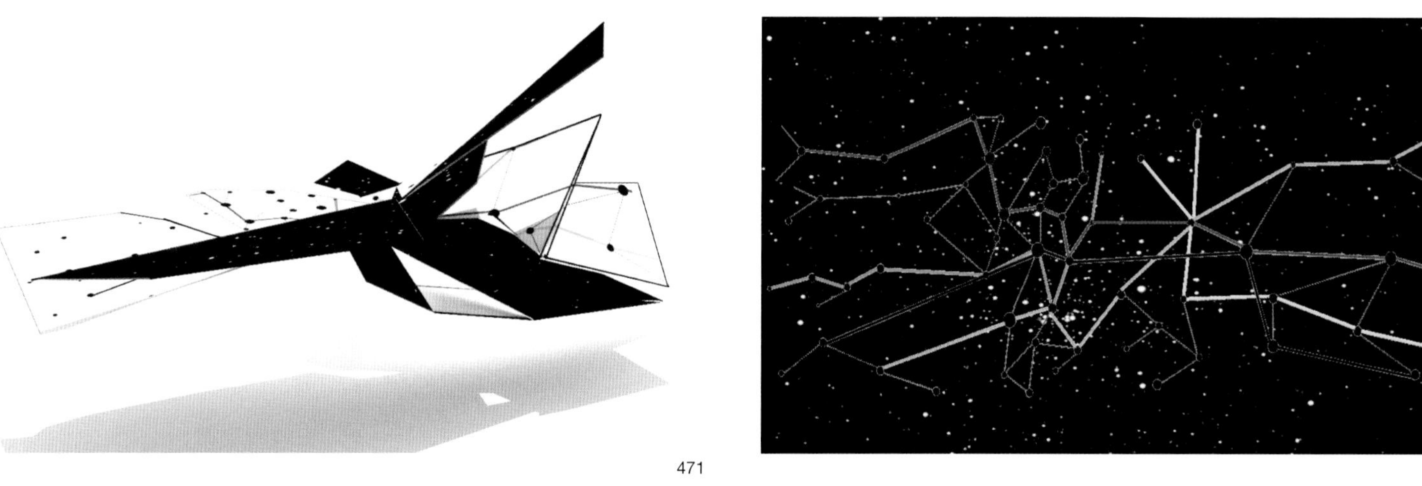

471

472

473

471 472 473 Folding, unfolding and dissection of notated elements that are derived by an analytical drawing of star constellations

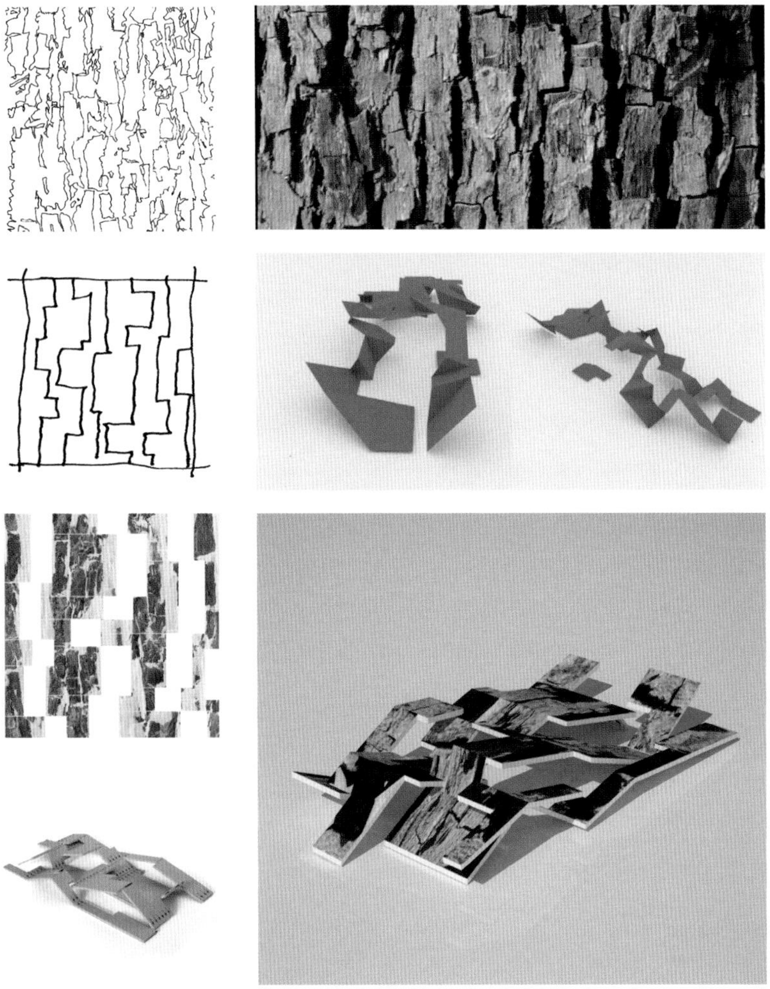

474

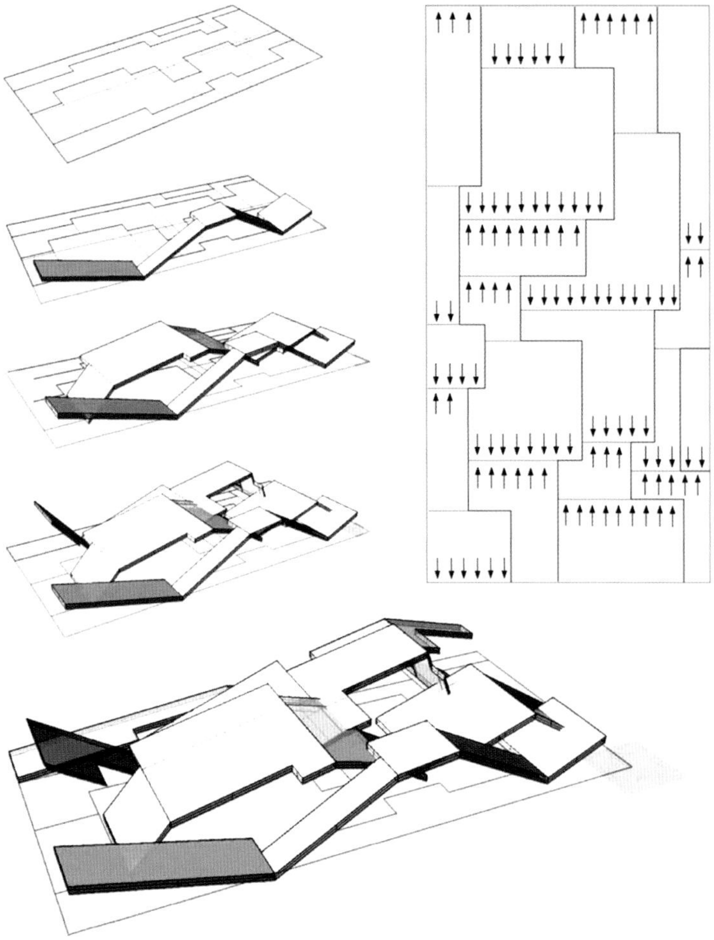

475

476

474 Tracing and graphical abstraction of a bark texture
475 Resulting folding morphology

476 Rendering of the fold based on the analytical process from fig. 474 - 475

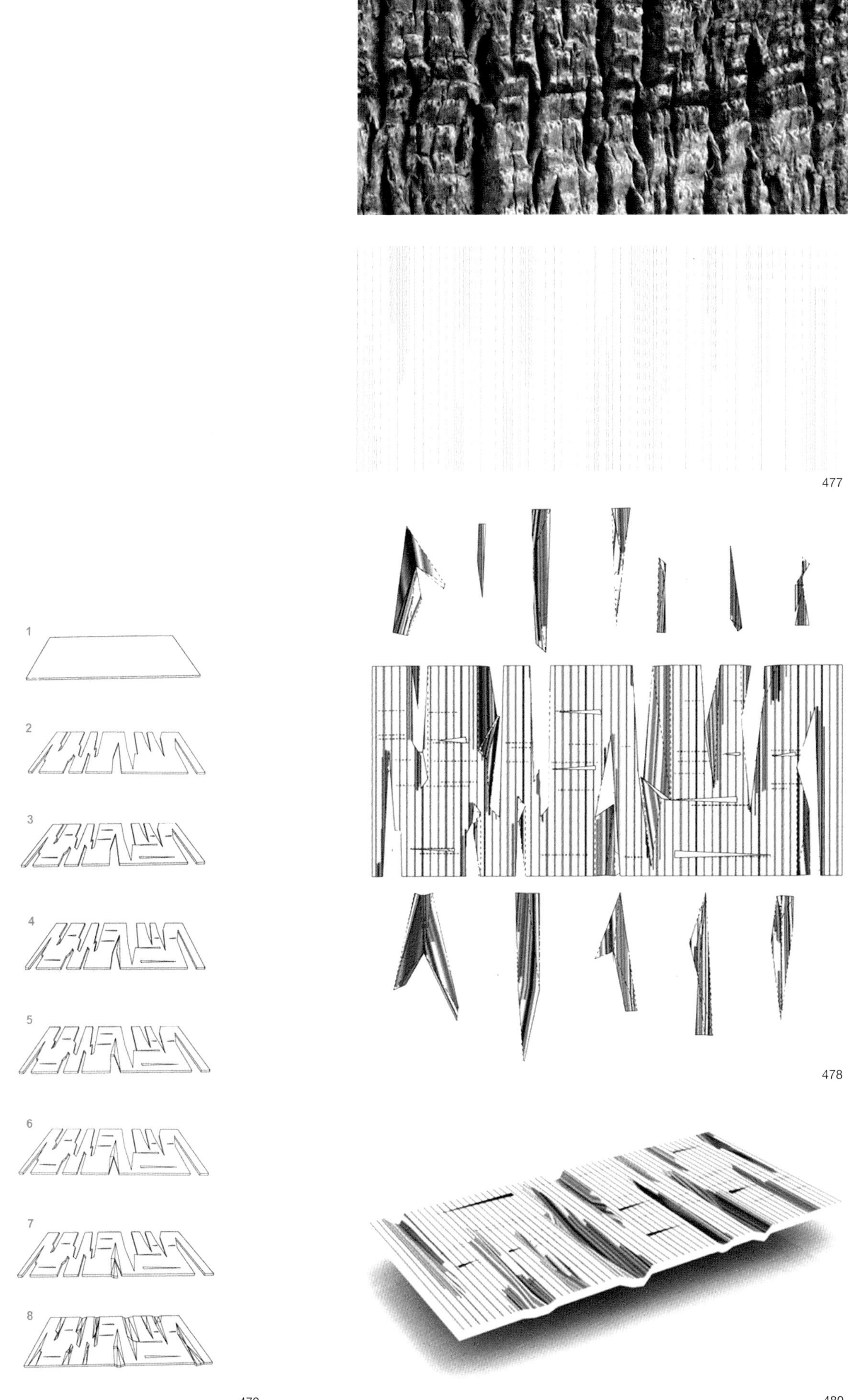

477 Image of a bark-texture and resulting abstracted graphical rendition
478 Documentation of the design assembly
479 Morphology of the transformation
480 Perspective of final spatial result

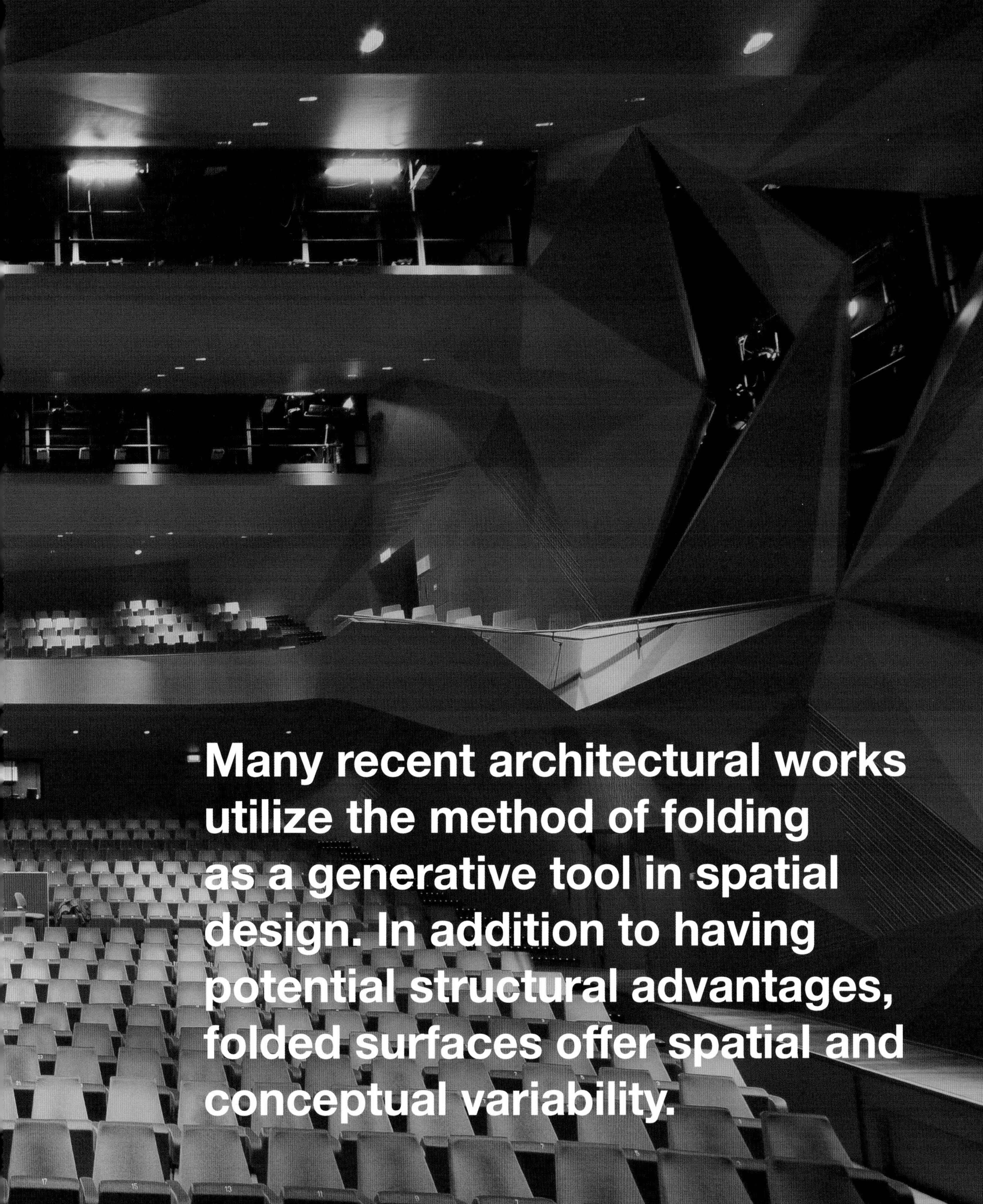

Many recent architectural works utilize the method of folding as a generative tool in spatial design. In addition to having potential structural advantages, folded surfaces offer spatial and conceptual variability.

Chapter 10: Folds and Foldings

fold as spatial philosophy

sculptural folding

folding dynamics

conceptual folds

constructing a fold

folding evolution

diagrammatic transformations

Folding as a method for spatial generation is an established theme in architectural design. It is a different way to apply spatial thinking on a plane or surface: making surface adjustments to define space under structural conditions. In the 1950s, geometric ideas and experiments like the Vector Equilibrium by Buckminster Fuller introduced the idea of folding into architecture and the build environment. (ref. 10.1)

In the 1960s and 1970s, Ronald D. Resch was one of the first to work with digital three-dimensional tesselated structures and folds in order to generate spaces and structural spans through self-supporting modular structures. (ref. 10.2)

At the same time, the fold was discussed philosophically by Gilles Deleuze. Based on this philosophy, further connections were being made within the deconstructivist movement, mainly by Peter Eisenman. In this line of thinking, the fold has the potential of bringing disconnected spatial elements together in a "mix" that aims for the integration of these elements. In his Architectural Design essay "Folding in Architecture," Greg Lynn argues for the possibility of complexity without heterogeneity, with the help of a "smooth pliant mixture." (ref. 10.3)

Although the philosophical view of the fold in connection to architectural space is fascinating, current architectural practice during the last fifteen to twenty years has moved towards a more pragmatic and technical approach when adopting the fold as a design concept. These recent architectural examples depart from philosophical implications of folded space in favor of a more formal aesthetic approach that incorporates equally intriguing fluent spatial effects. After two decades, the folded plane is still a valid formal entity in contemporary architectural design, often used to achieve dynamic spatial effects and to expose more ephemeral conditions such as movement and circulation patterns inside a building.

The Theatre Agora in Lelystad by UNStudio (fig. 9.0 - 9.5) is a good example of the application of folding in architecture. Like many of UNStudio's works, the floating space and the continuum that opens up through the perceptive potential of the folded spaces create an important theme within the building's concept: they dynamically follow the vertical movement of the visitors through the building, finally opening up to a skylight. This central space conveys a very fluid, elegantly enclosed, and at the same time spacious impression. Simultaneously, the formal

Page 222 223:
Main Auditorium, Agora Theater
Lelystad, The Netherlands, UNStudio
Ben van Berkel and Caroline Bos

10.1 Amy C. Edmondson: A Fuller Explanation: The Synergetic Geometry of R. Buckminster Fuller

10.2 Resch, Roland D.: The topological design of sculptural and architectural systems

10.3 Greg Lynn: Folding in Architecture

9.1 Staircase and open foyer space

9.2 Exterior view. The facades sharp angles are covered by orange steel plates and glass

9.3 Main Auditorium

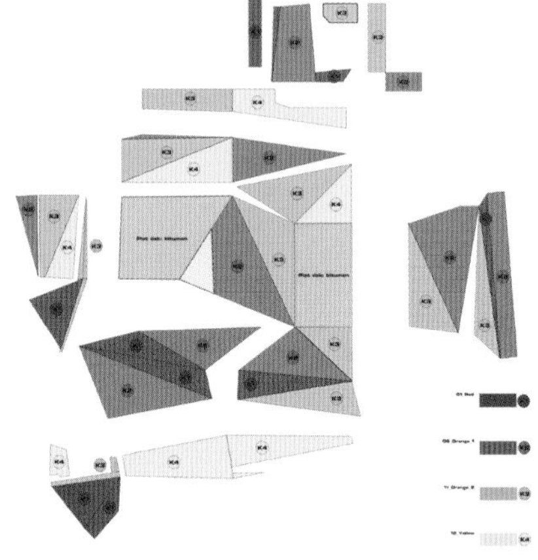

9.4 Diagram of the foldout for the façade and roof surface

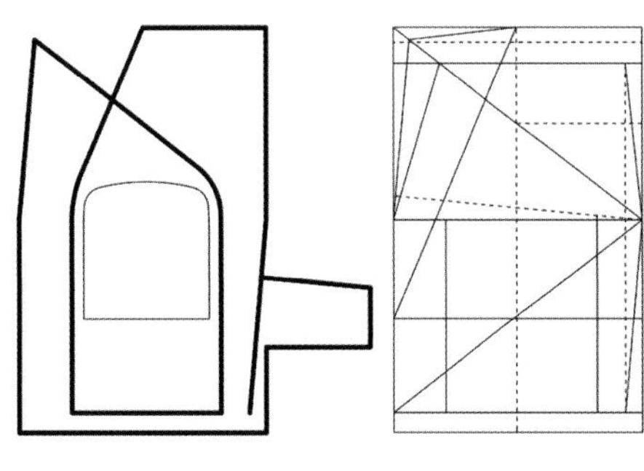

9.5 Concept drawings

language of the folded interior space enables a connective association with the exterior, between inside and outside.

In the technical realm, many characteristics of the fold bring pragmatic advantages. For example, the folded surfaces throughout the auditorium of the Theatre Agora help to control the acoustics.

The architecture of Frank O. Gehry, (fig. 9.6) often shows the formal phenomena of folding, which is closely related to his design process that often utilizes paper as a model building material. (ref. 10.4)
Interesting spaces and forms create a poetic appeal that is characteristic to his distinct and personal architectural language. For Rem Koolhaas' Seattle Public Library (fig. 9.7), the fold is more the result of a conceptual process in which the single and 'introverted' programmatic entities of the building are bridged and held together by spanned surfaces. These planes create spaces of their own, containing the more 'extroverted' public and impressive open areas of the building, blurring the boundaries of public and private, inside and outside.

Another feature of the fold is structural integrity. In this case, the fold has the potential to become much more than just a formal entity. This kind of

Images on this page:
Agora Theatre Lelystad, The Netherlands. UNStudio, Ben van Berkel and Caroline Bos

10.4 among other materials of course but in this case we are concentrating on paper as this chapter is discussing folding techniques

9.6 InterActiveCorp Headquarters, New York. Frank O. Gehry and Associates

9.7 Seattle Public Library, Rem Koolhaas. OMA

9.8 Tate Pier, London. Detail of folded space. Marks Barfield Architects

application can be observed inside the Yokohama International Port Terminal by Foreign Office Architects.

An issue with the execution of some of these otherwise fluid spaces is that the constructive and structural aspects of the architecture are fairly conventional in their assembly. A wall has different requirements than a ceiling or a floor of a building. In order for the impression to be continuous throughout the structure, a homogenous surface can only achieved through a seamless cladding of the same material.

The contradiction in the physical execution of folded buildings has the potential to be solved through contemporary research in the area of intelligent, performative materials and adaptive surfaces. Structural surface experiments by architectural researchers like Achim Menges correspond in part to this contemporary development in architectural academia that is finding its references in recent architectural history and theory (ref. 10.5). Through Menges's holistic approach in constituting aesthetics, theory, and construction, it may one day be possible to technically execute Greg Lynn's idea of a "smooth pliant mixture" in a less formal manner. Until then, the evolution of the fold and the constant development of this architectural design method under applied theoretical or technical aspects will not be fully concluded.

The student works in this chapter deal with the idea of the fold by using the methods of tracing and mapping that were described in chapter nine. In the first step, the students were asked to try out different folds in paper to develop ideas about the spatial and structural potential of the technique, and to test possibilities and limitations for architectural design applications. (ref. 10.6)

This step was an important part of the exercise, because it gave students an understanding of the tectonic properties of the composition, which would then be rendered digitally. In the second step, the students were asked to find a texture or condition that is represented in an image and analyze it through a mapping technique highlighting specific phenomena trough an overlaid drawing. In the third step, the parameters of drawing and image were projected onto three-dimensional space in order to achieve points that could be connected to form surfaces. These surfaces together open up a complexly folded space that follows examined parameters, resulting in diagrammatic transformations of space.

10.5 Michael Hensel /Achim Menges Morpho-Ecologies: Towards Heterogeneous Space In Architecture Design

10.6 Petra Schmidt / Nicola Stattmann: Unfolded: Paper in Design, Art, Architecture and Industry

481

481 Folding studies: Paper folds and sketches

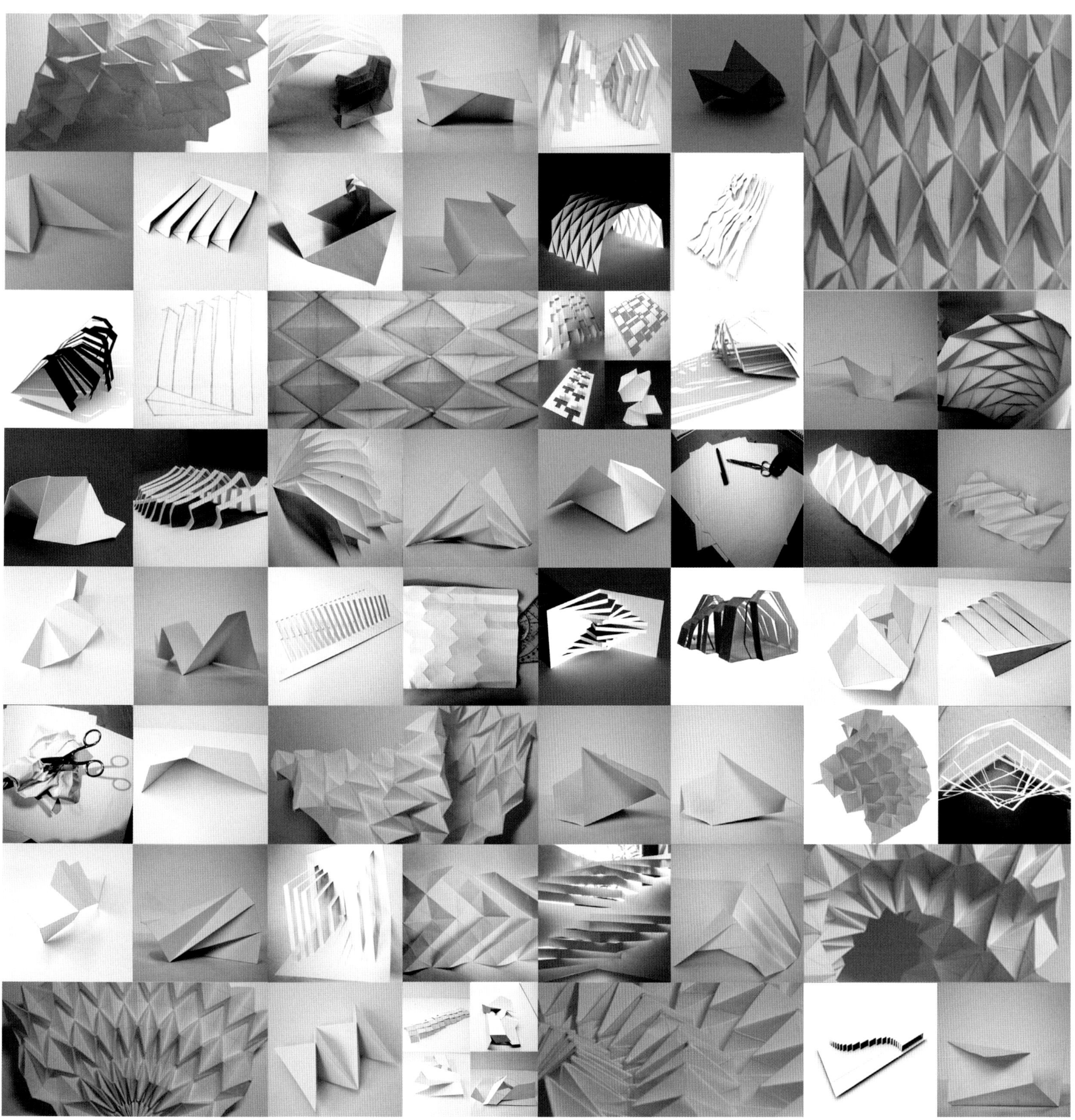

482

482 Folding studies: Paper folds, sketches, and renderings testing the potential of folding as a space generating entity

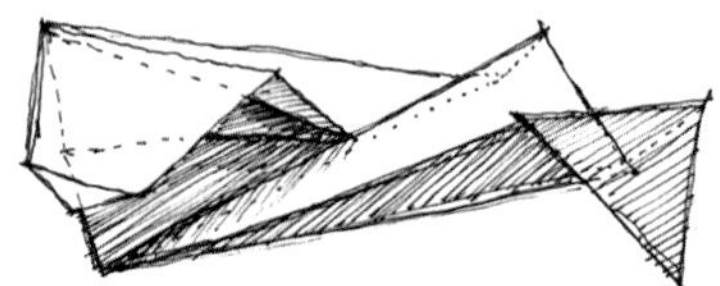
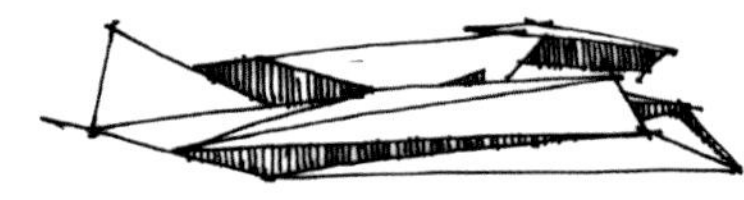
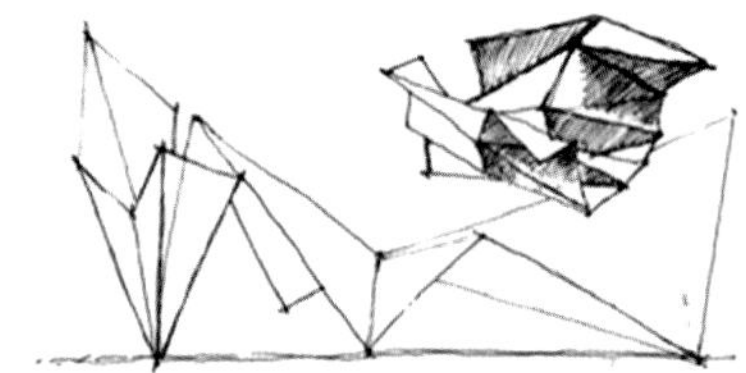
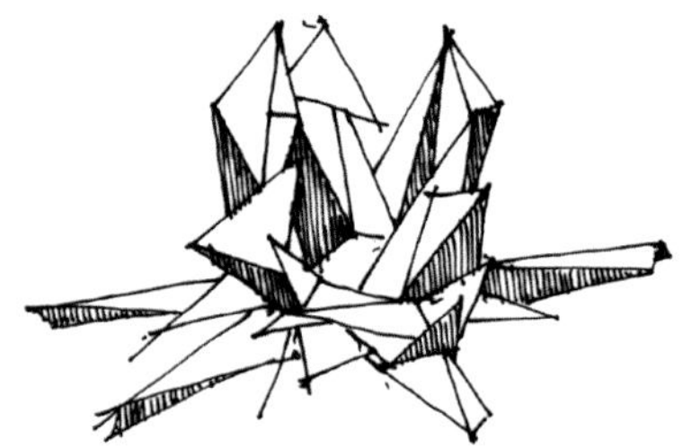
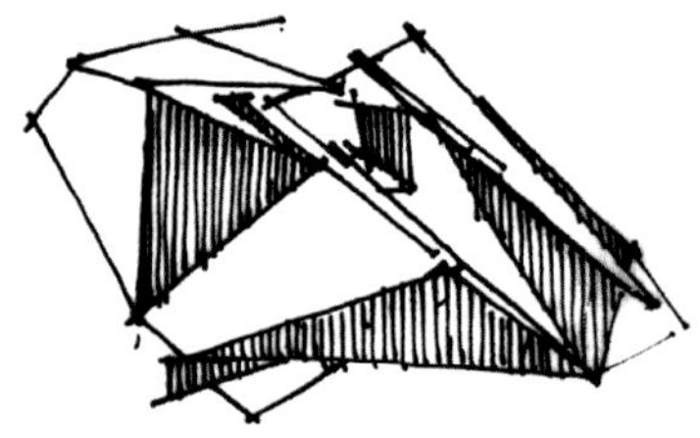
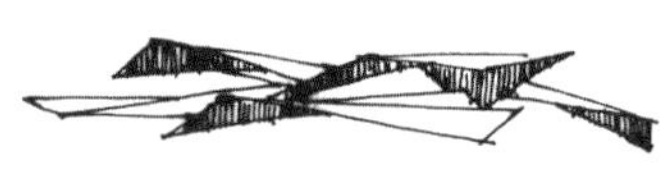
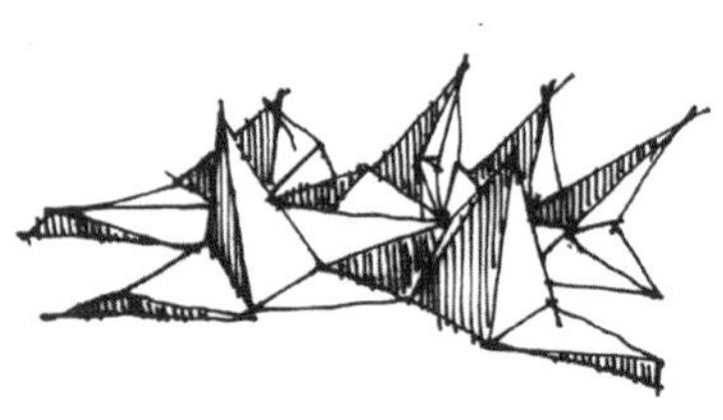
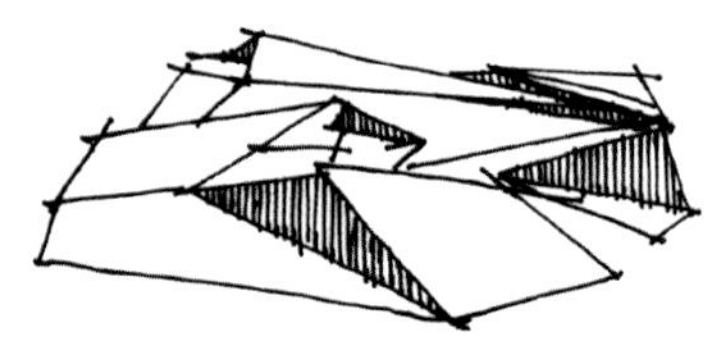
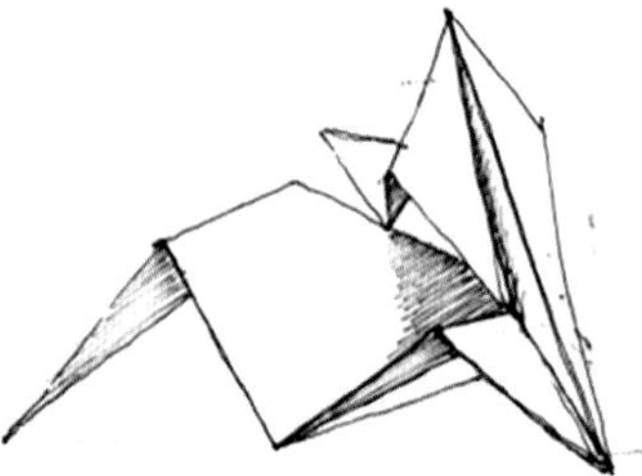
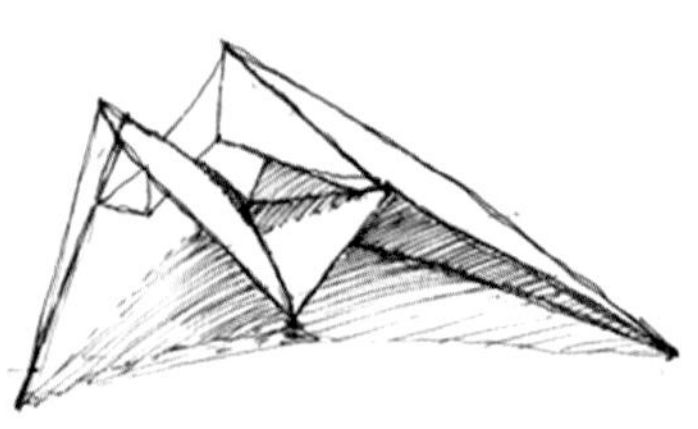
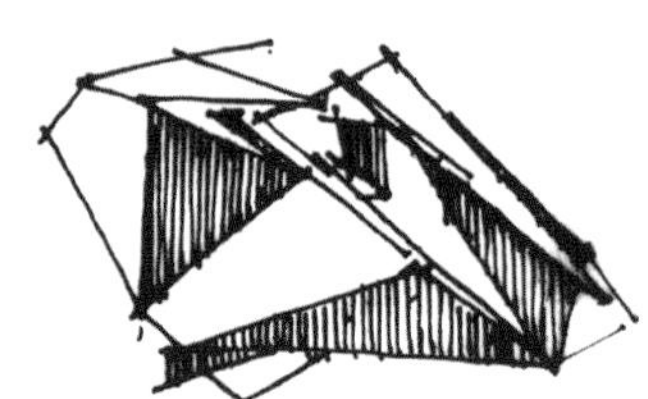
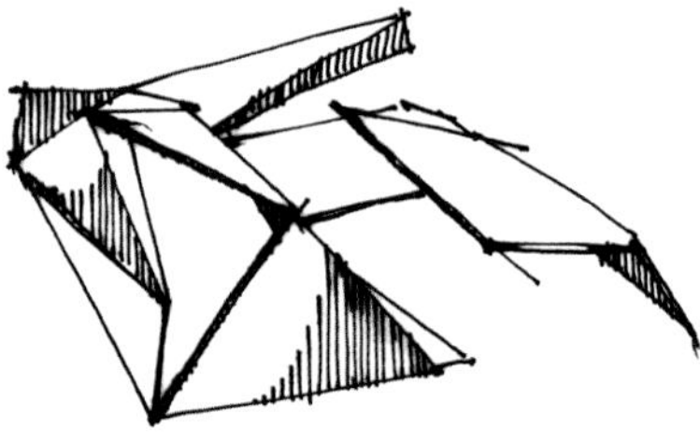

483

483 Freehand sketches of different folding stages and possible design options

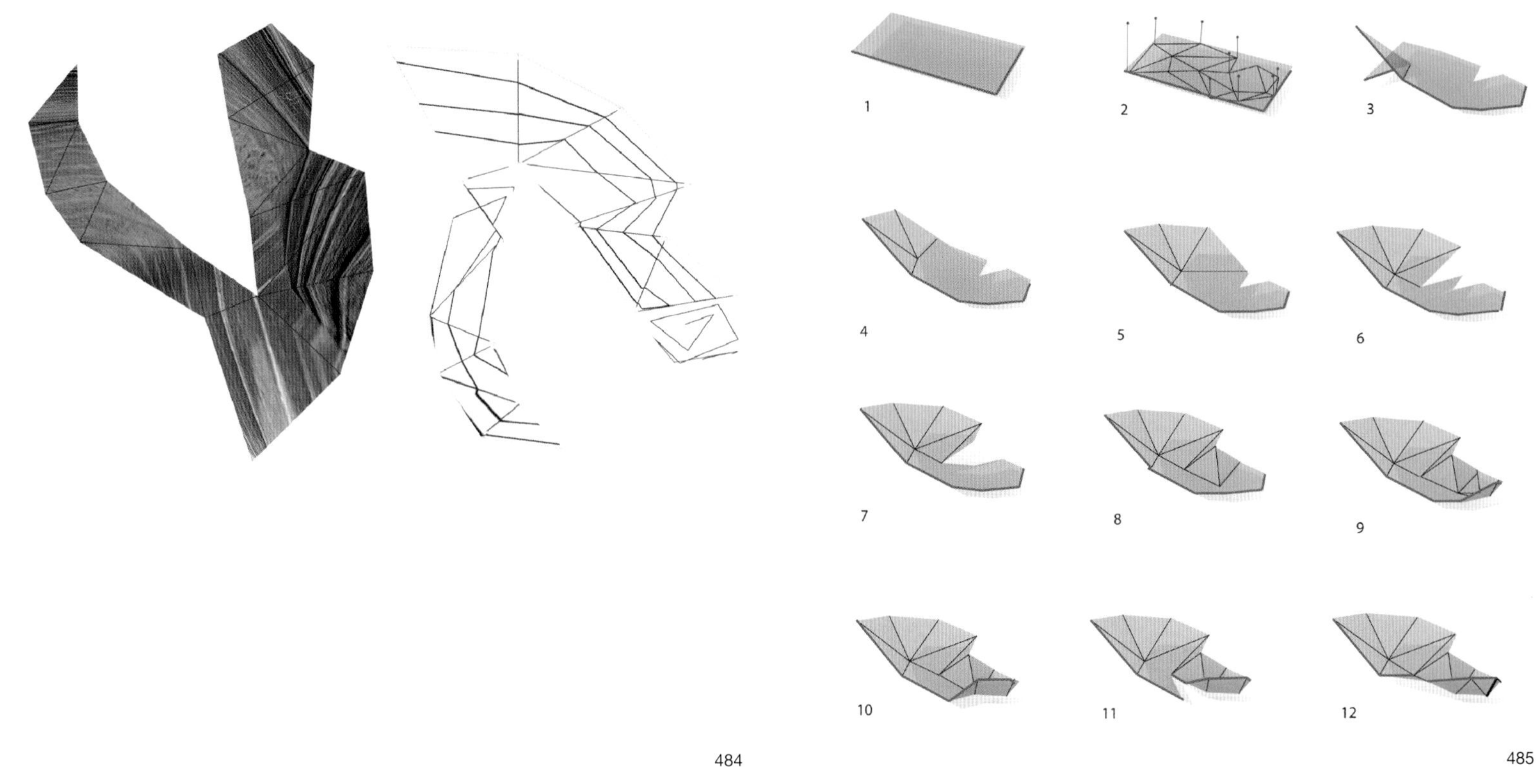

484

485

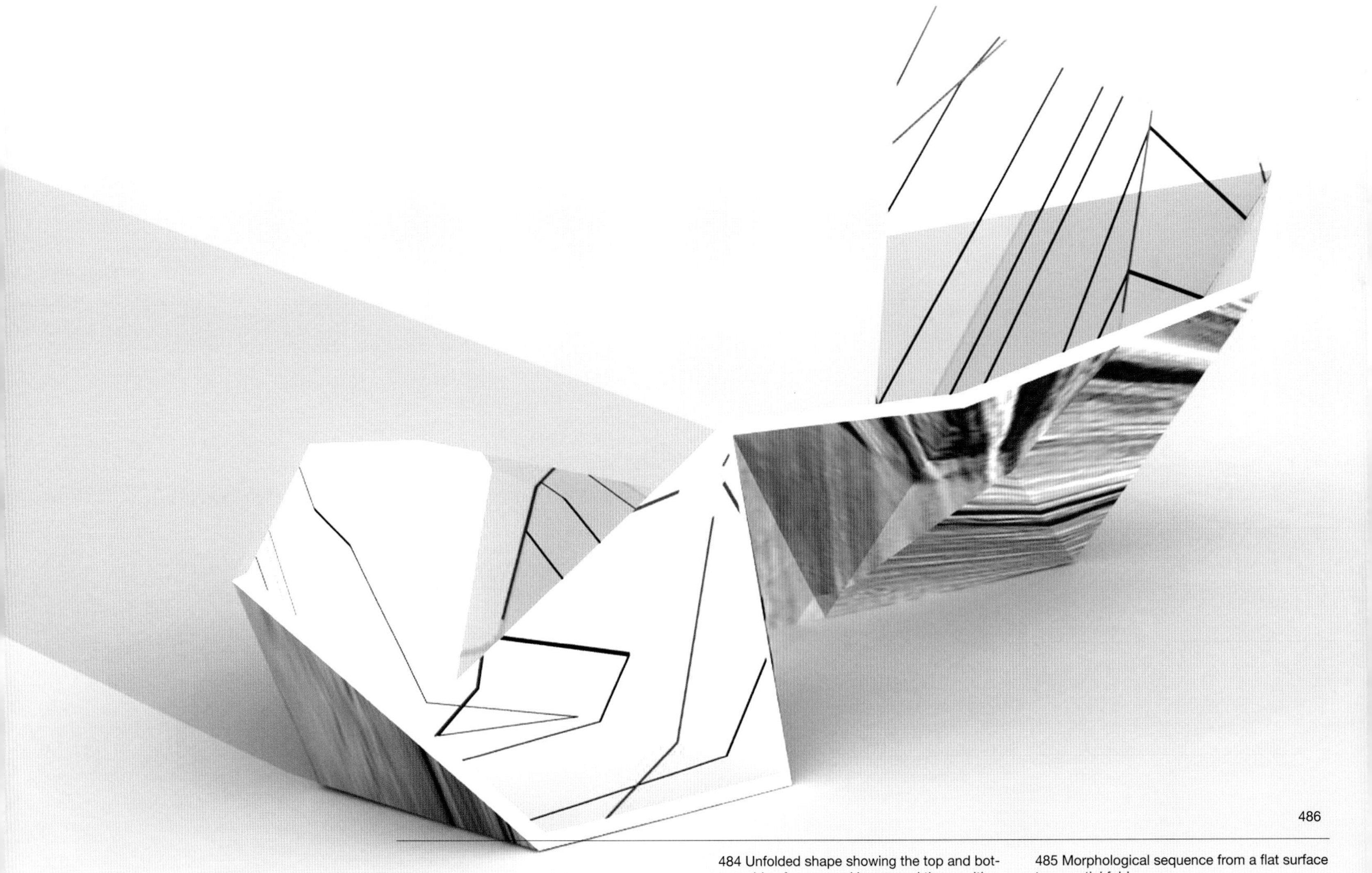

486

484 Unfolded shape showing the top and bottom side of a mapped image and the resulting abstraction in a generative notational drawing

485 Morphological sequence from a flat surface to a spatial fold

486 Final fold derived from a rock strata texture

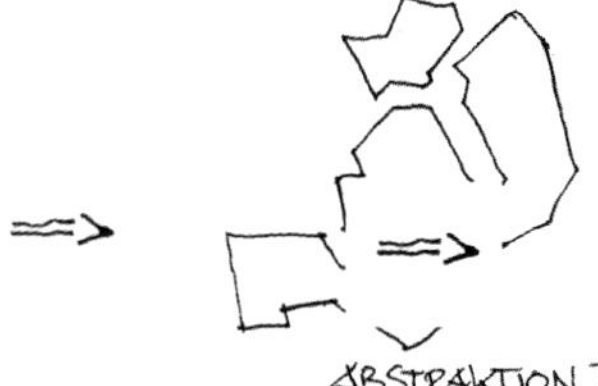

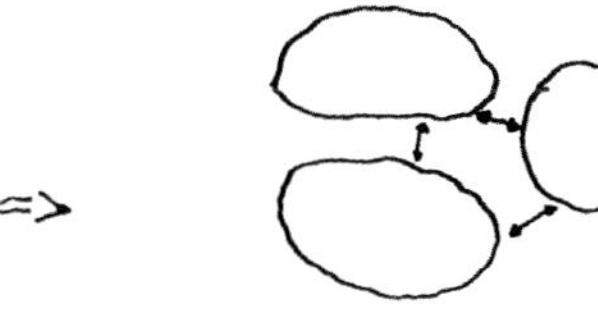

487

488

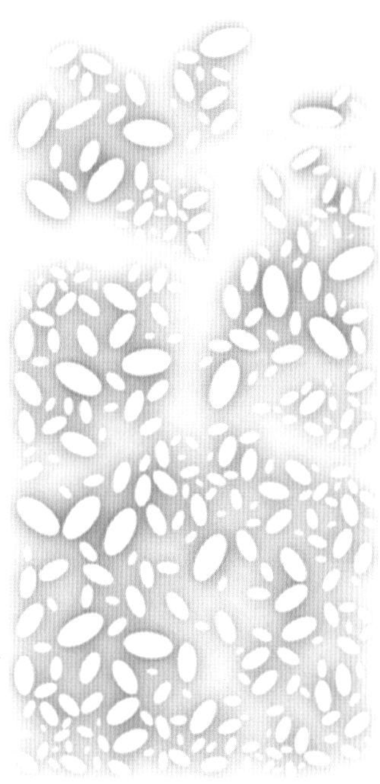

489

487 Conceptual strategic sketches based on the analysis and abstraction of an African village structure

488 Rendering of folded surface with elliptical openings derived by the mapping technique

489 Pattern structure, displaying the figure ground relationship of the mapped village

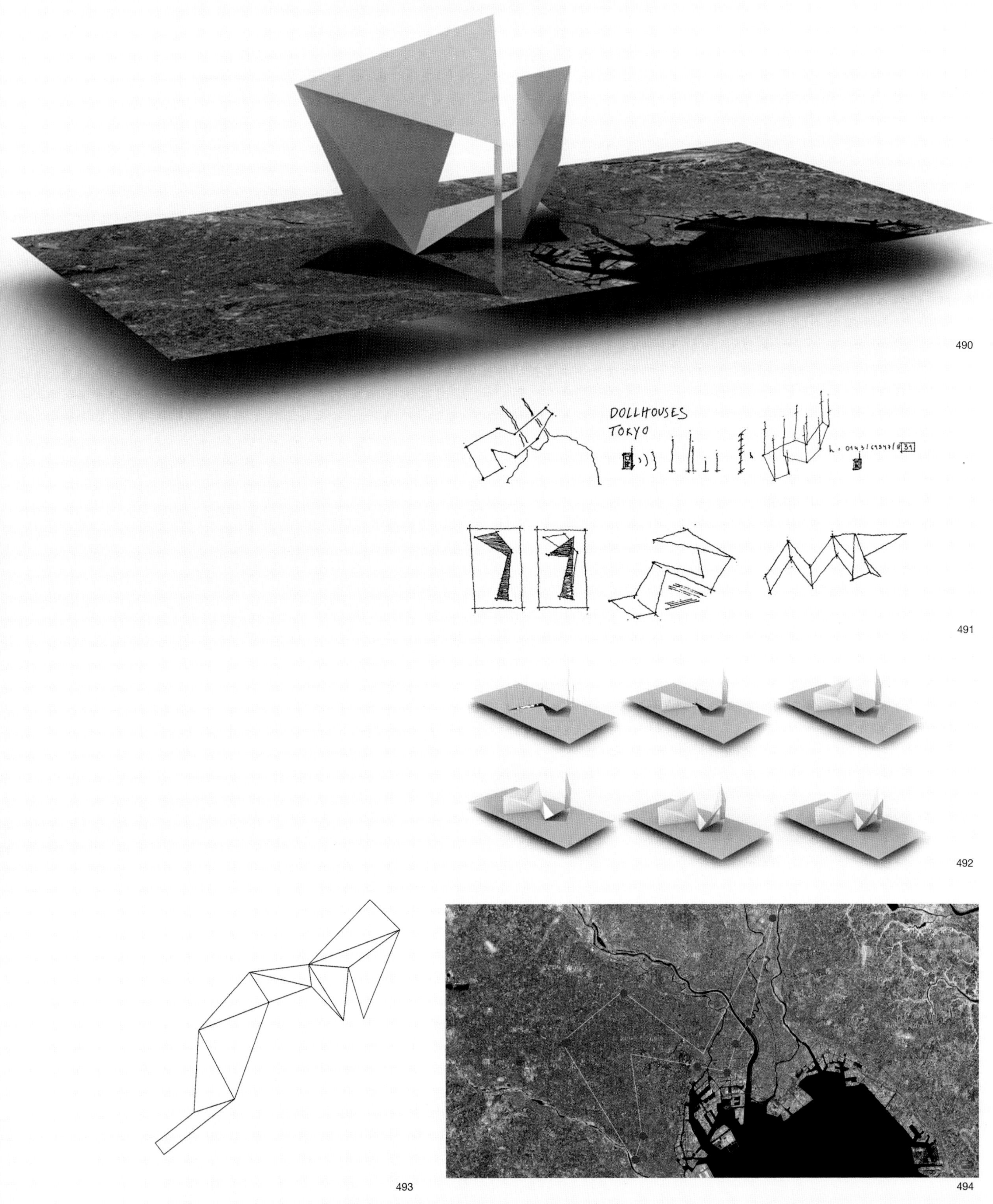

490

491

492

493

494

490 Folding based on points on the city map of Tokyo

491 Conceptual sketches illustrating the idea
492 Morphology of the folded surface
493 Unfolded surface

494 Different locations within Tokyo are marked on the map. The various heights of the fold are derived from the last two digits of the phone numbers at this location

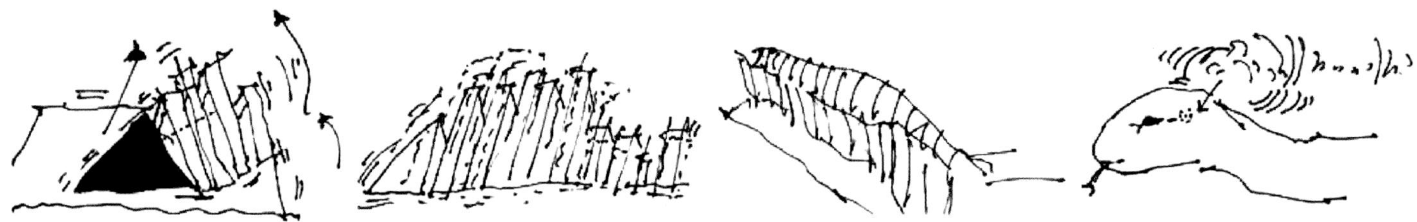

495

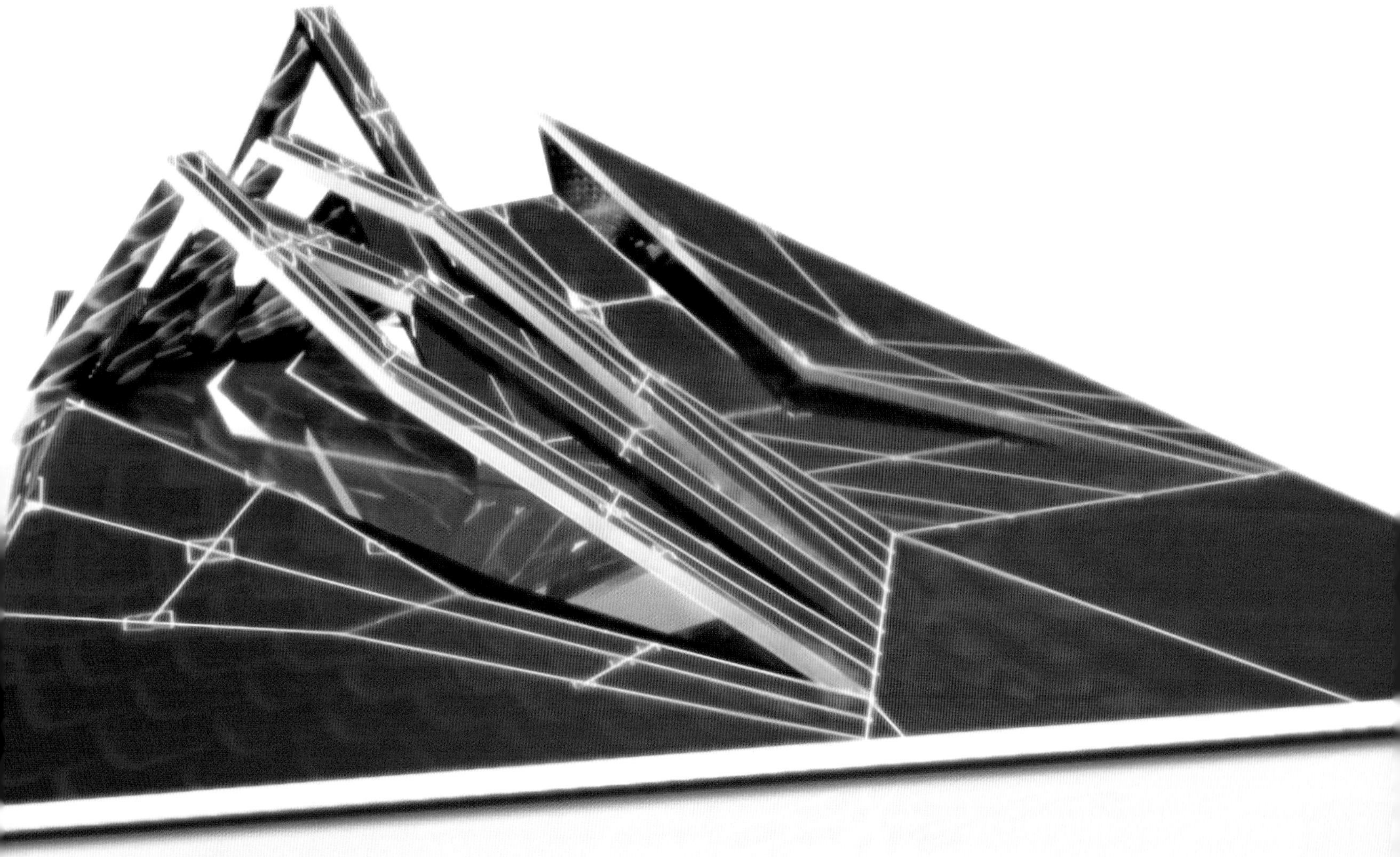

496

495 Conceptual sketches for a folded structure that is inspired by the texture of a snakeskin

496 Folding with mapped snakeskin texture. The green and red on the bottom- and upper surface gives the composition an interesting complementary color contrast

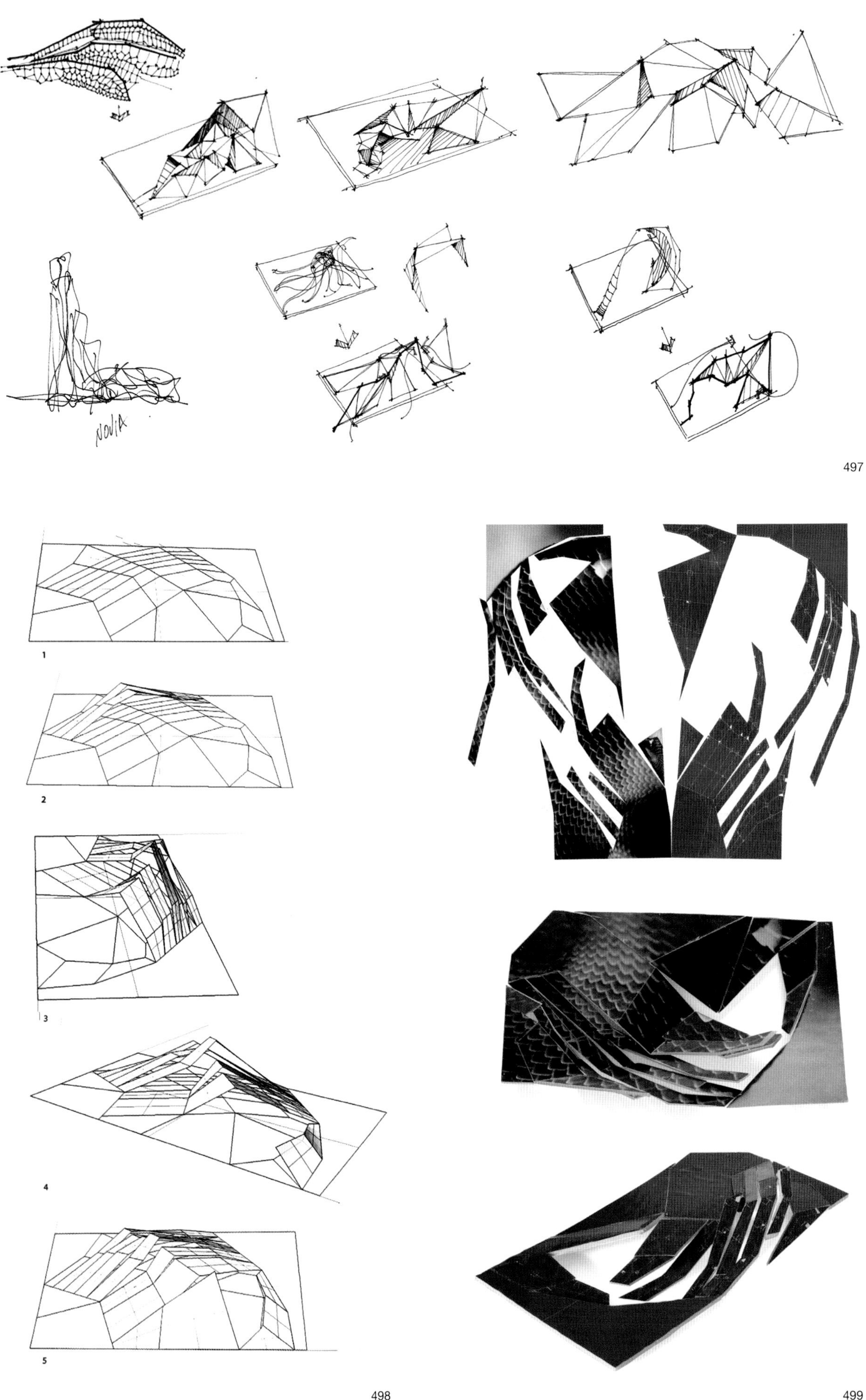

497

498

499

497 Conceptual design sketches

498 Morphological sequence from surface to fold

499 Rendering of the unfolded surface and photos of the physical model

500

501

502

503

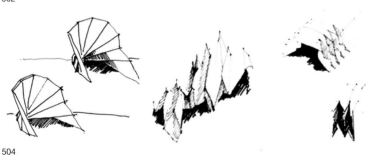

504

500 Rendering of the morphological sequence
501 Folding study rendering
502 Base mapping and cutout plane unfolded

503 Folding derived from spatial observations on the relationship of different destinations on a city map

504 Some rough initial sketches illustrating folding strategies

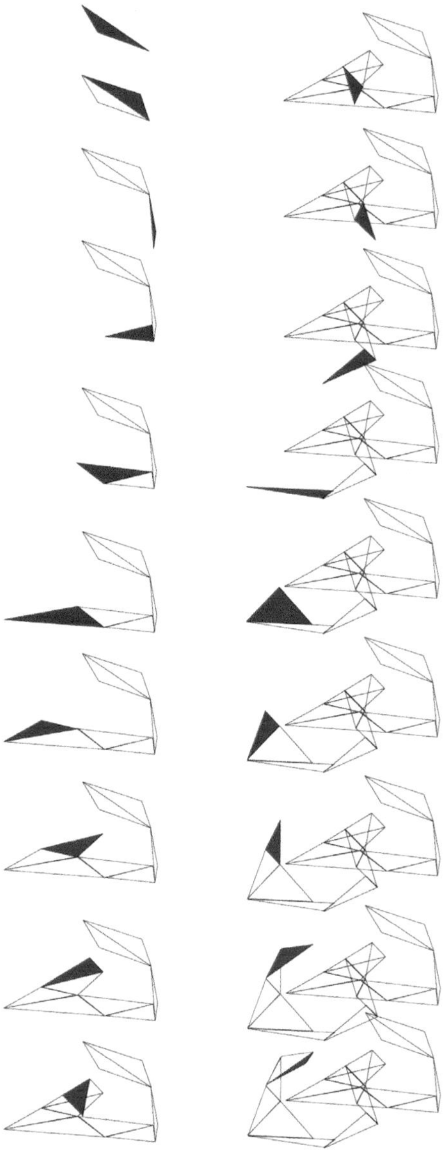

505

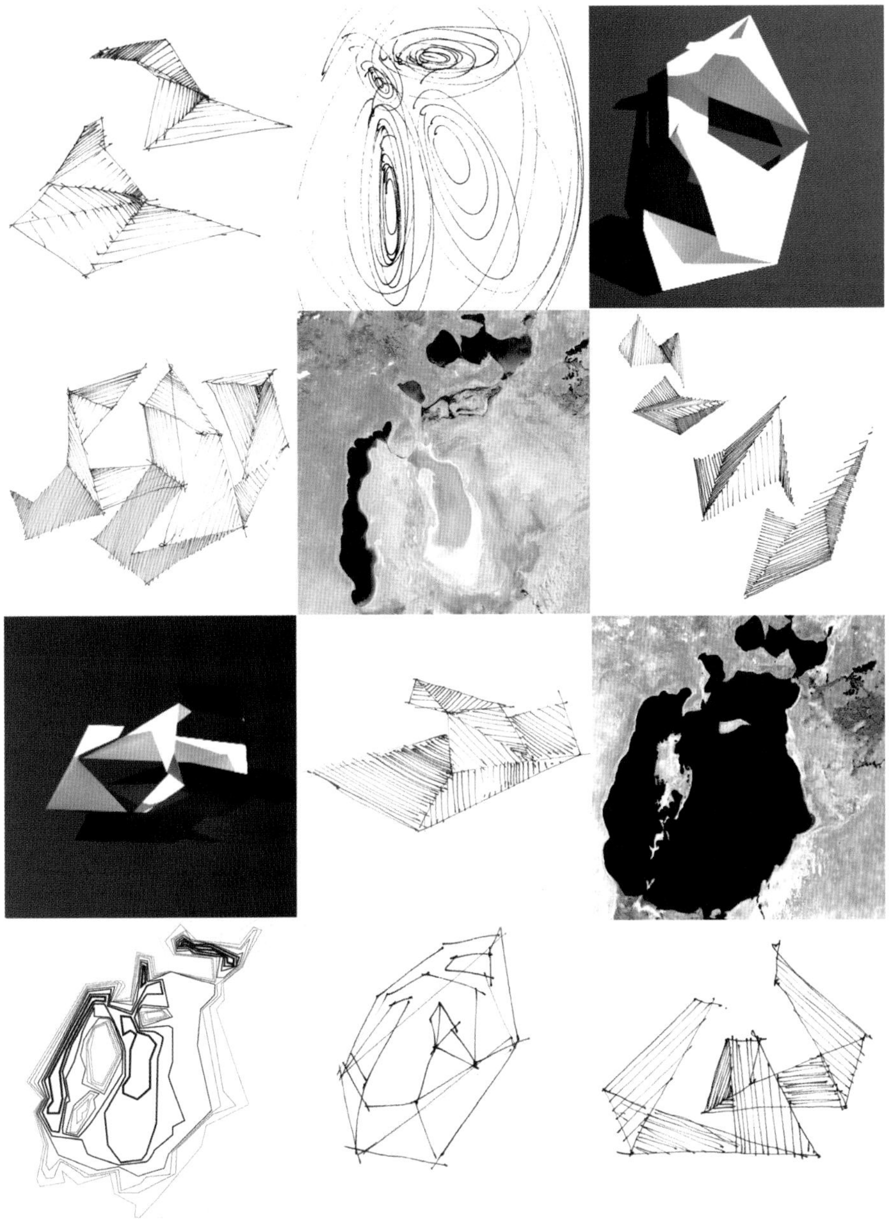

506

507

508

505 Sequence displaying the folding process

506 Development of a folded surface inspired by a topographical analysis of a specific site

507 Unfolded surface with a mapped generative drawing
508 Rendering of the final fold

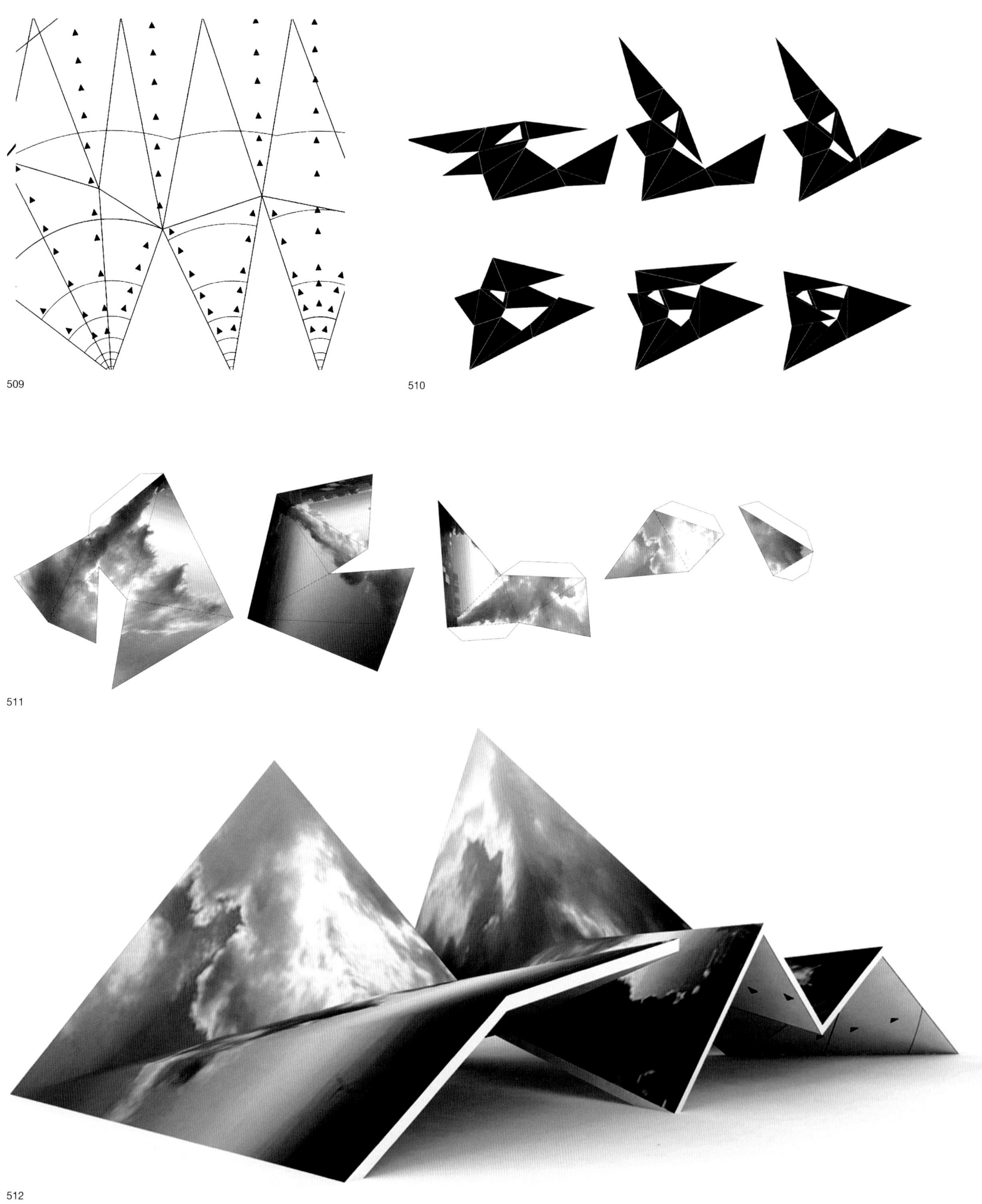

509 2D diagram with folding instructions
510 Morphological sequence
511 Dismantled surfaces for physical assembly of fold
512 Rendering of the final fold based on cloud densities

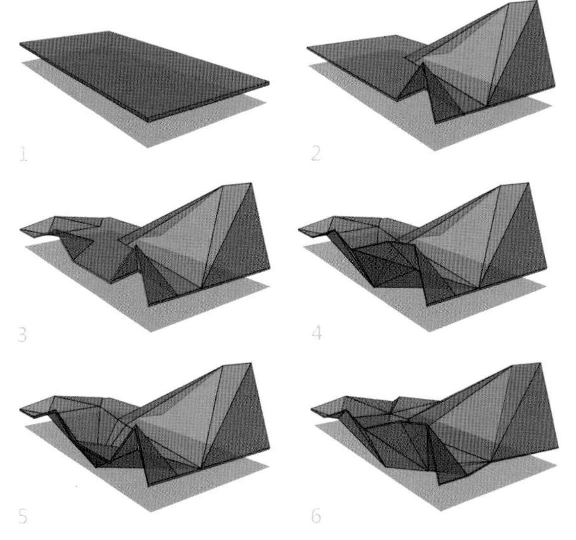

513

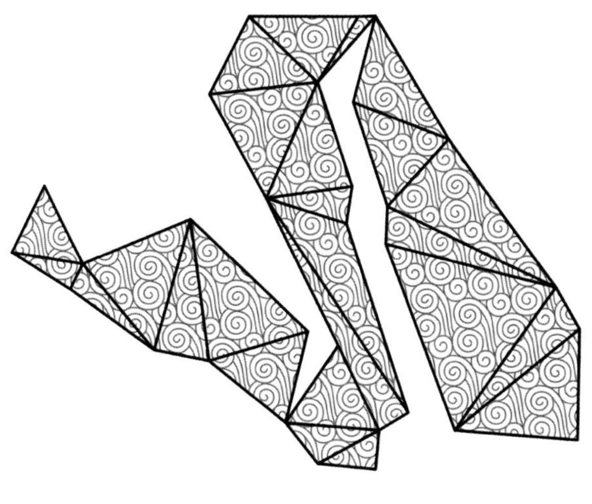

514

515

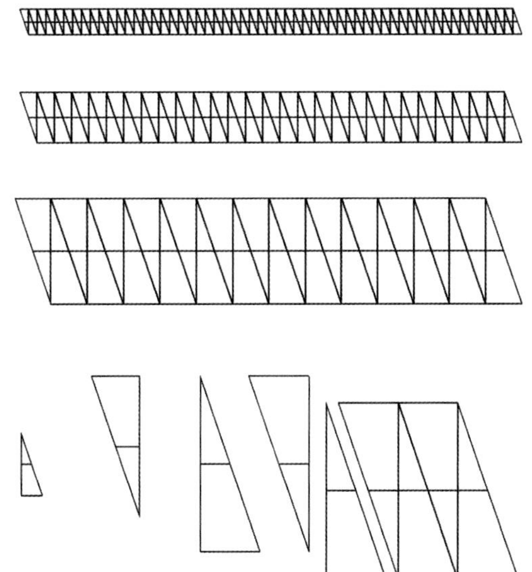

516

517

518

513 Folding morphology
514 Unfolded surface
515 Fold

516 Flattened folding plan for fig. 515
517 518 Renderings of shading studies for a folded space

SONY

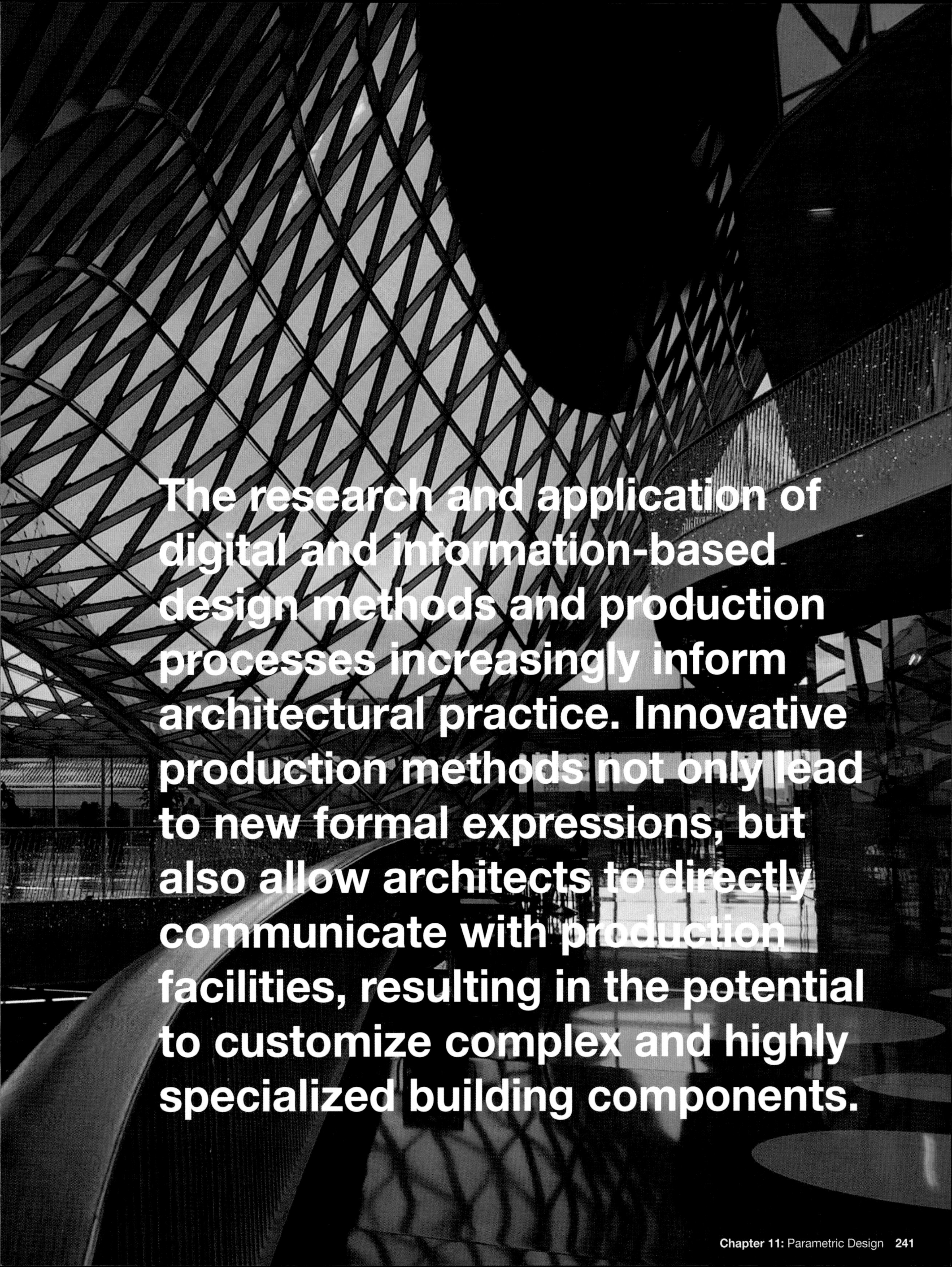

The research and application of digital and information-based design methods and production processes increasingly inform architectural practice. Innovative production methods not only lead to new formal expressions, but also allow architects to directly communicate with production facilities, resulting in the potential to customize complex and highly specialized building components.

Chapter 11 : Parametric Design

Flexibility, Change, and Adaptation
by Moritz Fleischmann

definition

physical simulation

object-oriented programming

parametric modeling

material behavior

In his book *Elements of Parametric Design*, Robert Woodbury (ref. 11.1) describes the term "parametric design" as computer-aided design systems that are capable of "represent[ing] designs that change with their input data."

This short description does not capture every aspect of what one might consider parametric design, and could be misunderstood as design that solely emerges via data input. It unveils, however, some of the term's central aspects: flexibility, change, and adaptation in a computer-based design system.

Parametric design is the subject of numerous publications. Despite the fact that computer-aided design and its effects on design methodology have recently gained a lot of attention both in academic and professional circles, the concept of parametric design software is not new. In fact, the ancestor of modern CAD software, called "Sketchpad," (ref. 11.2) developed by Ivan Edward Sutherland in 1963 for his doctorate at Massachusetts Institute of Technology, was already parametric in its inception. Beyond the concept of parametric design and object-oriented programming, Sutherland proposed a method for incorporating physical simulation to help inform the design process.
The recent development of object-oriented programming environments such as Processing and commercial software such as Bentley's Generative Components, McNeel's Grasshopper, and their scripting and programming functionalities have had a major impact that led to a renaissance parametricism. (ref. 11.3)

The examples provided are the results of a workshop that explored parametric modeling concepts in combination with principles of physics and their simulation. In this workshop, students were required to develop a design tool with

Page 240 241:
MyZeil, Shopping Mall, Frankfurt am Main, Germany, Massimiliano Fuksas Architetto

11.1 Woodbury, R.; Elements of Parametric Design, Routledge
11.2 also known as "Robot Draftsman"

11.3 www.processing.org
www.bentley.com/en-US/Products/GenerativeComponents/
www.grasshopper3d.com

11.1 Installation of a Tension Active Structure (Cable Net with membranes & compressive members) at the Architectural Association School of Architecture (AA) in London

11.2 Roof of the Shiliupu Ferry Terminal, Shanghai. Xian Dai Architectural Design (Group) Co., Ltd

integral physical simulation in order to develop a computer-based design environment with seamless interaction between physical simulation, the designer, and geometric forms. After developing a simple mass-and-force simulation in Processing, approaches were made to realistically simulate material behaviors by alignment of various material properties as they were derived from stress-testing machines. In recognition of the advantages of the digital over analog scale modeling, different generative and creative physically based design processes were explored through the investigation of tension-active structures.

The development of tension-active structures is challenging from a designer's point of view. One method that was utilized in the past—and still is widely common— is to use physical experiments to „form find" the shapes of these structures. This method requires extremely precise tests in material behavior and knowledge, of the specific properties of a certain material, as the forms are established based on scale models. The aim of the seminar was to develop an alternative computer-based design approach through the means of parametric (constraint-based) modeling.

During the seminar, after learning the concepts and syntax of the programming software Processing, the students developed a spring-based particle system and embedded it into a program which generated connections between individual springs based on their local stresses. The result was a seemingly complex mesh topology, which was based on a single simple rule. The software program's particle system used idealized linear abstraction of physical rules such as forces, gravity, and mass for the simulation of tension (and later on compression and bending). Each part of this environment was accessible

11.3 EMP Museum Seattle, façade detail. Frank O. Gehry and Associates

11.4 Façade Detail, MyZeil, Shopping Mall, Frankfurt am Main, Germany. Massimiliano Fuksas Architetto

11.5 Kunsthaus Graz, Peter Cook and Colin Fournier

to the designer. The option to embed specific material properties, derived from the stress-testing machine available to the students at the university, was developed in parallel. In the case of the cable nets, the relationship of strength and elasticity were important.

Through tests, this ratio was determined and an evolutionary algorithm was written to match the specific nonlinear curve of elasticity of the tested material. In a second step, the ability to simulate compressive members was introduced into the program. This was achieved by manipulating the spring's parameters such as rest-length and strength. Lastly, members that would buckle under compressive load were simulated as well. Therefore, each compressive member was re-assembled into a truss-like configuration to act in tension and compression. This method was also applied to higher dimensional forms, showing that it could be used for the simulation of thin plate deformations.

In these cases, all forces, compression, tension, and bending interact and contribute to the system's behavior. Finally, the group of students developed a graphical user interface and finished the seminar with short presentations that developed a concept for the installation of a full-scale prototype at the university.

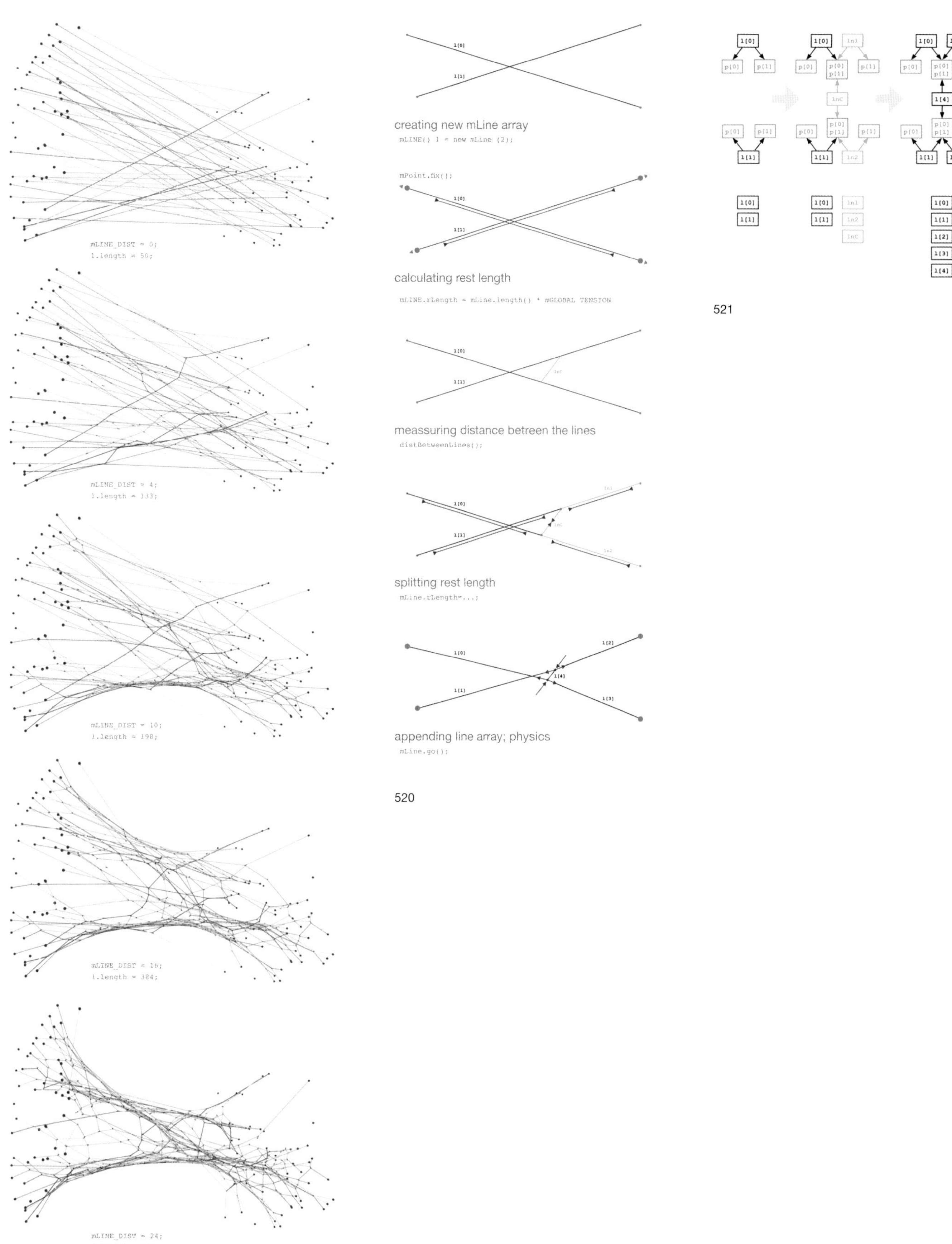

519 Particles tension: Simple simulation of a physical particle system that deals with spatial positions and forces. Points can be connected to lines, acting as springs. Depending on the load of the spring, a certain force acts on both of its end points. The acceleration of every point is then calculated by the resulting force that acts on it and its mass. By repeating this process, the system automatically tries to find the state of balance of all forces. It is possible to implement different material properties within this simulation.

520 Connections: The sketch automatically generates connections between lines, when they fall below a certain distance.

521 Data structure. One-dimensional „Line-Array“

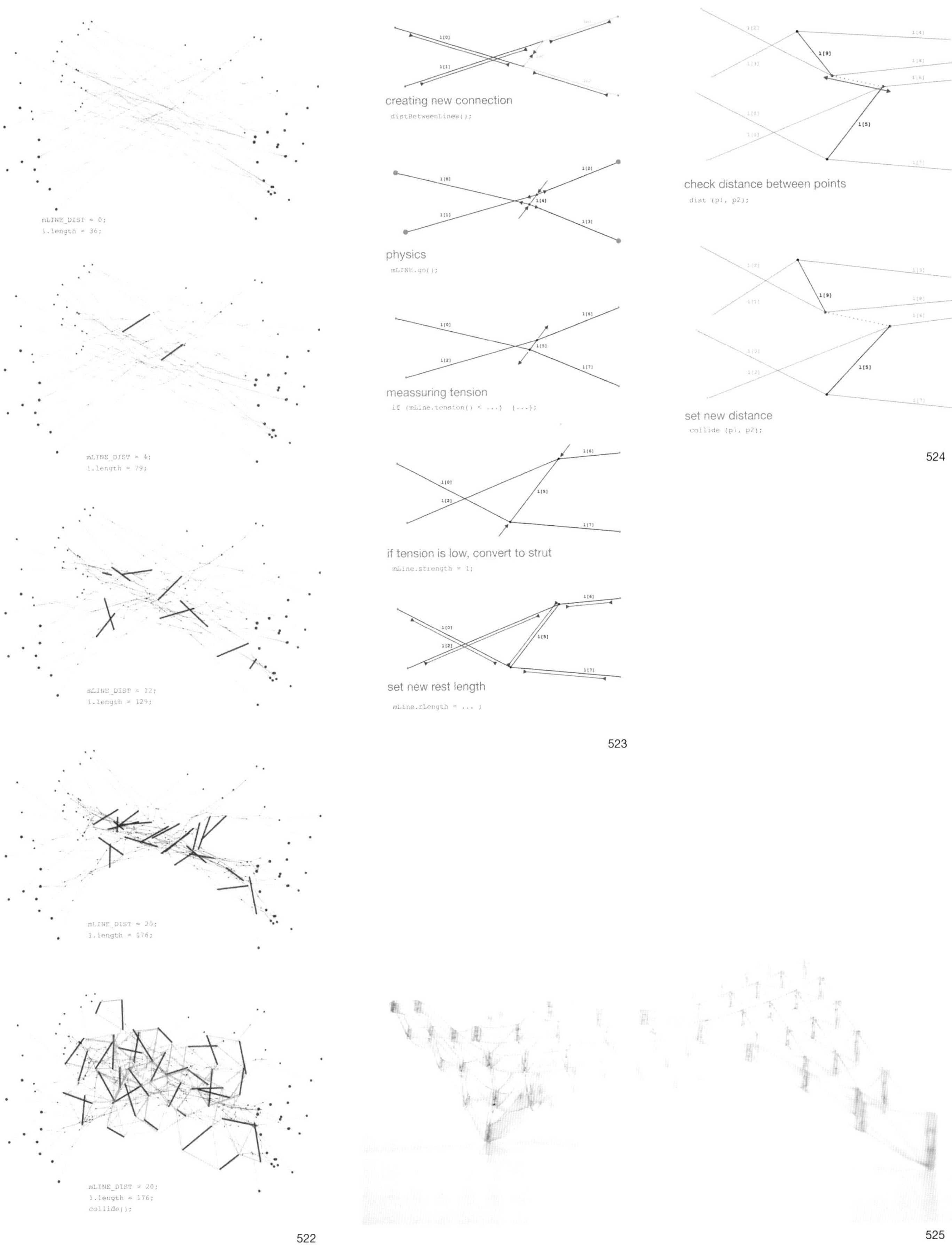

522 Particles collision. In a second version of the sketch struts were implemented in the simulation. The properties of the struts are based on the same principles such as the tensioned elements but have a fixed length.

523 Struts. When the tension between line connections falls below a certain value, lines are converted to struts by the connection generating function

524 Collision. In a second step a radius is assigned to the end points of all struts, colliding with each other

525 Physical model

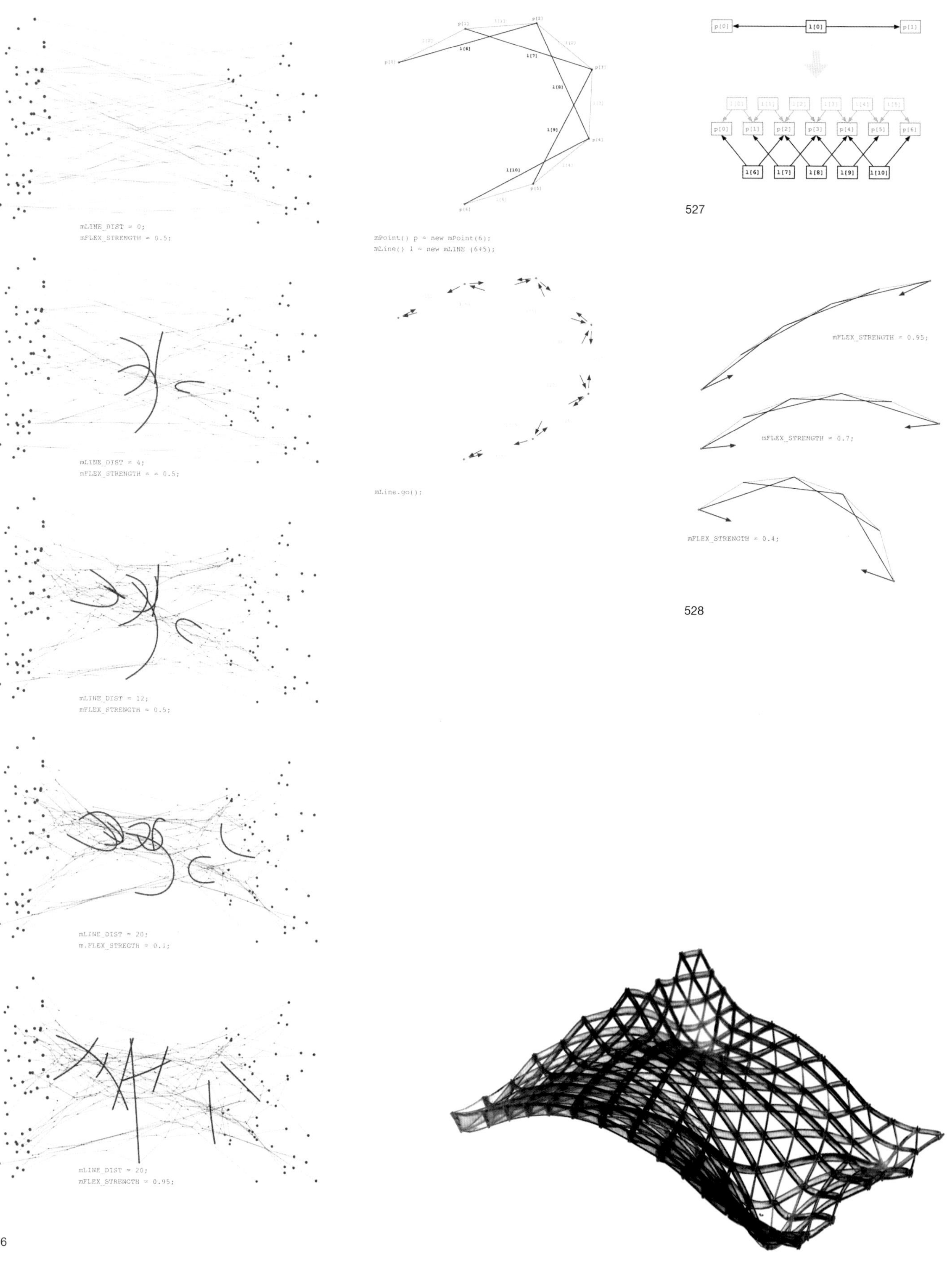

526 Bending particles. The flexural elements are a combination of compression- and tensional elements. The members in tension tend to balance the deformation (state of rest).

527 Diagram of the data structure: Conversion from a strut to a flexural element

528 Strength. By altering the strength values of different spring types, the stiffness of the element can be affected. Bending properties of certain materials can be measured and transferred into the simulation.

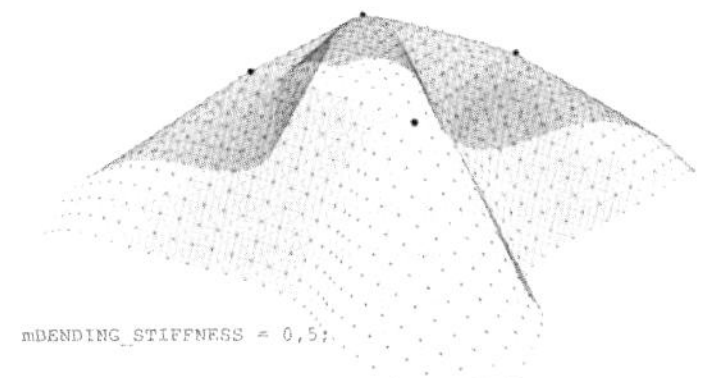

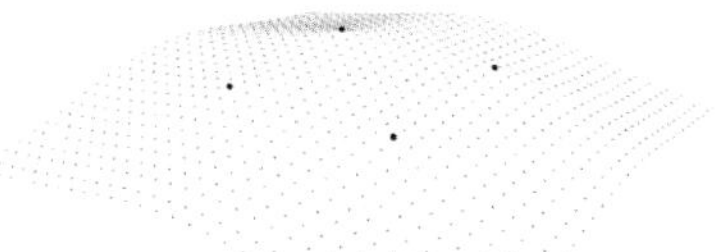

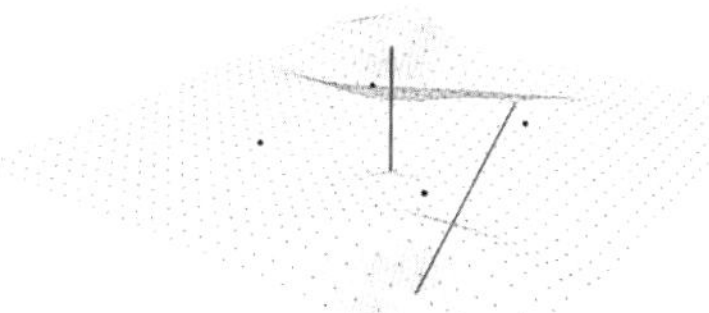

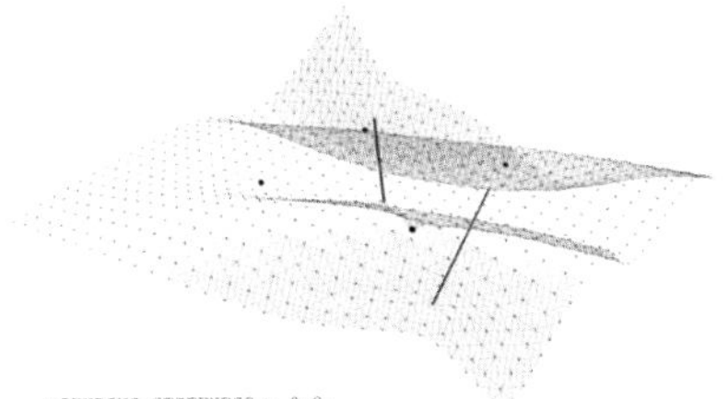

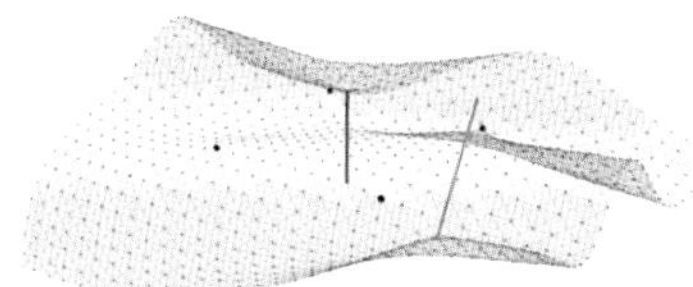

529

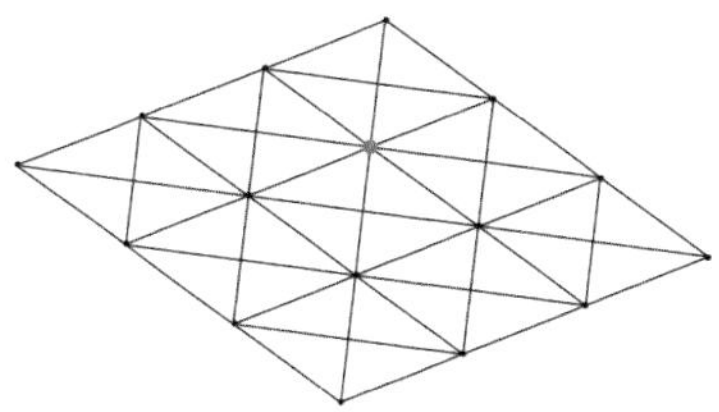

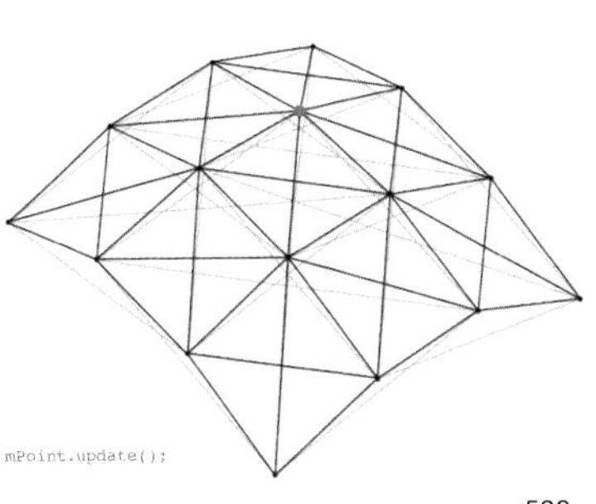

530

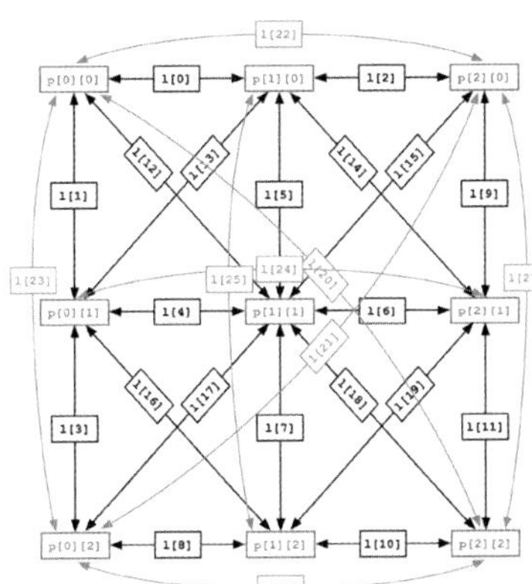

531

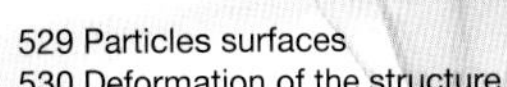

529 Particles surfaces
530 Deformation of the structure

531 Diagram of the data structure: Arrangement of a 3 x 3 point grid

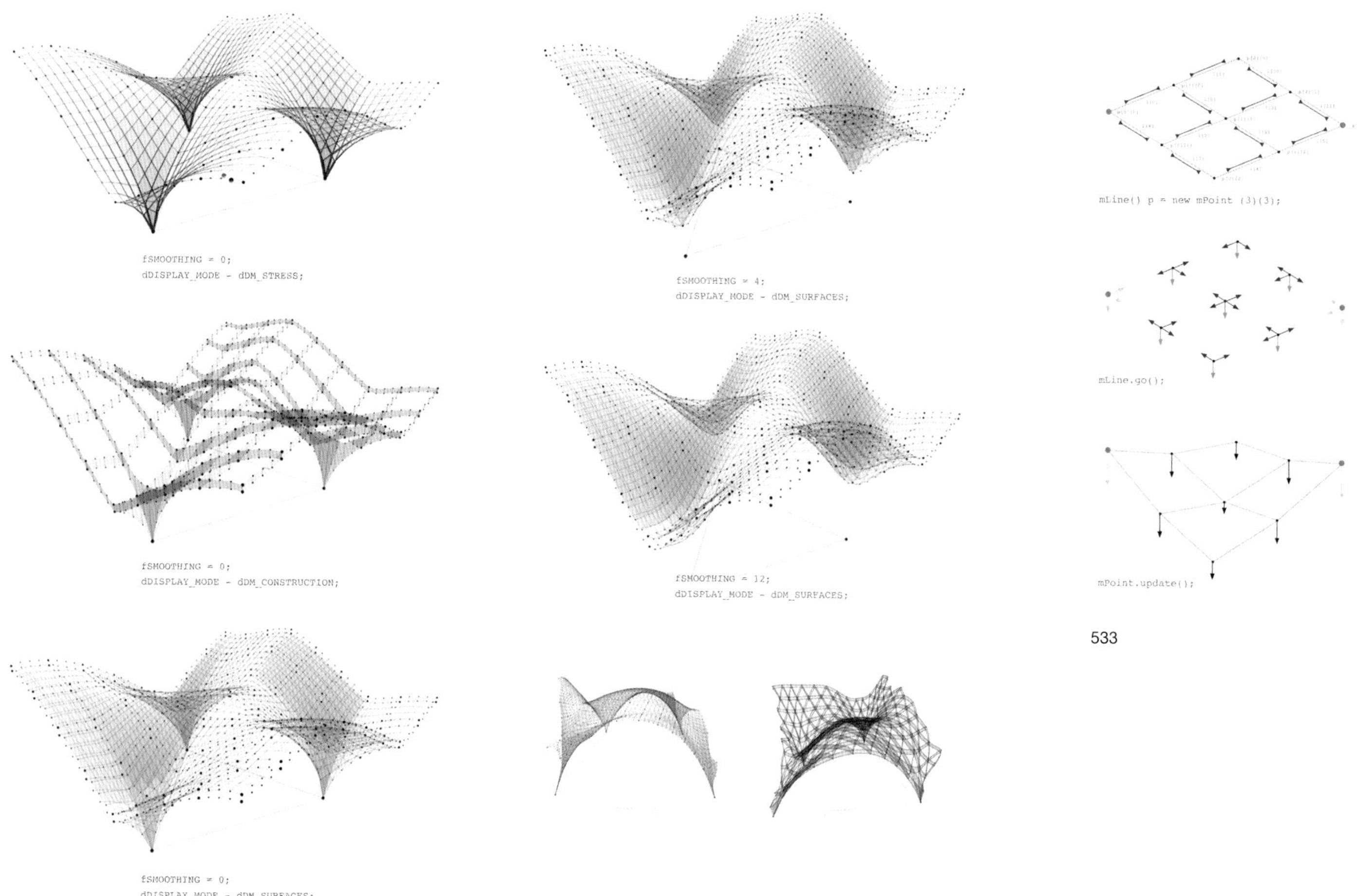

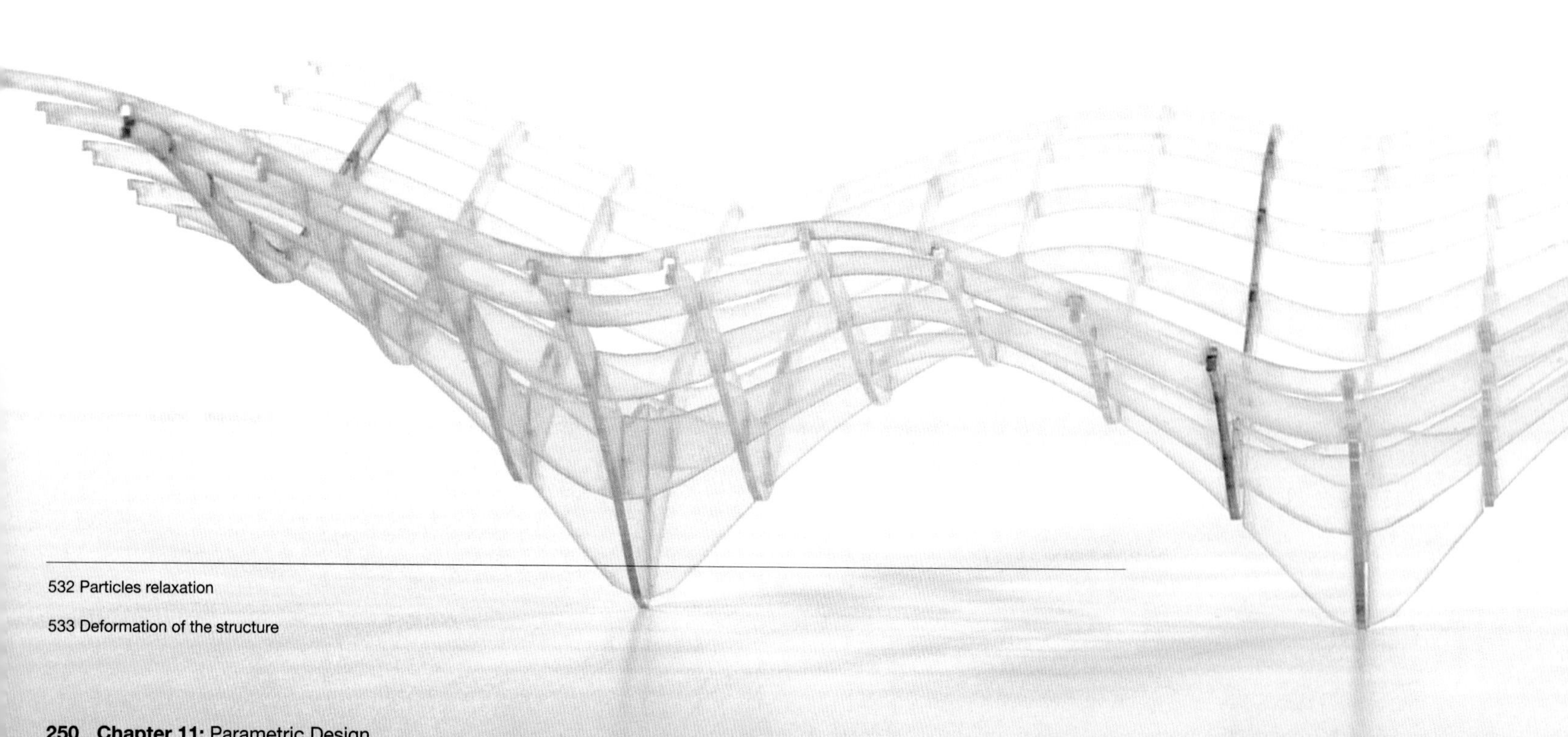

532 Particles relaxation

533 Deformation of the structure

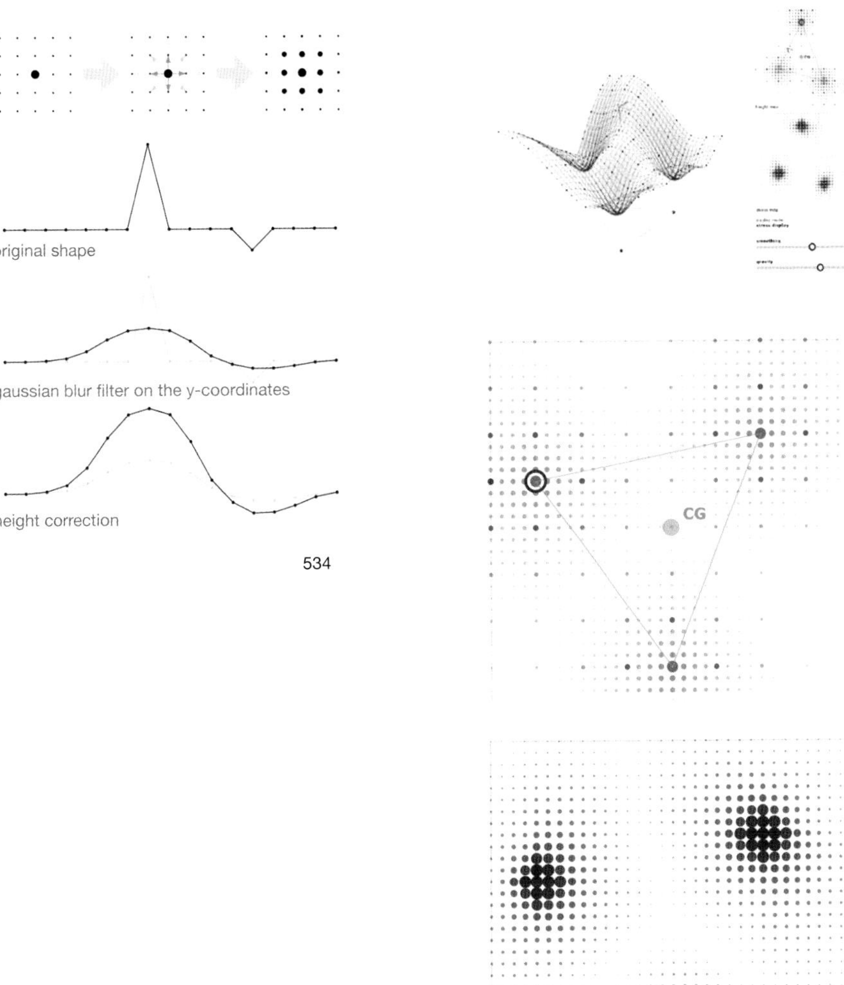

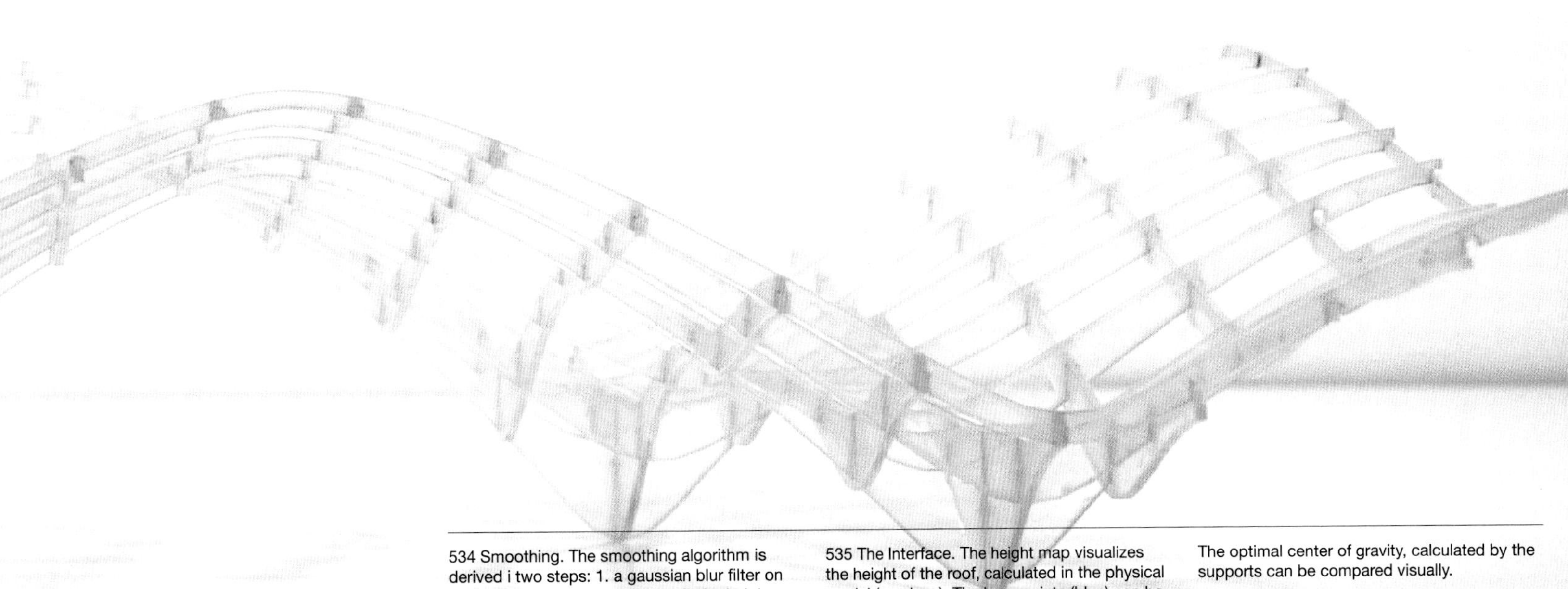

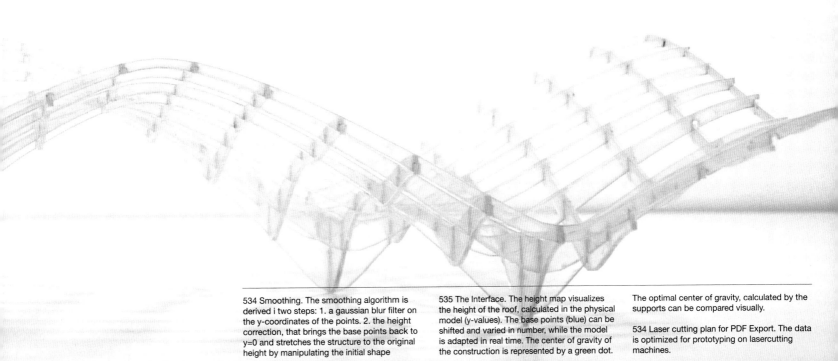

534 Smoothing. The smoothing algorithm is derived i two steps: 1. a gaussian blur filter on the y-coordinates of the points. 2. the height correction, that brings the base points back to y=0 and stretches the structure to the original height by manipulating the initial shape

535 The Interface. The height map visualizes the height of the roof, calculated in the physical model (y-values). The base points (blue) can be shifted and varied in number, while the model is adapted in real time. The center of gravity of the construction is represented by a green dot. The optimal center of gravity, calculated by the supports can be compared visually.

534 Laser cutting plan for PDF Export. The data is optimized for prototyping on lasercutting machines.

Appendix

Imprint

Authors
Mark Mückenheim
Juliane Demel

Guest Authors
Moritz Fleischmann
Tobias Klein

Edited by:
Mark Mückenheim
Juliane Demel

English language edits:
Vasilena Vasilev and Pamela Worth

Graphic Design:
Juliane Demel and Mark Mückenheim based on an initial concept by David Welbergen

Chair for Principles of Architectural Design / Visiting Professor:
Mark Mückenheim

Research Assistants / permanent Teaching Staff:
Juliane Demel
Peter Schmid
Maren Weitz

Teaching Staff:
Carla Baumann
Dietmar Dasch
Julian Dostmann
Robert Eichler
Urs Fridrich
John Friedmann
Fleur Kamenisch
Lena Lendzian
Martin Langner
Sarah Michels
Kristina Moehring
Georg Räß
Carolin Riesselmann
Veronika Pöllmann
Marija Tokic
Simon Vorhammer
Juni Ngoc Dung Vuong
Carlos Wilkening
Ivalina Yapova
Christoph Ziegler

Teaching Assistants:
Andreas Schulze
Boryana Yancheva

Guest Teachers:
Peter Dell'Uva
Moritz Fleischmann
Tobias Klein
Dietmar Koering
Dennis Vlieghe

Administrative Staff / Office of the Chair for Principles of Architectural Design:
Christine Engelmann
Marti Heidkamp

Research Assistants of the Chair
Harry Dobrzanski
Florian Hartinger

Authors:

Mark Mückenheim is the founder and principal of MCKNHM Architects BDA (www.mcknhm.com) in Düsseldorf, Germany. He has lectured and acted as a guest critic at numerous institutions in Germany and abroad. Among other schools, he taught for more than six years at the distinguished RWTH Aachen before being appointed as a visiting professor for principles of architectural design at the Technical University Munich from 2009 to 2012. His award winning work has been featured in various international book and journal publications and has also gained reputation through a number of exhibitions in Germany and abroad. Educated in Germany, the United States, and England, sponsored by a Fulbright scholarship and a DAAD grant from the German government, Mückenheim received his Master of Architecture from Parsons School of Design, New York, and his Graduate Diploma in Architecture at the Bartlett School of Architecture, University College London.

Juliane Demel is an assistant professor and research assistant at the Architecture department, chair for principles of architectural design at the Technical University Munich. Before her teaching engagement at the TUM, she worked at CAUPD in Beijing, where she conducted a research on Chinas sustainable development for the reconstruction of the earthquake effected area Beichuan under sustainable aspects. Educated in Germany and at the University of Auckland in New Zealand, she received her Diploma in Architecture and Urban Design from the University Braunschweig, Germany.

Guest Authors:

Tobias Klein is one of the founders of the design and research network Horizon (www.horhizon.com) he is currently teaching as a Course Master of the first year studio at the Architectural Association, runs a media studies class at the AA and is teaching the postgraduate studio ADS1 at the Royal College of Art together with Roberto Bottazzi. He has taught, lectured and given workshops internationally. His work, which is exploring the relation between actual and virtual in CAD/CAM technologies, is exhibited internationally and published in various books and journals. He studied Architecture at the RWTH Aachen, Germany, the University of Applied Arts in Vienna, Austria (master class of Wolf D. Prix), and finished his studies at the Bartlett School of Architecture where he received his Graduate Diploma and Master of Architecture.

Moritz Fleischmann is a doctoral candidate at the Institute for Computational Design (ICD) of Prof. Achim Menges at the University of Stuttgart. Fleischmann participated in numerous lectures and conferences on biology and computation. His work with his design groups morse and his own Architectural Research Network (ARN) together with Sean Ahlquist is exhibited and published internationally. Fleischmann studied architecture at the ETH Zürich and the RWTH Aachen in Germany, where he obtained his Dipl.-Ing. degree. He then received his Master's Degree from the Architectural Association after joining their Emergent Technologies & Design program as a DAAD scholarship holder.

Image credits

Introduction

p.7, fig. 0.1
Leonardo da Vinci. Vitruvian Man. Wikipedia, Wikimedia Foundation Inc., published on 14. Sept. 2010. Web. Date of access: 12. Sept. 2011. >http://de.wikipedia.org/w/index.php?title=Datei:Da_Vinci_Vitruve_Luc_Viatour.jpg&filetimestamp=20100914054557<

p.7, fig. 0.2
Wikipedia User: Thermos. Parthenon from south. Wikipedia, Wikimedia Foundation Inc., published on 1. Aug. 2011. Web. Date of access: 12. Sept. 2011. >http://de.wikipedia.org/w/index.php?title=Datei:Parthenon_from_south.jpg&filetimestamp=20110731233326<

p.8, fig. 0.3
Wikipedia User: Tobi 87. Cathedral of Cologne, Germany. Wikipedia, Wikimedia Foundation Inc., published on 12. May 2009. Web. Date of access: 12. Sept. 2011. >http://commons.wikimedia.org/wiki/File:Kölner_Dom.jpg?uselang=de<

p.8, fig. 0.4
Sujit Kumar. St. Patrick's Cathedral, NYC. Wikipedia, Wikimedia Foundation Inc., published on 7. Aug. 2008. Web. Date of access: 12. Sept. 2011. >http://commons.wikimedia.org/wiki/File:St._Patrick%27s_Cathedral,_New_York_1.jpg<

p.9, fig. 0.5
Ott, Jörg. Façade of the Guggenheim Museum. Bilbao, Spain. Frank O. Gehry and Associates

p.10, fig. 0.6
Kersting, Peter. Casa da Musica. Porto, Portugal. OMA

p.10, fig. 0.7
Demel, Juliane. Cuandixia, China

p.11, fig. 0.8
Wood model of Tokyo Apartments. Suo Fujimoto. Image courtesy Suo Fujimoto Architects

p.12, fig. 0.9
Demel, Juliane. Zollverein School of Management and Design, Essen. Kazuyo Sejima + Ryue Nishizawa / SANAA

p.13, fig. 0.10
Baan, Ivan. Serpentine Gallery Pavilion, London. Kazuyo Sejima + Ryue Nishizawa / SANAA

p.13, fig. 0.11
Demel, Juliane. Zollverein School of Management and Design, Essen, Germany. Kazuyo Sejima + Ryue Nishizawa / SANAA

1 Primary Elements of Design – Points

p. 14 – 15, fig 1.0
Orkelbog-Andresen, Leif. Danish Pavillon, World Expo Shanghai 2010, Shanghai. BIG Architects

p. 18, fig. 1.1
Frodesiak, Anna. A Longji terrace in Longsheng county, Guilin, China. Wikipedia, Wikimedia Foundation Inc., published on 28. Sept. 2009. Web. Date of access: 21. Feb. 2012. >http://commons.wikimedia.org/wiki/File:St._Patrick%27s_Cathedral,_New_York_1.jpg<

p. 18, fig. 1.2
South side of the Aachener of cathedral, around 1900. Wikipedia, Wikimedia Foundation Inc., published on 22. Jun. 2008. Web. Date of access: 12. Sept. 2011. >http://it.wikipedia.org/wiki/File:Aachen_Dom_um_1900.jpg<

p. 18, fig. 1.3
Wikipedia User: Surfsupusa. Fallingwater in Summer. Wikipedia, Wikimedia Foundation Inc., published on 31. Aug. 2007. Web. Date of access: 21. Feb. 2012. >http://en.wikipedia.org/wiki/File:Fallingwater_in_Summer.jpg <

p. 19, fig. 1.4
Mückenheim, Mark. Atomium, Brüssel

p. 19, fig. 1.5
Mückenheim, Mark. Interior facade with glass mosaic. „Five Courtyards", Munich. Herzog & de Meuron

p. 19. fig 1.6
Orkelbog-Andresen, Leif. Interior of the Danish Pavillon, World Expo Shanghai 2010, Shanghai. BIG Architects

2 Primary Elements of Design – Line to Surface

p. 30 – 31, fig. 2.0
Mückenheim, Mark. Dee and Charles Wyly Theatre, Dallas, Texas. REX | OMA

p. 34, fig. 2.1
Mückenheim, Mark. Towing Ropes of the Erasmus Bridge Rotterdam. UN Studio, Ben van Berkel and Caroline Bos

p. 34, fig. 2.2
Mückenheim, Mark. Alianz Arena, Munich. Herzog & de Meuron

p. 34, fig. 2.3
Demel, Juliane. Public record office, Basel Liesthal. EM2N

p. 35, fig. 2.4
Demel, Juliane. Rail Switchtower, Basel. Herzog & de Meuron

p. 35, fig. 2.5
Mückenheim, Mark. Temppeliaukion church, Helsinki. Timo and Tuomo Suomalainen

3 Pattern Development – Texture

p. 50 – 51, fig. 3.0
Mückenheim, Mark. De Young Museum, San Francisco. Herzog & de Meuron

p. 54, fig. 3.1
Mückenheim, Mark. Structured and textured façade. De Young Museum, San Francisco. Herzog & de Meuron

p. 54, fig. 3.2
Mückenheim, Mark. Concrete façade panels with embossed texture, University Library Utrecht, the Netherlands. Wiel Arets

p. 54, fig. 3.3
Mückenheim, Mark. Translucent façade panels, University Library Utrecht, the Netherlands. Wiel Arets

p. 55, fig. 3.4
Mückenheim, Mark. Arts Centre De Kunstlinie, Almere City, the Netherlands. Kazuyo Sejima + Ryue Nishizawa / SANAA

p. 55, fig. 3.5
Demel, Juliane. Wall covering. French National Library, Paris. Dominique Perrault

p. 55, fig. 3.6
Mückenheim, Mark. Wooden wall paneling, Kolumba Museum, Cologne. Peter Zumthor

4 Spatial Patterns – Structure

p. 68 - 69, fig. 4.0 Demel, Juliane. Olympic Stadium Beijing, “Birds Nest”. Herzog & de Meuron

p. 72, fig. 4.1 Grobe, Hannes / AWI. Marine microfossils. Wikipedia, Wikimedia Foundation Inc., published on 25. Dec. 2007. Web. Date of access: 12. Sept. 2011. > http://simple.wikipedia.org/wiki/File:Marine-microfossils-major_hg.jpg<
Source: Grobe, H., Diekmann, B., Hillenbrand, C.-D.(2009). The memory of the Polar Oceans, In: Hempel, G. (ed) Biology of Polar Oceans,

p. 72, fig. 4.2
Mückenheim, Mark. Espacio de las Artes at Santa Cruz de Tenerife, Spain. Herzog & de Meuron

p. 72, fig. 4.3
Demel, Juliane. Olympic Stadium Beijing, “Birds Nest”. Herzog & de Meuron

p. 73, fig. 4.4
Demel. Juliane. CCTV Tower, Beijing. OMA

p. 73, fig. 4.5
Demel, Juliane. Façade element. Institute du Monde Arab, Paris. Jean Nouvel

p. 73, fig. 4.6
Demel, Juliane. National Aquatics Center, Beijing. PTW Architects

5 Compositions on Typography and Color

p. 88 - 89, fig. 5.0
Mückenheim, Mark. CMYK House, Moers, Germany, MCKNHM Architects Mark Mückenheim in cooperation with Frank Zeising

p. 92, fig. 5.1
N.N. Dorisches Gebälk.1883, Verlag E. A. Seemann, Leipzig. Wikipedia, Wikimedia Foundation Inc., published on 17. Feb 2007. Web. Date of access: 27. Feb. 2012. >http://de.wikipedia.org/w/index.php?title=Datei:Antike_Polychromie_1.jpg&filetimestamp=20070217225856<

p. 92, fig. 5.2
Mückenheim, Mark. Visitors Center Ruhr Museum, Essen, Germany. OMA

p. 92, fig. 5.3
Mückenheim, Mark. Yellow Elevators Seattle Library, Seattle. OMA

p. 93, fig. 5.4
Wikipedia User: Schlaier. Museum Brandhorst, Munich, Maxvorstadt, Kunstareal, main entrance. Wikipedia, Wikimedia Foundation Inc., published on 24. Dec 2009. Web. Date of access: 27. Feb. 2012. > http://de.wikipedia.org/w/index.php?title=Datei:Museum_Brandhorst_außen3.jpg&file timestamp=20091224120456<

p. 93, fig. 5.5
Mückenheim, Mark. WoZoCo, Amsterdam. MVRDV

p. 93, fig. 5.6
Demel, Juliane. Public street, Hongkong

p. 94, fig. 5.7
Chris LaBrooy. Helvetica

p. 94, fig. 5.8
Chris LaBrooy. Helvetica

p. 94, fig. 5.9
Johann David Steingruber. Architectural alphabet, 1773

p. 95, fig. 5.10
Mückenheim, Mark. New York Times Building, New York. Renzo Piano

p. 95, fig. 5.11
Kersting, Peter. Casa da Musica, Porto, Portugal. OMA

p. 95, fig. 5.12
Mückenheim, Mark. Neon text installation ‚Joanna (chapter one)‘ by Cerith Wyn Evans at the palazzo delle esposizioni, Venice Architecture Biennale 2010. Text taken from ‚the changing light at sandover‘, a poem by american poet, James Merrill

6 Architectural Transformations – Surface to Volume

p. 118 - 119, fig. 6.0
Demel. Juliane. Zollverein School of Management and Design, Essen, Germany. Kazuyo Sejima + Ryue Nishizawa / SANAA

p. 122, fig. 6.1
Mückenheim, Mark. Ordrupgaard Museum extension, Charlottenlund, Denmark. Zaha Hadid Architects

p. 122, fig. 6.2
Mückenheim, Mark. Detail Porsche Museum, Stuttgart, Germany. Delugan Meissl Associated Architects

p. 122, fig. 6.3
Mückenheim, Mark. Staircase Museum Küppersmühle, Duisburg, Germany. Herzog & de Meuron,

p. 123, fig. 6.4
Kersting, Peter. Detail Casa da Musica, Porto, Portugal. OMA

p. 123, fig. 6.5
Mückenheim, Mark. Detail De Kunstlinie Theatre and Arts Centre, Almere, Netherlands. Kazuyo Sejima + Ryue Nishizawa / SANAA

p. 123, fig. 6.6
Mückenheim, Mark. Detail Kunsthaus Graz, Austria. Peter Cook and Colin Fournier

7 Volumetric Alterations

p. 152 - 153, fig. 7.0
Baan, Iwan. Wooden House, Kumamoto, Japan. Sou Fujimoto

p. 156, fig. 7.1
Aachen Cathedral. Floorplan. image is taken from: Georg Dehio/Gustav von Bezold: Kirchliche Baukunst des Abendlandes. Stuttgart: Verlag der Cotta'schen Buchhandlung 1887-1901, Plate No. 40.

p. 156, fig. 7.2
Fowelin, Johann. VM Houses, Copenhagen. BIG Architects

p. 156, fig. 7.3
Mückenheim, Mark. New Museum, New York. Kazuyo Sejima + Ryue Nishizawa / SANAA

p. 157, fig. 7.4
Wikipedia User Meckimac. Antelope Canyon, Navajo Tribal Park, Arizona, USA. Wikipedia, Wikimedia Foundation Inc., published on 14. Jan 2005. Web. Date of access: 27. Feb. 2012. >http://de.wikipedia.org/w/index.php?title=Datei:Lower_Antelope_Canyon_478.jpg&filetimestamp=20050114093424<

p. 157, fig. 7.5
Mückenheim, Mark.Bruder Claus Field Chapel, Mechernich, Germany. Peter Zumthor

p. 157, fig. 7.6
Demel, Juliane. Schaulager / Laurenz Foundation, Basel, Switzerland. Herzog & de Meuron

8 Spatial Ornaments

p. 186 - 187, fig. 8.0
Pierre Charron. Hylozoic Ground by Philip Beesley. Installation at the Venice Architecture Biennale 2010

p. 190, fig. 8.1
Beesley, Philip. Hylozoic plan diagrams. Eights generation. Hylozoic ground, Canada Pavilion. 12th International Architecture Exhibition, la Biennale di Venecia, Venice, 2010

p. 190, fig. 8.2
Beesley, Philip. Filter cluster assembly diagram. Filter cluster elevation. Hylozoic ground, Canada Pavilion. 12th International Architecture Exhibition, la Biennale di Venecia, Venice, 2010

p. 190, fig. 8.3
Beesley, Philip. Hylozoic plan diagrams. Hylozoic ground, Canada Pavilion. 12th International Architecture Exhibition, la Biennale di Venecia, Venice, 2010

p. 191, fig. 8.4
Wikipedia Uder Jebulon. Alhambra, Granada, Spain. Wikipedia, Wikimedia Foundation Inc., published on 19. Aug. 2010. Web. Date of access: 27. Feb. 2012. > http://commons.wikimedia.org/wiki/File:Pavillon_jardines_del_Partal_Alhambra_Granada.jpg<

p. 191, fig. 8.5
Tobias Klein. Drawing of a speculative reinterpretation of Sir Christopher Wren' St Pauls Cathedral, London

p. 191, fig. 8.6
Tobias Klein. Physical model of speculative spatial intervention inside the Dome of Sir Christopher Wren' St Pauls Cathedral, London

9 Tracing, Mappping and Notation

p. 204 - 205, fig. 9.0
Demel, Juliane. Art installation at the Architekturbiennale 2010 in Venice

p. 208, fig. 9.1
World weather map jan 25 1878. Source: Popular Science Monthly Volume 16. Wikipedia, Wikimedia Foundation Inc., published on 15. Aug 2010. Web. Date of access: 13. Feb. 2012.>http://commons.wikimedia.org/wiki/File:PSM_V16_D306_World_weather_map_jan_25_1878.jpg<

p. 208, fig. 9.2
Down Syndrome Karyotype. By courtesy of: National Human Genome Research Institute. Wikipedia, Wikimedia

Image credits

Foundation Inc., published on 23. June 2006. Web. Date of access: 13. Feb. 2012. >http://commons.wikimedia.org/wiki/File:Down_Syndrome_Karyotype.png<

p. 209, fig. 9.3
A NASA photograph of aircraft contrails, taken from I-95 in northern Virginia, January 26, 2001 by NASA scientist Louis Ngyyen. Wikipedia, Wikimedia Foundation Inc., published on 12. Dec 2008. Web. Date of access: 13. Feb. 2012. >http://es.wikipedia.org/wiki/Archivo:Sfc.contrail.1.26.01.JPG<

p. 209, fig. 9.4
Eadweard Muybridge. Woman walking downstairs, late 19th century. Wikipedia, Wikimedia Foundation Inc., published on 26. Mar 2008. Web. Date of access: 13. Feb. 2012. > http://de.wikipedia.org/w/index.php?title=Datei:Muybridge-1.jpg&filetimestamp=20050326094820<

p. 209, fig. 9.5
Wide-area map that presents Osaka city subway. Wikipedia, Wikimedia Foundation Inc., published on 17. Mar 2007. Web. Date of access: 13. Feb. 2012. >http://commons.wikimedia.org/wiki/File:Wide-Area_Map_of_Osaka_City_Subway.png?uselang=de<

10 Folds and Foldings

p. 222 - 223, fig. 10.0
Baan, Iwan. Main Auditorium, Agora Theater Lelystad, The Netherlands. UNStudio, Ben van Berkel and Caroline Bos

p. 226, fig. 9.1
Baan, Iwan. Staircase and open foyer space, Agora Theater Lelystad, The Netherlands. UNStudio Ben van Berkel and Caroline Bos

p. 226, fig. 9.2
Richters, Christian. Exterior view, Agora Theater Lelystad, The Netherlands, UNStudio, Ben van Berkel and Caroline Bos

p. 226, fig. 9.3
Baan, Iwan. Folded acoustic paneling, Main Auditorium, Agora Theater Lelystad, The Netherlands. UNStudio, Ben van Berkel and Caroline Bos

p. 226, fig. 9.4
Diagram of the foldout for the façade and roof surface, Agora Theater Lelystad, The Netherlands. UNStudio, Ben van Berkel and Caroline Bos

p. 226, fig. 9.5
Concept drawings, Agora Theater Lelystad, The Netherlands. UNStudio, Ben van Berkel and Caroline Bos

p. 227, fig. 9.6
Mückenheim, Mark. InterActiveCorp Headquarters, New York. Frank O. Gehry and Associates

p. 227, fig. 9.7
Mückenheim, Mark. Seattle Public Library. Rem Koolhaas, OMA

p. 227, fig. 9.8
Mückenheim, Mark. Tate Pier, London. Detail of folded space. Marks Barfield Architects

11 Parametric Design

p. 240 - 241, fig. 11.0
Demel, Juliane. MyZeil, Shopping Mall, Frankfurt am Main, Germany. Massimiliano Fuksas Architetto

p. 244, fig. 11.1
Moritz Fleischmann & Sean Ahlquist: Installation of a Tension Active Structure at the Architectural Association School of Architecture (AA), London

p. 244, fig. 11.2
Demel, Juliane. Roof of the Shiliupu Ferry Terminal, Shanghai. Xian Dai Architectural Design (Group) Co. Ltd.

p. 245, fig. 11.3
Mückenheim, Mark. EMP Museum Seattle, façade detail. Frank O. Gehry and Associates

p. 245, fig. 11.4
Demel, Juliane. Façade Detail, MyZeil, Shopping Mall, Frankfurt am Main, Germany. Massimiliano Fuksas Architetto

p. 245, fig. 11.5
Mückenheim, Mark. Kunsthaus Graz. Peter Cook and Colin Fournier

We took great care in referencing all of the student works included in the book. Please excuse any unintentional errors that may have occurred. If you have any comments or concerns, please contact us or the publishers.

1 Primary Elements of Design – Points

p. 20, fig. 1	Hannes Goetz, Frieder Knoeller
p. 20, fig. 2	Lea Bothe, Sabrina Weisenbach
p. 20, fig. 3	Felix Oberfrank, Sebastian Schützdeller
p. 20, fig. 4	Magdalena Stadler, Laura Zalenga
p. 20, fig. 5	Martina Boeer, Nadja von Mark
p. 20, fig. 6	Teresa Rettig, Lina Weber
p. 21, fig. 7	Martina Boeer, Nadja von Mark
p. 22, fig. 8	Moritz Dürr, Leonard Schrage
p. 23, fig. 9	Carina Pfeuffer, Lisa Scheibenzuber
p. 23, fig. 10	Christopher Irlbeck, Jörg Schwarz
p. 23, fig. 11	Nadine Grzonka, Pascal Steinbach
p. 23, fig. 12	Carolin Haslinde, Laura Strähle
p. 24, fig. 13	Lukas Blaschke, Florian Ludwig
p. 24, fig. 14	Max Becker, Bernadette Keller
p. 24, fig. 15	Marina Kolb, Mona Stöckl
p. 24, fig. 16	Cornelius Neckenig
p. 25, fig. 17	Daniel Büscher, David Frauenkron
p. 25, fig. 18	Max Becker, Bernadette Keller
p. 25, fig. 19	Teresa Rettig, Lina Weber
p. 26, fig. 20	Thomas Böck, Theresa Eckert
p. 26, fig. 21	Yvonne Mößmer, Leonard Strübin,
p. 26, fig. 22	Gösku Köksoy, Elisabeth Reischl
p. 26, fig. 23	Felix Oberfrank, Sebastian Schützdeller
p. 26, fig. 24	Rebecca Seifert, Julia Bawej
p. 26, fig. 25	Thomas Böck, Theresa Eckert
p. 27, fig. 26	Christopher Irlbeck, Jörg Schwarz
p. 28, fig. 27	Elena Giannitsopoulos, Josephine Köhler
p. 28, fig. 28	Asa Bovonwattanangkul, Luis Michal
p. 28, fig. 29	Katharina Hoekstein, Andeas Martin Honold
p. 28, fig. 30	Philipp Krüpe, Esen Yildirim
p. 29, fig. 31	Peter Prey, Markus Titze
p. 29, fig. 32	Kevin Kraus, Sandra Panzer
p. 29, fig. 33	Alexandra Troschke, Alexandra Stepan
p. 29, fig. 34	Verena Engel, Marion Gillhuber
p. 29, fig. 35	Peter Prey, Markus Titze
p. 29, fig. 36	Adrian Pigat, Lorenzo Trevisan Volta

2 Primary Elements of Design – Line to Surface

p. 36, fig. 37	Alisa Kellner, Julia Rosenfeld
p. 36, fig. 38	Teresa Rettig, Lina Weber
p. 36, fig. 39	Gösku Köksoy, Elisabeth Reischl
p. 36, fig. 40	Kristin Janda, Simone Theresia Hirmer
p. 37, fig. 41	Felix Oberfrank, Sebastian Schützdeller
p. 37, fig. 42	Nadine Grzonka, Pascal Steinbach
p. 37, fig. 43	Kevin Kraus, Sandra Panzer
p. 37, fig. 44	Sabrina Bauer, Stephanie Fusseder, Anna Brähler, Judith Stoppert
p. 38, fig. 45	Maximiliane Hurnaus, Livia Klemencsics
p. 38, fig. 46	Xaver Felixberger, Tugkan Akkoc
p. 38, fig. 47	Susanne Julinek, Julia Schallerer
p. 38, fig. 48	Maria Pfeiffer, Adrian Retzer
p. 38, fig. 49	Sebastian Deutinger, Laura Pastior
p. 38, fig. 50	Jonathan Bürgel, Simon Rott
p. 38, fig. 51	Leonard von Aster, David Bruckmüller, Ferdinand Grund, Larissa Müllner
p. 39, fig. 52 – 54	Hannes Goetz, Frieder Knoeller
p. 39, fig. 55	Nicolas Nabers, Benedikt Schmid
p. 40, fig. 56	Max Becker, Bernadette Keller
p. 40, fig. 57	Moritz Dürr, Leonard Schrage
p. 40, fig. 58	Dominik Cosentino, Roberta Mayerle
p. 40, fig. 59	Rebecca Brehm, Susanne Dykiert
p. 40, fig. 60	Yuichiro Yamada, Markus Heimbach
p. 40, fig. 61	Max Becker, Bernadette Keller
p. 41, fig. 62	Jing Dong, Chao Wu
p. 42, fig. 63	Gilles Dostert, Robert Geist
p. 42, fig. 64	Jonas Geisel, Sebastian Hacker
p. 42, fig. 65	Lukas Völker, Maria Schuster
p. 42, fig. 66	Leonard von Aster, David Bruckmuller, Ferdinand Grund, Larissa Müllner, Katharina Strobel, Inka Szewczyk
p. 43, fig. 67	Daniel Büscher, David Frauenkron
p. 44, fig. 68	Schuh, Jennifer, Jenny Tran
p. 45, fig. 69	Lea Bothe, Sabrina Weisenbach
p. 45, fig. 70	Carolin Haslinde, Laura Strähle
p. 45, fig. 71	Philipp Böhlke
p. 45, fig. 72	Felix Oberfrank, Sebastian Schützdeller
p. 46, fig. 73	Gregor Doetsch, Theresa Pudzich
p. 46, fig. 74	Adrian Pigat, Lorenzo Trevisan Volta
p. 46, fig. 75	Alexandra Schäfer, Carolina Weber
p. 47, fig. 76	Alexandra Schäfer, Carolina Weber
p. 47, fig. 77	Helena Hirokawa, Benjamin Leiffheidt
p. 47, fig. 78	Sabrina Bauer, Stephanie Fusseder
p. 47, fig. 79	Leonard von Aster, Ferdinand Grund
p. 48, fig. 80	Alisa Kellner, Julia Rosenfeld
p. 48, fig. 81	Laura Behrends, Theresa Blöhmer
p. 48, 49 fig. 82, 83	Dominic Kim, Lena Kohl

3 Pattern Development – Texture

p. 56, fig. 84, 85, 86	Helena Hirokawa, Benjamin Leiffheidt
p. 57, fig. 87 – 90	Karolina Sciborova, Simone Schneider
p. 58, fig. 91 – 94	Lukas Völker, Maria Schuster
p. 59, fig. 95 – 98	Christine Egold, Alissa Homma
p. 60, fig. 99, 100, 101	Kathrin Stretz, Nora Walter
p. 61, fig. 102 – 105	Chang Jeong, Jong We Nah
p. 62, fig. 106, 107, 108	Carolin Schöllhorn, Clara Köhler
p. 62, fig. 109, 110, 111	Annabel Romero, Meruert Zharekesheva
p. 62, fig. 112, 113, 114	Charlotte Reith, Larissa Müllner
p. 63, fig. 115, 116, 117	Nicola Bötsch, Verena Hollfelder
p. 63, fig. 118, 119	Laura Grünberger, Elisabeth Mariutti
p. 63, fig. 120, 121	Anna Hering, Markus Kiefl
p. 64, fig. 122, 123	Katharina Fink, Emmanouela-Sofia Melliou
p. 65, fig. 124 – 127	Quirin Mühlbauer
p. 66, fig. 128 – 131	Alisa Kellner, Julia Rosenfeld
p. 67, fig. 132, 133, 134	Anna Brähler, Saskia Ehlers

Credits

4 Spatial Patterns – Structure

p. 74, fig. 135 – 138	Sarah Fischer, Corinna Wiest
p. 74, fig. 139, 140	Constantin Bungau, Philipp Hartmann
p. 75, fig. 141 – 144	Angéla Németh, Franziska Vogl
p. 76 - 77, fig. 145 – 148	Christopher Irlbeck, Jörg Schwarz
p. 78, fig. 149, 150, 151	Max Becker, Bernadette Keller
p. 79, fig. 152 – 156	Philipp Böhlke, Marcus Wallbaum
p. 80, fig. 157, 158, 159	Daniel Büscher, David Frauenkron
p. 81, fig. 160, 161, 162	Timo Baier
p. 81, fig. 163, 164	Mario Hristov Gyurov, Christian Oehl
p. 82, fig. 165, 166. 167	Cecilia Böger, Cornelius Neckenig
p. 83, fig. 168, 169	Christopher Förch, Amir Ojalvo
p. 83, fig. 170, 171	Teresa Rettig, Lina Weber
p. 84, fig. 172, 173, 174	Jana Krischker,Viola Mraz
p. 85, fig. 175 – 178	Nadine Grzonka, Melanie Mayr
p. 86 - 87, fig. 179 – 183	Silviya Atanasova, Julian Christl, Philipp Gross, Maximilian Sirtl

5 Compositions on Typography and Color

p. 96, 97 fig. 184 – 187	Konstanze Winter, Hannes Englert
p. 98, 99 fig. 188, 189	Leo Bettini, Dominic Kim
p. 100, fig. 190, 191	Nadja Gebert, Christine Link
p. 101, fig. 192, 193, 194	Katharina Strobel, Inka Szewczyk
p. 101, fig. 195	Maximilian Buhler, Anette Magerhans
p. 102, 103 fig. 196 – 202	Leo Bettini, Dominic Kim
p. 104, fig. 203	Maria Maier, Birgit Steininger
p. 104, fig. 204, 205	Myriam Dautermann, Ralf Iberle, Kistina Bomhard
p. 105, fig. 206, 207, 208	David Bruckmüller, Quirin Mühlbauer
p. 106, fig. 209	Eva Brunner, Kristin Gräf
p. 106, fig. 210	Maximilian Buhler, Anette Magerhans Christina Denz, Juliane Gebauer, Julia Zima, Eva Brunner, Kristin Gräf
p. 107, fig. 211, 212	Ferdinand Grund, Sebastian Huth
p. 108, fig. 213, 214	Christiane Müller, Ferdinand Schachinger, Kathrin Schiele
p. 109, fig. 215	Max Lippsmeier, Beatriz Vilar
p. 109, fig. 216, 217, 218	Yuanyuan Zhang
p. 110, fig. 219	Lukas Kohmann, Roberto Urresti Grundlach
p. 111, fig. 220	Lukas Kohmann, Roberto Urresti Grundlach Khair Shakur, Michaela Supper
p. 112, 113, fig. 221, 222	Leonie Morano, Jamal Pourroy
p. 114, fig. 223, 224	Alexander Graf, Markus Huber
p. 114, fig. 225, 226	Susanne Dreyer, Martin Reitenbach
p. 115, fig. 227, 228	Constantin Hoffstadt, Lorenzo Trevisan Volta
p. 115, fig. 229, 230	Elitsa Bankova, Nikolina Paunova
p. 116,117 fig. 231	Thilo Konzok, Felicitas Weber

6 Architectural Transformations – Surface to Volume

p. 124,125 fig. 232 – 235	Luana Cortis, Anna Yeboah
p. 126,127 fig. 236 – 237	Kathrin Kühnhammer, Franziska Müller
p. 128,129 fig. 238 – 239	Constantin Bungau, Philipp Hartmann
p. 130, 131 fig. 240 – 241	Lukas Blaschke, Florian Ludwig
p. 132, fig. 242, 243	Vicky Klieber, Leonard Schrage
p. 132, fig. 244	Olga Osherova, Katharina Seela
p. 132, fig. 245	Christopher Förch, Amir Ojalvo
p. 133, fig. 246	Vicky Klieber, Leonard Schrage
p. 133, fig. 247	Christopher Förch, Amir Ojalvo
p. 134, fig. 248, 249	Chao Wu
p. 135, fig. 250, 251	Jana Hofmann, Katerina Stefanaki
p. 136, fig. 252	Lena Deggelmann, Susanne Gartner
p. 136, fig. 253	Moritz Rieke, Victoria Schweyer
p. 137, fig. 254, 255	Katharina Fink, Emmanouela-Sofia Melliou
p. 137, fig. 256, 257	Dominik Cosentino, Roberta Mayerle
p. 138, 139, fig. 258 – 262	Rolf-Stefan Enzel, Jonas Caspar Hahn, Nanjana Sterzig
p. 139, fig. 263	Johannes Prünte, Soroush Ramezanpour, Xing Zhang
p. 139, fig. 264 - 266	Stefan Mittermaier, Maksim Nedkov, Andreas Ordon,
p. 140, fig. 267 - 269	Moritz Kerschbaum, Patrik Halsdorf, Wenke Volkmann
p. 140, fig. 270	Stefan Mittermaier, Maksim Nedkov, Andreas Ordon,
p. 141, fig. 271, 272, 273	Manuel Gemoll, Iva Krolo, Annamaria Nickels
p. 141, fig. 274	Lacrimioara Buruga, Anna Aprath
p. 142, fig. 275 – 278	Maximilian Heidecker, Hanna Ruck, Katharina Stachowitz
p. 143, fig. 279	Alina Lozano Mora, Dalia Rava, Franziska Schlenk
p. 144, fig. 280	Noemi Barnet, Katharina Schimpf, Alexandra Tzenova
p. 145, fig. 281, 282	Elena Drefahl, Philipp Gross, Maximilian Sirtl
p. 145, fig. 283	Maria Bichtele, Saskia Nissen, Hanna Veit
p. 146, 147, fig. 284, 285	Rolf-Stefan Enzel, Jonas Caspar Hahn, Nanjana Sterzig
p. 148, 149, fig. 286, 287	Benedikt Bührle, Maximilian Kimmel, Bertram Landwerlin
p. 150, fig. 288, 289	Franziska Gehrmann, Kim Grabbe, Andreas Schulze
p. 150, fig. 290, 291	Denise Hafner, Jasmin Ostermeier, Yasmin Rahmanzadeh
p. 150, 151, fig. 292 – 294	Franziska Gehrmann, Kim Grabbe, Andreas Schulze

7 Volumetric Alterations

p. 158, 159, fig. 295 – 296	various students
p. 160, 161, fig. 297 – 300	Leonard von Aster, Larissa Müllner, Lukas Völker
p. 162, fig. 301	Leo Bettini, Dominic Kim
p. 163, fig. 302 - 306	Laura Behrends, Ferdinand Schmidt, Sven Wiebe, Felix Zeitler
p. 164, 165 fig. 307 – 315	Leo Bettini, Dominic Kim Anna Langenscheidt, Tobias Müller
p. 166, fig. 316 317	Raphael Hilz, Siona Wagner, Daniel Werle
p. 166, fig. 318 319	Patrik Halsdorf, Moritz Kerschbaum, Wenke Volkmann
p. 166, fig. 320 321	Raphael Hilz, Siona Wagner, Daniel Werle
p. 167, fig. 322 323	Johannes Prünte, Soroush Ramezanpour, Xing Zhang
p. 168, fig. 324 – 327	Alexander Richert, Laura Wollenhaupt, Johanna Zapf
p. 169, fig. 328 – 331	Michael Fox, Paul Kirchner, Benjamin Mooslechner, Annik Wolf,
p. 170, fig. 332, 333	Benjamin Becker, Cornelia Sirotek, Edda Zickert

Credits

p. 171, fig. 334, 335	Johannes Prünte, Soroush Ramezanpour, Xing Zhang
p. 171, fig. 336	Dorian Cani, Benjamin Süß, Dafni Skyrgianni
p. 172, fig. 337, 338, 339	Patrik Halsdorf, Moritz Kerschbaum, Wenke Volkmann
p. 172, fig. 340, 341, 342	Lisa Leitgeb, Daniel Mauracher, Yue Zhang
p. 173, fig. 343, 344, 345	Nicola Bötsch, Julian Kerkhoff, Tibor Bielicky, Carolin Friegel,
p. 173, fig. 346 347	Leo Bettini, Dominic Kim, Anna Langenscheidt, Tobias Müller
p. 173, fig. 348	Nicola Bötsch, Julian Kerkhoff, Tibor Bielicky, Carolin Friegel
p. 174, fig. 349 – 352	Maximilian Buhler, Eva Brunner, Carolina Weber, Nora Walter
p. 175, fig. 353 – 357	Elena Drefahl, Philipp Gross, Maximilian Sirtl
p. 176, fig. 358 – 363	Meike Braun, Andrea Endlein
p. 177, fig. 363 – 367	Ralk Iberle, Briant Sencan, Sebastian Völkl
p. 178, fig. 368 – 373	Benedikt Bührle, Maximilian Kimmel, Bertam Landwerlin
p. 179, fig. 374	Elisabeth Colwell, Darja Hense, Alexandra Maier
p. 179, fig. 375	Denise Hafner, Jasmin Ostermeier, Yasmin Rahmanzadeh
p. 179, fig. 376	Rosita Doneva, Johannes Romstätter, Moritz Schrödl,
p. 179, fig. 377 – 384	Ulrich Binder, Narges Ejtehadi, Maria Madjarova
p. 180, fig. 385 – 386	Alexander Richert, Laura Wollenhaupt
p. 181, fig. 387	Maximilian Helmreich, Stefan Imhof, Theresa Ludwig
p. 181, fig. 388	Natalia Oka, Magdalena Pfeffer, Georgina Simon-Seybold
p. 181, fig. 389	Franziska Gehrmann, Kim Grabbe, Andreas Schulze
p. 182, fig. 390, 391	Rolf-Stefan Enzel, Jonas Caspar Hahn, Nanjana Sterzig
p. 183, fig. 392 - 395	Sophie Frey, Nora Gazdag, Johannes Scholten, Benjamin Mühlbauer
p. 183, fig. 396 397 398	Dominik Buhr, Martin Hofmann
p. 184, fig. 399	Natalia Oka, Magdalena Pfeffer, Georgina Simon-Seybold Juliane Engelhart, Martina Ettenreich, Tatjana Ganz
p. 184, fig. 400	Various students
p. 185, fig. 401 402 403	Rebecca Burjack, Lisa Hüttinger, Sabrina Kösters, Kristina Miller
p. 185, fig. 404	Michael Fox, Paul Kirchner, Benjamin Mooslechner, Annik Wolf, Rebecca Burjack, Lisa Hüttinger, Sabrina Kösters, Kristina Miller
p. 185, fig. 405 406	Rebecca Burjack, Lisa Hüttinger, Sabrina Kösters, Kristina Miller

8 Spatial Ornaments

p. 192 – 193, fig. 407 408	Sofia Costamagna, Andreas Schulze,
p. 194 – 196, fig. 409 – 411	Paloma Huesca, Bertram Landwerlin
p. 197, fig. 412	Korbinian Luderböck, Carolin Berger
p. 198 – 199, fig. 413 414	Tsun Ning Chuang, Maximilian Kimmel
p. 200 fig. 415 – 423	Various Students
p. 201, fig. 424	Luisa Ebert, Franziska Militz
p. 202 – 203, fig. 425 – 230	Dominik Buhr

9 Tracing, Mappping and Notation

p. 210, fig. 431 – 435	Christiane Müller, Ferdinand Schachinger, Kathrin Schiele,
p. 211, fig. 436 – 438	Maria Schuster, Lukas Völker
p. 212, fig. 439 440 441	Janina Kuban, Stefanie Lutz
p. 212, fig. 442 443 444	Amelie Jasper, Ricarda Schindler
p. 212, fig. 445 446 447	Briant Sencan
p. 213, fig. 448 449	Sophie Frey, Nora Gazdag
p. 213, fig. 450 451	Kistina Bomhard, Ralf Iberle,
p. 213, fig. 452 453	Anna Hering, Markus Kiefl
p. 214, fig. 454 – 458	Karolina Sciborova, Simone Schneider Nicola Missel, Franziska Käuferle,
p. 215, fig. 459 – 461	Noemi Barnet
p. 216, 217, fig. 462 – 466	Maximilian Helmreich, Stefan Imhof, Theresa Ludwig
p. 218, fig. 467 – 470	Martina Schlusnus, Jana Hampe
p. 219, fig. 471 – 473	Alina Lozano Mora, Dalia Rava, Franziska Schlenk
p. 220, fig. 474 – 476	Ralf Grundel, Benjamin Jaschke, Christopher Martin
p. 221, fig. 477 – 480	Sarah Bachhuber, Carolin Henke, Susanne Slabon

10 Folds and Foldings

p. 228, fig. 481	Julia Bobardt, Sophie Kuchelmeister, Eva Vetter
p. 229, fig. 482	Various students
p. 230, fig. 483	Benedikt Bührle, Maximilian Kimmel Bertam Landwerlin
p. 231, fig. 484 485 486	Marie Keller, Sophia Necker, Niao Wu
p. 232, fig. 487 488 489	Alexander Richert, Laura Wollenhaupt, Johanna Zapf
p. 233, fig. 490 - 495	Rolf-Stefan Enzel, Jonas Caspar Hahn, Nanjana Sterzig
p. 234, 235, fig. 495 – 499	Elisabeth Colwell, Darja Hense, Alexandra Maier
p. 236, fig. 500 – 504	Franziska Gehrmann, Kim Grabbe, Andreas Schulze
p. 237, fig. 505 – 508	Natalia Oka, Magdalena Pfeffer, Georgina Simon-Seybold
p. 238, fig. 509 – 512	Johannes Romstätter, Moritz Schrödl
p. 239, fig. 513 514	Megi Gambeta, Hannes Hofmann, Yiran Wang
p. 239, fig. 515 516	Sabrina Appel, Valentin Zeller
p. 239, fig. 517 518	Alexander Richert, Laura Wollenhaupt, Johanna Zapf

11 Parametric Design

p. 246 – 251, fig. 519 – 531	Michael Mühlhaus, Nils Seifert

Credits

Albers, Josef. Interaction of Color. Yale University Press, 2006

Allen, Stan, Marc McQuade. Landform Building: Architecture's New Terrain. Lars Muller Publishers, 2011

Andersen, Paul / Salomon, David / Carson, David. The Architecture of Patterns. W. W. Norton & Company, 2010

Armitage, John / Virilio, Paul. From Modernism to Hypermodernism and Beyond (Theory, Culture & Society). Sage Publications, 2000

Aristotle, Metaphysica. Vol. VII 10, 1041 b. ca. 330 B.C

Arnheim, Rudolf. Art and Visual Perception: A Psychology of the Creative Eye, Fiftieth Anniversary Printing. University of California Press, 2004

Arnheim, Rudolf. The Dynamics of Architectural Form: 30th Anniversary Edition. University of California Press, 2009

Arnheim, Rudolf. Visual Thinking: Thirty-Fifth Anniversary Printing. University of California Press, 2004

Ayres, Phil. Persistent Modelling: Extending the Role of Architectural Representation. Routledge Chapman & Hall, 2012

Barrett, Cyril. An Introduction to Optical Art. Littlehampton Book Services Ltd, 1971

Bechtel, Robert B., Arza Churman. Handbook of Environmental Psychology. Wiley, 2002

Bechtold, Martin. Innovative Surface Structures: Technologies and Applications. Taylor & Francis, 200

Beesley, Philip. Hylozoic Ground: Liminal Responsive Architecture: Philip Beesley. Riverside Architectural Press, 2010

Berkel, Ben van / Bos, Caroline (ed.). Un Studio: Unfold. NAi Publishers, 2002

Berkel, Ben van. Delinquent Visionaries. 010 Uitgeverij, 1993

Borden, Iain, (ed.). Bartlett Designs: Speculating with Architecture. John Wiley & Sons, 2009

Bowers, John. Introduction to Two-Dimensional Design: Understanding Form and Function. Wiley, 2008

Conrads, Ulrich. The Architecture of Fantasy: Utopian Building and Planning in Modern Times. New York: Praeger, 1962

Craig, James, William Bevington, Irene Korol Scala. Designing with Type, 5th Edition: The Essential Guide to Typography. Watson-Guptill, edition, 2006

Critchlow, Keith / Nasr, Seyyed Hossein. Islamic Patterns: An Analytical and Cosmological Approach. Inner Traditions,1999

Doczi, Gyorgy. The Power of Limits: Proportional Harmonies in Nature, Art, and Architecture. Shambhala, 2005

Doczi, Gyorgy. The Power of Limits: Proportional Harmonies in Nature, Art, and Architecture Shambhala Pocket Classics, 2005

Edmondson, Amy C.. A Fuller Explanation: The Synergetic Geometry of R. Buckminster Fuller. Kindle Edition. Emergent World LLC, 2007

Elam, Kimberly. Geometry of Design, Revised and Updated (Design Briefs). Princeton Architectural Press, 2011

Ellis, Willis. D.. A Source Book of Gestalt Psychology The Gestalt Journal Press, 1997

Engel, Heino. Structure Systems. Hatje Cantz, 2007

Evans, Robin. Translation from Drawing to Building (AA Documents). MIT Press, 1997

Finger, Anke / Guldin, Rainer / Bernado,Gustavo. Vilem Flusser: An Introduction (Electronic Mediations). Univ Of Minnesota Press, 2011

Flusser, Vilem. Into the Universe of Technical Images (Electronic Mediations). Univ Of Minnesota Press, 2011

Flusser, Vilem. The Shape of Things. Reaktion Books, 1999

Flusser, Vilém: „Räume“ (in: außen räume innen räume. Der Wandel des Raumbegriffs im Zeitalter der elektronischen Medien, hg. von Heidemarie Seblatnig, Wien 1991, S. 75–83)

Flusser, Vilem. Writings (Electronic Mediations). Univ Of Minnesota Press, 2004

Foster, Hal. The Art-Architecture Complex. Verso, 2011

Fujimoto, Sou. Primitive Future. Inax Publishers, 2008

Garcia, Mark. The Patterns of Architecture: Architectural Design. Wiley, 2010

Gifford, Robert. Environmental Psychology: Principles and Practice. Pearson, 1996

Gissen, David, (ed.). Territory: Architecture Beyond Environment: Architectural Design. Wiley, 2010

Gleininger, Andrea / Vrachliotis, Georg. Pattern: Ornament, Structure, and Behavior (Context Architecture). Birkhäuser Architecture; 1 edition, 2009

Gleininger, Andrea / Vrachliotis, Georg. Simulation (Context Architecture). Birkhäuser Architecture, 2004

Gleiter, Jörg H.. Architekturtheorie heute. Transcript Verlag, 2008

Goldstein, Bruce E.. Sensation and Perception. Wadsworth Publishing, 2006

Bibliography

Gregory, Richard L..Eye and Brain. Princeton University Press, 1997

Harvey, Wilson. 1,000 Type Treatments: From Script to Serif, Letterforms Used to Perfection. Rockport Publishers, 2005

Hensel, Michael, Achim Menges, ed.: Morpho-Ecologies: Towards Heterogeneous Space In Architecture Design. AA Publications, 2007

Hensel, Michael / Menges, Achim / Weinstock, Michael: Emergent Technologies and Design. Routledge, 2010

Hoffman, Donald D.. Visual Intelligence: How We Create What We See. W. W. Norton & Company, 2000

Hoffman, Donald D.. Visuelle Intelligenz: Wie die Welt im Kopf entsteht. Klett-Cotta, 2001

Hofmann, Armin. Methodik der Form- und Bildgestaltung: Aufbau - Synthese - Anwendung. Niggli, 2009

Hrvol Flores, Carol A. Owen Jones: Design, Ornament, Architecture & Theory in an Age of Transition. Rizzoli, 2006

Ibelings, Hans. Supermodernism. NAi Publishers, 1998

Itten, Johannes. Design and Form: The Basic Course at the Bauhaus and Later. Van Nostrand Reinhold, 1976

Itten, Johannes. Gestaltungs- und Formenlehre: Vorkurs am Bauhaus und später. Christophorus-Verlag, 2007

Itten, Johannes. Kunst der Farbe. Ravensburg: Otto Maier Verlag, 1970

Iwamoto, Lisa. Digital Fabrications: Architectural and Material Techniques (Architecture Briefs). Princeton Architectural Press, 2009

Jackson, Paul. Folding Techniques for Designers: From Sheet to Form. Laurence King Publishers, 2011

Jones, Owen. The Grammar of Ornament, A&C Black, 2008

Joshi, Atri. Emergence in Architecture. Dissertation. School of Planning and Architecture

Kittler, Friedrich. Optical Media. Polity, 2010

Klanten, R. / Bourquin, N. / Ehrmann, S. / van Heerden. F.. Data Flow: Visualising Information in Graphic Design. Die Gestalten Verlag, 2008

Kolarevic, Branko / Malkawi, Ali (ed.). Performative Architecture: Beyond Instrumentality. Routledge, 2005

Koolhaas, Rem / Kuhnert, Nicolaus: Berlin, Offene Stadt, in: Lettre International Nr. 18, 1992, S. 39-43

Kopec, Dak. Environmental Psychology for Design. Fairchild Books, 2006

Lefebvre, Henry. The Production of Space. Wiley-Blackwell, 1991

Lim, Joseph. Bio-structural Analogues in Architecture. BIS Publishers, 2009

Lima, Manuel. Visual Complexity: Mapping Patterns of Information. Princeton Architectural Press, 2011

Lindinger, Herbert. Ulm Design: The Morality of Objects. The MIT Press, 1991

Loos, Adolf. Ornament und Verbrechen, Prachner Verlag, 2000

Loos, Adolf / Opel, Adolf. Ornament and Crime: Selected Essays. Gazelle Book Services, 1998

Lupton, Ellen. Thinking with Type, 2nd revised and expanded edition: A Critical Guide for Designers, Writers, Editors, & Students. Princeton Architectural Press, 2010

Lynn, Greg / Gage, Mark Foster / Nielson, Stephen / Rappaport, Nina (ed.). Composites, Surfaces, and Software: High Performance Architecture: Greg Lynn at the Yale School of Architecture. Yale School of Architecture, 2011

Lynn, Greg. Folding in Architecture (Architectural Design). Academy Press, 2004

Lynn, Greg. Mark Rappolt. Greg Lynn Form. Rizzoli, 2008

Matzner, Florian. Wolfgang Weilleder: House- Project. Ikon Gallery, 2006

May, John / Reid, Anthony (ed.). Buildings without Architects: A Global Guide to Everyday Architecture. Rizzoli, 2010

Menges, Achim. Material Computation: Higher Integration in Morphogenetic Design Architectural Design. John Wiley & Sons, 2012

Meredith, Michael / Aranda-lasch / Sasaki, Mutsuro (ed.). From Control to Design: Parametric/Algorithmic Architecture. Actar, 2008

Metzger, Wolfgang. Laws of Seeing. The MIT Press, 2009

Meyer, Adrian / Kuhlbrodt, Susanne / Aeberhard, Beat. Architecture a Synoptic Vision: A Prospectus of Developments from 1900 to Today. Birkhäuser, 2008

Miria Swain, Michael Stanley. Transfer: Wolfgang Weileder. Cornerhouse Publications, 2007

Moussavi, Farshid / Kubo, Michael (ed.). The Function of Ornament. Actar, 2006

Moussavi, Farshid. The Function of Form. Actar and Harvard Graduate School of Design, 2009

Mullins, Charlotte. Tate Modern Artists: Rachel Whiteread.

Tate, 2004

Nonaka, Ikujiro / Takeuchi, Hirotaka. The Knowledge-Creating Company, Oxford Univ. Press, 1995

Oxman, Rivka / Oxman Robert. The New Structuralism: Design, Engineering and Architectural Technologies (Architectural Design). Wiley, 2010

Padovan, Richard. Proportion: Science, Philosophy, Architecture. Taylor & Francis, 1999

Pallasmaa, Juhani. The Eyes of the Skin: Architecture and the Senses. John Wiley & Sons, 2005

Payne, Alina. From Ornament to Object: Genealogies of Architectural Modernism. Yale Univ Press, 2012

Polanyi, Michael. Tacit Dimension. University Of Chicago Press, 2009

Rajchman, John. Constructions (Writing Architecture). The MIT Press, 1998

Rajchman, John. The Deleuze Connections. The MIT Press, 2000

Reas, Casey/ McWilliams, Chandler. Form+Code in Design, Art, and Architecture (Design Briefs). Princeton Architectural Press, 2010

Reeh, Henrik. Ornaments of the Metropolis: Siegfried Kracauer and Modern Urban Culture. Mit Press, März 2005

Renner, Paul. Die Kunst der Typographie. Reprint der Ausgabe von 1940. Maro-Verlag, 2003

Renner, Paul. Ordnung und Harmonie der Farben. Eine Farbenlehre für Künstler u. Handwerker. Ravensburger Buchverlag G, 1982

Resch, Roland D. The topological design of sculptural and architectural systems. Published in: Proceeding, AFIPS '73 Proceedings of the June 4-8, 1973, national computer conference and exposition ACM New York, NY, USA, pages 643-650

Rudofsky, Bernard. Architecture Without Architects: A Short Introduction to Non-Pedigreed Architecture. University of New Mexico Press, 1987

Sandaker, Björn N. / Eggen, Arne P. / Cruvellier, Mark R.. The Structural Basis of Architecture. Routledge, 2011

Schmidt, Petra / Stattmann, Nicola. Unfolded: Paper in Design, Art, Architecture and Industry. Birkhäuser Architecture, 2009

Scholfield, P. H.. The Theory of Proportion in Architecture. Cambridge University Press, 2011

Shanks, D.R. & St. John, M.F. (1994). Characteristics of dissociable human learning systems. Behavioral and Brain Sciences 17 (3): 367-447

Smith, Virginia. Forms in Modernism: The Unity of Typography, Architecture and the Design Arts 1920s-1970s. Amphoto Books, 2005

Steingruber, Johann D. Architectonisches Alphabet 1773. Urania, 1997

Steingruber, Johann D. Architectural alphabet 1773. G. Braziller, 1975

Studinka, Felix, Andres Janser. Poster Collection 05: Typotecture : Typography As Architectural Imagery. Lars Muller Publishers; 2002

Terzidis, Kostas. Algorithmic Architecture. Architectural Press, 2006

Tschichold, Jan. Die Neue Typographie. Ein Handbuch für zeitgemäß Schaffende. Berlin: Verlag des Bildungsverbandes der Deutschen Buchdrucker, 1928

Tschichold, Jan. The New Typography: A Handbook for Modern Designers (Weimar and Now: German Cultural Criticism). English reprint from the 1928 original. University of California Press. 2006

Weinstock, Michael. The Architecture of Emergence: The Evolution of Form in Nature and Civilisation. John Wiley & Sons, 2010

Wentworth Thompson, D'Arcy. On Growth and Form. CreateSpace, 2011

Weston, Richard. 100 Ideas that Changed Architecture. Laurence King Publishers, 2011

Woodbury, R.. Elements of Parametric Design, Routledge, 2010

Zeisel, John. Inquiry by Design: Environment/Behavior/ Neuroscience in Architecture, Interiors, Landscape and Planning. W. W. Norton & Co. 2006

Bibliography

This book came to life in the fall of 2009, when I began as a Visiting Professor and Acting Chair for Principles of Architectural Design at the Technical University Munich (TUM) Faculty of Architecture, and Juliane Demel started out at our chair as a Research Assistant. This publication would not have been possible without Professor Tina Haase, artist and Chair for Visual Arts at the faculty, as she was the one who initially approached me for an academic engagement at the TUM. Above all, Juliane and I would like to thank her for the support we received throughout our time at the TUM.

We are also very thankful for the warm welcome we received from the members of the TUM faculty. During our engagement, our colleagues in the faculty and the many students that we taught each semester always gave us the feeling that our work was greatly appreciated. Almost all of the inspiring samples in this book come from the minds and hearts of our first- and second-semester students, while some of the works in the last chapters are from more advanced workshops. We would therefore like to thank all of the bright, talented, and highly motivated individuals with whom we have had the pleasure to work. Thank you all very much for your engagement with our research and positive attitude towards the challenging assignments you completed under our guidance.

We are also very grateful to the work of the research assistants, tutors, and teaching assistants of our chair. Thank you for going to great lengths to motivate students to always search for the best results and to always push their limits. Special thanks go out to our numerous guest critics and teachers we had during the last three years, most notably Moritz Fleischmann and Tobias Klein, who contributed their design expertise to both being visiting lecturers at our Chair and to being guest authors of two chapters of this book. We'd like to thank Rudolf van Wezel and everyone at BIS Publishers for their positive and motivating attitude.

Also, many thanks go out to Vasilena Vassilev, Assistant Professor of Architecture at Syracuse University, New York, for editing the English translation of this publication. We would also like to thank the architects who contributed their work to highlight the relevance of our students' design explorations, and to link practice with methodology and research. We are also very grateful to Ben Van Berkel, whose words and thoughtful remarks about our work now grace the back cover of this book. Finally, we would like to thank our families, close relatives, partners, and friends for their generous support and love: without you, none of this would have been possible!

Mark Mückenheim and Juliane Demel

Acknowledgements